Constructive
Classroom
Management

Constructive Classroom Management

Strategies for Creating Positive Learning Environments

Betty C. Epanchin
UNIVERSITY OF SOUTH FLORIDA, TAMPA

Brenda Townsend
UNIVERSITY OF SOUTH FLORIDA, TAMPA

Kim Stoddard
UNIVERSITY OF SOUTH FLORIDA, ST. PETERSBURG

Brooks/Cole Publishing Company
Pacific Grove, California

The trademark ITP is used under license.

Photo credits: 2, © Jeffrey Dunn Studios; **19,** © Bob Kalman/ The Image Works; **32,** © Tony Freeman/PhotoEdit; **58,** © Elizabeth Crews; **60,** © 1990 Jeffrey High/Image Productions; **70,** © Ken Karp/Omni Photo Communications; **76,** © Elizabeth Crews; **81,** © Elizabeth Crews; **98,** © Jeffrey Dunn Studios; **101,** © Elizabeth Crews; **114,** © Elizabeth Crews; **120,** © 1992 by Jeffrey High/Image Productions; **127,** Nita Winter Photography; **136,** Nita Winter Photography; **152,** © 1992 Jeffrey High/Image Productions; **170,** © Michael Siluk/ The Image Works; **175,** © Richard Hutchings/PhotoEdit; **180,** © Elizabeth Crews; **184,** © Elizabeth Crews; **203,** © Elizabeth Crews; **210,** © Elizabeth Crews; **218,** © Kim Stoddard; **220,** © Jeffrey Dunn Studios; **232,** © Elizabeth Crews; **235,** © Mark Richards/PhotoEdit; **262,** Nita Winter Photography; **278,** Nita Winter Photography; **290,** © Elizabeth Crews; **297,** © Elizabeth Crews; **308,** © Elizabeth Crews; **311,** © Elizabeth Crews; **324,** © Elizabeth Crews; **334,** © Alan Carey/The Image Works; **337,** © Alan Carey/The Image Works; **351,** © Elizabeth Crews.

Sponsoring Editor: Vicki Knight
Editorial Associate: Lauri Banks-Ataide
Production Services Manager: Joan Marsh
Production: Penna Design and Production
Manuscript Editor: Judith Johnstone
Permissions Editor: Lillian Campobasso
Interior Design: Detta Penna
Cover Design: E. Kelly Shoemaker, Laurie Albrecht
Cover Photograph: Gabe Palmer, The Stock Market
Photo Researcher: Diana Henry
Indexer: Alan Shaw
Typesetting: Graphic World, Inc., St. Louis
Cover Printing: Phoenix Color Corporation
Printing and Binding: Arcata Graphics, Fairfield

Brooks/Cole Publishing Company
A Division of Wadsworth, Inc.
Printed in the United States of America
10 9 8 7 6 5 4 3 2 1

Library of Congress Cataloging-in-Publication Data

Epanchin, Betty Cooper.
    Constuctive classroom management: strategies for creative
positive learning environments/Betty C. Epanchin, Brenda Townsend,
Kim Stoddard.
        p.   cm.
    Includes index.
    ISBN 0-534-22254-4
    1. Classroom management.   I. Townsend, Brenda.   II. Stoddard,
Kim.   III. Title.
LB3013.E63   1994   94-4309
371.5—dc20   CIP

Contents

Chapter 4

Structuring the Classroom for Success

Chapter 5

Promoting Positive Behaviors

Chapter 6

Reducing Undesirable Behaviors

Chapter 7

Promoting Prosocial Skills 180

Chapter 8

Involving the Group 210

Chapter 9

Assessing Individual Children
by Betty C. Epanchin and Lee Smith 232

Figures, Tables and Boxes

Figures

Tables

Boxes

Preface

*For every thousand
hacking at the leaves of evil,
there is one striking at the root.*
—Thoreau

For the past several decades, educators have been busily hacking away at disruptive student behavior—trying to find solutions to challenging student behavior, only to discover that the real challenges we face are systemic ones. Large numbers of children come to school unmotivated, angry at the adult world, and discouraged about their opportunities and realities. Many of our children are failing to graduate or are graduating with inadequate skills. They possess neither the social/personal nor cognitive skills to succeed in our fast paced business world. Our legal and correctional systems are overrun with juveniles, and our schools are no longer safe places for students or teachers. Our dominant culture is also undergoing radical changes as the American, Canadian, European white, male perspective is being transformed to incorporate gender, ethnic, religious, and social class diversity. Our everyday environment has expanded to include the world—not just our immediate neighborhood. Television, assisted by technologically advanced satellites, brings information about people from all over the world into our homes daily. Political boundaries, stable since World War II, are changing, and the world economy is threatened by local, national, and international needs. Schools reflect these social, political, technical, and economic issues; consequently, it follows that schools should also be undergoing radical reforms in teaching and learning.

While many of our schools are rethinking their assumptions and practices, many also continue to teach and to function much as schools did fifty years ago. Katzenmeyer (1993) reminds us that such schools are doing what they were designed to do—sort students. The problem is we can no longer afford such a model. We need our students to be productive, literate citizens. Unfortunately, the structures and practices in many of our schools are based on theories and research that have influenced thought for the past fifty years.

We need to rethink our schools so that at their core, they are enablers and facilitators for *all* children and their families. Such changes will require focusing on our roots—the fundamental beliefs upon which our schools operate. Rather than diagnosing what's wrong with a child or determining how to remediate, we need to be finding strengths and developing strategies and resources that can help children succeed. This does not mean that we have to discard what we have already learned about behavior management and discipline; rather, it means that we may use our knowledge and skills for different purposes.

We believe that education is not a cut-and-dried process. We don't believe that there is one "right" way to resolve every situation. Teachers make many complex, integrated decisions daily. We have chosen case studies to illustrate dilemmas and challenges that may confront any teacher.

Many effective strategies have been developed that can be applied within a different framework and can be used to provide students with the supports they need to succeed. More attention needs to be given to how we can teach children to be successful students and citizens, rather than how we can control them and make them learn what we want them to learn. More attention also needs to be given to how to create school environments that promote and support the learning community. Quality schools are places where children and teachers are engaged in joyful, meaningful learning, not places where teachers and administrators focus on control, and students conform and comply with authority's wishes while secretly yearning to escape. In quality schools, students discover that learning can be fun and order is created through harmony among the systems that influence and constitute schools, not from a "curriculum of control." This shift in thinking, from a focus on managing specific student behaviors to promoting constructive action with children, and in systems, means that teachers need to know not only how to help individual students succeed in school, but also how to help systems become more effective and supportive of their members.

In this book we have selected content that will prove useful and relevant to teachers as they construct systems of order in their classrooms. We have also tried to illustrate how teachers can pay thoughtful attention to the interacting systems that impact schools, classrooms, children

and teachers. Most of all, we have tried to include content that will help teachers create classrooms that inculcate a joy for learning, not a curriculum of control.

The first section focuses on system issues—what's wrong with our current system and ways of thinking and what do we need to do to help schools accommodate to our changing world. We've included content on school reform and on working with families so that they become our allies and partners. In the second section, we have focused on approaches to behavior management that are used in most classrooms with most students. These are the types of procedures that all teachers need to use to create order and harmony in their classrooms—prevention through structure and organization, supporting positive behaviors and discouraging problematic behaviors, working with groups of children, and dialoging in a meaningful way with students. The final section of the book includes strategies and approaches that are used with individual children when they are having particular problems. Again, our emphasis is on maintaining a positive focus, even during crises. We included the assessment chapter in this section because the content covered in this section includes assessment strategies for individual children. While teachers engage in continuous and ongoing evaluation of their teaching, the strategies included in this chapter are ones used as tools to solve specific problems. We also included a chapter on crisis management because no matter how well teachers plan to prevent problems, crises do arise and teachers need to be prepared to deal with them constructively. Finally, we close with a chapter on dealing with stress with a focus on helping teachers find a balance in their personal lives. While teachers may sometimes feel that much in their teaching world is beyond their control, dealing with their own stress is an area they can control. In order to survive in the field, teachers need to learn how to monitor, minimize, and control negative, unproductive areas.

Many people have helped in the creation of this volume. To all of them we extend our heartfelt gratitude. A few merit individual recognition and particular thanks. First, the contributing authors, Daphne D. Thomas (Chapter 3), Lee Smith (Chapter 9), and Terry Smith (Chapter 10), were wonderful to work with, sympathetic with our perspective and willing to accommodate our schedule. Their thoughtful and informed input strengthened our text significantly. Second, our colleagues who reviewed the manuscript: Linda Christianson, Eastern Montana College; Frances H. Courson, University of Charleston; Sharon Huntze, University of Missouri at Columbia; Timothy Landrum, Longwood College; Darcy Miller, Washington State University; and Michael Pullis, University of Missouri at Columbia; provided valuable, constructive feedback on early drafts of the book. Their comments were insightful and on target! Third, a few of our colleagues at USF, Bill Morse, Cathy Wooley-Brown, Ann Cranston-Gingras, Evie Engel, Reggie Lee, and MeMe Heineman read early drafts and provided help-ful feedback which helped us clarify our thoughts. The staff at Brooks/Cole have been wonderful! They have been professional, competent, supportive, and a lot of fun. Having a wonderful sense of humor seemed to be a gift that all shared and we certainly delighted in their good spirits. Vicki Knight, a long standing and valued friend and colleague, helped in the construction of this book and Joan Marsh selected a wonderful team of professionals. Detta Penna guided the production of the book, providing expertise, support and laughter. Judy Johnstone edited the manuscript. Kelly Shoemaker helped in the selection of the photos and design of the cover. Her enthusiasm was contagious. And Kathy Lee conscientiously proofread the final pages.

Finally, but hardly last, thanks to our families who tolerated our preoccupation with this project, provided support and encouragement when needed, and picked up the responsibilities we neglected because we were otherwise occupied. We extend our love and our thanks to Alex, Katherine, and Michael; Ronnie, Shelea, DeAndre, and Ronnie II; Tim, Katie, Kelly, and Andy.

Constructive Classroom Management

Chapter 1

Introduction

What a year! This class has been the most challenging for Mr. Bobrinski in six years of teaching. There is Dennis, who can't sit still, and Adam, who seems lost academically. Carmelita is distressingly volatile. Pia was devastated by her parents' nasty custody fight, especially when she had to testify in court. But, without doubt, Clyde has been the biggest challenge. A sullen 12-year-old boy, Clyde already had a drug problem when he entered Mr. Bobrinski's class. Clyde's family has disintegrated—his mother is dead and his father is in jail. It was never clear where Clyde was living, as he drifted from relative to relative during the school year.

Mr. Bobrinski feels that Clyde does remarkably well, considering all the problems he faces. Although he doesn't turn in homework regularly, Clyde performed better on the standardized tests this year and actually seemed interested in the lessons toward the end of the year. Whereas he terrorized the other kids at the beginning of the year, now they appear to like him. Clyde swears that he has stopped using drugs.

With high hopes, Mr. Bobrinski has anticipated that the end-of-year class picnic would allow the principal and the other kids' parents to observe the positive changes in Clyde. Instead of focusing on his problems, they would see how likeable he is. When Clyde asked who was chaperoning the picnic, Mr. Bobrinski used the opening to mention that he was looking forward to having the principal see how much progress Clyde had made. "I'm sure I can count on you to cooperate, can't I? You won't bring drugs or anything, will you?" From under the visor of his baseball cap, Clyde mumbled no.

At the picnic, however, Clyde's eyes are glassy and he is barely awake. Mr. Bobrinski is sick with disappointment. He alternates between feeling betrayed, worried, and furious. If Clyde is reported, he will be suspended. If Mr. Bobrinski does nothing, Clyde will think he can get away with the behavior. But maybe Clyde is upset about the coming separation. He shouldn't be punished for feeling upset, should he?

Mr. Bobrinski is finding it hard to think clearly because he feels both hurt and guilty. Maybe he set Clyde up by alluding to his drug problem. But he thought their relationship was solid enough that Clyde would be able to accept the no-drug request. Mr. Bobrinski really wants to talk with Clyde about his deliberately breaking the rules as well as his betrayal of their friendship, but privacy is a problem at the picnic. On the other hand, tomorrow is the last day of school and, like many kids, Clyde may not show up for the half-day session. What should Mr. Bobrinski do?

*L*ike Mr. Bobrinski, most teachers value relationships and want personal, positive relationships with their students and their families (Lortie, 1963; Goodlad, 1990); however, Johnson (1990) maintains that most of all teachers want to be regarded with respect. No matter what Mr. Bobrinski does, he risks a serious rupture in his relationship with Clyde. If Clyde is suspended, he will be sent to the juvenile detention home, which Mr. Bobrinski thinks is awful! Being the person to send Clyde there is hard to accept. On the other hand, if Mr. Bobrinski does not confront Clyde's problematic behavior in some way, he runs the risk of appearing either indifferent or inept. Mr. Bobrinski also runs the risk of criticism from his principal and the parents if he does not deal sternly with Clyde. For himself, Mr. Bobrinski needs some sort of resolution and closure. After spending so much personal energy on Clyde all year, having the relationship go sour at the end of the year is discouraging, perplexing, and demoralizing.

As this case illustrates, it takes considerable skill and personal maturity for teachers to develop caring, nurturing relationships with students like Clyde while also setting high standards. This is a book about such a challenge. The content we have included is typically called behavior management or classroom discipline because we discuss strategies that teachers can use to establish order and harmony in schools. This is *not* a book about controlling children. The techniques and ideas presented here are intended to help children learn academic content, self-control, and a sense of self-efficacy. They are also intended to suggest how teachers might work to make schools better places for children.

Many authors maintain that discipline is a learning and teaching tool (Brophy, 1986; Rosenshine, 1983), and that classroom management and teaching cannot exist independently from one another (Levin & Nolan, 1991). Nelsen (1993), however, notes that discipline can become an end in itself, and when this happens discipline becomes punitive. This book provides teachers with alternatives and options so that discipline and control do not become ends in themselves. We have no illusions that there are clear-cut answers about how to teach, but we do hope this book helps the reader think about important issues in education—especially those having to do with discipline and behavior management.

Attempting to create order and harmony in school is a monumental undertaking. It involves trying to persuade 600 or more students to be orderly, well-behaved, happy, and cooperative. It also requires that teachers find ways to help students focus on, and get excited about, learning and work. It involves motivating students to achieve and to cooperate with authorities. Additionally, it often includes trying to get 900-plus parents to be pleased with and supportive of the educational programs their children are receiving; 25 or more teachers to adhere to common expectations for all students; and a variety of related educational personnel to subscribe to the overall behavioral goals of the school. As children move from elementary to secondary school settings, the combinations of student–teacher, parent–teacher, administrator–educator, administrator–family, administrator–student, and student–academic content become even more complex. In reality, creating order and harmony in school for any length of time is probably an impossible dream—but we expect it of educators daily!

In addition to being extremely challenging, teaching is also gratifying. It involves assuming considerable personal and professional responsibility and making life-altering, complex decisions on a daily basis. Even though teachers are not highly paid, they are incredibly important people in the lives of children and their families. Teachers can help children grow and develop in healthy, positive ways, but they can also be very demeaning, hurtful, and destructive. In just one year a teacher can make life-long impressions on a child—positively or negatively.

Literature provides us with many vivid examples of how insensitive, ineffective teachers can misuse their power and become destructive disciplinarians. One of the most memorable examples is found in *To Sir, With Love* (Braithwaite, 1959). Rick, an Oxford-educated black engineer, takes a job teaching in one of London's poorest slum schools. Another faculty member, Mr. Bell, is a 40-year-old teacher struggling to establish control in his physical education class. Experienced with the Army Education Service, Mr. Bell is "something of a perfectionist and impatient of any one whose co-ordination was not as smooth and controlled as his own" (p. 153). One day a crisis erupts in Mr. Bell's class when one of the students, Richard Buckley, refuses to perform an assigned jump. Buckley, a chubby, awkward, rather inept boy, is well-liked and protected by his classmates. He does not request to be excused nor does he become defiant; he just does not attempt the vault. Enraged by Buckley's noncompliance, Mr. Bell nonverbally threatens Buckley, who responds by launching himself toward the vault, missing the jump, and hurting himself. The class is furious! One kid picks up the broken, metal-bound leg of the vault and threatens to hit Mr. Bell while screaming "You bloody bastard, you f---ing bloody bastard." Another kid summons Rick to break up the fight. After the crisis is abated, Rick asks Mr. Bell why he insisted that Buckley do the vault. Mr. Bell defensively replies, "I had to, don't you see; he just stood there refusing to obey and the others were watching me; I just had to do something." In Mr. Bell's view, teachers must dictate students' behavior in order to be in control, but he had no understanding of the *genuine* power teachers earn when they gain students' respect and admiration.

A heart-warming example of a teacher who used his power in a benevolent and wise manner, and who consequently was loved and revered by his students, is found in *Goodbye, Mr. Chips* (Hilton, 1934). Mr. Chips was a teacher who with time "began to feel a greater sureness; his discipline improved to a point at which it could become, in a sense, less rigid; he became more popular. When he first arrived at Brookfield, he had aimed to be loved, honored, and obeyed—but obeyed, at any rate. Obedience he had secured, and honor had been granted him; but only now came love, the sudden love of boys for a man who was kind without being soft, who understood them well enough, but not too much, and whose private happiness linked them with their own" (pp. 31–32).

Comparison of these two teachers illustrates the point that discipline can foster a positive working relationship between teacher and student when it is implemented fairly and thoughtfully. Fair and thoughtful discipline can help children learn organizational skills and pride in their ability to achieve. Over time, under such conditions, children come to love school and learning. Unfortunately, when discipline is oppressive, unfair, or insensitive, school can become an unpleasant, disliked activity that is overtly or covertly resisted. Morse (1993) attributes positive discipline to the ability of the teacher and the school to establish genuine authority that elicits respect and affection from students. Genuine authority is real power, earned through the demonstration of knowledge and the ability to help. Mr. Chips developed genuine authority through his skill and concern for his students' well being. Primitive authority, the kind that Mr. Bell invoked, bases power in bureaucratic rules and regulations. Principals can enforce rules through the power of their position, but they cannot force students to *internalize* principles. Children learn discipline through respect and admiration for it and the person who invokes it, not through naked power.

To create positive, productive learning environments in which discipline is wisely and fairly administered, we believe that teachers and other school personnel need to be:

☐ *excellent instructional leaders,* capable of stimulating students' thought and motivating students to become actively involved in the learning enterprise;

☐ *competent, caring, and ethical decision makers* who are affectively connected to their students and willing to act in order to create safe and affirming learning environments;

☐ *appreciative of multiple perspectives,* understanding that multiple realities may exist within a school. Judging that one perspective is "right" and others "wrong" or "inappropriate" can antagonize, alienate, and limit understanding, while learning about and affirming differences can enrich and strengthen the school climate;

☐ *sensitive to ethnic, gender, and religious differences,* realizing that heritage impacts people in profound ways that include language, attitudes, values, and expectations of self and others;

☐ *at ease with their own sense of self-efficacy and personal power* so that they can deal with the multitude of personal challenges to their beliefs and knowledge;

☐ *focused on their goals* so that they can react to immediate, short-term problems as well as think about and plan for long-term solutions;

□ *reflective in their practice* (Henderson, 1992), constantly evaluating and thinking about their teaching so that they learn from and grow in their profession;

□ *capable of a systems view of school,* acknowledging that school and classrooms are complex systems, intricately connected to other systems, particularly the families of children in school. When family and school work together, solutions that benefit the child are possible; when family and school are in conflict, the child usually suffers.

Limitations of Traditional Approaches to Behavior Management

In spite of the criticisms schools are currently facing, education during the twentieth century has made many advances. We have learned a great deal about teaching and learning, as evidenced by creative and productive programs that are being instituted around the world. We have created greater access to education, as evidenced by the increasing numbers of minority and exceptional children who are succeeding in school. We have learned much about dealing with challenging behavior, as evidenced by successful programs for many different groups of exceptional children. Some of our most significant lessons, however, have to do with the shortcomings of our current practice. While we have developed tools that are relatively effective in short-term control, we have not been able to engage all children in the educational process to the degree that we desire. We still have many children who are academic and behavioral failures. The following issues illustrate some of the current limitations in our practice.

Reactive Behavior Management Approaches

Much time and attention has been devoted to sorting out how to deal with a problem once it has occurred. Teachers have learned how to administer many consequences once a child has misbehaved, and in the process teachers have come to the realization that reactive discipline has the potential of creating negative, punitive interactions between teachers and students, which can lead to even greater problems. Students often perceive corrective feedback as criticism, nagging, or a reprimand and therefore blame the teacher for being unkind. This creates a cycle in which reactive feedback produces more anger and resentment, rather than solving a problem.

In reactive situations, students are not taught what to do instead of misbehaving. Research has consistently indicated that punishment may modify a specific behavior quickly but it does not ameliorate it (Sabatino, 1987). Furthermore, reactive approaches provide students with attention; thus, over time, students may learn to gain attention through misbehavior. When a problem develops in a classroom, it can become contagious. Once students are upset and acting out, even outstanding teachers can have difficulty managing the disruption. In Kounin's (1970) classic study, differences were not found between successful and unsuccessful teachers in how they dealt with classroom disruptions, but differences were found in how they dealt with students so as to prevent or de-escalate problems.

Dominance of the Technical, Rational, Mechanistic Paradigm

Especially since the 1970s, when behavioral technology began to dominate educational practice, considerable attention has been devoted to the technology of behavior management, the "what to do." By comparison, little attention has been given to the "whys" of an intervention, or the ethical, moral reasons for action. Justification for suggested interventions has rested in a "technical rational" position (Schon, 1987), also called an "objectivist view" or a "positivist philosophy." From the technical, rational position, truth is established by testing the "facts." "Facts" are the basis upon which conflict is resolved, and professional knowledge rests upon a foundation of "facts." "Facts" are seen as objective information, separate from the perceiver. Practitioners are instrumental problem solvers who select the technical means that best suits their particular purposes. In this view, rigorous professional practitioners solve well-formulated instrumental problems by applying theory and technique derived from systematic, preferably scientific, knowledge (Schon, 1987). This approach assumes that there is an objective reality that can be segmented and divided into understandable parts, that behavior can be understood and determined, and that learning depends upon accurate perception. Heshusius (1989) details the assumptions of this paradigm in Figure 1.1.

Limitations of this view are numerous, however. In practice, educational problems are not comparable to engineering problems. Unlike the incline of a hill that can be reliably measured, a child who is misbehaving will be perceived differently by different people. A teacher, a parent, a therapist, and a neighbor are likely to hold widely divergent views of the child's behavior, have different explanations of the child's problems, and recommend different interventions for the child. The "facts" in such a case are based on the perceptions of various people who are likely to view problematic situations in differing ways depending upon multiple, complex factors such as their ethnicity, education, age, gender, experience, or organizational role. Neither people nor problems come in neat packages that fit the theories. Each time people attempt to solve a problem, they frame (bias) the problem by what they select to attend to, to measure, to observe, and to try to understand. Selection in research is based on values held by the practitioner, often values derived from professional training and practice. Eisner (1990) observes that "educational policy is shaped by beliefs about the kind of

Figure 1.1 The Mechanistic Paradigm

Key Assumptions of the Mechanistic Paradigm

The nature of reality:

- ☐ is objective. Fact can be separated from value, the observer from the observed, the knower from the known
- ☐ is understood through a mathematical symbol system
- ☐ is reductionistic. The dynamics of the whole can be understood from the properties of the parts
- ☐ consists of components. Knowledge of pieces adds up to knowledge of the whole
- ☐ can be known with certainty with the gathering of sufficient data

The nature of progress:

- ☐ is deterministic. All events have direct causes and consequences
- ☐ is additive, incremental, sequential, and continuous, which leads to prediction and control
- ☐ is the same regardless of personal meaning and context

The nature of the organism:

- ☐ is reactive

Synchronized

Translations into Special Education Theory and Practice

- ☐ attempts to objectify knowledge and knowing; only that which can be reliably measured gains the status of formal knowledge; categorization of exceptionalities by objective diagnoses; right/wrong answers, errorless learning
- ☐ quantification and ranking (statistically significant findings, frequency counts, test scores) as indices of children's recall abilities; diagnostic testing
- ☐ learning equates lengthy sequences of processes, behaviors, and learning strategies; focus on deficits within the student
- ☐ isolated skill training, worksheets, bottom up approaches to literacy; task analysis; learning equates mastery of predetermined, known curriculum outcomes
- ☐ predictive instruments, search for causality in diagnosis; answers to problems lie in "more research" and "more data"
- ☐ causal linkages between diagnoses and instruction; task analysis, mastery learning; precision teaching; programmed and sequentialized materials; controlled vocabulary; daily charting; curriculum-based assessment; "individualized" education (meaning the same for all students but at their own pace)
- ☐ Behaviorism, stimulus control, reinforcement, input-output models; unidirectional control of curriculum by teacher

Source: Heshusius (1989).

knowledge one can trust and the kinds of methods one can use to get such knowledge" (p. 96).

As differences in perception, beliefs, values, and knowledge have been examined and studied, new ways of thinking about practice have emerged that consider not only the "facts" (the data) but also how knowledge is generated, the interpretation of "facts." These new understandings of educational problems are the basis for much thinking about school reform and school restructuring.

Another significant and related issue now getting more attention is ethics and ethical decision making. For the most part, educational decisions have traditionally been based on personal or political understandings of the "facts." Research on the efficacy of intervention has often served as the basis for action, with little or no attention given to the ethical implications of the action. Rarely have we asked "All things considered, what ought to be done?" (Howe & Miramontes, 1992). Increasingly, however, practitioners and researchers are recognizing the shortcomings of attending only to technology and the data when making decisions about educating people.

Failure to Focus on System Variables

For many decades, schools have operated on the belief that if a child misbehaves in school, it is the fault of either the child, the teacher, or the family. We have created policies that inform teachers and administrators about how they should respond to such "problems." Much of the professional literature dealing with behavior management issues rests on the assumptions that either the child or the teacher should be the target of change. Most behavior management texts have focused on specific child, teacher, or classroom variables that can be manipulated to increase desired behaviors and/or decrease undesirable behaviors. While such a focus may be necessary when planning specific, immediate interventions, it fails

to recognize the broader context in which schooling takes place; yet it is this context that often facilitates order or creates problems. Furthermore, school reform advocates charge that focus on specific child/teacher/classroom variables has the potential of becoming a "blame the victim" mentality, and that the real problems are not "bad" students, families, or teachers but rather a failure to understand the whole system and to see the implications of practice (Brown, 1991; Glasser, 1992; Nieto, 1992).

For example, some schools use authoritarian, "get tough," teacher-centered approaches that emphasize academic requirements and reduced student electives (Ravitch, 1983). Teacher authority and top-down administrative action are emphasized. Conformity to rules, passivity, mastery of sameness, and standardized expectations are mandated. Critical inquiry, independent thought, and creative and innovative action is discouraged (Brown, 1991). A "back to the basics" focus dominates this view, and reading, writing, and arithmetic are stressed. Relevance of the curriculum is not a priority. Pedagogy consists of stern discipline, frequent drills, homework, and class recitation. In these systems, poor achievement is typically attributed to students' lack of ability, teachers' lack of discipline, or school administrators' lack of control.

Shor (1986) adds an additional dimension. He equates authoritarian approaches with conservatives' efforts to maintain the status quo and protect their control over dissident voices such as students, the poor, and minority groups. He also sees career education and vocational education as strategies for reducing student unrest by focusing on education as a means of getting a job rather than a means of learning about one's world and becoming a critical thinker. Bullard and Taylor (1993) associate authoritarian approaches with the ethos of the late nineteenth century, when management wanted workers, especially immigrants and poor people, to be socialized to the work ethic of following orders and not questioning authority. This work ethic was part of the "scientific management" movement that treated workers as cogs in the machine—and the best worker came with no mind. In such a system, students who feel disenfranchised and bored by an irrelevant curriculum frequently become hostile and oppositional in school.

More progressive, child-centered educational approaches have emphasized the importance of students gaining greater control over their learning (Brown, 1991; Shor, 1986). Proponents of this view have sought to help students learn how to critically understand their society, to be creative, and to make education personally relevant and meaningful. Progressive schools seek to empower students by raising their consciousness of social, economic, and historical forces that are shaping our society. Students are encouraged to be meaning makers instead of passive receptacles of knowledge. Education is relevant and students have a sense of control and accomplishment; therefore their need to misbehave and oppose the system is significantly reduced. Historically, this educational approach has primarily been used in schools attended by children from more affluent backgrounds (Bullard & Taylor, 1993); consequently, disenfranchised children have often been denied access to an education that is empowering.

Inequitable Educational Practice

Another way in which minority and poor children have been denied access to an educational opportunity has been through school policies. Bureaucracies have been developed to insure the implementation of various laws designed to integrate our society and to create equal access to opportunities for all citizens; however, as politicians and academicians have adjusted policy, communities have "resegregated." Busing, magnet schools, and a variety of other solutions have been developed in an effort to counter "white flight" to suburban neighborhoods. Economic, racial, ethnic, and gender differences have been at the root of unequal, segregated educational practices.

Jonathan Kozol (1991) writes:

> I began to teach in 1964 in Boston in a segregated school so crowded and so poor that it could not provide my fourth grade children with a classroom. We shared an auditorium with another fourth grade and the choir and a group that was rehearsing, starting in October, for a Christmas play that, somehow, never was produced. In the spring I was shifted to another fourth

grade that had a string of substitutes all year. The 35 children in the class hadn't had a permanent teacher since they entered kindergarten. That year, I was their thirteenth teacher.

The results were seen in the first tests I gave. In April, most were reading at the second grade level. Their math ability was at the first grade level.

In an effort to resuscitate their interests, I began to read them poetry I liked. They were drawn especially to poems of Robert Frost and Langston Hughes. One of the most embittered children in the class began to cry when she first heard the words of Langston Hughes.

> *What happens to a dream deferred?*
> *Does it dry up*
> *like a raisin in the sun?*

She went home and memorized the lines.

The next day I was fired. There was, it turned out, a list of "fourth grade poems" that teachers were obliged to follow but which, like most first-year teachers, I had never seen. According to school officials, Robert Frost and Langston Hughes were "too advanced" for children of this age. Hughes, moreover, was regarded as "inflammatory."

I was soon recruited to teach in a suburban system west of Boston. The shock of going from one of the poorest schools to one of the wealthiest cannot be overstated. I now had 21 children in a cheerful building with a principal who welcomed innovation. (p. 2)

In the fall of 1988, Kozol returned to the public schools, spending two years traveling from system to system, visiting many schools and talking to many students. What startled him most in his visits was "the remarkable degree of racial segregation that persisted almost everywhere" (p. 2). He observed, "I knew that segregation was still common in the public schools, but I did not know how much it had intensified. . . . Most of the urban schools I visited were 95 to 99 percent nonwhite. In no school that I saw anywhere in the United States were nonwhite children in large numbers truly intermingled with white children" (p. 3).

He described urban schools as "extraordinarily unhappy places." He noted "With few exceptions, they reminded me of garrisons or outposts in a foreign nation. Housing projects, bleak and tall, surrounded by perimeter walls lined with barbed wire, often stood adjacent to the schools I visited. The schools were surrounded frequently by signs that indicated DRUG-FREE ZONE. Their doors were guarded. Police sometimes patrolled the halls. The windows of the schools were often covered with steel grates" (p. 5).

Children who attend schools like the ones Kozol describes had behavior problems. They are described as children with little initiative, poor study habits, low achievement, and "wilted-looking" (Kozol, p. 230); yet their voices indicate their desire for inclusion and recognition.

In an elementary school in Anacostia, a little girl in the fifth grade tells me that the first thing she would do if somebody gave money to her school would be to plant a row of flowers by the street. "Blue flowers," she says. "And I'd buy some curtains for my teacher." And she specifies again: "Blue curtains."

I ask her, "Why blue curtains?"

"It's like this," she says. "The school is dirty. There isn't any playground. There's a hole in the wall behind the principal's desk. What we need to do is first rebuild the school. Another color. Build a playground. Plant a lot of flowers. Paint the classrooms. Blue and white. Fix the hole in the principal's office. Buy doors for the toilet stalls in the girls' bathroom. Fix the ceiling in this room. It looks like somebody went up and peed over our heads. Make it a beautiful clean building. Make it pretty. Way it is, I feel ashamed." (p. 181)

Bullard and Taylor (1993) suggest that schools sometimes expect poor students to bring duller minds and to be from broken families, thus lowering achievement standards. Teachers are not expected to cover as much material; the curriculum is "dumbed down." Grade inflation takes the pressure off teachers as well as students. Tracking of students is more common and pervasive in such schools. When some children are prohibited from being included in the full, intended curriculum—no matter what the cause—children of all backgrounds suffer.

Not only are there ethnic and social class differences that create tensions, there are also gender issues that have stimulated conflict. Brown and Gilligan's (1992) work with young adolescent girls highlights the subtle yet powerful forces that operate in our culture. They interviewed 100 girls over a 5-year period as they moved through adolescence, documenting the social pressures young girls face as they become women. Prior to adolescence, young girls "speak freely of feeling angry, of fighting or open conflict in relationships, and take difference and disagreement for granted in daily life" (p. 4). Adolescence is the crossroad where young girls begin to "not know," to be unwilling to be outspoken because they fear they will endanger their relationships. Brown and Gilligan observed that outspoken young girls become silent women who avoid conflict rather than risk the loss of relationship. Thus they see adolescence as a time of disconnection or repression as girls face the choice of changing the way they relate and the way they know, so that they can be the way they are expected to be in relationships as women "with men." Ethnic, racial, and gender differences are at the core of our current efforts to restructure or reform schools.

Stigmatization and Isolation of Children with Special Needs

Since the passage of PL 94-142, educational services for children with disabilities have increased significantly (between 11 and 12% of the total school enrollment are receiving services that they would not have received prior to implementation

of the law); there has been a substantial increase in funding for special education programs; and, for the most part, children all over the country have access to services (Gartner & Lipsky, 1992).

While more services are available, the potential for stigma and isolation in segregated classes is also greater. The model that currently exists is one that entails identifying children whose behavior or achievement differs from the school norm. An assumption is made that there is something wrong with the child; yet research consistently indicates that minorities and students whose socioeconomic status differs from the norm are the children who are disproportionately referred for services (Skrtic, 1991).

Additionally, research studies indicate that decisions about special education classification are not only functions of child characteristics but also involve powerful organizational influences (Skrtic, 1991; Reynolds, 1991; Morsink, Soar, Soar, & Thomas, 1986). Apparently classification decisions are affected by availability of programs and space; incentives for identification, range, and kind of competing programs and services; number of professionals; and federal, state, and community pressures (Keogh, 1990). Furthermore, some researchers have reported that the teaching approaches used in special education classrooms are not significantly different from the ones used in general education classrooms (Morsink, Thomas, & Smith-Davis, 1987).

Given the imperfect system of providing services to children with disabilities, it is especially important that systems be cautious about placing children in pull-out or segregated programs, and that they monitor carefully to insure that children are benefitting. In writing about their son's experience with special education services, Lori and Bill Granger (1986) observed, "The trap of special education is . . . a beguiling trap. Children of special education are children of Small Expectations, not great ones. Little is expected and little is demanded. Gradually, these children—no matter their IQ level—learn to be cozy in the category of being 'special.' They learn to be less than they are" (pp. 26–27).

Loss of Connection and Caring in Educational Environments

One of the most comprehensive and enlightening studies about the problems of schools is found in the research of Mary Poplin and her colleagues at the Institute for Education in Transformation at the Claremont Graduate School in California (Poplin & Weeres, 1992). They spent 18 months studying four representative urban/suburban public schools. They interviewed people inside the schools—students, teachers, custodians, secretaries, security guards, administrators, parents, day-care workers, cafeteria workers, school nurses, and others—asking open-ended questions about their school. Starting with the question What is the problem of schooling? they conducted extensive interviews, compiled the data,

and returned for a second round of investigation. Data from the original interviews were shared and groups were asked to respond. The purpose of this second round of discussion was to verify that their data accurately reflected the ideas and thoughts of people within the schools.

A major conclusion drawn from their data was "the heretofore identified problems of schooling (lowered achievement, high dropout rates and problems in the teaching profession) are rather consequences of much deeper and more fundamental problems." Using multiethnic student voices to answer their questions about the problems of schooling, they concluded with the words of one high school student who replied "This place hurts my spirit" (Poplin & Weeres, 1992, p. 11).

They noted that relationships dominated all participant discussions about issues of schooling in the United States. As one elementary parent stated, "I want schools in which they can pay attention to each student's special needs and abilities. No such school can have regular classes of 34 pupils!" (p. 31). Poplin and Weeres also note that no group inside the schools felt adequately respected, connected, or affirmed and that the ruptures of relationships among people inside schools were one of the most dominant themes found in their data. On the positive side, they found that all participants wanted authentic, honest, and frequent communication within and among groups.

It is interesting to note that initially all the groups interviewed felt they themselves were caring, but that other groups were indifferent; however, evidence suggested a different interpretation. All groups reported care and concern for the youth in their schools, all groups affirmed the importance of education, and all supported the importance of relating to one another. The authors reported that "the demands placed on schools to attend to policies and practices that have little to do with relating to one another in authentic and honest ways, inhibit people from coming to know and relate productively with one another" (p. 27).

While many in the study reported negative views of schools, most also noted that they wanted to make schools better places for students. For example, an elementary teacher said "No one ever taught me how to have a really serious conversation with children. It's not that I don't want to, I don't know how to, I'm afraid" (p. 46). Students also voiced the desire to improve.

Other authors as well have emphasized the importance of schools' creating an academic atmosphere characterized by supportive, connected relationships in which students and faculty feel safe to take risks in learning, and these relationships need to be sustained over time (Katzenmeyer, 1992). Teachers must take time to attend to students and their needs and be willing to discuss ideas or examine problems. They also need to look for the good in students, not look for and confirm their flaws (Buber, 1965).

In her discussion of care in the classroom, Noddings (1992) suggests that the needs of students must drive our thinking. She suggests that teachers should stop asking How can we get kids to learn math? How can we make all our kids ready for college? How can we keep kids in school even though they hate it? Instead, Noddings thinks, teachers should shift their thinking, share their power, and be more sensitive to individual differences in students. She thinks teachers should be asking How can my subject serve the needs of each of these students? How can I teach so as to capitalize on their intelligences and affiliations? How can I complete the caring connection with as many students as possible? How can I help them to care for themselves as well as for other humans, animals, the environment, and the wonderful world of ideas?

Caring and nurturing are complex processes, evidenced in many different ways, as Noblit (1993) reminds us. He describes the classroom of a second grade teacher, Pam, who was known for setting high standards as well as for being loved by her students. School lore indicated that each year she told her students they would love her more once they left her class. Noblit chose to study her class because she did not conform to his notion of care. Her classroom was not a democratic, nurturing classroom; rather, he described her as being "in charge of" what her students did.

He spent one day a week for an entire year in her classroom in an effort to understand how she conveyed care. After extensive observations, he reported that discipline in Pam's class was evidenced in a number of ways. Routines helped the children know what was expected of them and therefore often kept them out of trouble. "Instruction" had a dual meaning. On the one hand, instruction was about teaching the subject matter. On the other hand, it was about a meticulous process of making sure everyone knew what and how to do whatever was being assigned. . . . Teacher talk was laced with reminders and admonitions to the students to prevent more serious infractions. Finally, when all else failed and "a student blatantly violated one of the written classroom rules (cooperation, consideration, communication, concentration) he or she . . . lost the right to free time during the day" (p. 29). According to Noblit, however, the worst infraction of all was to laugh if someone did not know the right answer to a question. "It was not a written rule, but all the children knew it." He reported that "this violation made all the children, and myself, drop our heads in apparent shame" (p. 30). Discipline was rarely an issue in Pam's class; rather, it was taken for granted. The children knew she expected them to behave, and largely they did. This was true even though Pam was likely to be assigned the children with major discipline problems.

Noblit attributes her success in conveying care and concern as well as in setting high expectations to her ability to use her power in an ethical, fair manner. Pam created an emotionally safe, secure classroom environment in which children could depend on her to be present, to be consistent in her demands, and to be fair. She used her power to promote her students' success.

Emphasis on a Curriculum of Control

In their national examination of programs for children with behavior disorders, Jane Knitzer and her colleagues also found ruptures in caring relationships (Knitzer, Steinberg, & Fleisch, 1990). They attributed this rupture in relationships, at least in part, to the quality of educational programs available to all children in both general and special education, noting that a common variable underlying the overwhelming majority of classes and school structures is the emphasis on control. While Knitzer and her colleagues found this emphasis on control in both special education and regular education, they saw it as an even more central part of the structure in classrooms for children labelled emotionally

Educational reformers criticize the "teacher-lecture, student-swallow" model of classroom instruction. As can be seen in this picture, students are easily distracted and prone to disruptiveness when forced to be in passive learning situations for long periods of time.

or behaviorally handicapped. They reported "The often more subtle and implicit mechanisms of control in regular education become explicit, clearly visible and widely supported as 'necessary.' Too often the dominant curriculum is not the traditional academic curriculum, nor is it about concepts, thinking, and problem solving. Instead, the curriculum is about controlling the behaviors of the children" (p. 25). To illustrate how the curriculum of control is implemented, Knitzer and colleagues (1990) described the following incidents.

For at least 20 minutes, seven fourth and fifth graders practiced going out to recess. Repeatedly they got in a line and tried to be silent in the hall. Because they spent so much time practicing how to go outside, they never got there!

A similar incident was seen in an urban school where special education children sat and watched the other children play basketball. When asked, their teacher explained that "they fight too much when they play" (p. 28), thus both the joy of play and a critical opportunity to learn more self-control were denied through overcontrol. The research team also noted that "too often, potentially interesting, 'fun' aspects of school have been deleted, because students have not handled them well in the past and/or because other needs seem more pressing" (p. 29).

There appears to be a similar reward system for teachers. In many schools teachers report that a quiet class is highly regarded by administrators (Zabel, 1992). Knitzer and co-workers (1990) suggest that few supervisors, administrators, or even parents look much beyond the quiet.

Polly Nichols (1992) concurred with Knitzer's observations about a curriculum of control, pointing out that "the use of power is often effective at intimidating students who need control least and is seldom effective with students whose behavior is most unproductive" (p. 7). She cited the research of Deci, Nezlek, and Sheinman (1981), who investigated the differential effects of rewards administered for control purposes and rewards administered for teaching children about their behavior. These authors found that rewards given to control behavior actually decreased intrinsic motivation, but rewards administered in a way that emphasized positive competence rather than control did not undermine intrinsic motivation. It was predicted that there would be a correlation between measures of children's self-esteem and teachers' orientation toward control. The authors reasoned that students with more autonomy would have greater intrinsic motivation and would view their classrooms more positively. They further reasoned that the more positively students view their classrooms, the higher their self-esteem will be. Their findings strongly supported their hypotheses.

Nichols also cited the work of Allen and Greenberger (1980) in observing that the "less control a person has over objective events, the more satisfaction he or she draws from destructive acts" (p. 8). She noted "Students who experience failures in school are more likely to act in deviant ways to increase, at least temporarily, their feelings of power and self-determination. One high school student reported to an interviewer that each time he passed a locker he had smashed, he thought with pride, 'There's my little destruction to this brand new school.' He had made his mark of control on his environment" (p. 8). How much better it would be if schools were enabling students to be competent, productive citizens in our world. Instead of controlling students, schools need to be teaching students how to belong and succeed.

Lack of Relevance and Rigor in Educational Programs

At the turn of the century, good jobs that paid well were available for laborers, regardless of whether they could cipher their names. Now, however, workers are needed who can read, handle sophisticated computers, solve problems, and think. Now we want workers who have initiative. By the year 2000, it is anticipated that over half of the nation's jobs will require skills and knowledge beyond the high school level and over a third will require at least college level skills and knowledge. Not only will there be fewer jobs for unskilled laborers, these jobs will be low paying jobs. A more demanding, more technical curriculum is needed that also is appropriate for a much broader proportion of the population. We can no longer afford to sort out large numbers of school failures.

Merely raising standards in what we are currently doing is unlikely to lead to improvement. We need a different way of thinking and of involving students in the learning process. Noddings (1992) suggests that we do not need to cram

"Give a man a fish, you feed him for a day...
...teach a man to fish, you feed him for life"
~ CHINESE PROVERB

students' heads with specific information and rules; rather, we need to help them learn how to inquire and seek connections.

Such an approach is consistent with the holistic, constructivist approach that maintains meaning is constructed by each person as new knowledge is connected to existing knowledge. Learning is no longer seen as acquiring knowledge, but as an active construction of knowledge. In this view learning is not a receptive act, but a creative one. This "change of lens," as Mary Poplin (1993) describes it, means that teachers interact with children in authentic ways as they make meaning of learning experiences. Knowledge is not viewed as static, something the experts know and students have to learn; it is created. As we learn, we change old knowledge with our new understandings.

In the constructivist approach, teachers are learners and facilitators of others' learning, not the ones who give the knowledge to students. Poplin (1993) believes that the single most important function of a teacher is to know how her students think, so she or he can create new experiences that can be related to the students' ways of thinking. She also thinks the curriculum should be connected to what students already know. It should be geared toward the students' developmental needs (what they are developmentally ready to learn). As much as possible, it should also be experientially based and it should be interesting to the students.

As Crowell (1989), Heshusius (1989), Piaget (1959), Poplin (1988, 1993), Reid (1988), and Rhodes (1991) explain, other tenets of holistic or constructivist thought are:

1. Errors are opportunities to teach, not behaviors to punish, and they are an essential element of the learning process.

2. Learning is transformational, not additive. As we learn about things, our understanding changes or transforms the way we view the thing. We do not learn by merely adding facts together.

3. All people are learners, always actively searching for and constructing new meanings.

4. The best predictor of what and how someone will learn is what they already know.

5. Learning often proceeds from whole to part to whole.

6. Learners learn best from experiences about which they are passionately interested and involved.

7. Learners learn best from people they trust.

8. Experiences connected to the learner's present knowledge and interest are learned best.

To implement this approach, we need teachers who are so comfortable with what they know and who they are that they can move beyond a self-consciousness with their teaching to an intense involvement in learning. They need to be able to encourage their students, to be willing to discuss matters about which they have no specific training, and to help students create and learn to investigate. We need to empower teachers if we want them to empower students. However, teacher empowerment does not happen in schools where the principal dictates policy and teachers' voices are not valued (Barth, 1991).

Loss of Teacher Voice

As Darling-Hammond (1993) points out, teaching is not routine. To be effective, teachers need to be able to vary techniques in relation to student needs. Teachers need to make many decisions about their students' learning styles, ability levels, stages of cognitive and psychological development, and experience with subject matter. These decisions are based upon teachers' knowledge of child development, learning theory, curriculum approaches, and assessment procedures. When administrators or school boards require teachers to follow a fixed set of prescriptions, as so often happens, their ability and motivation to adapt their instruction to their particular teaching situation is diminished. Under such circumstances, we are unlikely to have high-level teaching.

When students perceive school as relevant, interesting, challenging, rewarding, and welcoming, they rarely engage in destructive, oppositional, disruptive behavior. However, the reverse is also true. When teachers do not feel empowered to teach children rather than a curriculum, they are more likely to be confronted by more behavioral problems.

Unfortunately the literature repeatedly suggests that far too many teachers believe they lack the support and the sanction to be innovative. Too many schools exist that have conflicting explicit and implicit goals. For example, teachers are assigned classes with children who are having serious behavioral difficulties. The teachers are given the responsibility for organizing programs that will help the students improve behaviorally. Yet, when the child misbehaves, the administration may suspend the child without consulting the teacher. Even though the teacher disagrees with the administrative action, the teacher is expected to support the administration's position. This is both frustrating and discouraging to teachers. It undermines their sense of purpose and their sense of control. Additionally, it allows no comfortable means of evaluating practice and discussing how to improve.

Not only does control over teachers hamper their work with students, but it also interferes with their ability to be leaders and change agents. As Betts (1992) notes, we have attempted to treat education as a unitary system, but in reality it is highly pluralistic with many conflicting goals. By treating education as a unitary system, we have been forced to make unsatisfactory compromises both conceptually and in practice. We need teachers to be well informed, willing to take risks, and capable of creative problem solving. We also need to provide them with work environments that support their problem solving.

Management literature suggests that productive work conditions are ones in which people feel that their work is purposeful, that it has meaning beyond just earning a paycheck, that there is a collective commitment to the work, and that progress and improvement are evident (Schmoker & Wilson, 1993). Schools are needed that have a shared vision and understanding of purpose, that support risk taking and individualization, and that encourage teamwork and shared decision making.

Addressing Hard Questions Through School Reform

With so many issues that need attention, it is not surprising that we are in a period of school reform and restructuring. Spring (1989) notes that during almost every decade in the twentieth century large groups of people have complained that American public schools were failing. He suggests that when the conservatives are in power liberals criticize their laissez-faire attitudes, and when liberals are in power conservatives criticize their spending and idealism.

Banathy (1991) suggests the following reasons our reform efforts have been largely unsuccessful:

1. They have been piecemeal and incremental.

2. Solution ideas have not been integrated within the system.

3. Our study of education has used a discipline-by-discipline approach.

4. Our thinking has been reductionistic and within the boundaries. We have not been thinking "outside the box" when developing solutions.

If current efforts at educational reforms are to be more than "window dressing," most agree that fundamental changes are needed that put the needs of students and their families at the heart of the reform (Kozol, 1991; Barth, 1991; Bullard & Taylor, 1993; Glasser, 1992). A debate is currently underway about how this reform is best accomplished (Fuchs & Fuchs, 1991). For example, Stainback and Stainback (1991) advocate total restructuring of our current system of providing services, while Kauffman (1993) argues for less radical change through thoughtful adjustment to our current system. Chapter 2 deals with these issues in greater depth.

Conclusions

Finding a Balance

While we develop the future, we also need to attend to the present. Our culture is changing. It is becoming more complex, diverse, and multifaceted. The power base is shifting. White, middle-class men are no longer the only ones with power. Women, minorities, and persons with disabilities are all groups that are developing a voice in our culture. This shift in the power base is also reflected in schools. Teachers and school administrators are trying to sort out how to maintain order while shifting some of the power.

Our schools need teachers who can deal with the shifting sands of our society, who understand the issues that undergird our current reform debate, who know what they believe and why, and who will actively work to promote reform in schools where it is needed (Fullan, 1993). Our schools also need teachers who know how to deal with day-to-day challenges in a manner that is compassionate, child-centered, ethical, and informed—consistent with our best knowledge.

To do this, teachers will have to balance the interests of a number of persons and determine priorities. Such decisions are difficult. Usually there are no clear-cut, "right" ones. Furthermore, there are multiple criteria for making decisions, many of which take time to evaluate. For example, referring to the case presented at the beginning of this chapter, if Mr. Bobrinski wants Clyde to learn about the importance of honesty in a relationship, it is unlikely that there will be any way of clearly determining whether his action was wise, at least not in the short term. Instead, Mr. Bobrinski must act in accord with his own personal moral standards, his understanding of his professional ethics, his school's regulations, the law, and his professional knowledge. Sometimes, perhaps often, he may have to consider to whom he is most responsible: his student or class, his family, his colleagues, the school district (his employer), or himself and his own needs and ideals. He will feel conflicted and may want help in making such decisions. Certainly he needs to develop tools that will help him meet the challenges of teaching.

In this book we have sought to present challenges. We have not glossed over the tough issues teachers face. We have selected case material that illustrates real world situations, rather than what we sometimes call best practice. We have also selected studies that were based on qualitative data obtained from teachers as well as on traditional quantitative research data, because we wanted to reflect *qualitatively* the types of challenges teachers face. We want our readers to debate the cases. We believe there are multiple ways of thinking about our cases. It has been our experience that teachers are best prepared to implement positive, constructive behavior management programs when they have practiced problem solving around these complex issues. Successful teachers are people who have found a way to match their actions to their personal values and beliefs. They are genuine—comfortable with themselves—and free to share themselves. They are powerful people who can share their power with others.

Underlying Assumptions of the Text

We have sought balance between solutions that work in the classroom today and system-level solutions that will take time to achieve, between concrete behavior management strategies and more abstract and nebulous relationship interventions, and between teacher as authority and limit setter and teacher as friend and facilitator. We have emphasized the importance of a shift in thinking, from behavior management or classroom management as strategies for managing children's behavior, to approaches that enable children to succeed in school. This shift in thinking is associated with several important assumptions:

1. The most effective approach to discipline is creating a school that has enriched, stimulating, activity-oriented learning environments where students are successful and feel valued. As Bullard and Taylor (1993) note, "A school where all children learn is the best school for all children. In an equitable school, where teaching for learning for all occurs, there are far less discipline problems. More students are highly motivated to study and learn, because they know they will get a fair shot at the target" (p. 10).

2. Schools must have the expectation that all children *can* learn, achieve, behave, and cooperate. It is not acceptable to excuse, avoid, or dismiss

children because they are different, or because they have disabilities or social, psychological, or physical stressors. Not all children may meet the same standards, but they can all meet *some* standards.

3. There is no curriculum standard or behavioral practice that is always best. Rather than relying on a state-adopted curriculum standard, teachers need to use standards that fit their students. This does not mean that teachers ignore mandates given them by the state; rather, state standards serve as a road map. Teachers, like travelers, stop and take the time for repairs. They also take detours that enrich the trip. With success, students may progress and one day meet the state standards. With repeated failure, they are likely to spend their energies disrupting and opposing school, often getting pushed out by disciplinary or safety rules, or they may give up in despair over their failures and eventually drop out of school.

4. Schools and teachers need to give careful attention to developing and using educational approaches that accommodate individual and cultural styles and preferences. Much of the current practice in schools reflects a dominant-culture orientation, and too frequently children get the message that their own heritage and culture is inferior. Differences need to be seen as strengths and points of enrichment, not as problems to be accommodated.

5. Teachers, administrators, and other school personnel need to start with an examination of themselves when they develop individual or classroom plans for students. When they view a child as the problem, they create the potential for failure. Rather than search for the deficits in the child, they should frame their task as capitalizing on strengths or on improvements and they should ask themselves How can I view this situation or this child more constructively and empathetically? What can I do to make the classroom more positive?

6. The most effective interventions, whether designed for individual children or for entire classes, occur within a context that supports the intervention. Children are part of the classroom system and classrooms are part of larger systems that must be considered when planning interventions.

We believe that creating positive, productive classrooms and schools requires a fundamental shift in thinking from an orientation towards what is wrong with a child or a teacher to a way of thinking about strengths the child, the teacher, and the school possess. The question is not What's wrong? Rather, it is What can we do to support or enable success? As a parent of a child with disabilities succinctly told school officials, "We spend our days looking at what our children can do. You spend your days talking about what they cannot do. The school system should listen to us."

Discussion Questions and Activities

1. In the case presented at the beginning of the chapter, what do you think Mr. Bobrinski should do and why? If you were in such a situation, what would you do?

2. Schools have both a formal and an informal (or hidden) curriculum. The concept of the hidden curriculum refers to the unplanned, unintentional lessons that are taught in school. For example, when the class bully hits another child and the teacher or the school does nothing to protect the victim, a message is conveyed that it is OK to victimize others. If most of the children who get in trouble are from a minority background, children in the school may believe people from that minority background are troublemakers. When the names of all children who receive free lunch are read out loud, the message is conveyed that they are different; if the teacher's attitude is disdainful, the children also learn that receiving free lunches is bad. Children often translate such messages in personal ways ("If it is not good to receive free lunch, and I receive free lunch, then I am not good"). Think back to your own schooling and the lessons you learned from the hidden curriculum.

3. If local schools agree, visit a classroom and shadow one of the "trouble-makers" all day. Look for actions, policies, or patterns that support this child's role as a troublemaker. Pay particular attention to patterns of behavior. Under what type of circumstances does this student seem to get into trouble and what happens when this student misbehaves? Where or who are the student's supports in the school? How does the school seem to feel about the child's family?

4. William Glasser (1985) states: "All living creatures, and we are no excep-tion, only do what they believe is most satisfying to them. The main reason our schools are less effective than we would like them to be is that, where students are concerned, we have failed to appreciate this fact" (p. 8). Do you agree or disagree? Have a debate in your class between those who support this statement and those who do not.

Self-Reflection

Much of the content in Chapter 1 has to do with setting one's personal vision for teaching. To help you with that task, answer the following questions.

1. What kind of school would you want your child to attend? Describe the curriculum, the type of teacher, the school atmosphere, behavioral expec-tations, and the evaluation strategies that will be used. In your ideal school, who makes the decisions about these features?

2. What kind of teacher do you want to be? Why did you decide to become a teacher? What are your best qualities as a teacher? What qualities do you most need to develop in order to be the kind of teacher you want to be?

3. Describe the culture in which you grew up. How did your family interact (paying particular attention to the language you and your family used)? Describe your family rituals and ceremonies and your feelings about them. Describe a typical dinner at your home when you were growing up. What were your family's expectations for you and how were these expectations conveyed? What actions were praised/valued and which ones were punished in your home? Compare your own background with someone who seems quite different from you, looking for subtle differences in your experiences. Think about how these affect your outlook and perception of others.

4. Teachers touch lives permanently—sometimes in caring, helpful ways and sometimes in hurtful, destructive ways. Think about your teachers. Who was the best and why was he or she the best? Who was the worst and why? Write a letter to both (you may never mail it), telling them how you remember them and the way they treated you and what you liked or disliked about that treatment. Do the lessons you learned from these two teachers guide your own teaching?

References

Allen, V. & Greenberger, D. (1980). Destruction and perceived control. In A. Baum & J. Singer (eds.), *Advances in environmental psychology: Vol. 2, Applications of personal control* (pp. 85–109). Hillsdale, NJ: Erlbaum.

Banathy, B. (1991). *Systems design of education: A journey to create the future.* Englewood Cliffs, NJ: Educational Technology Publications.

Barth, R. (1991). *Improving schools from within.* San Francisco: Jossey-Bass.

Betts, F. (1992). How systems thinking applies to education. *Educational Leadership, 50,* 38–41.

Braithwaite, E. (1959). *To Sir, with love.* Englewood Cliffs, NJ: Prentice-Hall.

Brophy, J. (1986). Classroom management techniques. *Education and Urban Society, 18,* 182–84.

Brown, L. & Gilligan, C. (1992). *Meeting at the crossroads: Women's psychology and girls' development.* New York: Ballantine.

Brown, R. (1991). *Schools of thought.* San Francisco: Jossey-Bass.

Buber, M. (1965). Education. In Martin Buber, *Between man and man* (pp. 83–103). New York: Macmillan.

Bullard, P. & Taylor, B. (1993). *Making school reform happen.* Boston: Allyn & Bacon.

Crowell, S. (1989). A new way of thinking: The challenge of the future. *Educational Leadership, 47* (1), 60–63.

Darling-Hammond, L. (1993). Reframing the school reform agenda: Developing capacity for school transformation. *Kappan, 74,* 752–61.

Deci, E., Nezlek, J. & Sheinman, L. (1981). Characteristics of the rewarder and intrinsic motivation of the reward. *Journal of Personality and Social Psychology, 40,* 1–10.

Eisner, E. (1990). The meaning of alternative paradigms for practice. In E. Guba (ed.), *The paradigm dialog.* Newbury Park, CA: Sage.

Fuchs, D. & Fuchs, L. (1991). Framing the REI debate: Abolitionists versus conservationists. In J.W. Lloyd, N. Singh, & A. Repp (eds.), *The regular education initiative: Alternative perspectives on concepts, issues, and models* (pp. 241–55). DeKalb, IL: Sycamore.

Fullan, M. (1993). Why teachers must become change agents. *Educational Leadership, 50,* 12–17.

Gartner, A. & Lipsky, D. (1992). Beyond special education: Toward a quality system for all students. In T. Hehir & T. Latus (eds.), *Special education at the century's end: Evolution of theory and practice since 1970.* Cambridge, MA: Harvard Educational Review.

Glasser, W. (1986). *Control theory in the classroom.* New York: Harper & Row.

Glasser, W. (1992). *The quality school.* New York: HarperCollins.

Goodlad, J. (1990). *Teachers for our nation's schools.* San Francisco: Jossey-Bass.

Granger, L. & Granger, B. (1986). *The magic feather.* New York: Dutton.

Henderson, J.G. (1992). *Reflective teaching: Becoming an inquiring educator.* New York: Macmillan.

Heshusius, L. (1989). The newtonian mechanistic paradigm, special education, and contours of alternatives: An alternative. *Journal of Learning Disabilities, 22,* 403–415.

Hilton, J. (1934). *Goodbye, Mr. Chips.* New York: Bantam.

Howe, K. & Miramontes, O. (1992). *The ethics of special education.* New York: Teachers College, Columbia University.

Johnson, S. (1990). *Teachers at work: Achieving success in our schools.* New York: Basic Books.

Katzenmeyer, W. (1993). Schools for the 21st century: What should they be like? Presented at the Florida TED/DOE Conference in Tampa, FL, February 11–12, 1993.

Kauffman, J. (1993). How we might achieve the radical reform of special education. *Exceptional Children, 60,* 6–16.

Keogh, B. (1990). Learning disabilities: Diversity in search of order. In M. Wang, M. Reynolds, & H. Walberg (eds.), *The handbook of special education: Research and practice, Vol. 2.* Oxford: Pergamon.

Knitzer, J., Steinberg, Z. & Fleisch, B. (1990). *At the schoolhouse door: An examination of programs and policies for children with behavioral and emotional problems.* New York: Bank Street College of Education.

Kounin, J. (1970). *Discipline and group management in classrooms.* New York: Holt, Rinehart & Winston.

Kozol, J. (1991). *Savage inequalities: Children in America's schools.* New York: Crown.

Levin, J. & Nolan, J. (1991). *Principles of classroom management: A hierarchical approach.* Englewood Cliffs, NJ: Prentice-Hall.

Lortie, D. (1963). *Schoolteacher: A sociological study.* Chicago: University of Illinois Press.

Morse, W. (1993). Personal communication.

Morsink, C., Soar, R.S., Soar, R.N. & Thomas, R. (1986). Research on teaching: Opening the door to special education classrooms. *Exceptional Children, 53,* 32–40.

Morsink, C., Thomas, C. & Smith-Davis, J. (1987). Noncategorical special education programs: Process and outcomes. In M. Wang, M. Reynolds, & H. Walberg (eds.),

The handbook of special education: Research and practice, Vol. 2. Oxford: Pergamon Press.

Nelsen, J. (1993). *Positive discipline in the classroom.* Rocklin, CA: Prima Publishers.

Nichols, P. (1992). The curriculum of control. *Beyond Behavior, 3,* 5–11.

Nieto, S. (1992). *Affirming diversity: The sociopolitical context of multicultural education.* New York: Longman.

Noblit, G. (1993). Power and caring. *American Educational Research Journal, 30,* 23–38.

Noddings, N. (1992). *The challenge to care in schools: An alternative approach to education.* New York: Teachers College, Columbia University.

Piaget, J. (1959). *The construction of reality in the child* (translated by M. Cook). New York: Basic Books.

Poplin, M. (1988). Holistic/constructivist principles of the teaching/learning process: Implications for the field of learning disabilities. *Journal of Learning Disabilities, 21,* 401–416.

Poplin, M. (1993). A practical theory of teaching and learning: The view from inside the new transformative classroom: Contributions of constructivism. Presentation at the TED/DOE Conference in Tampa, FL, February 1993.

Poplin, M. & Weeres, J. (1992). *Voices from the inside: A report on schooling from inside the classroom.* Claremont, CA: Institute for Education in Transformation at the Claremont Graduate School. Funded by the John W. Kluge Foundation.

Ravitch, D. (1983). *The troubled crusade: American education 1945–1980.* New York: Basic Books.

Reid, D. (1988). Reflections on the paradigmatics of a paradigm shift. *Journal of Learning Disabilities, 21,* 417–20.

Reynolds, M. (1991). Classification and labeling. In J.W. Loyd, N. Singh & A. Repp (eds.), *The regular education initiative: Alternative perspectives on concepts, issues, and models* (pp. 29–42). DeKalb, IL: Sycamore.

Rhodes, W. (1991). The paradigm change. In W. Rhodes (ed.), *Out at the edge: An education sourcebook on the new paradigm.* Collection available from the author.

Rosenshine, B. (1983). Teaching functions in instructional programs. *The Elementary School Journal, 83,* 335–51.

Sabatino, D. (1987). Preventive discipline as a practice in special education. *Teaching Exceptional Education, 19,* 8–11.

Schmoker, M. & Wilson, R. (1993). Transforming schools through total quality education. *Kappan, 74,* 389–95.

Schon, D. (1987). *Educating the reflective practitioner.* San Francisco: Jossey-Bass.

Shor, I. (1986). *Culture wars: Schools and society in the conservative restoration 1969–1984.* Boston: Routledge & Kegan Paul.

Skrtic, T. (1991). *Behind special education: A critical analysis of professional culture and school organization.* Denver: Love.

Spring, J. (1989). *The sorting machine revisited: National educational policy since 1945.* New York: Longman.

Stainback, W. & Stainback, S. (1991). A rationale for integration and restructuring: A synopsis. In J.W. Lloyd, N. Singh & A. Repp (eds.), *The regular education initiative: Alternative perspectives on concepts, issues, and models,* 225–39. DeKalb, IL: Sycamore.

Zabel, M. (1992). Responses to control. *Beyond Behavior, 4,* 2.

Creating Positive, Productive School Climates

It is Tuesday afternoon and Karen must prepare for the midwinter parents' night at Middlesex School. She dreads the entire affair! All she really wants to do is go home and curl up with a good book. More and more, Karen feels that teaching is just a job that interferes with her private life.

It wasn't always like this. At Juniper Elementary, Karen was voted Teacher of the Year. She loved teaching at Juniper, where teachers and administrators worked as a team. There she was encouraged to be innovative, and if an idea proved unsuccessful, she was still supported by the administration and her co-workers. Karen team taught with two other people, and she loved the challenge of working with colleagues. She even wrote a few grant proposals for special projects. Two of her proposals had been funded, with one featured in the local newspaper and the other presented to the school board. It was invigorating to work at a school like Juniper, and Karen felt herself learning and growing in many ways. She still keeps in touch with the principal and several colleagues who were her friends at Juniper.

Karen was disappointed when her husband was transferred, but she found a job almost immediately at Middlesex, which is considered one of the best schools in the area. Unfortunately, after teaching there Karen doesn't think it's so wonderful. Middlesex teachers don't work together, and some of them are actually nasty in their criticism of each other. Staff meetings are sterile, tending to focus on issues that have little to do with teaching children, and when 3:45 clicks on the clock, all the teachers close their notebooks, clearly indicating they are ready to leave. Mr. Dinkmeyer then takes their cue and stops droning on about filling out forms.

Mr. Dinkmeyer is a passive person devoted to smooth paper flow, who avoids the more challenging issues dealing with the needs of children. Just before the winter holidays, Karen approached him about finding the funds so that the family of one of her students would be able to buy their kids a few gifts. Mr. Dinkmeyer's response was that giving them money would be inappropriate and Karen was not to meddle.

Karen does not agree with Mr. Dinkmeyer's way of administering the school. Everything is dictated from above. The curriculum is boring, and the students predictably respond by being difficult to control. When they misbehave, Mr. Dinkmeyer insists that they be sent to his office. Following a rigid system, he suspended two of Karen's students. The parents were angry at Karen for the suspensions, and she was angry with Mr. Dinkmeyer, although she felt it would be unprofessional to reveal her feelings to the parents. The disgruntled parents griped to others, who then complained to Mr. Dinkmeyer about Karen. Because of this unrest and dissatisfaction, Mr. Dinkmeyer asked Karen to explain the discipline system this evening at parents' night. Karen feels that he has passed the buck, and she really dreads having to present a system with which she is not in sympathy to a potentially hostile audience.

Karen is sorry she was so open with Mr. Dinkmeyer in the beginning. If she had just closed her door, she could teach pretty much as she wants; that's what a lot of the other teachers seem to do. Because Mr. Dinkmeyer knows what is going on in her class, he feels free to dictate her actions. If he would just let her teach in her own way, she wouldn't have discipline problems. How she wishes she were at her old school, where she felt like a good teacher and enjoyed both administrative and parental support!

*O*ne of the naive assumptions we sometimes make in education is "as long as you have a good teacher, nothing else matters"; however, Karen's situation illustrates how the structure and climate of a school impact teachers and their students. Karen appears to have changed from a "teacher of the year" to a passive, discontented conformist. Issacson and Bamburg (1992) maintain that "despite personal differences, individuals are likely to behave in similar ways when they operate in a given system" (p. 44). In schools that have an authoritarian principal, teachers tend to be passive and conforming, whereas in schools where the principal establishes a democratic atmosphere by encouraging the expression of opinions and by sharing responsibility, teachers tend to be more assertive, independent, and innovative. Likewise, when schools create rigid rules for students, students tend to find ways of circumventing the rules, often while appearing to conform.

The purpose of this chapter is to review the impact of school structures on school climate and school effectiveness. Much of the school reform literature is based on findings about characteristics of schools that have been successful in creating positive, productive learning environments that welcome children, families, instructional personnel, and support staff.

Research on Positive, Productive Schools

Traditionally, research on effective schools has focused on input variables: budget, textbooks and available teaching supplies, teacher salaries, level of teacher training, quality of school facility, and family background of students. These variables have been assessed against output variables, the most common being student achievement on standardized tests. Consistently, the findings of such studies have indicated that family background is the most powerful predictor of student achievement (Coleman et al., 1966; Jencks et al., 1972). Critics charge that many of the schools' positive results are a function of the population they serve rather than what the schools actually do. For example, Coleman and colleagues (1966) observed:

> Schools bring little influence to bear on a child's achievement that is independent of his background and general social context. . . . This very lack of an independent effect means that the inequality imposed on children by their home, neighborhood and peer environment are carried along to become the inequalities with which they confront adult life at the end of school. Equality of educational opportunity must imply a strong effect of schools that is independent of the child's immediate social environment, and that strong independence is not present in American schools. (p. 325)

While more recent research on school effectiveness has not refuted earlier research, it has changed focus. Lezotte (1993) believes the definition of effective schools should include the concept of equity. The vision of a quality school that is emerging is one in which there is the "joint presence of quality (acceptably high levels of achievement) and equity (no differences in the distribution of that achievement among the major subsets of the student population)" (Lezotte, 1993, p. 305). Stated differently, equitable, quality, productive schools are schools where students from impoverished backgrounds achieve proportionately to students from privileged backgrounds.

The focus of more recent investigations into school effectiveness has been centered on the question When input data are held constant, what processes contribute to increased student outcomes? The results of these studies have been surprisingly consistent. Effective schools have the following elements:

☐ A vision and mission, a sense of purpose, that is understood and shared by all members of the school.

☐ Stimulating and safe learning environments where students and teachers can explore and learn together and take risks without fear of failure.

☐ A pluralistic perspective and authentic, meaningful ties to the community.

☐ An expectation that all students will learn and achieve. High expectations—opportunities to learn should abound.

☐ Interaction between teachers and students that provides students with frequent feedback and teachers with formative measures of progress. In such a system, students and teachers are constantly receiving information that is necessary to learn and to teach.

☐ Principals who are visible and involved in the instructional program and who support and provide instructional leadership to teachers in the school.

☐ Teachers who are empowered to make instructional decisions, to participate actively in school governance, and who feel a sense of ownership, investment, and pride in their school.

☐ Clear and frequent communication among all school components.

☐ A system of evaluation that enables participants to adjust the program and plans to accommodate individuals' needs.

Importance of a Shared Vision, Mission, and Philosophy

Most state departments of public instruction require schools to develop a mission and philosophy and to have them on file in the department as well as in the local district. Accrediting bodies also require this. Too often, however, these documents are prepared by a few administrators and serve only for compliance. It can be a time-consuming process to develop consensus among staff members about their educational beliefs, their goals for the school, and their preferred course of action, yet these form the operating principles that guide work. Teachers and administrators may feel it is a waste of time to talk about such abstract concepts as vision, mission, and philosophy; however, schools that do not have a shared vision, mission, and philosophy are more vulnerable to conflict and dissention (Chrispeels, 1992).

Table 2.1 illustrates the type of questions that groups need to ask themselves as they begin to develop a vision. Typically, each person in the group completes the sentence stems privately. When the group convenes, each person shares his responses and the group discusses all responses until consensus is reached. The final product needs to embody values of the whole school if it is to be taken seriously. It cannot be a top-down decision; therefore selection of the group to develop the vision and mission is very important. Group members need to be representative of the school at large. Parents representing minority groups within the school should be present, as should the teachers and support personnel. If the principal, assistant principal, and a few of the most established teachers create the vision and mission, it will be just like many others that sit in notebooks on shelves, gathering dust.

While vision, mission, and philosophy overlap, there are important distinctions. *Vision* refers to our ideas about an ideal (for example, the kind of school we want for our children). Visions set direction, they focus on the future. *Mission* refers to purpose, the raison d'etre. Mission statements are brief statements about why an organization exists and its overarching goal(s). *Philosophy* refers to the underlying belief system, the principles that guide our actions. Sergiovanni (1990) adds "covenant" to this grouping. *Covenant* is the shared values and expectations.

Barth (1991a) believes that "vision unlocked is energy unlocked" (p. 151). Actualizing visions creates synergy—a force greater than the component parts.

Table 2.1 Developing a Vision for Seaside Elementary School

At Seaside, we believe that . . .

Schools should provide children with . . .

The curriculum should . . .

Teachers should . . .

Students should . . .

Parents should . . .

Individual differences should . . .

Teaming relationships should . . .

Cultural diversity . . .

The communication and interaction among staff should . . .

The relationship between general and special education should be . . .

Resources should be allocated . . .

We are able to recruit and retain quality staff because . . .

Our programs are successful because . . .

Missions and philosophies provide guidelines for making tough decisions. Barth suggests that "all of us begin our work in education with 20/20 personal vision about the way we would like a school to be. This is what we value and are prepared to work and even fight for" (p. 148). He believes personal vision is why most people become educators, but he maintains that "by about December of our first year, something devastating and apparently inevitable begins to happen. Our personal vision becomes blurred by the well-meaning expectations and lists of others. Superintendents, state departments of education, and universities often all but obliterate the personal visions of teachers and principals with their own abundant goals and objectives" (p. 148). In Barth's opinion, the greatest tragedy is to be caught every day in the position of doing something one does not want to do or does not believe in. He suggests that "too many educators are playing out this tragedy, functioning as assembly-line robots whose main business is production, not learning" (pp. 150–51). In his opinion, "this condition, above everything else, diminishes both learning and professionalism in the public schools" (p. 151).

Some schools develop their shared vision, mission, and philosophy as a staff while others have their mission developed prior to the initial funding of the program. Staff in programs that are assigned a specific mission still need to establish a shared understanding of the underlying philosophy and the vision—a commitment to a vision about how to realize the mission.

Regardless of how a belief system is developed, it is critically important that individuals within the organization reach consensus about the basic issues. As Glickman (1992) maintains, "In order for a school to be educationally successful, it must be a community of professionals working together toward a vision of teaching and learning that transcends individual classrooms, grade-levels, and departments. The entire school community must develop a set of principles, not simply as an exercise but to establish a covenant to guide future decisions about goals, staffing, scheduling, materials, assessment, curriculum, staff development, and resource allocation" (p. 24).

As Sergiovanni (1990) points out, some school covenants (mission/vision/philosophy) also include operational platforms that provide the rules and standards for living and working together. Examples of the content found in vision statements of schools engaged in restructuring are described next.

Meeting individual needs through the teaching and learning process. Programs built on this value emphasize the importance of being guided by the needs of children and their families. Typically, the programs protect teacher flexibility in decision making and they avoid decisions made only for administrative convenience. Teachers are not expected to move large numbers of children through prefabricated curricula with a goal of obtaining uniform outcomes. Individual, human needs rather than standardization are valued and teaching is seen as an art—not a technology that can be applied regardless of the human beings using it. Likewise, children are not objects on an assembly line that have to be treated alike, but people with individual needs who are worthy of respect. Edwards and Young (1992) articulate this position very well:

> Social, emotional, physical, and academic growth and development are inextricably linked. As the social supports for children weaken, teachers have to devote much more time and energy to noninstructional demands. Teachers' and administrators' primary responsibility is instruction, but, as a practical and moral matter, they cannot ignore the social and psychological dimensions

of their students' lives. Changing social contexts demand changing practices. This view not only stretches the boundaries of parent/school involvement but redefines its purpose: not just higher academic achievement, but the well-being of children in its fullest sense. (p. 78)

Involving the community in serving the child and family. There is an African proverb that states "It takes a village to raise a child." Adhering to this wisdom, some schools that are engaged in restructuring have acknowledged that no one agency can meet all the needs of some children and their families. These schools are essential parts of their communities because they focus on serving the whole child by creating alliances with the community and working closely with community agencies. Called "full-service" or "comprehensive local schools" (Sailor et al., 1989), these schools serve as the coordinating vehicle for all children's services, including medical care, social service, public housing, legal aid, and foster care, as well as educational categorical program resources. Characterized by a high degree of shared decision making and site-based management, these programs seek to provide case management to families in a coordinated, personal manner, enabling schools to concentrate more on educational issues. Sailor (1991) observes that "if school is a place where children of poverty are viewed negatively by teachers and administrators, and where parents are held accountable for these perceived problems by being furnished with detention slips, requests to come in for disciplinary discussions, threats of suspension, and so on, then parents will come to view the school as mainly a place of bad news and harassment" (p. 16). On the other hand, if school is a neighborhood institution where advocates work to help families obtain services, then school is viewed positively and families are supportive of school efforts.

Schools that are part of a comprehensive system of service provision usually have incorporated a commitment to multiagency, multidisciplinary consultation in their vision and philosophy statements. Individuals within such schools function as service brokers working in multiple settings to secure the types of services needed. To function successfully in this role, they must find ways to work in partnership with persons from other agencies. Policies that restrict the sharing of information and funding of services must be addressed. Through such models, professionals are finding ways to collaborate and cooperate to serve the whole child and the family, rather than compete with other agencies for diminishing local, state, and federal monies.

Diverse instructional and curricular approaches. Schools that value individualization also value diversity in curricular and instructional approaches. They recognize that many of the children who are the most disruptive and challenging are students who learn best through channels not typically emphasized in schools. Bruner (1967) provides a vivid illustration of this in his description of a sixth grade class in the Bedford-Stuyvesant district of New York City. He instructed the class to move in such a way as to demonstrate what freedom means.

> . . . After some hesitation, a tall student stood and walked heavily forward to the front of the room. I heard the audible reaction of the other students and saw the look of dismay on the teacher's face. The student stopped, stood straight, and announced that he was about to demonstrate Freedom! He began to take a long stride across the room. Halfway through the stride he came to a shattering stop. A look of panic crossed his face, and, for all purposes, his right foot was riveted to the floor. His body lurched forward, then backward, but his right foot stayed locked to the floor. He jerked and lunged, but the foot wouldn't budge. He tried to pry the foot loose with a nearby chair—he commandeered a broomstick, which also failed to move the foot. We were all transfixed by the performance. Then his entire body relaxed. He smiled widely at us all, bent over, and deftly slipped his right foot out of its shoe and walked away with a lilt—leaving the "anchored" shoe behind. The class broke into applause, the teacher relaxed, and the student took several bows and returned to his seat. I asked if he could tell us what his movements told us about what freedom means. He said, "Sometimes you have to give up something that matters to you so that you can have it [freedom]." (p. 65)

Later, his teacher told Bruner that this student was the problem student of the school and that he virtually held the class hostage to his whims. The teacher also said this was the first assignment he had voluntarily engaged in since school started.

Traditionally, schools have placed a great deal of value on the traditional, symbolic, logical approach to learning. Like the student just described, many students who do not learn easily through this approach assume that they are the problem. They consider themselves "dumb" and they rebel in school, when the problem is the school's not valuing the way they learn best. As Samples (1992) observes, "Reading about art is vastly different from doing art. All the modes of knowing are vital throughout life and should be given equal weight" (p. 66).

Individualization is a way to insure that more children succeed in school. Jericho Middle School in New York has developed a program that not only recognizes individual differences and disabilities but also focuses on developing strengths and aspirations. Believing that all children have dreams and secret ambitions, many of which are dashed by early failures (or perceived failures), this school has instituted a policy that minimizes failure. For students at Jericho, participation in extracurricular activities is based on interest rather than ability. Any student who wants to be involved in an extracurricular activity may do so, as long as she or he fulfills the requirements of the activity (obtaining a uniform, attending games). Students with physical disabilities may be full members of the cheerleading squad if they are willing to make the necessary time commitment (Betts, 1992).

Inclusive schooling. Inclusion refers to the process of developing school communities that nurture, support, and welcome the educational and social needs of all students attending the school (Stainback & Stainback, 1990). Some authors have defined inclusion as educating all children in the mainstream (Stainback & Stainback, 1991) and this issue has created considerable controversy. Critics of full-inclusion models charge that the rights of children with disabilities will not be protected if they are only served in the mainstream; that the services and needed supports for children with disabilities to succeed in general education will disappear as budgets are cut; and that general education programs are not prepared to serve children with disabilities (Hocutt, Martin, & McKinney, 1991; Kauffman, Gerber, & Semmel, 1988; Fuchs & Fuchs, 1991). Advocates of inclusion maintain that many children in need of services are not being served because of artifacts in the identification process (Wang, Walberg, & Reynolds, 1992). Additionally, they note that the cost of serving individual children with special needs has been so intense that funds for improving classroom instruction have been depleted (Case, 1992). They believe that doing away with categorical programs and assigning responsibility for student progress to teams of teachers will be a successful and cost-effective solution. Wang and colleagues (1992) maintain that many strategies currently exist that will enable schools to respond more effectively and efficiently to all students' needs. For example, Wheelock (1992) describes structures that have been developed within the school day and the school calendar to give students who need extra help time to practice and more opportunities to learn. Instead of failing a grade or being segregated from the mainstream in pull-out programs, students are assigned extra periods for review or extended days or school years.

Regardless of the position taken regarding full inclusion, most support the concept of minimizing differences among children by focusing on similarities or on common human characteristics, rather than on disabilities. Creating schools where "everyone belongs, is accepted, supports, and is supported by his or her peers and other members of the school community in the course of having his or her educational needs met" (Stainback & Stainback, 1990, p. 3) is a widely accepted vision even though disagreements exist about the particulars of how this vision should be accomplished. Table 2.2 outlines the initial steps suggested by Sapon-Shevin (1990) for constructing a caring, inclusive school.

High expectations and meaningful involvement for all children. High expectations are included in almost all visions of excellence. Bill Honig (1987), former superintendent of California schools, observed "When you demand the best, at first your students will wrestle with you; they'll squirm and angle and look for any leverage point they can use to escape, until they realize you're determined

Table 2.2 Creating Inclusive Schools

1. *Take the labels off students and off classrooms.* Refer to people by name, not by label. It is not the LD class, it is Mrs. Sung's class.

2. *Take the labels off teachers.* Teachers should be responsible not just for a small group of students; they are responsible for all students in the school. Some teachers have a specialization in an area such as individualization of instruction or behavior management, which means they share their knowledge and skills with others through collaboration and working together.

3. *Develop a school philosophy that focuses on caring and inclusion of diverse students.* Affective and social concerns are sensitively attended to through scheduling, goal setting, and evaluation. Time is allotted for building relationships, and goals for social outcomes are established and evaluated alongside academic goals.

4. *Include all people who work in the school.* Cafeteria workers, school bus drivers, and secretaries are all critical components of the school and should be included in inservices and celebrations.

5. *Build the school as a community.* Expect participation in activities such as assembly, celebrate accomplishments, and encourage school spirit. School-wide birthday celebrations, a school-wide newsletter that includes everyone's accomplishments, and school color days are all strategies for building community.

6. *Honor diversity.* Draw attention to diversity and celebrate the differences among people in the school community. Celebrate the widest possible number of holidays: Chinese New Year, Native American holidays, Syttende Mai, etc. Educate children about disabilities, focusing on positive responses to differences.

7. *Think about curriculum broadly.* Promote sharing materials and projects across grade levels and ability levels. Establish school-wide yellow pages or offer miniworkshops after school on different topics taught by persons within the community.

8. *Stress cooperation rather than competition.* Have cooperative learning groups rather than individual competitive assignments. Teach cooperative games rather than competitive sports in physical education. Assign peer tutors or "book buddies" ("olders teaching youngers"). Plant a Good Deed Tree on which notes telling about acts of kindness may be placed. Pay for substitutes so teachers can visit each others' classes. Disperse classes for children with disabilities throughout the building rather than in trailers or an isolated wing away from most of the school.

9. *Empower everyone in the school.* Create committees that are as diverse as possible. Then a broad base of people will understand issues and feel responsible for solutions to problems. Challenge the whole school: Kids are being teased on the playground. What can we do? Place children in small groups/families and make a rule that children must ask their group for help before they can ask the teacher for help. When power is shared and spread around, everyone acts more powerfully.

10. *Think, dream, plan, and keep a sense of humor.* There are unlimited ways that schools can become more welcoming and inclusive. Teachers, administrators, students, and families just have to think about them.

Source: Sapon-Shevin (1990).

that they are going to learn. Then they'll do it, and do it joyfully, because they know you care enough to make things tough on them now for their own good later" (p. 19). He tells of taking a group of "emotionally handicapped" students on a camping trip in the California Sierras. He describes them as children who basically have "no self-control or tolerance for pain" and who "can be very disruptive in class." Yet, to Honig's amazement, around the campfire at night these holy terrors began talking about their teachers, and it was clear that the one they admired most was "the school crank, a tough old cop-on-the-beat who asked no quarter and gave none in his presentation of grammar, Edgar Allan Poe, and difficult vocabulary lists. On the other hand, the 'nice' teachers—the ones who passed everybody whether they deserved it or not—came in for a hiding. At intimate times like that evening around the campfire one discovers how kids really feel. They just aren't that dumb. Even the baddest of the bad actors knows that teachers who are 'nice' to them in school are really killing their chances to make it in the outside world" (p. 20). While some may argue that it is possible to be "nice" and also have high standards, it is hard to argue with the position that accomplishing tasks that are difficult is gratifying and affirming of one's competence.

The critical issue is not demanding that students *do* work, but rather helping them *become meaningfully engaged* in their work. Haberman (1991) reports seeing a variety of instructional techniques used in urban schools, including direct instruction, cooperative learning, peer tutoring, individualized instruction, computer-assisted learning, behavior modification, student contracts, media-assisted instruction, scientific inquiry, lecture/discussion, tutoring by specialists or volunteers, and even the problem-solving units common in progressive education. However, he notes that in spite of the broad range of instructional approaches a teacher could select, there is a typical form of teaching that has become accepted as basic. Furthermore, he maintains that since he first started observing in urban schools in 1958, this style has become even more entrenched. Now, he notes that a "teacher in an urban school of the 1990s who does not engage in these basic acts as the primary means of instruction would be regarded as deviant" (p. 291). The teaching acts that constitute the core of Haberman's urban teaching style are:

1. giving information,
2. asking questions,
3. giving directions,
4. making assignments,
5. monitoring seatwork,
6. reviewing assignments,
7. giving tests,
8. reviewing tests,
9. assigning homework,

10. settling disputes,
11. punishing noncompliance,
12. making papers, and
13. giving grades. (p. 291)

Haberman maintains that this directive pedagogy of poverty is evident at all levels and in all types of classrooms. "Unfortunately, the pedagogy of poverty does not work. Youngsters achieve neither minimum levels of life skills nor what they are capable of learning. The classroom atmosphere created by constant teacher direction and student compliance seethes with passive resentment that sometimes bubbles up into overt resistance. Teachers burn out because of the emotional and physical energy that they must expend to maintain their authority every hour of every day. The pedagogy of poverty requires that teachers who begin their careers intending to be helpers, models, guides, stimulators, and caring sources of encouragement transform themselves into directive authoritarians in order to function in urban schools" (p. 291).

The few teachers who gain control through a trusting relationship and involvement in meaningful learning activities are effective, according to Haberman (1991). For them, control is a *consequence* of their teaching, not the prerequisite. He proceeds to detail criteria for what he believes to be good teaching. In his view, the criteria set forth in Table 2.3 reflect high expectations. He notes that changing schools and giving up the pedagogy of poverty can only be done with widespread cooperation and commitment from teachers, administrators, parents, and community. He further notes that each group will have to give up its current limited scope of responsibility, its safety net, in order to make such a change happen, and he wisely questions whether people are willing to take such risks.

A pluralistic perspective.   A pluralistic approach to education is based on the assumption that all groups have strengths that contribute to the fabric of a society. Pluralism is based on the existence of cultural compatibility; that is, the perspectives of all individuals are incorporated, appreciated, admired, accepted, and used in the search for desired societal outcomes.

Children enrolled in public schools represent diverse ethnic, socioeconomic, religious, political, and geographic backgrounds. Positive, productive schools find ways of negotiating among the diverse interests of families served by the school so that no one perspective or body of knowledge dominates the culture to the detriment of others. Unfortunately, data currently being reported in many different sources (Lewis, 1992; Brown, 1991; Kozol, 1991) suggest that many, if not most, schools still have policies and practices that are predominantly based in white, middle-class perspectives. Many low-income, minority children do not have access to rigorous, college-preparatory educational programs. Women and minorities have strongly criticized existing textbooks as being highly biased toward a masculine, Western culture rooted in a commitment to rational inquiry.

Table 2.3 Criteria of Good Teaching

According to Martin Haberman (1991), good teaching is going on when students are engaged in the following . . .

- ☐ involved with issues they regard as vital

- ☐ involved with explanations of human differences

- ☐ being helped to see major concepts, big ideas, and general principles (not engaged in learning isolated facts)

- ☐ planning what they will be doing

- ☐ involved with applying ideals such as fairness, equity, or justice to their world

- ☐ actively involved (Doing an experiment is better than reading about it or watching it being done.)

- ☐ involved in real-life experiences such as field trips and community resources

- ☐ involved in heterogeneous groups

- ☐ challenged to think about ideas in a way that questions common sense or widely accepted assumptions, that relates new ideas to previously learned ones, or that applies an idea to the problems of living

- ☐ redoing, polishing, or perfecting their work

- ☐ involved with the technology of information access

- ☐ encouraged to think about their lives and how they have come to believe and feel as they do

Source: Haberman (1991).

Price (1992) reports that he was an adult before he learned that the Russian poet Pushkin and the French author Dumas were black. While their works are widely published in popular texts, their heritage is not. When the focus of most texts is on the accomplishments of white, Western males, the assumption is made that they are the superior group, the group that has made the most significant contributions to our culture. In reality, seminal contributions to our culture have also been made by minorities and women. Recognizing these contributions and valuing their importance in our lives is a way of affirming pluralism.

On a more personal level, schools that are able to understand and respond sensitively and flexibly to children of different cultural heritages are more successful in helping children achieve in school. James Comer, a well-known Yale child psychiatrist, reports that three of his childhood friends dropped out of school because they had neither the personal self-confidence nor the social skills to adapt to the dominant culture in their schools. Comer (1988) attributes his own success largely to his parents, who helped him feel confident and helped him acquire the necessary social skills to succeed in school. Positive schools do not depend upon the families of minority children to teach the children how to adapt to the school; rather, the schools are flexible, creative, and caring in how they adapt to the children.

Shade and New (1993) discuss schools' need to learn sensitive responses to subtle troubles based on ethnic differences. "The perspective of many African Americans is an amalgamation of both African and Anglo-Saxon beliefs, attitudes, customs, and practices designed to facilitate acculturation and adaptation to a racially stratified society. This cultural orientation differs significantly from that of the middle-class Anglo-Saxon community. . . . School culture, no matter where the institution is located, has a carefully defined behavioral norm that seems to have emanated from the early religious schools. It requires conformity, passivity, quietness, teacher-focused activities, and individualized, competitive noninteractive participation of students. The ideal student in this culture sits quietly in his or her own seat, looks only at the teacher, answers the questions when called on, and performs the required work in the manner prescribed" (p. 318).

Such norms can create conflict for African American children, who frequently have an active approach to learning that involves (1) a preference for moving around the room and talking to their neighbors rather than staying in their seats and being quiet, (2) a more spontaneous style of calling out rather than raising their hands, (3) unwillingness or indifference to completing their work unless they receive help from the teacher. When middle-class, Anglo teachers perceive such children as disruptive, a vicious cycle is set in motion. The children feel the teacher is "racist, mean, punitive, and unwilling to help them learn . . . a personal rejection" (Shade & New, 1993, p. 318). Teachers provide more negative feedback for behavior and academic pursuits, and they concentrate on controlling the classroom environment. As efforts to control behavior escalate, these children tend to be disproportionately represented in the suspension, expulsion, and discipline statistics. Even more damaging are teachers' lowered evaluations of students' potential and their lowered expectations for students' academic performance. Shade and New (1993) point out that "the variations in approach to behavior, communication, perceiving, and thinking are not differences that affect students' ability to learn. They represent a diversity of opinions and ideas about how to function. Teachers must realize that the desired outcomes can be the same for all children. There exists, however, variation in how these outcomes can be achieved" (p. 324).

The point has been made repeatedly that visions shape the policies and practices of schools. If the collective school culture conveys mistrust of minority children or fear of children with disabilities, teacher practice will reflect that view, independent of individual teachers' compassion and concern. If schools do not take the time to establish a shared vision, mission, and philosophy, there is no collective guide for action. Teachers then act upon their own individual values and beliefs, and often these beliefs are not consciously considered by the individual, but are developed through the experiences of life. It is through these subtle but powerful messages that prejudices and biases are developed and institutionalized within schools. Schools frequently manage their collective discomfort through bureaucratic overcontrol. Under such conditions, rampant cynicism develops (Issacson & Bamburg, 1992) and the school is rudderless (Senge, 1990). In contrast, developing a shared vision helps transform difficult challenges into creative acts.

Organizational Structures of Positive, Productive Schools

As discussed in Chapter 1, historically schools have been top-down, bureaucratic organizations, where teachers have worked in isolation from each other (Goodlad, 1984; Lortie, 1975; Sarason, 1971) and often antagonistically with their administrators. Rules and regulations have been developed by advisors to legislators, curriculum specialists, district-level administrators, and supervisors. The requirements generated by these rules and regulations have often been overwhelming and have taken up large amounts of time with students. Teachers have frequently complained they have little power to implement programs and practices they particularly like. They have felt undervalued and overworked, mistrustful of large organizations and impersonal bureaucracies (Johnson, 1990). Furthermore, schools within highly centralized organizations tend to emphasize conformity and compliance over variation and independence and to reinforce the preeminence of an administrative hierarchy that excludes teachers and parents from important decision making. Such schools have also been found to alienate students (Poplin, 1993).

Curriculum developers and publishers have worked hard to develop "teacher proof" materials—materials that teachers could not "mess up." Poor teachers were seen as the problem, and this attempt to protect the profession from its weaker members further reduced teachers' opportunities to create. Teachers were like workers on the assembly line and a standardized curriculum was the tool they used to produce their products—educated students.

Schools involved in restructuring recognize the shortcomings of this model and realize that when teachers feel uncertain about their craft, their self-esteem and sense of self-efficacy is threatened (Rosenholtz, 1989). When teachers face challenges such as teaching children who come from backgrounds different from their own or children who do not learn as the teacher expects, teachers often resort to "safe," known teaching strategies unless they have organizational support to help them try new approaches and learn new interventions. Organizational research has focused on structures that can shape and influence school climate. Consistently findings have indicated that supportive, affirming, collegial climates are more conducive to risk taking and the acquisition of new skills (Bullard & Taylor, 1993; Henderson, 1992; Noddings, 1992; Poplin & Weeres, 1992; Sarason, 1990).

Decentralized organizational models. More democratic, pluralistic, collaborative organizational models are emerging. For example, Roland Barth (1991a) describes good schools and healthy workplaces as communities of learners, where "students and adults alike are engaged as active learners in matters of special importance to them and where everyone is thereby encouraging everyone else's learning" (p. 9). These schools are also communities of leaders, "where students, teachers, parents, and administrators share the opportunities and responsibilities for making decisions that affect all the occupants of the school-house" (p. 9). He states, "I would welcome the chance to work in a school characterized by a high level of collegiality, a place teeming with frequent, helpful personal and professional interactions. I would become excited about life in a school where a climate of risk taking is deliberately fostered and where a safety net protects those who may risk and stumble. I would like to go each day to a school to be with other adults who genuinely wanted to be there, who really chose to be there because of the importance of their work to others and to themselves. I would not want to leave a school characterized by a profound respect for and encouragement of diversity, where important differences among children and adults were celebrated rather than seen as problems to remedy. . . . I'd like to work in a school that constantly takes note of the stress and anxiety level on the one hand, and standards on the other, all the while searching for the optimal relationship of low anxiety and high standards" (pp. 9–10).

A number of organizational reforms that enable instructional personnel, administrators, and families to work cooperatively and collaboratively in improving educational programs for children are currently being implemented. These initiatives involve decentralized decision making, professional collaboration across disciplines and within schools, shared-decision making, and inclusive, democratic service delivery.

Variously described as empowerment, site-based management, school-improvement teams, and participatory management, these initiatives involve important stakeholders in the decision making process. Rather than superintendents, supervisors, and principals setting policy and prescribing action for teachers and students to follow, school-based teams are being constituted and charged with the responsibility for making decisions about school curricula, priorities for resource allocation, and guidelines for developing and implementing instructional programs. As Glickman (1992) points out, however, merely shifting the responsibility for making decisions does not solve school problems. He maintains that to be effective, site-based or shared decision-making teams need to develop the following:

1. *A clear vision, a covenant,* to guide their decision making. (The importance of this was discussed earlier in this chapter.)

2. *A process for making decisions,* much like a constitution, that details

   (a) the types of decisions that will be made by the team (Will the site-based team focus on discipline policies, instructional practices, and equitable school routines such as bus duty, but not on personnel issues?)

(b) the roles of various persons (How does the principal relate to the site-based team?)

(c) selection procedure for the teams (Are members appointed or elected?)

(d) the decision-making mechanism to be used by the team (Are decisions reached by voting or by consensus? Does anyone have veto power?)

3. *A mechanism for acquiring information* upon which good decisions may be made. Teams cannot make competent decisions without relevant and valid data upon which to make their decisions. Most effective site-based teams are focusing on school improvement efforts. Without information about how children responded to an intervention, no reasonable decision can be made about the effectiveness of the intervention.

4. *Effective planning and prioritizing.* With the complexity of issues facing schools, school-based teams can be seduced or distracted from their primary mission. Productive teams are effective in setting priorities and maintaining their focus. This enables resources such as staff development activities and collaboration times to be matched to priorities.

Without these conditions, Glickman (1992) believes that a number of educational reforms currently receiving national attention such as whole language, interdisciplinary curriculum, cooperative learning, interactive technology, nongraded schools, heterogeneity, and authentic assessment will "burn bright for a few years, then fade away—to reappear in the next cycle following another 'back to basics' movement" (p. 27).

Goodlad (1991) also emphasizes the importance of teams understanding the rationale for an action and a structure within which to operate. With a common understanding and a commitment to a democratic decision-making process, he believes schools can become a community of professionals with diverse personal values and ideologies, who struggle to become responsible stewards for the vision of their institution (Goodlad, 1991), independent from irrelevant practices imposed from external authority figures. Without such frames, however, he questions whether reform efforts are worth the inevitable confusions and conflicts.

A number of authors (Barth, 1991a; Kessler, 1992) have reported that faculties who are involved in such meaningful endeavors tend to be highly motivated and committed to school improvement efforts, even when the actions required run counter to teachers' self-perceived interests. After several years of participating in a shared decision making model, Robert Kessler (1992), a

California school district superintendent, observed that dealing with the disagreements that arose during their team discussions "is unconditionally preferable to the system I have been used to. After having an adversarial environment for many years, the district now has open communication and an atmosphere of developing trust. Teachers and principals can focus their attention on improvements in curriculum and school programs. . . . I believe that making a mutual commitment to work by consensus and to base decisions on the best interest of kids is a model that can work anywhere" (p. 38).

Staff development as a tool for altering school climate.   The Augusta Project (Showers, 1990) illustrates how collaborative inservice and peer coaching can be used to produce change in the teaching workplace. This project grew out of the conviction that staff development is a critical element in school reform. This project, based in a middle school in Richmond County, Georgia, involved the implementation of a comprehensive staff development program in instructional innovations designed to reach all students. This school was selected because its student body contained large numbers of so called at-risk children. At least half of the students were receiving attention from the special education services. Some of the essential elements of the project were:

1. In order for the project to be instituted in the school, 80% of the faculty had to agree to participate.

2. Each teacher signed a written commitment to participate in all aspects of the project which included:

    (a) two weeks of summer training during both academic years,

    (b) regular practice with peers during the remainder of the summers,

    (c) use of the training content during the academic years,

    (d) work with peer study coaching teams during the years on implementation of the training content, and

    (e) periodic videotaping in their classrooms.

Content taught in the training sessions and practiced during the coaching sessions included cooperative learning, inductive learning, concept attainment, and mnemonic strategies. The ultimate goal of the project was to encourage teachers to use more active teaching and learning techniques and to become more involved with all students, but particularly with the ones exhibiting academic deficits. These interventions were selected because research indicated they are effective with low-performing students.

At 6-week intervals assistance was provided in order to address observed teacher problems and to extend documented teacher skills. Noting the isolation in which most classroom teachers work, Showers (1990) hypothesized that providing opportunities for substantive collegial interaction (coaching) would increase the thoughtful integration required to use new knowledge, behaviors, and materials. Observations of the teachers supported this hypothesis. At first the teachers tended to imitate the exact model they had seen demonstrated, but as the year progressed, most developed new and more appropriate, individualized uses of the strategies. By the middle of the second year, 60% were using the strategies at better than average levels of skill. Additionally, disciplinary referrals decreased notably and achievement test scores indicated a rate of growth at the national average whereas previously it had been significantly below the average.

Showers (1990) reported observing enormous communication gaps between the regular and special educators as well as remarkably similar perceptions of and attitudes towards students. "The pessimistic attitudes of many teachers about the possibility of improving student learning are not intractable, but success by colleagues has little apparent effect on such attitudes" (p. 39). For teachers to change the way they think about students, they apparently need to see their own students succeed with a new approach.

Outcomes rather than compliance. Traditionally, schools have operated within a top-down system in which administrators developed policy and procedures based upon their interpretation of state and federal law. Good principals ran schools that were in compliance with these policies and procedures. Good employees did what they were told to do. Little if any of the evaluation efforts focused on *how* these policies and procedures impacted the quality of education for the children in the school. For example, IEPs were monitored to determine whether they were in the proper folders, had the necessary component parts, were completed within the specified time period and were signed by the necessary people. Rarely were IEPs monitored to determine whether they really focused on important issues for the child, whether they were realistic, and whether the child was actually making progress on his goals. Stated differently, *we have focused on compliance, not on quality of outcome.*

When we have asked questions about quality, we have typically used criteria such as performance on group achievement tests, which critics charge is an inadequate criterion. For evaluation purposes, school reform efforts are moving away from achievement test scores to more authentic measures (such as portfolios) because they are a better qualitative indication of what the child or the program has accomplished. Additionally, an evaluation model that emphasizes outcome provides schools with greater flexibility regarding how they accomplish their goals. Teachers and schools can decide how they can best accomplish their goals, given their particular strengths and weaknesses. However, these approaches also have problems. Most of the authentic outcomes are very time consuming to review, we do not have good evaluation criteria, and it can be difficult to understand data obtained from portfolios. People not familiar with schools do not know whether a story written by a fourth grader is exceptional or average.

Instituting outcome-based evaluation systems and assigning responsibility for accountability to schools or to teachers also involves developing systems for continuous monitoring of quality indicators. Staff need to know when difficulties are developing so they can be easily remedied. Additionally, staff are always striving to be better; therefore systems for obtaining feedback about the school need to be in place and groups need to be assigned the responsibility for analyzing the feedback and planning proactive interventions to address identified needs.

Teachers' Roles in Positive, Productive Schools

School reform is based upon an assumption that teachers' roles will change. In the school restructuring literature, teachers are no longer seen as imparters of knowledge who dictate what happens in the classroom; rather they are facilitators of learning. They no longer close their classroom doors and work in isolation; rather they co-teach, collaborate, consult, function on teaching teams, participate in school governance, and enable themselves and others to learn and acquire skills. Teachers do not have to have the answers, but they need to know where and how to find them. Teachers do not dictate action without input from others; rather they lead discussions with children and collaborate with other teachers in deciding how best to deal with different situations.

Structures that promote professional collaboration among teachers include co-teaching, consultation models, and teacher assistance teams.

Co-teaching.   Co-teaching (Budoff, 1988a, 1988b) involves the integration of special education students into general education classes that are co-taught by both the special and general education teachers. The two teachers cooperatively plan and teach, placing emphasis on improving classroom instruction. Co-teaching enables both teachers to share their expertise and learn from each other. This model appears to be particularly effective when the mutual goal for both teachers is to improve their own skills and knowledge while also providing quality instruction in an inclusive setting for a group of children with a broad range of abilities.

Collaborative consultation models.   Collaborative consultation models (Fuchs & Fuchs, 1988; Idol, 1993; Idol, Paolucci-Whitcomb, & Nevin, 1986) have been developed that involve professionals working together to improve services for children and their families. These models are based on a collegial relationship between consulting teacher and another teacher. Their relationship is characterized by mutual trust and open communication, joint approaches to problem identification, pooling intervention resources, and shared responsibility for evaluation.

Research on the efficacy of collaborative consultation has been promising. Tindal, Shinn, Walz, and Germann (1987), in their study of the Pine County model, concluded that collaborative consultation between regular and special educators increased the likelihood of success for mildly handicapped students in regular educational classrooms. Similar results were obtained by Self, Benning, Marston, and Magnusson (1991). Other studies have suggested that consultation can significantly reduce the number of subsequent referrals for special education (Graden, Casey, & Bonstrom, 1985; Ritter, 1978).

Teacher assistance teams. Teacher assistance teams (Chalfant, Pysh, & Moultrie, 1979; Graden, Casey, & Christenson, 1985) are similar to cooperative consultation in the way they function, but they differ in their initial structure. These are usually school-based, interdisciplinary teams that work with general education teachers to help children be successful in general education settings. Generally these teams work with the general education teacher, providing support and information about a particular child until the child is referred for special education.

While current educational literature emphasizes the need for reform, it also reminds us of the difficulties inherent in change. As with many of the changes discussed in this chapter, teachers will need to shift their ways of thinking in order to contribute to the restructuring efforts. Johnson (1990) describes some of the obstacles that teachers will face when creating collegial, collaborative environments: functioning as collaborator as well as teacher, sharing their relationships with students, finding time to work with others, and being willing to share ideas with colleagues. Like many other authorities, Johnson believes that until teachers overcome their fear of these changes and actively take charge of their own professional relations, teaching will remain isolated work; however, like others, Johnson also believes that the responsibility for creating more collegial schools is not teachers' alone. Concurring that change will be difficult, Barth (1991b) queries whether teachers can maintain an already overloaded, complex, and demanding classroom while also designing and accepting a new vision of schooling. He equates the challenge to redesigning a 747 in flight, but then he reminds us that ". . . even a tiny insect can make its presence felt in a dramatic way to a very large animal" (p. 128). He and other authorities advocating school reform believe it possible, if schools develop a clear and inspiring vision and belief system to guide their actions.

Curriculum Reform

Curriculum involves both content and method, thus reforming the curriculum involves changing both what and how we teach. Many creative efforts are currently underway that involve reforming both curriculum content and teaching methodology. These reforms are in reaction to pressing social and political problems as well as changing views of knowledge and learning.

Changes in curriculum content.   Schools are the social institution designed to prepare future citizens of the society, and they are often given responsibility for addressing social ills. Curriculum is the vehicle through which these problems are addressed. For example, in the early 1900s our public schools were responsible for inducting large numbers of immigrant children into the American way of living and preparing them to work in our factories. As was pointed out in Chapter 1, our schools then focused on standardization and conformity. Sorting out the factory workers from the managers and the academicians was the task of schools in the early 1900s. Now our needs have changed radically. Our schools have become overly standardized and bureaucratized, and unable to respond constructively to our diversity, to the violence and alienation in our society, and to our technological needs.

Efforts to reform our curriculum are addressing these problems. Curriculum reform efforts include: a renewed interest in character education, support for instruction in multicultural issues, efforts to learn about and reduce racism, an emphasis on community-referenced content, and development of communication and information-seeking skills through the use of technology.

Character education programs have existed in schools for centuries. As Teddy Roosevelt observed, "To educate a person in mind and not in morals is to educate a menace to society" (quoted in Lickona, 1993). Schools of the 1990s are revisiting this issue in response to a number of problems: violence among our youth, increasing dishonesty, growing disrespect for authority, peer cruelty, a resurgence of bigotry in schools, a decline in the work ethic, sexual precocity, declining civic responsibility, increase in self-destructive behavior, and a general ethical illiteracy. When these problems first appeared, many tried to blame them on broken families or adverse socioeconomic conditions; however, these problems exist in all groups of young people from many differing backgrounds. Blaming a broken family or a student's low socioeconomic status are no longer acceptable explanations. Action is needed.

The current interest in character education has support from leaders in business, labor, government, faith communities, and families, not just from educators. Lickona lists a number of strategies that may be used for promoting character education (Table 2.4).

Multicultural education is another example of curriculum reform that has gained support from persons interested in social reform. Unfortunately, numerous examples of racism and its resultant problems are found in modern society. Problems faced by American cities illustrate the negative impact of racism— socially, morally, and economically. Molnar (1993) believes that as educators we need "to ensure that school and classroom activities help all children understand the many ways in which racism has shaped their lives and affects their

Table 2.4 *Strategies for Character Education*

Set a good example. Model caring and treat students with respect.

Create a moral community in school. Help students learn to value their fellow classmates, have respect for others, and feel responsible for contributing to their well-being.

Practice moral discipline. Create opportunities for students to practice moral reasoning and voluntary compliance with rules.

Develop a democratic classroom environment. Teach students to make decisions that take into account the well-being of all members.

Teach values through the curriculum. Literature, history, and science all lend themselves to teaching values, as do other commercially available programs such as *Facing History and Ourselves* and *The Heartwood Ethics Curriculum for Children.*

Use cooperative learning. Develop students' ability to appreciate and work with others.

Encourage moral reflection. Discuss and debate ethical, moral issues that arise in literature, research, and everyday life.

Teach conflict resolution. Help children learn to negotiate and resolve conflicts in a constructive manner.

Recruit the help and support of parents and community people. Develop a broad base of support for character education.

Work to create and maintain a school and community climate based on care and concern for all members. Develop a schoolwide ethos of ethical concern through school discipline policies, schoolwide activities, and student government activities.

experiences and understanding of the world. Schools can help children learn about the strengths and contributions of minority group members and their cultures. Schools can help children recognize the wounds that racism inflicts on all of us and can help them learn to appreciate, instead of fear, people different from themselves. These are lessons worth teaching. Again" (p. 59).

Changes in curriculum methodology.   Not only has the curriculum content changed, so too has our view of learning and teaching. As discussed in Chapter 1, many educators are shifting from a view of learning centered on teachers and their dispensation of a predetermined body of knowledge to a view of learning that is student centered and builds on students' backgrounds, experience, knowledge, and interests. From this perspective, learning should be active, meaningful, purposeful, and holistic. Students should not be required to be passive listeners, dealing with fragmented content that seems irrelevant to them. These shifts in approach to teaching and learning are reflected in all areas of instruction. In mathematics, there is a renewed emphasis on the use of manipulatives and a greater focus on problem solving. In science, innovative curricula emphasize hands-on experimental approaches that are integrated with math and other subjects. Writing is being taught as a process and skills such as punctuation, capitalization, and grammar are taught in the context of writing, not as isolated subject matter. Literature-based reading programs are replacing basal readers and reading and language arts are now being taught through a whole language approach. This shift from mastering basic skills to acquiring critical literacy also involves using integrated, thematic, contextualized, developmentally based curricula. Wiske and Levinson (1993) describe two classroom scenarios that illustrate how this can be done while using the *Curriculum and Evaluation Standards for School Mathematics* published by the National Council of Teachers of Mathematics (NCTM).

Lamont Stewar's geometry class:

I begin with a concrete example. When we were ready to start parallelism, I raised the question of the parking lot at the high school, whether it could be restriped to hold more cars. The kids measured lines, turning radii, angles. Then they proposed ideas. They were doing a heck of a lot of math.

But I have to give a departmental exam, and sometimes it's a real challenge to get to the right point at the right time. Also, it's hard to give a grade to projects submitted by groups. Is it fair to give a high grade to someone who is a marginal member of a productive group?

Olivia Green's geometry class:

I start a unit by asking the students what they know and then posing a problem for them to investigate in the computer labs next to my classroom. They create certain figures, usually working in pairs, take measurements, and make and test conjectures. Then, we talk about their findings.

As can be seen in these scenarios, curricula can be based on core concepts and taught through induction rather than didactic instruction. Furthermore, progress can be assessed through open-ended approaches rather than multiple-choice tests. Advocates of this approach believe that students learn to apply their knowledge and to be strategic in approaching tasks, framing what they need to know, identifying resources they will need, organizing information, and creating a project. This shift in teaching approach from "teacher lecture/student swallow" (p. 11, Wiske & Levinson, 1993) to guided inquiry stems from concern that mastery of discrete subject disciplines does not prepare students to be problem solvers and information users; but to recite what they have memorized (Brown, 1991; Bullard & Taylor, 1993).

The general education literature seems to be endorsing these approaches; however, special educators seem more divided. Some have been somewhat hesitant to employ these approaches, fearing that children with special needs need more direct instruction. A number of educators, however, see the shift to more active, student-centered learning as a means of introducing greater flexibility in the classroom (Stainback & Stainback, 1992). The supporters of reform believe that as general education classrooms become more flexible, they are better equipped to adapt to individual needs and to meet the needs of many children currently identified as disabled. It is too early to know how effective these reforms will be; however, early reports are promising (Chrispeels, 1992). Teachers who are philosophically sympathetic with the reform efforts should not hesitate to employ some of the innovative approaches as long as students are carefully monitored to be certain that all students are progressing and that all students feel valued, welcomed, and worthwhile.

Examples of Positive, Productive, Restructured Schools

Examples of such schools are briefly described here in an effort to illustrate how schools are successfully developing missions that focus on children's strengths, that invite children to learn and to achieve, and that minimize the need for intrusive behavior management through their excellent educational programs.

Accelerated Schools

Henry M. Levin, a Stanford professor of education and economics, has developed the Accelerated Schools model in which he focuses on bringing "at-risk" students into the academic mainstream by the end of their elementary school years. Levin believes "the way you define children has an awful lot to do with the way you work with them" (Brandt, 1992, p. 20). If you see a child as "at risk" of failure, your view emphasizes potential for failure. Accordingly, your intervention will focus on remediation or fixing a problem. If, however, you see a child as having talents, you will foster these strengths. Levin, therefore, recommends that children be exposed to enriched, stimulating educational environments that are also connected to their experiences, culture, and community. There are 300 schools in 25 states that have undertaken this model. He reports that as schools succeed with the philosophy, they are able to turn their school around.

Levin does not offer a pre-packaged model, but a process that involves the entire school in creating a "dream school"—the type of school you want for your own child or grandchild or child dear to you. This vision-building process is a time-consuming one that far exceeds the development of a mission statement. Levin observes that most schools have mission statements, but that in many schools the mission has little bearing on the decision making. He wants schools to develop visions that are "in the hearts" of the staff and that are a set of beliefs that drive daily behavior. He describes Accelerated Schools as nice places to be for kids and for adults. People are smiling and talking. The schools are noisy because there's a lot of word building going on. There's a "can do" attitude. The focus is on strengths—the kids' talents, the teachers' skills and interests, things that can

Productive schools invent ways of promoting a pluralistic perspective in academic and social activities.

be done. The kids' natural curiosity is encouraged. By the fourth year in the program, a dramatic gain is seen in test scores, but these scores are seen as a byproduct of the educational experience rather than one of its goals.

Etobicoke, Ontario

Rexford Brown in 1991 compiled descriptions of classrooms and school districts' policies as a means of illustrating different ways in which schools can reform and improve or maintain the status quo, which in Brown's view will contribute to the continued decline of public education. Etobicoke represents excellence in a number of areas: policy framework, curriculum, innovation, and incorporation of multicultural concerns. The district serves a school population that includes students from working-class, blue-collar families, from white, middle-class families, and from the so-called new Canadian families (Jamaicans, West Indians, Pakistani, and Asian Indians). Brown's description underscores a number of interesting features that distinguish Etobicoke from the traditional American system.

There is a fundamental difference in attitude and outlook. Teachers are regarded with respect; students are incorporated in the decision making; families are valued; multicultural differences contribute to the "great Canadian mosaic" rather than to the "melting pot"; curriculum is broadly defined, focused on thinking and problem solving, not atomized and laid out as bits of knowledge and skill; and evaluation is based on outcomes, not minimum competencies and basic skills as measured on standardized tests. Teachers help children and groups of children learn and work within a multicultural environment; they are not the "sage on the stage." Learning approaches are child-centered (children advance at their own pace), flexible, and experience-based. Minorities and poor children receive as much challenge as majority students. Condescending, patronizing, "dumbing down" remedial materials are rare. Multiculturalism, supported firmly by policy, pervades the curriculum and positively influences the attitudes of teachers and students alike. Teachers are selected foremost because they care about children *and* they possess the knowledge and skills of a good teacher. They are good observers and capable of implementing active learning approaches. In this system, teachers are also given more responsibility but held accountable for their decisions. They select the textbooks and learning resources they use, and they are ultimately responsible for what goes on in their classroom.

One teacher's self-description illustrates her vision and hopes. "I think I'm a teacher, in the true sense of the word. I think I teach children to learn and to love learning as much as I love learning. I'm . . . over twenty-nine and still taking courses. And . . . I hope these guys will for the rest of their lives, too. And I believe I teach kids to like themselves. That's important" (Brown, 1991, p. 218).

An illustration of fundamental differences in system perspectives is found in the fact that data are not even collected on percentages of minorities, children in poverty, and children on welfare in Etobicoke because they are not needed. Trust in teachers is evidenced by the position that "teachers know" who needs help. School districts don't need to predict ahead of time which groups are at risk for not benefiting from the educational program. They trust that teachers will do their job, and they hold teachers accountable for doing so.

Special education students are "advancement students." Not only is the name different, the form and substance is different from many special education programs in the States. Classes are real tutorials, with three or four students at a time. Class time is spent on focused, intensive instruction that has a goal of improving the students' skills in three months—one or two years at most. It is not a chronic placement. Equal attention is paid to protecting the child's self-confidence and self-esteem.

When asked about the impact of the child-centered, active-learning, positive approach in Etobicoke, administrators reported that they don't have graffiti on their walls, they have an increasing number of students who are graduating, and

Active learning activities that require children to solve meaningful problems promote construction of knowledge.

their graduates are increasingly skilled. In schools where students are helped to achieve meaningful goals and to feel good about themselves and their accomplishments, the need for behavioral control is minimized. Students are too busy being students.

Inquiring Schools

Inquiring Schools (Calfee & Wadleigh, 1992) grew from a model for developing critical literacy, Project READ. This project was designed collaboratively with a school district to accomplish two major goals:

1. to shift from a basic skills approach to critical literacy, defined as the capacity to use language in all its forms to think and to communicate; and

2. to move toward responsive instruction, and away from the lockstep approach of preplanned textbooks.

Along the way, the project evolved as teachers began to apply the structures and strategies for critical literacy in a number of school areas. "The path to empowerment—literate inquiry—was neither bureaucratic nor managerial, but educational" (p. 28). Calfee and Wadleigh point out that most schools must undergo a paradigm shift in order to become an inquiring community. Typically, schools have chaotic agendas and are short on time. People work in isolation, and a top-down system of management is in place.

Inquiring school communities focus on the curriculum and place improved classroom practice as their central agenda. The problem-solving strategies associated with critical literacy are used in all grades. Additionally, inquiring schools are also characterized by professional collaboration across all grades and school roles, and by shared decision making. In the Inquiring Schools model, "shared knowledge became shared power. Classroom teachers who can explain themselves to visiting colleagues gain a sense of expertise and efficacy that marks them as professionals. It is not enough to do, nor even to know—the key to professional leadership is the capacity to explain" (p. 30). In the Inquiring Schools model, teachers are assuming responsibility in all aspects of school life, including schoolwide discipline programs, curricular innovations, teachers' own inservice training and professional development activities, and school organization. At one of the schools, teachers developed a schoolwide program for integrating regular and categorical programs to achieve better student–teacher ratios. Their motivation came, not from bureaucratic mandates, but rather from their desire to improve their teaching and learning environment. Again, in such schools, teachers are more in control of their classrooms and more responsible for solving problems.

Conclusions

The professional literature contains a number of recommendations for dramatic changes in schools that will affect school atmosphere, school discipline, student behavior, and teachers' behavior. The power base that administrators have held for so long is being questioned and appears to be shifting. Initiatives that encourage teachers to have a powerful and influential voice in programming for students appear to be widespread. Students and their families are also being heard and recognized as having legitimate voices.

These changes present personal and professional challenges to teachers. Glasser (1986) suggests that some of these ideas "may be as new to you as the idea that the world was round or that the earth revolved around the sun was to your ancestors. So be patient. It will take time to realize that teaching is not doing things to or for students: Teaching is structuring your whole approach in a way that they want to work to learn" (p. 79). These shifts in thinking about schools and teaching will have dramatic consequences for teachers. Thus, as they plan a behavior management system, teachers need to think carefully about their beliefs, how they can fit into this rapidly changing world, and what they can do to influence the future.

Discussion Questions and Activities

1. A number of reform initiatives were discussed in this chapter: inclusion, site-based management, whole language, and constructivism. Select one of the topics and research it in greater depth. Have a class debate on the topic. Be certain that the strengths and the drawbacks of each position are examined.

2. View the film *Why Do These Kids Love School?* and discuss how closely schools in the film fit your vision of the ideal school.

3. With the permission of the school administration, interview both students and faculty in your school, asking them the simple question posed by Poplin and her colleagues (1992), "What's wrong with schools?" Compile their responses. What were their dominant themes?

4. Observe in an inner-city or low-income school. Do you see evidence of Haberman's "pedagogy of poverty"? What kinds of expectations do teachers seem to have for the students? Do you think the students receive subtle negative messages about school and themselves?

5. Evaluate the quality of instruction in your school using the following scale adapted from Newmann and Wehlage (1993).

Standards for Authentic Instruction

Use of higher order thinking (Students are expected to manipulate and transform information in order to synthesize, generalize, explain, hypothesize or interpret. Students do not engage in recitation of factual information and other repetitive routines.)

Depth of knowledge (Students deal with central ideas and construct explanations of complex concepts. Students get more than a trivial understanding of important concepts.)

Connectedness to the world (Does the content have meaning beyond the classroom? Students are able to address real-world problems and apply knowledge to their own personal experience.)

Substantive conversation (There is considerable conversation about the ideas of the topic, students share their thoughts. This is not a lecture-driven class in which students merely answer questions the professor asks.)

Social support for student achievement (There are high expectations for student achievement, encouragement of risk taking, mutual respect among students, and assistance in achievement.)

Reflective Questions

1. Does your school have a clear vision and mission? Did you or some of your colleagues participate in developing it?

2. Have there been conflicts about your vision and mission? Do some members of your faculty disagree with aspects of the philosophy/vision/mission? What happens when these disagreements arise?

3. Do students feel loyal and proud to be at your school?

4. Are diverse learners welcomed and valued?

5. Are people from your community involved in your school? Is your school an open, welcoming place? How do you know? On what type of information do you base your answer?

6. Are high academic standards set for all students in your school? Are students supported in their effort and helped in their failures?

7. Do teachers criticize and gossip about students in the teachers' lounge? How do you respond, and how should you respond?

8. When students misbehave, does your school suspend them or are students put on in-school suspension and strategies developed to address the misbehavior?

9. When students miss a lot of school are they punished or does someone try to find out what the problem might be? Are they welcomed back or punished through the policy?

10. Is there a system for self-evaluation in place so that your school gets regular feedback about its operations?

11. Are students with disabilities valued members of your school community? Are classrooms labeled by the disability or by other means? Are students called by their disability or by their names?

12. Are you directive and controlling in the way you run your class or do you try to use democratic principles and incorporate student wishes and interests in your program?

13. Do substitute teachers tell you that your class runs itself when you are out or do your students only behave when you are present?

14. What types of activities are you using to recognize and celebrate the ethnic, cultural, racial, religious differences among the students in your class? Are you involving parents and community people in these activities?

15. Do you feel that you have sufficient autonomy to make curricular and behavioral decisions about the students in your class?

16. How would you describe your school climate?

17. Are staff at your school focused on teaching and helping children? Do they talk about children at meetings? Do they work together to improve programs for children?

18. What type of curricular innovations are going on in your school? Has your principal supported efforts to reform curriculum? Have you had staff development activities to help teachers learn about curriculum innovations?

19. Do you feel that you know what is going on in your school? Is communication good?

20. Are you enjoying teaching? Do you find the school reform efforts exciting and invigorating? If not, why not? Think carefully about why you are in teaching.

References

Barth, R. (1991a). *Improving schools from within.* San Francisco: Jossey-Bass.

Barth, R. (1991b). Restructuring schools: Some questions for teachers and principals. *Kappan, 73,* 123–128.

Betts, F. (1992). How systems thinking applies to education. *Educational Leadership, 50,* 38–41.

Brandt, R. (1992). On building learning communities: A conversation with Hank Levin. *Educational Leadership, 50* (1), 19–23.

Brown, R. (1991). *Schools of thought.* San Francisco: Jossey-Bass.

Bruner, J. (1967). *Studies in cognitive growth.* New York: Wiley.

Budoff, M. (1988a). *The study of the co-teaching or team teaching model* (progress report 2). Cambridge, MA: Research Institute for Educational Problems, Inc.

Budoff, M. (1988b). *The study of the co-teaching or team teaching model—The characteristics of teams that work and don't work* (progress report 3). Cambridge, MA: Research Institute for Educational Problems, Inc.

Bullard, P. & Taylor, B. (1993). *Making school reform happen.* Boston: Allyn & Bacon.

Calfee, R. & Wadleigh, C. (1992). How Project READ builds inquiring schools. *Educational Leadership, 50* (1), 28–32.

Case, A. (1992). The special education rescue: A case for systems thinking. *Educational Leadership, 50* (2), 32–34.

Chalfant, J., Pysh, M. & Moultrie, R. (1979). Teacher assistance teams: A model for within-building problem solving. *Learning Disability Quarterly, 2,* 85–96.

Chrispeels, J. (1992). *Purposeful restructuring: Creating a culture for learning and achievement.* Bristol, PA: Falmer Press.

Coleman, J.S., Campbell, E.Q., Hobson, C.J., McPartland, J., Mood, A.M., Weinfeld, F.D. & York, R.L. (1966). *Equality of Educational Opportunity.* Washington, DC: U.S. Government Printing Office.

Comer, J. (1988). *Maggie's American dream: The life and times of a black family.* New York: NAL–Dutton.

Darling-Hammond, L. (1993). Reframing the school reform agenda: Developing capacity for school transformation. *Kappan, 74,* 752–61.

Edwards, P. & Young, L. (1992). Beyond parents: Family, community, and school involvement. *Kappan, 74,* 72–80.

Fuchs, D. & Fuchs, L. (1988). Mainstream assistance teams to accommodate difficult-to-teach students in general education. In J.L. Graden, J.E. Zins & M.J. Curtis (eds.), *Alternative delivery systems: Enhancing instructional options for all students* (pp. 49–70). Washington, DC: National Association of School Psychologists.

Fuchs, D. & Fuchs, L. (1991). Framing the REI debate: Abolitionists versus conservationists. In J.W. Lloyd, N. Singh, & A. Repp (eds.), *The regular education initiative: Alternative perspectives on concepts, issues, and models* (pp. 241-55). Dekalb, IL: Sycamore.

Fullan, M. (1993). Why teachers must become change agents. *Educational Leadership, 50,* 12–17.

Gartner, A. & Lipsky, D. (1992). Beyond special education: Toward a quality system for all students. In T. Hehir & T. Latus (eds.), *Special education at the century's end: Evolution of theory and practice since 1970.* Cambridge, MA: Harvard Educational Review.

Gay, G. (1993). Ethnic minorities and educational equality. In J. Banks & C. Banks (eds.), *Multicultural education: Issues and perspectives,* 2nd ed. Boston: Allyn & Bacon.

Glasser, W. (1986). *Control theory in the classroom.* New York: Harper & Row.

Glasser, W. (1992). *The quality school.* New York: HarperCollins.

Glickman, C. (1992). The essence of school renewal: The prose has begun. *Educational Leadership, 50* (1), 24–27.

Goodlad, J. (1984). *A place called school.* NY: McGraw Hill.

Goodlad, J. (1990). *Teachers for our nation's schools.* San Francisco: Jossey-Bass.

Goodlad, J. (1991). A study of the education of educators: One year later. *Kappan, 73,* 311–316.

Graden, J.L., Casey, A. & Bonstrom, O. (1985). Implementing a prereferral intervention system. *Exceptional Children, 51,* 487–96.

Graden, J.L., Casey, A. & Christenson, S.L. (1985). Implementing a prereferral intervention system: Part I. The model. *Exceptional Children, 51*(5), 377–84.

Haberman, M. (1991). Pedagogy of poverty versus good teaching. *Kappan, 73,* 290–294.

Hayek, R.A. (1987). The teacher assistance team: A pre-referral support system. *Focus on Exceptional Children, 20*(1), 1–7.

Henderson, J.G. (1992). *Reflective teaching: Becoming an inquiring educator.* New York: Macmillan.

Hocutt, A., Martin, E. & McKinney, J. (1991). Historical and legal context of mainstreaming. In J.W. Lloyd, N. Singh, & A. Repp (eds.), *The regular education initiative: Alternative perspectives on concepts, issues, and models.* Dekalb, IL: Sycamore.

Honig, B. (1987). *Last chance for our children: How you can help save our schools.* Reading, MA: Addison-Wesley.

Idol, L. (1993). *Special educator's consultation handbook* (2nd ed.). Austin, TX: PRO-ED.

Idol, L., Paolucci-Whitcomb, P. & Nevin, A. (1986). *Collaborative consultation.* Austin, TX: PRO-ED.

Issacson, N. & Bamburg, J. (1992). Can schools become learning organizations? *Educational Leadership, 50* (3), 42–44.

Jencks, C., Smith, M., Ackland, H., Bane, M., Cohen, D., Gintis, H., Heyns, B. & Michelson, S. (1972). *Inequality: A reassessment of the effects of family and schooling in America.* New York: Basic Books.

Johnson, S. (1990). *Teachers at work: Achieving success in our schools.* New York: Basic Books.

Kauffman, J. (1993). How we might achieve the radical reform of special education. *Exceptional Children, 60,* 6–16.

Kauffman, J., Gerber, M. & Semmel, M. (1988). Arguable assumptions underlying the Regular Education Initiative. *Journal of Learning Disabilities, 21,* 43–52.

Keogh, B. (1990). Learning disabilities: Diversity in search of order. In M. Wang, M. Reynolds & H. Walberg (eds.), *The handbook of special education: Research and practice, Vol. 2.* Oxford: Pergamon.

Kessler, R. (1992). Shared decision making works! *Educational Leadership, 50* (1), 36–38.

Knitzer, J., Steinberg, Z. & Fleisch, B. (1990). *At the schoolhouse door: An examination of programs and policies for children with behavioral and emotional problems.* New York: Bank Street College of Education.

Kozol, J. (1991). *Savage inequalities: Children in America's schools.* New York: Crown.

Lewis, A. (1992). A tale not widely told. *Kappan, 74,* 196–97.

Lezotte, L. (1993). Effective schools: A framework for increasing student achievement. In J. Banks & C. Banks (eds.), *Multicultural education: Issues and perspectives*, 2nd ed. Boston: Allyn & Bacon.

Lickona, T. (1993). The return of character education. *Educational Leadership, 51* (3), 6–11.

Lortie, D. (1963, 1975). *Schoolteacher: A sociological study.* Chicago, IL: University of Illinois Press.

Molnar, A. (1993). Racing the racial divide. *Educational Leadership, 50* (8), 58–59.

Morsink, C., Soar, R., Soar, R. & Thomas, R. (1986). Research on teaching: Opening the door to special education classrooms. *Exceptional Children, 53,* 32–40.

Morsink, C., Thomas, C. & Smith-Davis, J. (1987). Noncategorical special education programs: Process and outcomes. In M. Wang, M. Reynolds & H. Walberg (eds.), *The handbook of special education: Research and practice (Vol. 2).* Oxford: Pergamon.

Newmann, F. & Wehlage, G. (1993). Five standards of authentic instruction. *Educational Leadership, 50* (7), 8–12.

Nieto, S. (1992). *Affirming diversity: The sociopolitical context of multicultural education.* New York: Longman.

Noddings, N. (1992). *The challenge to care in schools: An alternative approach to education.* New York: Teachers College, Columbia University.

Poplin, M. (1993). A practical theory of teaching and learning: The view from inside the new transformative classroom: Contributions of constructivism. Presentation at the TED/DOE Conference in Tampa, FL, February 1993.

Poplin, M. & Weeres, J. (1992). *Voices from the inside: A report on schooling from inside the classroom. Part One: Naming the problem.* The Institute for Education in Transformation at the Claremont Graduate School. Funded by the John W. Kluge Foundation.

Price, H. (1992). Multiculturalism: Myths and realities. *Kappan, 74,* 208–213.

Reynolds, M. (1991). Classification and labeling. In J.W. Lloyd, N. Singh & A. Repp (eds.), *The regular education initiative: Alternative perspectives on concepts, issues, and models* (pp. 29–42). DeKalb, IL: Sycamore.

Ritter, D. (1978). The effects of a school consultation program upon referral patterns of teachers. *Psychology in the Schools, 15,* 239–243.

Rosenholtz, S. (1985, May). Effective schools: Interpreting the evidence. *American Journal of Education,* 352–88.

Rosenholtz, S. (1989). *Teachers' workplace.* New York: Longman.

Sailor, W. (1991). Special education in the restructured school. *Remedial and Special Education, 12,* 8–22.

Sailor, W., Anderson, J., Halvorsen, A., Doering, K., Filler, J. & Goetz, L. (1989). *The comprehensive local school: Regular education for all students with disabilities.* Baltimore: Brookes.

Samples, B. (1992). Using learning modalities to celebrate intelligence. *Educational Leadership, 50* (2), 62–66.

Sapon-Shevin, M. (1990). *Support networks for inclusive schooling.* Baltimore: Brookes.

Sarason, S. (1971). *The culture of school and the problem of change.* Boston: Allyn & Bacon.

Sarason, S. (1990). *The predictable failure of school reform.* San Francisco: Jossey-Bass.

Schmoker, M. & Wilson, R. (1993). Transforming schools through total quality education. *Kappan, 74,* 389–95.

Schon, D. (1987). *Educating the reflective practitioner.* San Francisco: Jossey-Bass.

Searl, S., Ferguson, D. & Biklen, D. (1985). The front line . . . teachers. In D. Bicklin, ed. *Achieving the complete school:* Strategies for Effective Mainstreaming. New York, Teacher's College Press.

Self, H., Benning, A., Marston, D. & Magnusson, D. (1991). Cooperative teaching project: A model for students at-risk. *Exceptional Children, 58,* 26–34.

Senge, P. (1990). *The fifth discipline: The art and practice of the learning organization.* New York: Doubleday.

Sergiovanni, T. (1990). *Value-added leadership: How to get extraordinary performance in schools.* San Diego: Harcourt Brace Jovanovich.

Shade, B. & New, C. (1993). Cultural influences on learning: Teaching implications. In J. Banks & C. Banks (eds.), *Multicultural education: Issues and perspectives,* 2nd ed. Boston: Allyn & Bacon.

Shor, I. (1986). *Culture wars: Schools and society in the conservative restoration 1969–1984.* Boston: Routledge & Kegan Paul.

Showers, B. (1990). Aiming for superior classroom instruction for all children: A comprehensive staff development model. *Remedial and Special Education, 11*(3), 35–39.

Skrtic, T. (1989). Excellence and equity in public education: The adhocratic school organization. Testimony given at the hearings conducted by the National Council of Disability, Washington, DC, June 7, 1989, as part of its study, The Education of Students with Disabilities: Where Do We Stand?

Skrtic, T. (1991). *Behind special education: A critical analysis of professional culture and school organization.* Denver: Love.

Spring, J. (1989). *The sorting machine revisited: National educational policy since 1945.* New York: Longman.

Stainback, W. & Stainback, S. (1990). *Support networks for inclusive schooling: Interdependent, integrated education.* Baltimore: Brookes.

Stainback, W. & Stainback, S. (1991). A rationale for integration and restructuring: A synopsis. In J.W. Lloyd, N. Singh & A. Repp (eds.), *The regular education initiative: Alternative perspectives on concepts, issues, and models,* 225–39. Dekalb, IL: Sycamore.

Stainback, S. & Stainback, W. (1992). *Curriculum considerations in inclusive classrooms: Facilitating learning for all students.* Baltimore: Brookes.

Tindal, G., Shinn, M., Walz, L. & Germann, G. (1987). Mainstream consultation in secondary settings: The Pine County model. *The Journal of Special Education, 21,* 94–106.

Wang, M., Walberg, H. & Reynolds, M. (1992). A scenario for better—not separate—special education. *Educational Leadership, 50* (2), 35–38.

Wheelock, A. (1992). The case for untracking. *Educational Leadership, 50* (2), 6–10.

Wiske, M. & Levinson, C. (1993). How teachers are implementing the NCTM standards. *Educational Leadership, 50* (8), 8–11.

Other Resources

Film: *Why Do These Kids Love School?* Produced by Dorothy Fadiman. Pyramid film & video. P.O. Box 1048, Santa Monica, CA 90406.

Curricula:

Facing History and Ourselves is an 8 week Holocaust curriculum for 8th graders. Write Facing History and Ourselves, National Foundation, 25 Kennard Rd., Brookline, MA 02146.

The Heartwood Ethics Curriculum for Children uses multicultural children's literature to teach universal values. Write the Heartwood Institute, 12300 Perry Highway, Wexford, PA 15090.

Chapter 3

Family—School Partnerships in a Pluralistic Society

Ms. Green is very frustrated with the lack of parental participation in activities at her school and the limited contact she has with the parents of children in her classroom. The Parent–Teacher Organization (PTO) was dissolved because of poor attendance at the monthly meetings. Parents rarely attend parent conferences unless their children are re-entering school following a suspension. The Individualized Education Plan (IEP) meetings are usually teacher directed and parents are asked to do little more than sign documents. The school restructuring plan called for home–school–community partnerships, but very little is being done to facilitate the process—especially with those "hard to motivate" parents.

Ms. Green has minimal contact with her parents through IEPs and suspension conferences, but she wants more time to get to know them and involve them in educational planning for their children. She specifically needs help with children who have behavior problems in her classroom. Recently, she implemented a new behavior management plan. Full parental cooperation is necessary in order to reinforce appropriate classroom behaviors. These behaviors could also generalize to the home environment; this would involve restructuring some of the ways parents relate to their children. Parents would also learn how to better organize their households around the needs of their children.

To introduce the new behavior management plan, Ms. Green planned a special parents' night just for the parents of those enrolled in her class. She carefully prepared a special invitation on brightly colored paper and solicited the children's help:

"Children, may I have your attention please? I have a special request of you today and I need your full cooperation. I have planned a special parent's meeting for next Wednesday night from 7 to 9. I would like you personally to deliver these notes to your mothers and fathers and urge them to come to school. At the meeting I will be sharing our new behavior management plan and I would like your parents to be aware of the changes and to involve them in helping you manage your behavior at home."

The children were all quite willing to deliver the invitations and assured Ms. Green they would urge their families to participate. She began to prepare for the meeting by developing her personal philosophy of behavior management and preparing a checklist of appropriate classroom behavior management practices. She made copies of these materials for each of the parents. She believed that many of the behavior management practices could be reinforced in the home if parents were given proper instructions on how to adapt their relationships and the home environment to facilitate good behavior management. She planned a get-acquainted activity in order for the parents to get to know each other and share their concerns and expectations for their children's behavior. She then structured small-group activities, assigning each parent to one of the tables that coincided with a basic component of her behavior management plan. She has 25 students in her class this semester, so each of the four tables would have at least five persons (assuming that each child would have at least one parent in attendance).

Table 1 would examine the classroom rules for movement and noise and activity levels. These rules are designed to restrict movement in the classroom without permission, maintain a reasonable noise level for teaching and learning, and help the children to self-monitor their physical contact with other students. The parents' task would be to construct similar rules for the home environment. They would address rules for homework, play, and family time; responsibilities for household chores, like disposing of the trash and caring for the yard; conduct at the dinner table, and appropriate behaviors for when guests are visiting; noise levels for the television, stereo, and radio; physical contact with siblings; and horseplay with dad.

Table 2 would review the classroom rules for communicating with the teachers and classmates. These rules address respect for adult supervision and teach children to respect the rights and properties of their classmates. The parents' task would be to construct home rules that reinforce the kind of relationship Ms. Green is trying to create in the classroom. Table 3 would work on spelling out rewards and penalties for the home that were similar to those the children received at school. Table 4 would work on behavior expectations outside the classroom in the halls, cafeteria, and on the bus. The parents would develop comparable expectations for conduct in the neighborhood, while visiting friends and family, or during worship services. Each group would be told to identify specific activities they could practice at home that would support the classroom philosophy and behavior management components they had examined. Ms. Green would then compile all of the activities from the four groups and distribute them to the parents as a packet at a later date.

As the meeting day approached, Ms. Green again urged the children to remind their parents of the meeting. She personally phoned all the homes in which there were telephones and left reminder messages with the children or child-care person when she could not reach a parent. She was very excited about the meeting and shared her ideas with several of the other teachers. She was pleased with the extra effort she'd made in planning the meeting, and looked forward to meeting with and educating the parents on appropriate behavior management practices.

On the day of the meeting Ms. Green readied the classroom and, with the assistance of the children, prepared refreshment for the parents. She had the children display some of their class work on their desks so parents could see some of the academic and social progress made since the implementation of the new behavior management plan. She also prepared a chart displaying each child's progress to date in meeting the self-management goals she and the students had negotiated.

Around 7:10 P.M. the first parents arrived. They were three grandmothers who had no transportation of their own, but were able to coordinate transportation through their weekly support group for grandmothers of cocaine-exposed children. One of the grandmothers had immigrated from Cuba only three years ago and spoke very little English. Ms. Green was pleased that these women attended, but wondered why the mothers hadn't come, as they too lived at home with their children. Shortly after the grandmothers, several couples and four single women arrived who appeared to have come directly from work, some still in uniforms, others in business suits and dresses. They obviously had not seen their children or had dinner. They were followed by three older siblings of students whose mothers and/or fathers worked at night or were absent from the home, leaving them to provide the primary supervision of their siblings.

A family friend of a child with a serious behavior problem attended; the mother of this child was in night school and worked on weekends, and the friend cared for the child most of the time. An uncle and aunt arrived; they were raising a child because the biological mother was incarcerated and the father was unemployed. Two sets of foster parents arrived. Each had children placed in their homes by the Protective Services Agency and were very much committed to working with the school for as long as the children were in their custody. Most of the other families represented at the meeting were headed by single parents; single mothers, single fathers, or other relatives

attended the meeting either alone or with their partners.

Although Ms. Green was delighted with the attendance, she is quite concerned about the wide range of family structures represented in her classroom. She wonders what effect these differing family forms have on the level of parent participation in the PTA and other home–school activities. She wonders how this affected the parents' reception to her plans for the meeting.

Ms. Green is also concerned about how late some of the families must arrive home from work and how feasible it is to expect them to structure and monitor some of the behavior management activities she has in mind. Further, she wonders how feasible it is for her to tell the parents how to redefine their relationships with the children when the chronological ages, relationships to the children, and the life-cycle stages of the "parents" in her group are so varied. "Home" is not the same for all of the children, and many of the parent–child relationships are unique and complex, unlike the traditional family constellations she expected.

These differences made it almost impossible to talk about home–school partnerships in a general sense. Yet, her time and school resources are limited and don't permit the diversification the group obviously needs.

*M*s. Green's classroom is an excellent example of how family life in America has changed. However, the practices embedded in her plan for family involvement do not reflect the diversity of American families in either form or function. Many of her assumptions about how families function are rooted in a series of myths that have been accepted as truth and have guided our thinking in the past. These myths continue to influence the policies and practices that guide present day home–school partnerships. They are based on nostalgic images of families that do not consider social class and cultural variations. Zinn and Eitzen (1990) and Walsh (1993) have identified several such myths that influence our expectation of families. A discussion of these myths can enhance the development of a philosophy of behavior management reflective of the unique needs of children with behavior problems and their families.

The Myth of a Stable, Harmonious Family of the Past

Contemporary families are frequently compared to nostalgic representations of families of the past that were thought to be intact, stable, well adjusted, and happy. These families included multigenerational households that shared one domicile or lived in close proximity to each other. This myth suggests that most of the problems encountered by these families were solved by family members with limited help from the outside. Zinn and Eitzen (1990) and Walsh (1993) challenged this notion. They pointed to problems families have historically confronted in this country, such as children born outside of marriage, spousal desertion resulting in single-parent families, limitation in economic resources requiring outside assistance, and incidences of child abuse and neglect requiring legal and judicial involvement. Those problems were very similar to the ones confronted by families today. When we evaluate contemporary family life based on nostalgic images of the past we limit our ability to develop positive home–school partnerships with families in crisis or those experiencing life-cycle transitions. These families are often referred to as "broken," "troubled," or "dysfunctional." Our models for working with these families often reflect a view of pathology or deviance. We fail to recognize many of the adaptations families make to accommodate the crises or transitions they are experiencing.

The Myth of Separate Worlds

The belief that the worlds of work and family (and school) are independent has fostered the myth of separate worlds. This myth suggests that families are self-sufficient and capable of maintaining a private refuge, separate and apart from their work. It also suggests that the responsibilities inherent in family membership can be separated from the responsibilities as an employee in the work force. This myth has been challenged, particularly as women have entered the work force. The boundaries of home and work often overlap. This is indicated by the rise in workplace day-care centers and requests for flexible work schedules more compatible with family responsibilities for child and elder care. Employer fringe-benefit packages are changing to respond more to the health and educational needs of all family members, not just the employee.

Family life is intertwined with the many institutions, including schools. Parents' ability to participate in a child's education is highly contingent on his or her work (hours, location, and leave privileges) and on other family responsibilities. The income derived through employment provides the economic base for the total family and when it is jeopardized the entire family unit suffers. In planning for parent partnerships, schools have attempted to accommodate the schedules of working parents by delaying school meetings until evening or individually scheduling parent–teacher conferences during, or immediately following, the school day. This sometimes can accommodate the traditional work environment that is stable and predictable. However, shifts in our economy—resulting in many changes in the types of jobs held by parents—will require us to reconsider many of our traditional home–school practices. Later in this chapter we will discuss some of the changes in employment patterns and the shifts in family structures that challenge many of the ways we have conceptualized parent participation.

The Myth of the Monolithic Family Form

The typical nuclear family headed by a male with a wife and dependent children continues to serve as the prototype family structure (Walsh, 1993). This model of family life has been frequently portrayed by the media and is rigidly implanted in the educational and social policies that guide many of our practices. Fewer than 10% of all U.S. families live in their original nuclear families, and over 80% of children under 18 will spend a portion of their school years in a single-parent family (Norton & Glick, 1986). American families now take many different forms, including, but not limited to, the nuclear family structure. To rely exclusively on the nuclear family model ignores the vast array of structures present among families today. These include:

- ☐ A multi-generation family in which a grandmother who works outside the home serves as the head of the household, which includes both her children and grandchildren

- ☐ A combined-sibling household, in which adult siblings share a domicile and rear their children together as co-parents

- ☐ A biological custodial father who has remarried and is sharing childrearing responsibilities with his new wife and the absent biological mother

- ☐ A nonbiological kin rearing a child while the parent is away from the home

Each of these arrangements violates many of the assumptions embedded in the nuclear family model, but they nevertheless are examples of families represented in schools today. In developing home–school partnerships we will encounter an increasing number of families having variant family structures who will challenge many of the traditional roles we have assigned to "parents." In our attempts to involve these families we must use language that is inclusive of the range of family structures and develop practices that address the changes in parental gender and family configurations.

Schools need to recognize and welcome families with diverse structures and configurations.

The Myth of Family Consensus

The myth of family consensus is manifested in many of the popular press and television portrayals of family life. In these idealized presentations, family conflicts are usually resolved through discussion, within a short period of time, and with minimal effort or help from outside. In reality, families are constantly balancing the full spectrum of human emotions:

> The family can provide bonds of living, caring, and belonging. Yet emotional relationships inevitably contain negative feelings as well as positive ones. This combination of love and antagonism sets intimate relationships apart from less intimate ones. The family contains a captive participant audience. No other institutionalized setting in industrial society gives this richness and texture to an individual's life. (Zinn & Eitzen, 1990)

Our pluralistic society includes a range of families with many different communication styles and interactional patterns. These various styles and patterns are often reflected in the communication of feelings and expectations, as well as the approach to the resolution of conflicts (Moos & Moos, 1975, 1976). When we work with families, we must be prepared to encounter a variety of family climates consistent with the family's style and cultural traditions. Additionally, other demographic factors such as social class, family structure, and gender role expectations will contribute to family climate (Tolson & Wilson, 1990). Each family is different, and when we apply universal standards we limit our abilities to identify the wide array of contributions families can make toward their children's education.

The Diversity of American Families
Family Ethnicity

Kumabe, Nishida, and Hepworth (1985) characterized family ethnic groups as "a collection of people who conceive of themselves as being alike by virtue of their presumed common ancestry and cultural heritage (race, religion, or national origin) and who are regarded by others to be part of such a group." Changing demographic patterns have emphasized the need for greater awareness and understanding of cultural and ethnic diversity among families (Boyd-Franklin, 1989; McAdoo, 1993; Paul & Simeonsson, 1993). Recognition of this need is evident in a growing body of literature on the nature and expressions of culture diversity and the implications of such diversity for the provision of educational services (Banks & Banks, 1993; Nieto, 1992) and culturally sensitive home–school partnerships (Chavkin, 1993). An appreciation and respect for cultural diversity among educational professionals has become an important priority. Responses to this priority have taken the form of recommendations to understand cultural diversity (Anderson, 1991) and to develop cross-cultural competences in working with Asian American, African American, Mexican (and Spanish origin) American, and Native American families (Baca & Cervantes, 1989; Lee, 1989; Marfo, 1991; Lynch & Hanson, 1992; Harry, 1992; Paul & Simeonsson, 1993).

Special education has traditionally served disproportionately high numbers of minority children (Mercer, 1973; Reschley, 1988; Harry, 1992). This has been due, in part, to perceptions that children deviating from the norms and the modal culture are deviant or deficient and thus prime candidates for special education programs. Comparative studies that employed these perceptions fostered a knowledge base rooted in a deficient orientation. This knowledge base has resulted in school policies and practices that seek to remediate or compensate for perceived deficits. McLoyd (1990) encourages the study of minority children and their families in their own right, without the need for a "control" group of

Anglo-American children and families to derive and interpret an adequate research base on minority children.

The school–family partnership outlined in the Education for All Handicapped Children (1976) and the Individuals with Disabilities Education Act (1991) provides a mechanism by which schools can gain a better understanding of the linguistic and cultural experiences of all children served, including minority children.

One function of families is to transmit and shape cultural attitudes, behaviors, and patterns (Zinn & Eitzen, 1990). In the development of effective home–school partnerships we can construct a bridge to better access the culture of the home. Having this knowledge, school personnel can better understand the diversity of behaviors, learning styles, and interactional patterns of the children in schools today.

Asian American Families

Asian American families are an extremely diverse group. They originated from the Asian continent but from three distinct regions—East Asia, Southeast Asia, and South Asia. Each of these regions is characterized by unique national heritage, language, beliefs, customs, and practices. The dominant groups in the United States include Chinese, Filipinos, and Japanese. However, persons of Cambodian, Guamanian, Asian Indian, Indonesian, Korean, Laotian, Malaysian, Pakistani, Vietnamese, and Samoan descent are also included in this classification. The Japanese American population constitutes the largest subgrouping, approaching 1 million, many of whom were born in the United States (McAdoo, 1993). The majority of people in the remaining subgroups immigrated to this country. The recency and nature of child/family's immigration, as well as their economic resources and degree of social support, are critical factors in assessing the educational needs of Asian American children. Additionally, effective home–school partnerships will be dependent on the linguistic characteristic of the child/family and the school's ability to provide interpreters and cultural mediators to facilitate communication. Most important, knowledge of the *specific* cultural and family needs is critical because of the wide variability among Asian American families.

African American Families

African American families compose the largest ethnic minority group in the United States. However there exists wide variability among these families in socioeconomic status, family structure, and childrearing practices and beliefs. The history of slavery in America and the injustices and discrimination that followed are important elements to consider in understanding and working with African American families. The constant battles with racism and discrimination that many of these families still endure often interferes with the establishment of effective home–school partnerships. The adaptations made by these families to accommodate the discriminatory structures that surround and define their lives often are inconsistent with some expectations for home–school partnerships. It is critical, however, that we do not lose sight of the rich and diverse cultural traditions that define African American families and, to the greatest extent possible, incorporate these issues into our work with families. An area of considerable importance is the interdependence and multigenerational texture of many African American families. The involvement of extended family members and other kinship networks in the parenting and educating of African American children requires that we extend our parental involvement models appropriately to include these structures.

American-Indian Families

Contemporary American-Indian families emanated from a variety of tribal groupings spread throughout the United States. Each group has its own unique geographic distinctions, tribal histories, religious beliefs, and practice. Eight different language groupings categorize the Indian language. Included among these groups are Iroquoian, Muskogean, Caddoam, and Athapaskan (Joe and Malach, 1992). However, the uniqueness associated with each group is often rooted in a core value system shared collectively by most tribes of like or similar descent (Sipes, 1993). Values which some American-Indian tribes share include harmony with nature, the rhythmic-circular nature of time, the extended nature of the family structure, and the ultimate value of the group rather than the individual (Joe and Malach, 1992). When Europeans invaded this continent in the fourteenth century they forcibly removed American-Indians from their land and tried to force them to reject tradtional customs. Many families were separated and thousands of lives were lost in this process. The hardships experienced by many of these families resulted in the mass relocations of communities to reservations established throughout the United States, Canada, and Alaska. However, American-Indians are now located in each of the 50 states. Some continue to observe traditional customs and practices while others have migrated to various rural and urban communities and have experienced varying degrees of acculturation into these communities. As with most ethnic groups, it is critical that we understand the tribal and family customs and the degree of acculturation of each American-Indian family before making assumptions regarding family life and child-rearing practices. Home–school partnerships will be greatly enhanced by our knowledge of the history, languages, and values of the American-Indian families in our schools, as well as our willingness to allow for the individual variation in family form and functioning inherent in this group.

Latino and Hispanic-American Families

Latino and Hispanics are the fastest growing ethnic group in the United States. They represent a variety of nationalities who have immigrated to the United States from Cuba, Mexico, and Puerto Rico, as well as several Central, South American, and Caribbean countries. At the end of the Mexican-American war, a large segment of Mexico was annexed to the United States and now constitutes Texas, New Mexico, Colorado, and California. Many Mexican families living in these regions remained and became U.S. citizens. They continue to share a rich heritage with both Mexico and the United States. Other Mexicans immigrated to this country long after the war due to the close proximity of Mexico to the United States (Zuniga, 1993). A significant number of Cubans and Mexicans came to this country as part of a labor force created by Congress to support the agriculture, fishing, and food processing industries. These "migrant workers" continue to travel from state to state in search of work and economic and social gains. They often experience many hardships due to inadequate housing and limited health care provided by their employers. This is sometimes the result of their illegal citizenship status and the lack of due process procedures to protect them.

Most families identified as Latino and Hispanic are familiar with the Spanish language. This communality has served as the basic characteristic that categorizes this group. It is important to note that considerable local, regional, and national variations in dialects, colloquialisms, speech fluency, and body language exist among members of this group. Language is part of a communication system which must be understood within a social-cultural context in how the family uses the language. Whether it is the dominant form of communication or used only under specific circumstances must be considered before designing family interventions that incorporate a translator or cultural mediator.

Harry (1993) suggests that in addition to a common language, persons of Latino and Hispanic descent are likely to share a world view grounded in a religious ideology, with wide-spread Christianity. This is sometimes manifested in the strong respect some children hold for their family members, particularly grandparents. She stressed the interdependence of children with their parents and the elderly. This is often intertwined with a respect for and obedience to the religious doctrine and the customs of their native country. In working with families of Latino and Hispanic descent it will be important to be aware of the emphasis placed on the group identity rather than individual accomplishments. Home–school collaborators must recognize this characteristic and be prepared to incorporate multiple family members when planning home interventions; and design interventions which are facilitative of family growth as well as the needs of the children in our classrooms.

These variations in beliefs, language, and practices emphasize the importance of recognizing the within-group variations present across Latino and Hispanic families. Additionally, the family's social class, recency of immigration, and degree of acculturation are factors which interact to help clarify our understanding these families.

Economic Variability

Zinn and Eitzen (1990) identified several economic shifts that have had a tremendous impact on the economy and financial bases of many families. They include the technological advancements in microelectronics that produced the computer chip. This revolutionary communication system has transformed our economy into the service/information age. Computers have eliminated many of the mid-level, semi-skilled jobs held by heads of households and created the need for lower-paid, manual workers to support the robotic-based manufacturing systems implemented by many companies.

The globalization of our economy has resulted in increased competition. Goods and services that traditionally were manufactured and distributed solely by U.S. companies must compete in the world marketplace. This has resulted in substantial decreases in profits for many American corporations. Layoffs, reductions in force, and mergers have generated high unemployment rates in the steel, automobile, and textile industries.

The shift from an economy based on the manufacturing of goods to one based on service and information has resulted in a major increase in service jobs. In the past, family members were employed in the production of goods. Now they are primarily employed in service-related occupations as office workers, retail clerks, restaurant cooks and waiters, custodial workers, and security guards. The limited numbers of persons remaining in manufacturing jobs are highly skilled and technologically sophisticated. Many of the families affected by economic shifts lacked the financial resources to return to school for the re-education necessary to compete for these jobs.

In the development of effective home–school partnerships, we must consider the impact of these recent economic shifts on families. One major result has been an increase in female labor force participation. Women entered the workforce en masse in the mid-1970s and their presence has steadily increased. Work is an absolute necessity for many women in dual-earner families, due to the economic hardships just discussed. Many of the shifts have resulted in unemployment or underemployment for males in these families. Additionally, the rise in separation and divorce rates during the 1960s and 1970s forced many women to join the workforce with limited education or training. This has resulted in an over-representation of working mothers in unskilled and semi-skilled jobs.

Family Structure Variability

Family structure is a second variable that is often an important consideration in the development of home–school partnerships. Much of the previous research has focused on the disproportionate number of families living in female-headed, single-parent households, the many stressors associated with solo parenting, and the coping mechanisms employed by these families (Reichle, 1987; Schillings, Kirkham, Snow, & Schinke, 1986). While such families are often defined as dysfunctional on the basis of marital status alone, a single-parent family structure in itself does not constitute dysfunctionality. In this regard, Bristol (1987) lists several methodological caveats that should be considered when working with these families: the absence of a father from a single-parent home; persons other than parents contributing to child-rearing in single-parent families; socioeconomic differences between one-parent and two-parent families; the nature of single-parent families (all single-parent families are not alike); and the long-term coping strategies of single parents. The deficit model of single parenting as a broken home fails to advance understanding of how to serve these families. It is not useful to assume that outcomes for all single-parent families will be unfavorable any more than to assume that outcomes for all two-parents will be favorable. (Bristol, 1987) The rapid growth in single-parent families in recent years has caused providers of special education services to examine the assumptions that have guided home–school interventions. Many of these assumptions were derived from earlier contributions (Moynihan, 1965) that described single-parent families as dysfunctional matriarchal structures whose major deficits were the absence of males as the heads of the household. Such assumptions need to be examined on historical as well as contextual grounds.

Another family structure represented in school today is the extended family. These kinship networks have a major historical significance for several ethnic groups, specifically African American, Asian American, and Hispanic families. Many of these families have a shared sense of connectedness that goes beyond the traditional parent–child–sibling relationship peculiar to the nuclear family. They are characterized by a commitment to the well-being of the total family, including biological and nonbiological relationships. Referring to the current context, Hines and Boyd-Franklin (1990) conclude, "The reliance on a kin network, not necessarily drawn along 'blood lines,' remains a major mode for coping with the pressures of an oppressive society" (p. 87).

Many families maintain strong alliances with their kin networks, due in part to economic hardship, as well as to their shared experiences associated with racism and discrimination. Extended families have traditionally provided support to adolescent and other never-married mothers, as well as nuclear families in crises such as incarceration, drug and alcohol dependency, and spousal abuse (Martin & Martin, 1985; Stevens, 1984; Jackson, McCullough & Gurin, 1988). More recently, extended families have emerged as alternate family structures whose members are pursuing higher education, saving to purchase housing, or encountering serious elder- and childcare difficulties. "Ours is by no means a tradition limited to respect for the bonds uniting the members of the nuclear family. In a landmark case supporting the recognition of grandparents and grandchildren occupying a domicile, Justice Powell stated that the "tradition of uncles, aunts, cousins, and especially grandparents and grandchildren sharing a household along with parents and children has roots equally venerable and equally deserving of constitutional recognition" (*Moore v. City of East Cleveland*).

There is considerable variation within the extended family structure among families. Unlike the traditional nuclear family, extended families are not dependent on domicile, biological ties, or male presence for definition. Billingsley (1968) has provided a framework categorizing extended families into four types: (a) subfamilies, (b) families with secondary members, (c) augmented families, and (d) nonblood relatives. Subfamilies are composed of two or more individuals and may take on any of the following forms:

(a) The "incipient extended family," which consists of a married couple with no children of their own who take in other relatives.

Families and schools can form very effective partnerships by focusing on developing life skills, confidence, and responsibility.

(b) The "simple extended family," which consists of a married couple with their own children who take in other relatives.

(c) The "attenuated extended family," which consists of a single, abandoned, legally separated, divorced, or widowed mother or father living with his or her children, who take into the household other relatives. (Billingsley, 1968)

Families with secondary members "take in" relatives and kin (primarily children and elderly persons) to provide refuge during a family crisis or during transition in the family life cycle (Hill, 1993). They include "minor relatives" (nieces, nephews, cousins, grandchildren, and younger siblings); relatives close in age to the primary parent; elders of the primary parent (aunts, uncles); and parents of the primary family (p. 34).

Augmented extended families are an important part of the kin network. In these families, children are cared for in homes in which they have no biological relationship to the head of the household, nor are they related by marriage, ancestry, or adoption (Hill, 1972). These children were often neighbors, church members, students, or playmates invited to join a family because of the need for a better home. That is, families share their resources and space with others to provide for a better quality of life. Extended families often make room for such children in their homes and adjust their own lives to meet the needs of the "new" children.

The nonblood extended family is a structure sometimes found among African American families. It is characterized by a series of individuals who are regarded as family members but have no biological ties. Stack (1974) refers to these members of the African American extended family as "fictive kin." This network includes "play mama," godmothers and godfathers, neighbors, and church members. These fictive kin play a major role in the family network but are often inappropriately labeled as family supports by school personnel unfamiliar with African American extended family structures.

The variability in family structures present in schools today is also reflected in the rise in blended and reconstituted families. These families are created when one or both remarried spouses have childrearing responsibility for a child or children from a previous marriage or relationship. They are characterized by an extensive network of households intertwined in a web of relatives and kinship groups from the previous marriages. Many of these relationships are still significant in the lives of the children and/or the spouses. New sibling relationships are also formed if the remarriage results in children. Zinn and Eitzen (1990) view the challenges these family face as particularly stressful, in that our society has not established roles for many of the new relationships inherent in remarriages:

Society has not provided a useful way to handle these complex social roles. The language even fails. What does the child who has a "mom" call her or his stepmother? There is no term in the English language to describe a child's relationship to the woman his or her father remarried after he divorced the child's mother. What are the rights and duties of the child and this woman to each other? What is "home" to a child whose remarried parents share her or him in a joint custody arrangement? What people constitute the child's "family"? (Zinn & Eitzen, 1990)

In addition to negotiating roles and the usual family issues—housing, work and school, transportation and scheduling—new families in these very complex structures must focus immediately on the establishment of the family as a unit. The building of family trust and unity is typically a developmental process that begins at birth and matures as the marriage and children develop. In blended and reconstituted families, parents must immediately begin this process in order to establish a definition of the new unit. This can be complicated when the children in these families are at varying stages of development (preschool, adolescence, young adulthood) or if the children did not participate in the decision to blend the families. The children may have difficulty adjusting to their new parent figure. The parents' childrearing and behavior management practices may also suffer.

Another variant of family structure is reflected in the growing number of foster care families (Hochstadt, Jaudes, Zimo, & Schachter, 1987). This family structure is established when a child is placed in an approved home by the state as a result of the absence of family members and/or a cessation of parental rights. These families are headed by both biological and nonbiological kin and include single- and two-parent heads of household. The use of foster grandparents for infants and young children is also a common practice in many states. Foster parents receive training and financial subsidies for the care of children, and work in conjunction with an assigned caseworker from the agency placing the child in their home. Foster care families are often providers for children who have severe medical and behavioral problems or whose parents were substance abusers. Foster families will often care for a group of siblings from one home or for one or more children from different homes. Foster care placements can be short- or long-term. Recent changes in placement laws have emphasized the value of permanent placements for some children to assure greater continuity of care and family commitment to life-long development. These families, however, must always be prepared for a transition in the child's life that could result in a change in placement or a reunification with the original parent(s) or other family members. The intensity of the relationship between foster parents and the children in their care is often equal to that of other kinships. Many children adjust to their new family environments and their parents work closely with the school. However, in some situations, foster families encounter children in various stages of crisis or others whose emotional and physical condition prevent them from developing the necessary bonds and communication for healthy parent–child relationships. These families often require counseling and other types of assistance from human service providers, including the school, in the development of their relationships. School personnel sometimes find it difficult to establish home–school partnerships with families of children placed in foster care when the child is in crisis. The assumptions we have traditionally held regarding parent–child relationships and parental responsibility for home follow-through may not be appropriate for this population. However it is critical that models for home–school relationships become flexible enough to accommodate diverse family structure. As home–school partnerships are designed, the case manager and foster parents must be involved. This will insure that the child's behavioral history, as well as current transition issues, are considered.

The families we have discussed represent alternate family structures in which members have adapted roles and responsibilities in response to their unique circumstances and needs (Walsh, 1993). Considerable variation exists within these groups of families who challenge previous assumptions about typical family functioning. Socioeconomic status and level of social support are critical factors to consider in determining the functionality of these families (Bristol, 1987; Reichle, 1987; Thomas, 1989). To view these families as dysfunctional based solely on family structure without considering the degree of success they may have attained in areas such as communication, household management, childrearing—as well as the level of family cohesion and adaptability—can greatly impact the potential for successful home–school partnerships. Epps (1985) cautions us:

> Each group must be understood from the context of its historical experience and current circumstances. The influence of race, ethnicity, and class on socialization patterns and family style must be viewed from a variety of per-spectives, free of the implicit ethnocentrism that idealized the middle-class Anglo-European life styles.

Families as Educational Partners

Let us recall Ms. Green as we discuss how family diversity impacts home–school partnerships. It is evident, from Ms. Green's efforts to engage parents in the implementation of her new behavior management system, that she is committed to parent–teacher partnerships. Her strategies for involving parents were con-structive, and appropriate for some of the families. She actively sought their support of her students, one of the best "home–school resources" available to her. She sent written notices to their homes and followed up with telephone contacts when feasible. She made the classroom attractive and welcoming for the parents, and attempted to link the classroom environment to the home environment. However, many of her assumptions of home–school interactions were based on traditional notions of family functioning.

Each of the assumptions represents a view about the level and degree of family involvement in education. As we examine the changing nature of American families, we must consider how these changes impact home–school partnerships, particularly as they relate to helping children manage their behavior through constructive, positive learning environments.

The assumptions reflected in Ms. Green's plans suggest that parents should know school-appropriate behaviors and that they should be willing and able to incorporate these behaviors into their relationships with their children, family, and community. From this view, if a child is having behavioral difficulties at school, parents should direct the majority of their attention and energy toward remediating the child's behavior. If families comply with this expectation, managing the child's behavior takes priority over other family responsibilities.

Family life, however, is not simplistic. Families are a series of interlocking subsystems, and changes in one subsystem automatically impact other subsystems (Minuchin, 1974; Turnbull & Turnbull, 1990). If we understand children's behavior from the perspective of families, we see behavior in the context of interrelating subsystems. Schools typically focus only on the parent–child subsystem. Although that subsystem is very important, there are other critical subsystems: siblings, spouse or partner, extended family, and nonbiological kin. Together these subsystems form the total family unit, and people representing all of these subsystems could be taking care of children in Ms. Green's class. Some of these parenting relationships may be formal and some may be informal. Some include persons very close in age to Ms. Green's students, while other parenting figures may be in a later stage of their lives where schools have become foreign places. It is only when we have become knowledgeable about these relationships that we are well equipped to identify our home partners accurately. Furthermore, we cannot construct relevant home interventions and activities until we understand the child caregiving relationships we are attempting to influence.

Ms. Green might have facilitated this process by encouraging family members to assist in defining the components of the plan that would enhance family/community life as well as appropriate behaviors for school and the classroom. She might have asked the families to identify successful behavior practices used in the home for all of the children and explored with the group how some of those practices might be beneficial for classroom and school behavior management. More specifically, exploring family expectations for movement, noise level, and adult–child supervision might engage family members in the process of defining the problem and developing a solution.

Professionals in the field of special education often enter into relationships with parents from a hierarchical position of authority (Harry, 1992). This is based on a number of factors, including the specialized clinical and instructional training professionals receive, the organizational structure of the schools and classroom environments, and the nature of the student–teacher relationship. These factors have contributed to the belief that professionals are more knowledgeable and objective than parents on matters relative to children and schooling and that parents should be willing to learn from professionals and return home to teach their children. This hierarchical view of the relationship of teacher to parents ignores the adult nature of teacher–parent relationships and the wealth of knowledge and information that parents bring to the relationship by virtue of their intimate and historical relationship with the child. In the hierarchical view, parents are expected to take and implement professional advice, often without question, and defer most educational decision making to school personnel (Turnbull & Turnbull, 1990). When they do this they are considered cooperative, positive parents. When they do not, they are often termed "noncompliant," or worse, "noncaring."

Ms. Green's development of her behavior management philosophy independent of parental input is an example of the hierarchical expectations of parental deference. The needs of the classroom and school are quite different from the needs of families, children, and communities. Family behavior-management philosophies are shaped by a number of factors including parent–child relationships, cultural norms and traditions, living space, and degree of adult supervision (Turnbull & Turnbull, 1990). For Ms. Green's behavior-management philosophy to reflect co-ownership with the families, they should be involved throughout the process, and not be limited to home implementation of so-called best practices.

A third assumption that is problematic for Ms. Green is reflected in her expectation of a universal family form. She was quite surprised by the wide array of family structures present among her students. In her initial instruction to the students she reminded them to encourage their "mothers and fathers" to attend the meeting and stressed the importance of full "parental" participation. Demographers Norton and Glick (1986) predicted that more than 86% of school-age children will spend some portion of their lives in a non-nuclear family. The majority of these children will grow up in families headed by women who are employed outside of the home in semi-skilled or service jobs. Many of these women will work shifts that are not compatible with the school day or Ms. Green's evening meeting. Additionally, they will not have the benefit packages that would permit them to miss work and attend a school meeting or participate in a school-based training session. This means that the childcare persons Ms. Green spoke to on the telephone are critical links to the home–school partnerships we are attempting to establish and not merely babysitters "watching the children" until the parents return.

Families experiencing major stressors in their lives often seek alternate home environments for their children. These transitions may be the result of marital dissolutions (desertion, separation, divorce). Additionally, the sudden death of one parent, or the loss of employment, housing, or transportation may lead to the temporary (yet sometimes long-term) separation of school-age children from their families. In some cases the child welfare agencies and juvenile court system may remove a child from the home and temporarily place her or him with other families (or in holding facilities) while evaluating the original home environment.

These new family groupings have created a range of kinship relationships in families that have major implications for home–school partnerships (Takas, 1993).

The grandparents present in Ms. Green's group, as well as the adolescent siblings in attendance, reflect the multigenerational parenting occurring in many families (Beck & Beck, 1989; Pearson, Hunter, Ensminger, & Kellan, 1990). This has major impact on home–school partnerships, in that the nature of the parent–child relationship changes as a result of the chronological age and life experience of the "parent." A universal nuclear view of families fails to recognize the variant adult–child and child–child relationships in families that can still be supportive of educational goals.

The substance-abuse epidemic has redefined the role of primary caregiver in some families (White, 1992). Many of the children identified as behavior disordered will have been prenatally exposed to toxic substances (alcohol, cocaine, tobacco), but more important, the degree of a parent's addiction or incarceration may limit the abilities of biological parents to care for their children. Siblings, foster-care parents, and other relatives and family friends have become our educational partners. We must begin to include the perspective of these sometimes short-term and transitional parents in our plans for home–school partnerships. This will include expanding our definitions of parents and considering the range of relationships present in the home environments of the children we serve.

Planning for Family Involvement in Behavior Management

Parents have a long history of participation with schools in educational planning for their children (Walberg, 1984). Their active involvement has been associated with many positive outcomes (Bronfenbrenner, 1974; Bloom, 1981; Moles, 1987; Walberg, 1984). They include improved parent–child communication, improvement in the attitude of the student toward school, an increase in school attendance, and a decrease in school drop-out rates (Comer, 1986). However, much of the parental participation in schools has been limited to middle-income families from majority backgrounds (Chavkin, 1993).

The over-representation of middle- and upper-class families in home–school activities and limited representation of lower-income, minority families has been of great concern to many interested in pluralistic models of family involvement (Chavkin, 1993). Comer (1986) examined some of the more traditional approaches for involving minority families and found that many have chosen not to participate in school activities like parents' night, parent-teacher associations, and parent/child banquets because of discomfort with school protocol. He attributes this to a long history of negative experiences with school systems. He calls for a greater flexibility on the part of school systems in dealing with families from diverse ethnic, educational, and income backgrounds. This should include a range of opportunities for involvement in educational programing.

The participation of families in the development and implementation of effective behavior management plans requires a re-examination of existing school policies and practices to determine the extent to which they reflect the changes that have occurred throughout our society, particularly those related to families and schools. In the past, a lack of parental participation was attributed to a lack of interest on the part of the parents in their child's education. A review of many of the existing practices suggests that the models for family participation were based on the assumptions of nuclear family structure and functioning (in which the father worked outside of the home and the mother remained in the home to care for the children and the household). These assumptions have failed to recognize the variability in family characteristics and functioning present in schools today.

One of the areas that has historically inhibited effective home–school partnerships has been the scheduling and location of "parent activities." Most of our traditional activities require parents to come to the school and meet in groups or individually with teachers and other school personnel. These activities generally occur during the school day or on weekday evenings. Rich (1993), in her work at the Home School Institute, suggested that we must now consider the impact of work on parenting, particularly on women. Scheduling on-site activities fails to acknowledge the multiple issues many families must negotiate in order to participate while maintaining employment. These issues include parent schedules (which change dependent on employers' needs), limited or no leave privileges, and the distance between school and work. Additionally, many of these families must rely on public transportation. They must also consider childcare needs of other children in the family, as well as responsibilities for elderly family members. In some rural and suburban areas, families face transportation dilemmas that restrict their mobility in the late evening. Parents in large urban areas with high crime rates may have concerns for personal safety when activities are scheduled in the evening.

The shifts in family structure and functioning have created the need for a broader definition of parenting and a redesign of parent involvement activities. Rich (1993) maintains that we should seek parental involvement in the child's total education well beyond the classroom and school setting. Her proposal would shift the emphasis from any one academic subject to include parents as partners in the building of successful life skills including confidence, responsibility, initiative, and perseverance skills that all children need to be successful in school—and which can be done through a variety of approaches. Rich (1993) suggested a mobilization plan to ensure educational success that would mobilize the family's role. She emphasized the importance of an educational infrastructure that includes funding and commitment to ensure success. Her mobilization includes three phases:

Phase I: Set the stage with an information campaign on the importance of parents as educators. Conduct an extensive local media campaign informing the community of the importance of home–school partnerships. All parents need reassurance that they play an important role and have strength to help their child achieve. Utilize public-service announcements available through community-relevant radio/television stations, back-of-the-bus-signs, grocery bags, church bulletins. The advertisements should emphasize Home **+** School **=** Learning and should include pictures of a variety of family members and structure involved in educational activities with their children. These images should represent a variety of family variables including ethnic, language, social class, and gender roles. "Families need information presented in varied ways, not just through print alone. This enables more parents to be reached, especially those with limited education. (Rich, 1993)

Phase II: Establish a parent–education delivery system.

1. Prepare teachers to work with parents. Utilize principles of adult education and cultural pluralism to prepare to work with parents as educational partners. Most teachers are very committed to working with parents, but the need for home–school partnerships will require that we relate to parents as adult learners from diverse backgrounds with world views unique to their life experiences.

2. Provide ways for families to help one another. Some parents may benefit from affiliation with a network of parents with similar interests and educational concerns. It may be helpful for the school to assist in organizing the initial meeting and provide a gathering place for these families. However, it is critical that the parent group reflect the diversity of families present in the school and that families provide the leadership in setting the agenda for the organization.

3. Establish a family education corps. Utilize family involvement dollars to hire additional school staff to provide the home–school connections that are necessary to meet the needs of parents whose work schedules are not compatible with the school day. These staff should be trained to work with a variety of family forms including grandparents, foster care workers, and nonbiological kin, whose ideas of parenting may be different from traditional expectations.

4. Provide support to schools from all who care about children. Parent–school partnerships should begin as soon as possible and include the full network of family service providers. The influence of work in the lives of family members has created an immediate parents/childcare network very early in the lives of some children. Transitions planning between the hospital, childcare community, and the school can provide an initial con-

tact with families that may facilitate the development of the home–school partnerships early in the lives of children.

5. Involve the wider community (and the total family). Make home–school partnerships a community-wide activity. Seek the assistance of groups of citizens who have the most to gain from families and schools working together. Senior citizens are one of the fastest growing groups in our society. Because of early retirement, many grandparents and other kin are seeking second jobs with shorter work weeks. They may be excellent home–school liaisons to assist in home–school partnerships with working parents. Take advantage of plant closings, mergers, and down-sizing to involve unemployed parents in the school. Suggest that they use this time as an opportunity to reconnect with their child's educational needs. As they return to work, help families identify ways that they can remain connected with the school.

Conclusions

Families are complex units composed of many different subsystems. Events at school impact these systems to the extent that a child reacts at home. Teachers designing interventions for children, especially for ones having behavioral problems, need to be particularly sensitive to the transactions between children

---

Pre-Conference Family Questionnaire

In preparation for our conference, I would like to have some information so that we can use our time productively. Please complete the questions listed below and send them in by _____ . If you have any questions or concerns, this will give me time to get the answers for you. Thank you!

1. How does your child feel about school this year?

2. What seems to interest him/her most about school?

3. What does she/he seem to dislike most?

4. In your opinion, what are your child's greatest strengths or talents? (These do not need to be school related.)

5. Are there areas in which you think your child needs to improve? Have you or others tried to help him/her in these areas? What has worked? What has not worked?

6. Sometimes school life contradicts or interferes with home life. Has that been the case in your home?

7. Do you have any questions about school this year?

8. Do you have any other concerns or questions? Can you think of a question I should have asked but forgot to?

and their caregivers. Teachers need to know, and have some understanding of, the families of their students, including knowledge of how they are different, and teachers must remember that families are not all alike. Neither a teacher nor a school can dictate a family's behavior or response. Rather, school personnel need to learn how to adapt to the many different family practices represented in each classroom. Schools also need to be flexible and capable of working with the many family subsystems that provide care to children and thereby influence children's growth and development.

Discussion Questions and Activities

1. Construct an activity that would elicit family input in the development of a home–school behavior management philosophy.

2. Generate a list of issues you consider as problems in contemporary families' lives. Reflect on the four myths discussed at the beginning of the chapter. How do the myths influence our definitions of family problems?

3. Design a family involvement activity for children whose family members' work schedules and transportation limitations prohibit their attendance at the annual parents' night. Construct activities allowing these families to share in the excitement of the new school year. More specifically, develop a way to engage them in the planning process without losing valuable family income.

4. Many persons (other than parents) provide after-school and evening care for children with behavior problems. Design an activity for the children to identify the family members (neighbors or relatives) who care for them outside of school. What factors would you consider in structuring home–school partnerships when a child's older sibling provides after-school and evening care?

5. How does the family's ethnicity and socioeconomic status influence the design of culturally sensitive home–school activities?

Reflective Questions

1. Does your school welcome all families, even those who are different? How are families welcomed? How effective is the welcoming?

2. Do teachers judge who the "nice" families are, or are teachers accepting of a multitude of caregiving relationships?

3. Do school practices reflect the expectation of traditional families (two

parents)? For example, are mothers supposed to be grade mothers or are family members invited to be helpers in the classroom?

4. Are children made to feel that their family is not as good if their family is different from most families?

5. Do families and teachers interact regularly about school, school events, and children's successes as well as challenges?

6. Are families blamed, perhaps subtly, for children's failures and difficulties?

7. Are parents encouraged to participate in school committees like school advisory committees?

8. Do 75% of the parents in your school attend parent–teacher conferences? If not, what seems to be the problem? (Disinterested parents is not an acceptable response.) What could the school do to involve and welcome the parents?

9. Have parents and teachers reached an understanding and agreement regarding completing and monitoring homework?

10. Are parents aware and supportive of your school's disciplinary policy?

11. Does the administration respect and work with parent groups and parents in general?

12. Do faculty members feel secure that most parents will support their discipline efforts?

13. Are families invited to attend school events such as sports events, plays, concerts, and award assemblies? Are all different kinds of families actively involved in school events?

14. Are events held at varying times to accommodate families' work schedules?

15. Does your school celebrate a multitude of ethnic and religious holidays, involving families in the celebrations and teaching everyone about our many traditions?

16. Do teachers conduct home visits? Why or why not? Might they be helpful, or are there other mechanisms by which teachers can get to know families?

17. Are before-school and after-school programs sensitive to both school and family needs?

18. Do parents receive regular and adequate information about school activities?

19. Do families receive agendas prior to meetings so they can be prepared? Do teachers know about family questions and concerns before meetings so they can have satisfactory answers?

20. When parents are upset about something at school, are they heard and helped in an understanding, nondefensive manner?

References

Anderson, N.B. (1991). Understanding cultural diversity. *American Journal of Speech Language Pathology, (41)*, 121-54.

Baca, L. & Cervantes, H. (1989). *The bilingual special interface.* (2nd ed.) Columbus, OH: Merrill.

Banks, J.A. & Banks, C.A. (1993). *Multicultural education: Issues and perspectives.* Needham Heights, MA: Allyn & Bacon.

Beck, R.W. & Beck, S.H. (1989). The incidence of extended households among middle-aged black and white women. *Journal of Family Issues, 10,* 147–68.

Billingsley, A. (1968). *Black families in white America.* Englewood Cliffs, NJ: Prentice-Hall.

Bloom, B. (1981). *All our children learning: A primer for parents, teachers, and other educators.* New York: McGraw-Hill.

Boyd-Franklin, N. (1990). *Black families in therapy: A multisystems approach.* New York: Guilford.

Bristol, M.M. (1987). Methodological caveats in the assessment of single-parent families. *Journal of Division for Early Childhood, 11,* 135–42.

Bristol, M.M., Reichle, N.C. & Thomas, D.D. (1987). Changing demographics of the American family: Implications for single-parent families of young handicapped children. *Journal of Division for Early Childhood, 12,* 56–69.

Bronfenbrenner, U. (1974). *Is early intervention effective? A report on longitudinal evaluations of preschool programs, Vol. 2.* Washington, DC: U.S. Department of Health, Education, and Welfare.

Chavkin, N.F. (1993). *Families and schools in a pluralistic society.* Albany, NY: SUNY Press.

Comer, J. (1986). Educating poor minority children. *Scientific American, 259,* 42–48.

Epps, E. (1985). Foreward. In M. Spencer, G. Brookins, & W. Allen (eds.), *Beginnings: The social and affective development of black children* (pp. xiii–xv). Hillsdale, NJ: Erlbaum.

Harry, B. (1992). *Cultural diversity, families, and the special education system: Communication and empowerment.* New York: Teacher's College Press, Columbia University.

Hill, R. (1972). *Strengths of black families.* New York: Emerson Hall.

Hill, R. (1993). *Research on the African-American family.* Boston: William Monroe Trotter Institute, University of Massachusetts at Boston.

Hines, P. & Boyd-Franklin, N. (1982). Black families. In M. McGoldric, J. McPearce, & J. Giordano (eds.), *Ethnicity in family therapy* (pp. 84–107). New York: Guilford.

Hochstadt, N.I., Jaudes, P.K., Zimo, D.A. & Schachter, J. (1987). The medical and psychosocial needs of children entering foster care. *Child Abuse and Neglect, 11,* 53–62.

Jackson, J., McCullough, W., & Gurin, G. (1988). Family, socialization, environment, and identity in black Americans. In H. McAdoo (ed.), *Black families,* 2nd ed. (pp. 252–63). Beverly Hills, CA: Sage.

Joe, D., Malach, P. (1992). Families with Native-American roots. In E. Lynch and M. Hanson, *Developing cross-cultural competencies: A guide for working with young children and their families.* Baltimore: Paul H. Brooks.

Kumabe, K.T., Nishida, C., & Hepworth, D.H. (1985). *Bridging ethnocultural diversity in social work and health.* Honolulu: University of Hawaii, School of Social Work.

Lee, A. (1989). A socio-cultural framework for the assessment of Chinese children with special needs. *Topics in Language Disorders, 9*(3), 38–44.

Lynch, E.W. & Hanson, M.J. (1992). *Developing cross-cultural competence: A guide for working with young children and their families.* Baltimore: Brookes.

Marfo, K. (1991). *Early intervention in transition: Current perspectives on programs for handicapped children.* New York: Praeger.

Martin, J. & Martin, M. (1985). *The black extended family.* Chicago: University of Chicago Press.

McAdoo, H. (Ed.). (1988). *Black families.* Beverly Hills, CA: Sage.

McAdoo, H. (1993). *Family ethnicity: Strength in diversity.* Newbury Park, CA: Sage.

McLoyd, V. (1990). Minority children: Introduction to the special issue. *Child Development, 61,* 263–66.

Mercer, J. (1973). *Labeling the mentally retarded child.* Berkeley: University of California Press.

Minuchin, S. (1974). *Families and family therapy.* Cambridge: Harvard University Press.

Moles, O. (1987). Who wants parent involvement? *Education and Urban Society, 19,* 137–45.

Moore v. City of East Cleveland

Moos, R.H. & Moos, B.S. (1975). Families. In R.H. Moos (ed.), *Evaluating correctional and community settings* (pp. 263–287). New York: Wiley.

Moos, R.H. & Moos, B.S. (1976). A typology of family social environments. *Family Process, 15,* 357–71.

Moynihan, D. (1965). *The Negro family: The case for national action.* U.S. Department of Labor: Office of Planning and Research.

Nieto, S. (1992). *Affirming diversity: The socio-political context of multi-cultural education.* New York: Longman.

Norton, A.J. & Glick, P.C. (1986). One-parent families: A social and economic profile. *Family Relations, 35,* 9–17.

Paul, J.L. & Simeonsson, R. (1993). *Children with special needs.* Fort Worth, TX: Harcourt Brace Jovanovich.

Pearson, J.L., Hunter, A., Ensminger, M.E. & Kellan, S.G. (1990). Black grandmothers in multigenerational households: Diversity in family structure and parenting involvement in the Woodlawn community. *Child Development, 61,* 434–42.

Reichle, D. (1987). Stress, support, and quality of parenting: Comparison of black, never-married and previously-married mothers of handicapped children. Unpublished dissertation. Chapel Hill, North Carolina: The University of North Carolina at Chapel Hill.

Reschley, D. (1989). Minority over-representation and special education. *Exceptional Children, 54,* 316–23.

Rich, D. (1993). Building the bridge to reach minority parents: Education infrastructure supporting success for all children. In N.F. Chavkin (ed.), *Families and schools in a pluralistic society* (pp. 235–44). Albany: SUNY Press.

Sameroff, A.J. & Chandler, M.J. (1975). Reproductive risk and the continuum of caretaking casuality. In F.D. Horowitz (ed.), *Review of child development research* (pp. 187–244). Chicago: University of Chicago Press.

Schillings, R., Kirkham, M., Snow, W. & Schinke, S.P. (1986). Single mothers with handicapped children: Different from their married counterparts? *Family Relations, 35*, 69–78.

Sipes, D.S. (1993). Cultural values and American-Indian families, In Nancy Chavkin, *Families and schools in a pluralistic society.* Albany, New York: SUNY Press.

Stack, C.B. (1974). *All our kin: Strategies for survival in a black community.* New York: Harper & Row.

Stevens, J. (1984). Black grandmothers' and black adolescent mothers' knowledge about parenting. *Developmental Psychology, 20*, 1017–1025.

Takas, M. (1993). Kinship care: Developing a safe and effective framework for protective placement of children with relatives. *Zero to Three, 13*, 12–17.

Thomas, D. (1989). Focus on families: Assessing young black children with handicapping conditions within the context of their families. *SENGA, 1*, 18–23.

Tolson, T.F.J. & Wilson, M.N. (1990). The impact of two and three generational black family structure on perceived family climate. *Child Development, 61*, 416–28.

Turnbull, A. & Turnbull, H. (1990). *Families, professionals and exceptionality: A special partnership.* Columbus: Merrill.

Walberg, H.J. (1984). Families as partners in educational productivity. *Phi Delta Kappan, 65*, 397–400.

Walsh, F. (1993). *Normal family processes.* (2nd ed.). New York: Guilford.

White, E. (1992). Foster parenting the drug-affected baby. *Zero to Three, 13*, 13–17.

Wilkinson, D. (1993). Family ethnicity in America. In H.P. McAdoo (ed.), *Family: Strength in Diversity.* Newbury Park, CA: Sage.

Zinn, M.B., & Eitzen, D.S. (1990). *Diversity in Families.* (2nd ed.). New York: Harper-Collins.

Zuniga, M. (1992). Families with Latino roots. In E. Lynch and M. Hanson, *Developing cross-cultural competencies: A guide for working with young children and their families.* Baltimore: Paul H. Brooks.

Chapter 4

Structuring the Classroom for Success

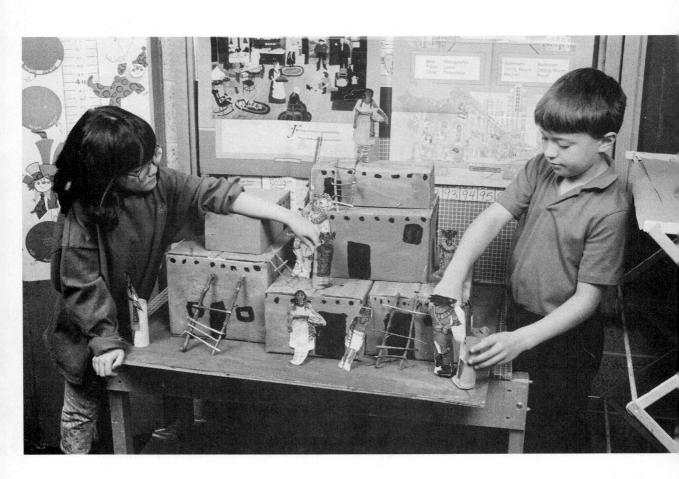

Mrs. Albritton began her career teaching ten students in a self-contained exceptional education classroom within a public school setting. A fulltime paraprofessional assisted her. The classroom was large and open with lots of light, its floor covered with brand new indoor/outdoor carpeting to muffle footsteps as students moved easily about. New study carrels and a well-designed room readily accommodated learning centers for science and social studies. Walls lined with cabinets and electrical outlets allowed ready access to materials and audio equipment as well as numerous computers.

Scheduling was never a problem for Mrs. Albritton because the principal believed that exceptional education was a priority and allowed her first choice in scheduling changes. Mrs. Albritton's students represented a wide range of abilities, but she felt confident in meeting their needs because of the fine physical plant, available materials, and administrative support, all undergirded by her own excellent teaching skills. For three years Mrs. Albritton was in heaven, knowing she had the best job in the school. She loved teaching!

Then Mrs. Albritton was transferred to another school. In the new setting she shared her teaching space with the librarian. The room felt very cramped when all 20 kids were in attendance, and despite having twice as many students she was assisted by a paraprofessional only three days a week. To make matters worse, while Mrs. Albritton was attempting to teach her new class there was constant traffic through the room. As other classes entered and left the library to exchange books they also exchanged glances with her easily distracted students.

In her new situation, Mrs. Albritton had to think creatively to make up for the lack of flexibility in her classroom design. Every inch of space was precious, so only the most immediately necessary materials were out. Mrs. Albritton had to teach her students to structure the day for themselves rather than having it structured for them. She recruited volunteers, plus her own and other students, to help complete tasks not readily accomplished without the daily support of her paraprofessional. Scheduling in this much larger school was a problem because the principal could not give priority to her class. Though Mrs. Albritton still loves teaching, her days tend to be hectic as she runs interference for her students while attempting to uphold her own high standards of education.

With thoughtful advanced planning about how to utilize the space, schedule,
curriculum, and people in a classroom, a teacher can develop a positive learning environment for students. Mrs. Albritton is only one example of many such teachers who have learned to be flexible and creative in meeting the needs of students.

This chapter will address the following elements, all of which require careful consideration to assure a supportive environment for learning:

- ☐ Space within the classroom
- ☐ Scheduling
- ☐ Tempo and pacing
- ☐ Methods for keeping students engaged in learning activities
- ☐ Creating a positive climate

Space Within the Classroom

Mrs. Albritton's initial teaching placement was an ideal learning environment, but unfortunately many teachers have teaching situations more like Mrs. Albritton's second placement. In deciding how to use classroom space, there are several issues to consider. We know that crowding is associated with aggressive behavior, and that students respond positively when they have some type of personal space in the classroom. Thus, teachers need to arrange their space so as to avoid crowding, and they may need to advocate for appropriate class size given their space. They may also need to prioritize how space is used so that adequate student personal space is given a top priority. Once students have adapted to each other, their personal space can be reduced (Smith, Neisworth, & Greer, 1978) and more space can be used for learning centers and activity areas. In setting up the design of a classroom, a teacher needs to provide for the following:

- ☐ Personal student space
- ☐ Work area
- ☐ Teacher materials and space

Personal Student Space

Personal student space can easily be accomplished when students have their own desks. In classrooms where students must share desk space, the teacher needs to avoid student ownership of the desk and create other areas for personal supplies. These areas can be made through designing individual cubby holes. Bookshelves that are divided with masking tape can suffice. Shoe boxes, large round cans, hanging files, or large envelopes on a wall or board can also be used for personal space.

Students' personal space should be clearly marked, and rules for use of personal space delineated for all students. The personal space area is best located near where the students enter the room. The personal space can also be used as a means of communication for teacher and student. Teachers can leave notes to the student, assignments for the day, notes to be taken home, and returned assignments.

The personal space provides structure to the room. This is especially important in classrooms where numerous children share the same classroom and materials can be easily misplaced. By allowing students a personal area for their materials, the teacher can enhance their sense of belonging and develop their ownership of and commitment to the classroom.

Desk arrangement influences classroom interactions. In this class, the desk arrangement encourages peer interaction and teamwork.

Work Area

The working area includes the entire classroom. Different types of work occur in different sections of the room. They include:

- ☐ Large-group instruction
- ☐ Small-group instruction
- ☐ Independent activities (learning centers)

Expectations for acceptable behavior in each setting need to be stated and acceptable behaviors need to be modeled. Emmer, Evertson, and Anderson's (1980) investigation of effective junior high school teachers emphasizes the importance of establishing expectations for classroom behavior and continual monitoring of expectations.

Large-group instruction. This space is utilized when the teacher needs the attention of the entire class. A sample floor plan for whole group instruction with adjoining work spaces is illustrated in Figure 4.1. In those classrooms where different levels of instruction occur at different times of the day, teachers need to utilize the same space for various levels of instruction. For those classrooms that have small learning groups and large-group instruction, chairs can be turned to accommodate the small group and the total-class instruction with minimal disruption. Any time furniture is moved it can be difficult to return it to the original space. Students need to be clear on expectations when moving furniture and teachers should demonstrate how the furniture is to be moved and returned to its original place. Using masking tape to mark the position of table legs on the floor will ease the transition and allow for optimal learning.

Small-group instruction. Small-group instruction is an effective strategy for the teacher to look more closely at each child's ability to grasp a skill (Carnine & Silbert, 1979). Small-group instruction is often utilized for a direct-instruction exercise with six students and a teacher at a semicircular table (Carnine & Silbert, 1979). Small groups can also involve two students at a learning station. When small groups are working side by side, it is imperative that the teacher set the tone for the work groups. Students must understand the noise level that is allowed, how much movement within the group can occur, and how much movement away from the group is acceptable. Small-group instruction (Carnine & Silbert, 1979) and peer-group pairing (Johnson & Johnson, 1986) can be used effectively if expectations are clearly delineated. Masking tape used as boundary markers on the floor can be an effective silent reminder. Teachers need a clear view of all working groups. Furniture should be spaced to allow the teacher to circulate throughout the room as the groups are working. This circulating allows the

Figure 4.1   Sample Floor Plan for Whole-Group Instruction

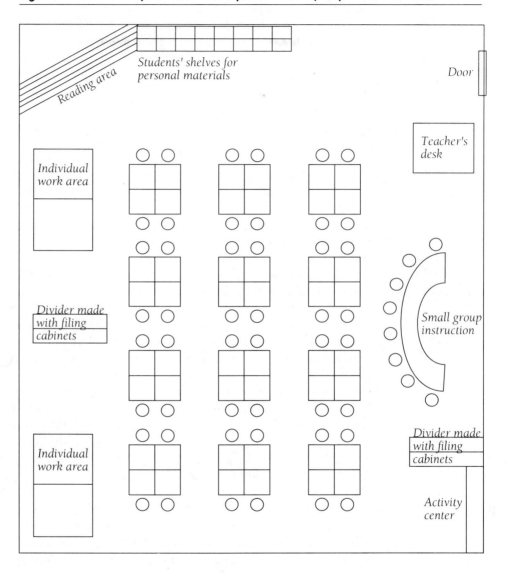

teacher to monitor the working groups quietly and to offer assistance where needed (Brophy & Evertson, 1976). Teachers often exclude potentially disruptive students from independent or peer-group activities because they fear these students will be unable to "handle" the process and inappropriate behavior will escalate. While this activity presents more of a challenge to both teacher and student, the student needs to learn to respond appropriately in these more independent activities and may benefit from the opportunity to practice appropriate social skills. Careful structuring of the room lays the groundwork for a positive working team.

Independent activities/learning stations.   Students working independently need to be able to stay on task without direct teacher instruction and with minimal teacher supervision. This requires that all learning stations or independent activities be easily accessible to students. All materials for the activity should be stored in boxes, cans, jars, baskets, or plastic containers. Keeping a list of the materials for each project ensures easy inventory when the teacher is reordering supplies.

The rules and directions for the station must be written on durable material and laminated. Directions should include set-up and clean-up. This ensures that the station or work area is ready for the next student. A sign-up sheet by the station with time-in and time-out can assist the teacher in spot checking any problems with misuse or damage of equipment. A timer set to allow a certain amount of time for each student also encourages effective transition from student to student.

The influx of electronic technology in the schools has been found to be an effective tool for enhancing education (Budoff, Thormann, & Gras, 1984). Keeping electronic equipment in good working order is essential. Teachers often report that learning stations are too disruptive for highly distractible students. When looking at the situation more closely, it is sometimes apparent that the student becomes disruptive because a piece of equipment is malfunctioning and/or inadequate materials are supplied within the learning station.

Many classrooms built before the age of technology are ill equipped to handle multiple outlets. The use of a plug strip is a relatively inexpensive investment for those classrooms with few outlets. If a student needs adult assistance in an independent activity and no one is available, the student can become disruptive or distracted while waiting. To ensure smooth running of the program, the teacher should periodically check the station and run through the activity to check on all materials and to see that all electronic parts are in good working order and all pieces of the activity are still in place and in order. As part of "classroom responsibility," a student can be selected to monitor the equipment, thus freeing the teacher from another daily task.

Teacher Materials

Increased time on task has been shown to affect academic achievement positively (Rieth, Polsgrove, & Semmel, 1981). Teachers who are organized with their materials can keep students' attention focused and reduce down time (Evertson et al., 1984). Teachers need to have quick access to all materials for the days' lessons. A written organizer for each lesson provides a quick visual reminder of necessary materials.

Advance organizers. An advance organizer is a quick visual cue for the teacher that highlights the necessary materials and sequence of events for a lesson. The example at the bottom of the page of an advance organizer is one means for maximizing instruction.

Teacher editions, or any book used daily, can be stored in a file box or on a bookshelf in the same spot every day. This enables the teacher to ask a student or other assistant to retrieve it easily. For small-group lessons, keeping all teaching materials next to your teaching area is most efficient. A rectangular cardboard box or "in" basket is effective for keeping materials that will be distributed for each lesson. If media equipment is to be used during a lesson, the teacher needs to be sure the equipment is in good working order and that it can be transported easily to the spot where it is to be used. Practicing the movement of equipment before or after school will avoid a loss of momentum and prevent any wait time. To keep students focused, the teacher must provide a smooth transition. Teachers need to model organization to their students and efficient handling of materials is one way to do that.

Advance Organizer for a Teacher on a Place-Value Math Lesson

Introduce concept   overhead projector
                     blue and red transparency pens
                     transparency sheets, water bottle, paper tissues
                     place-value cubes for teacher
                     place-value cubes for each student
                     teacher edition
Discussion and examples that express numbers using place value cubes
                     examples of numbers
Student guided practice using place value cubes
                     directions for using place-value cubes and working in groups
                     numbers for students to determine values
Student independent practice using place-value cubes
                     directions for assignment
                     time allocated for assignment

Management of paperwork.   Prompt feedback to students has been recognized as an effective means for improving academic achievement (Barringer & Gholson, 1979; Hughes, 1973). This feedback often occurs in written form through teacher responses on tests, class activities, and student projects. Unfortunately, even the most dedicated teachers begin to eliminate written feedback due to the voluminous amounts of administrative paperwork required at both the school and district level (Stoddard & Danforth, in press).

To complete necessary forms and provide feedback and communication to students requires a systematic effort by both the teacher and students. In the area of administrative paperwork, several strategies help in managing the workload:

- ☐ *A yearlong calendar* with due dates one week before reports are due enables a teacher to complete activities in a timely manner.

- ☐ *Necessary administrative paperwork* can be determined through discussion with veteran teachers and by calling the district office of the local school system. New teachers are often unfamiliar with the many paperwork requirements and advance planning will avoid unexpected deadlines.

- ☐ *Filing of important forms* issued from the district in separate files and in one location will assist the teacher in having ready access to forms when due dates draw near.

- ☐ *Using a word processing program* enables a teacher to save frequently used phrases, sentences, and paragraphs and have ready access to these items for use on student materials, parent materials, and district reports.

- ☐ *A to-do list* that is reviewed daily will help to prioritize necessary tasks and relegate unnecessary tasks to a different day.

Paperwork and grading can overwhelm a teacher to such a degree that grades are based on multiple-choice tests with little written interchange between the teacher and students. Teachers can provide students with prompt feedback through the following strategies:

- ☐ *Self-grading* by students provides them the opportunity to take responsibility for checking their own work. Self-grading can be completed by using "answer keys."

- ☐ *Class check* of the information provides a quick means of feedback to the students.

- ☐ *Written peer feedback* enables students to begin the process of evaluation. If this strategy is implemented, it is critical that the teacher train students as to the appropriate words to use in critiquing another's work.

Smooth transitions. Time on task and smooth transitions have clearly been demonstrated to improve academic achievement (Stallings, 1980). Transitions include small ones like the change in focus from a class lecture to student practice as well as large ones that involve the entire school or grade level like movement from lunch period to a specific class. By planning for transitions, teachers can effectively prepare and focus students for the next activity. Preparing students may include a simple verbal reminder or a chime that signals 15 minutes are left for completion of activities. When five more minutes have passed, the teacher gives another reminder (10 minutes are left) and finally, after another five minutes, the teacher states that five minutes are left and all students should be getting ready to move to the next activity. This brief verbal cue gives students time to prepare to complete activities and to realize that this activity will end and it is time to move on to something else.

Clear expectations about what is to be done at the conclusion of one activity and the beginning of the next will reduce confusion and shorten the wait time between activities. This also applies to a beginning activity that is highly motivating and independent of teacher instruction.

Effective organization of materials and space within the classroom will allow distracted students to increase their focus on the lesson and result in more efficient learning. Efficient movement in the classroom is enhanced when students can replace all materials themselves in a systematic way. This can be easily accomplished through labeling of shelves and marking exact placement for each item (an outline with masking tape or markers of the various items to be returned—small tape recorders, scissors, blocks, books, glue, games).

The organization of the desks can also enhance transition. This requires trial and error in many classrooms and creative problem solving when space is very limited. A teacher can easily determine effective transitions through a trial run with the assistance of three other adults, who move through the various activities in sequence.

Planning for transitions and preparing students for movement will decrease down time and increase valuable teaching minutes within the school day.

Scheduling

Many variables that affect student motivation are not under teacher control. Such problems might include poor nutrition, lack of sleep, parental neglect, and home stress. However many factors *can* be influenced by, or directly decided by, the teacher. These variables include the length of an activity and the type of learning the student is engaged in (independent seat work, small-group instruction, large-group instruction, passive learning, active learning, direct instruction, guided discovery, cooperative learning). These teacher-determined variables can affect the level of enjoyment of the task, the student's attention to task, and the amount of learning that occurs in the classroom (Brophy & Evertson, 1976).

In the case of Mrs. Albritton, one of the reasons the teacher was so happy in her first school was the scheduling priority given to her class. Preplanning times for specific activities will significantly reduce the number of disruptions (Peterson, Marx, & Clark, 1978). In preplanning the schedule, a teacher needs to consider the type of activity and the energy level of the students.

When planning a master schedule, the teacher needs to first think of all the general activities that occur in a given day: language arts, science, mathematics, physical education, music, art, lunch, transition time, and breaks. Strategically planned breaks and transition time from one activity to the next can dramatically affect the amount and quality of learning that occurs in the classroom. Once the general time schedule is determined the individual activities within each time frame can be scheduled. A balance of activities will enable even the most overactive student the structure to settle and work for a specific period of time and still allow the student time for movement. Planning not only gives the teacher structure, assurance, and management (McCutcheon, 1980), but it also gives students more control over their environment.

Scheduling the day for any group of students requires a well thought out plan based on the preceding considerations. Both the elementary and secondary settings have circumstances that result in unique scheduling problems.

Elementary Level

Scheduling use of the resource room at the elementary level is the most difficult of all scheduling procedures. Elementary schools do not have predetermined periods within the day and teachers must learn to juggle the scheduling of their students around activities such as homeroom, physical education, lunch, music, and art. It is imperative that students who are scheduled for the resource room do not leave their homeroom during the first part of the day. This is when most general education teachers spend time getting to know, and building rapport with, their students.

The schedule for leaving the general education classroom should be based on the needs of the student, not on the convenience of either the exceptional education or the general education teacher. If a student is receiving primary instruction for an academic subject in the resource room, then the time for that student to be pulled out is when the homeroom class is studying the same subject. Due to scheduling conflicts the best schedule cannot always be implemented. Both the general education teacher and the exceptional education teacher must be flexible in their scheduling requests. While the exceptional education student is in the general education classroom, the schedule must always provide for the student to be involved in a variety of activities and an active participant in the

---

Table 4.1 Chart of a Student's Day

Tina Callione's schedule (fourth grade SLD student)

8:15	homeroom
8:30	exceptional education room—reading
9:00	physical education
9:30	exceptional education room—reading
10:30	general education—science/social studies
11:30	lunch
12:00	exceptional education room—language arts
12:45	general education—mathematics
1:30	music
2:00	exceptional education room—check out for the day
2:15	dismissal

---

class. It is the responsibility of both the general education and exceptional education teacher to provide services to the student, and if there is an overlap of time in either setting the student must not be left idly waiting. At no time may either teacher view part of the time in their class as just a "holding pattern" until the student returns to "real" instruction.

The exceptional education student needs a structured day, and if the child's day is fragmented due to poor scheduling all the teachers involved need to re-examine the master schedule to determine if any changes can be made. A schedule as depicted in Table 4.1 details the activities an exceptional education student engages in during the day. The chart clearly indicates the type and length of time of each activity. This chart will assist teachers in determining if changes need to be made to ensure that the student is being exposed to a balance of learning activities.

Hall Traveling in the Resource Room Setting

Two problems particular to resource rooms at the elementary level are timeliness in arriving and leaving the resource room and hallway problems during the transition from one classroom to the next. The most efficient strategy is allowing each student to walk independently to and from class. This requires that the student be able to determine correctly the time to leave and return to class and that the student exhibits the skills to walk independently to the next class without being sidetracked by extraneous or mischievous activities. For those students who are unable to reach their destination successfully, the following strategies can be implemented—beginning with the least intrusive and ending with the most intrusive.

1. Taping a clock on the student's desk that indicates the correct time to leave for a class.

2. Cueing the student to remember that after a particular activity occurs the student should always leave and go straight to the next class.

3. Setting a timer or alarm clock that rings when the student should leave for class.

4. Selecting another student in the class to be the buddy who assists the student in remembering to leave on time and walking appropriately in the hall.

5. Having a paraprofessional pick up each student and return each student to the door of the classroom.

6. Having the exceptional education teacher schedule part of the day for "traveling" to pick up and return students to class.

Self-contained setting.   Scheduling is easier in a self-contained classroom because of the autonomy of the setting. The teacher must schedule time for all academic subjects and must be able to meet the needs of students with a wide level of abilities. Despite the connotation of a self-contained setting, the teacher must also consider schedules for mainstreaming the students into the general education classroom for particular activities when appropriate.

The master schedule for the self-contained classroom must also delineate how much time students are actually engaged in active learning. The scheduling chart in Table 4.2 illustrates what happens when a teacher attempts to individualize all teaching. As exemplified in the chart, a very small amount of time is spent in the instruction of any one student. By attempting to schedule all individual instruction the teacher may actually only teach a mathematics concept to one student for 3 to 5 minutes. Through a chart like the one in Table 4.2, a teacher can determine how much time is being spent with each student in direct teacher instruction, independent practice, learning stations/computers, working with peers, and working with the paraprofessional.

After analyzing the actual time scheduled for each activity, the teacher can adapt the schedule as appropriate. Teachers need to determine if 1 minute of individual math instruction is more effective than 50 minutes of small-group instruction. Many behavior problems can be eliminated if a student is involved in a variety of learning activities for an appropriate length of time.

Secondary Level

The secondary schedule typically follows the master schedule of the school. The beginning and ending times for class periods are predetermined and rarely

Table 4.2 Chart of Teaching Time for Each Student

Time	Bob R.	Tom M.	Mary L.	Anne R.	John W.
8:00	**math**	indep. wk.	indep. wk.	indep. wk.	indep. wk.
8:15	indep. wk.	**math**	indep. wk.	indep. wk.	indep. wk.
8:30	indep. wk.	indep. wk.	**math**	indep. wk.	indep. wk.
8:45	indep. wk.	indep. wk.	indep. wk.	**math**	indep. wk.
9:00	indep. wk.	indep. wk.	indep. wk.	indep. wk.	**math**
9:15	**reading**	indep. wk.	indep. wk.	indep. wk.	indep. wk.
9:30	indep. wk.	**reading**	indep. wk.	indep. wk.	indep. wk.
9:45	indep. wk.	indep. wk.	**reading**	indep. wk.	indep. wk.
10:00	indep. wk.	indep. wk.	indep. wk.	**reading**	indep. wk.
10:15	indep. wk.	indep. wk.	indep. wk.	indep. wk.	**reading**
10:30	**lang. arts**	indep. wk.	indep. wk.	indep. wk.	indep. wk.
10:45	indep. wk.	**lang. arts**	indep. wk.	indep. wk.	indep. wk.
11:00	indep. wk.	indep. wk.	**lang. arts**	indep. wk.	indep. wk.
11:15	indep. wk.	indep. wk.	indep. wk.	**lang. arts**	indep. wk.
11:30	indep. wk.	indep. wk.	indep. wk.	indep. wk.	**lang. arts**
11:30	lunch	lunch	lunch	lunch	lunch

overlap. The inherent scheduling problems found in elementary schools are not part of the scheduling difficulty at the high school level. The challenge for secondary teachers lies in scheduling the activities that are to occur within each class period for students with a wide range of abilities. Table 4.2 demonstrated the importance of charting the types of learning that each student will be exposed to during a particular class period. In addition, it is important for the exceptional education teacher to be knowledgeable about the type of learning environment the student will need throughout the day, both in exceptional education and general education classes. Through an analysis of the scheduling chart, the exceptional education teacher will be able to determine the amount of time a student is spending in a particular learning environment. After examining the scheduling chart the teacher may determine that a student with poor auditory ability is spending a significant portion of the day taking dictation notes in each class. The anger and frustration the student exhibits by the end of the day could be eliminated through modifying the schedule regarding type of classes or choice of activities for a particular class. This requires a cooperative effort among all the teachers with whom the student interacts daily. The teachers must be willing to adapt their schedules to accommodate the needs of the student.

An analysis of the schedule allows teachers to determine if modifications in scheduling can prevent problems from escalating. The initial time that scheduling and rescheduling requires will assist the teacher throughout the rest of the year with smoother transitions and fewer disruptions.

Tempo and Pacing Within the Classroom

In Mrs. Albritton's classroom, students were actively participating in a variety of activities with eagerness and anticipation of the next project. Effective teachers keep students motivated by teaching lessons that are thorough and providing quick-paced practice sessions (Rosenberg, O'Shea, & O'Shea, 1991). Students who are having difficulty learning new information or attending to task will not learn more quickly from a teacher who is providing the same information, in the same manner, at a slower pace. An effective explanation is clear and concise, and followed with a variety of successful practice activities that will ensure mastery of the concept.

A quick explanation of new material followed by a single worksheet or an assignment of a text page that needs to be completed in 5 minutes is a quick lesson—but not necessarily fast-paced and motivating. A teacher cannot teach each student at his or her own individual pace, but a teacher *can* provide each student with opportunity for repeated practice of a newly acquired skill until the student reaches mastery. A teacher must also provide enrichment activities for the student who reaches mastery quickly. Enrichment activities (Sindelar & Stoddard, 1991) can be of benefit for all students, not just those students labeled "intellectually gifted" or "advanced placement." Through enrichment activities a student can be provided with background knowledge that may otherwise be unavailable in the general class curriculum.

Keeping Students Engaged in Learning Activities

Higher academic achievement scores have been reported for students who spend increased time actively engaged in academic tasks (Bennett, 1978; Gump, 1974). In a 1-hour period of instruction, students spend approximately 30% of time working directly with teachers and 70% of time working independently, with peers, or with another adult (Rosenshine, 1980). In a study of second- and fifth-grade students, Rosenshine (1980) reported higher academic engagement by students involved in teacher-directed activity than for those doing independent seatwork.

Increasing the percentage of time in lessons involving teacher-directed activities to students with a wide range of abilities is viewed as an impossible task by many general education and exceptional education teachers. Teachers often report that a student does not "fit" into their particular class because the ability level of the student is at a much lower level than the other students in the class.

Teachers are identifying more and more students who do not "fit" into a particular class. This phenomenon indicates that the range of ability levels in exceptional education and general education is expanding, and teachers must now adapt their curriculum to fit the expansion rather than exclude students who do not fit into the mold of an average student.

Teaching by Topic Area

Teachers can instruct a large group of students with the understanding that the students will acquire different levels of competence. Teaching a particular concept like money does not require each student to pass the same set of objectives concerning knowledge and application of skills. The teacher determines the topic and sets objectives and evaluation criteria for a wide variety of levels. When teaching by topic, the teacher must involve all students actively in the 30-minute lesson rather than having them work independently for 25 minutes and finally receive a 3–5 minute lesson at their individual ability level. Through the practice of teaching by topic, students receive more direct instruction and are able to practice appropriate social skills for group lessons. These social skills include such activities as listening (in a large group) for instruction and direction; listening to other students' questions and comments; and appropriately waiting to respond or comment to the group. If students *only* receive one-to-one instruction, they learn to tune out the classroom because they know eventually the teacher will provide them with individual attention. Teaching by topic is one means by which teachers can efficiently provide direct instruction to students with a wide range of abilities.

Peer Grouping

Grouping students of varying abilities for tutoring and learning groups is an effective means for utilizing the wide range of abilities in a group to the advantage of students' learning (Ysseldyke, Thurlow, Christensen, & Weiss, 1987). Peer tutoring has been proven to be effective in improving the academic performance of the tutor/tutee dyad (Bloom, 1984; Greer & Polirstok, 1982) and is a means for structuring interaction between students who normally do not socialize (Valcante & Stoddard, 1990). Jenkins and Jenkins (1985) highlight in their study the improved social standing of students within a class as a result of peer tutoring groups. A comprehensive description of peer tutoring can be found in Chapter 8.

Using Volunteers

The efficient use of volunteers is an inexpensive solution when an additional "hand" is needed for a particular project or activity. Volunteers cannot be considered teachers or substitutes for teachers, but volunteers can work with students in reviewing reading assignments, reviewing information with the use of flashcards, playing games, or supporting students who need extra attention. Here are some teacher actions that can enhance the volunteer program:

☐ *Develop a volunteer manual* (by the teacher) in each classroom that states rules and procedures for the class and school, expectations for the volunteer, and any critical information about students (medical, special needs).

☐ *Match the ability and interest of the students to the volunteers,* which will encourage a positive experience for both participants.

☐ *Monitor the work of the volunteer* to pinpoint problem areas and avoid problems from arising.

☐ *Provide a daily feedback form and mailbox for volunteers* so that they can write down questions, reactions, and suggestions. This enables the busy teacher to respond when time is available, rather than on the spot. The teacher can return the form to the volunteer's mailbox in time for the next visit.

☐ *Show appreciation of the volunteer* through thank-you cards and notes by students and teachers. These small tokens of appreciation provide the

Senior citizens can be wonderful classroom volunteers.

volunteers with positive feedback and the knowledge that they are making a difference.

The initial set-up of the classroom volunteer program takes some time for the teacher. However, once the program has been established, the efficiency and learning opportunities for students are considerably expanded.

Creating a Positive Climate

The physical structure of the class can be designed to provide the most effective teaching practices, but the teacher still significantly influences what learning will occur in the classroom. Hiam Ginott states it best in his book *Teacher and Child* (1972): "I've come to a frightening conclusion that I am the decisive element in the classroom. It's my personal approach that creates the climate. It's my daily mood that makes the weather. As a teacher I possess a tremendous power to make a child's life miserable or joyous. I can be a tool of torture or an instrument of inspiration. I can humiliate or humor, hurt or heal. In all situations, it is my response that decides whether a crisis will be escalated or de-escalated and a *child humanized* or *dehumanized*" (pp. 15–16).

Awareness and respect for the diverse culture of students within a classroom will continue to be of paramount importance in the teaching profession. By the year 2000, it is projected that over 50% of the public school population will be from ethnically diverse backgrounds (Yates, 1988). Unfortunately most educators in the public school system come from the Anglo-American subculture. It is critical that teachers become aware of cultural differences, value those differences, and structure their classroom so all students will feel a part of it.

The case of Maria clearly demonstrates the misunderstanding that can occur on the part of both student and teacher concerning the structure of the classroom. Maria's parents were called in to school to discuss Maria's defiant behavior towards the teacher. After a very long discussion, the problem was finally uncovered. The teacher had asked Maria and several other students who witnessed a fight to come forward and say who started the incident. The teacher requested the students individually to look her in the eye to be sure they were telling the truth. When it was Maria's turn she could not look up at the teacher. After repeated attempts by the teacher to get Maria to respond, Maria was told that her parents would be called and that she would also have to stay for detention. Maria's parents explained that in their culture children do not look at the adult or authority figure when being reprimanded. To look up at the adult is disrespectful. Maria believed she was being respectful to her teacher, but in the teacher's eyes, Maria was being defiant. Misunderstandings like this are more common than most teachers realize. Through a clearer understanding of and respect for differences, a teacher may realize what was once viewed as defiant or inappropriate behavior may really be just a difference in background.

A teacher must never view a student as a stereotype of a particular ethnic background. This can happen when educators have limited knowledge about a particular ethnic group. A teacher with information about the learning styles of children from Hispanic backgrounds may create alienation in the classroom if this information is used indiscriminately as the educational strategy. Brown (1986) contends that in the Hispanic culture the emphasis is on the present rather than the future. From this a teacher may falsely assume that every Hispanic child in the class will only learn through an appeal to the students' most immediate needs and place no emphasis on planning for the future. This practice would be just as much a disservice to the students as ignoring their ethnic background.

A supportive climate makes each student feel valued. This value extends to the student's background. To enable a teacher to support and even celebrate differences in cultures requires an examination of the teacher's own background. This self-exploration will help the teacher to notice what personal values and ideas, gleaned from the teacher's culture, are incidentally being passed on to students. This awareness will also enable teachers to examine their own overt and hidden prejudices.

Teachers encourage a climate of acceptance of differences through their own statements, reactions, and comments to students, family members, and other professionals. In addition, teachers can foster a climate of celebrating differences through the following:

☐ Have students conduct research and report on various cultures and sub-cultures

☐ Invite individuals from various backgrounds as guest speakers

☐ Infuse multicultural education into the curriculum

☐ Seek parental input on school and classroom policies

☐ Encourage students to share their backgrounds in a supportive environment

Conclusions

Through problem solving and creative planning, teachers can meet the needs of their students. In Mrs. Albritton's case she utilized the space within her classroom for maximum efficiency and organized all materials so the items could be readily accessible. As an effective teacher, Mrs. Albritton used careful analysis to determine how the students' schedules could merge smoothly with the school's schedule. She was willing to give and take when necessary to allow a smooth transition for her students. Mrs. Albritton developed strategies to assist her students in the transition from period to period, allowing them to become responsible for their own behavior while facilitating that progress. Finally, Mrs. Albritton knows the importance of motivation in learning. Through the development of learning settings for individuals, small groups, and large groups, Mrs. Albritton was able to meet the needs of a diverse group of students effectively and efficiently.

Discussion Questions and Activities

1. Smooth transitions are enhanced when a teacher has clear expectations of students. Create a list of expectations necessary for moving the desks in the class from the present format to a circle format. Have a peer group follow your directions and achieve your expectations. At the end of the experience, have the group critique the means and methods utilized to create the circle format. Determine which verbal exchanges and actions enhanced a smooth transition and which impeded it.

2. Disruptive students are often removed from independent or peer-group activities because of the fear that they will be unable to "handle" the process and inappropriate behavior will escalate. As noted in the chapter, the inclusion of these students presents a challenge for the teacher and the student. However, the student needs to learn to respond appropriately in more independent activities and may benefit from the opportunity to practice appropriate social skills. In groups of three, determine three methods for incorporating the student in a learning center activity or peer-group activity that enhance the student's opportunity to be successful.

3. Advance organizers provide a quick visual reminder of the necessary materials for each lesson. Create an advance organizer for a science lesson on rock formations.

4. Interview a teacher to determine what paperwork is required for their particular school setting and collect sample forms the teacher developed to enhance effectiveness within the classroom. These forms may be designed for scheduling field trips, requesting academic assistance for a student, referring a student for a special program, parent communications, or discipline reports. Share the collection of forms with other preservice teachers and determine what forms may be useful for the beginning teacher.

5. As illustrated in Tables 4.1 and 4.2, a chart of a student's day can help the teacher determine how much time is spent in active learning. Develop a time chart for a selected student in a school setting. Shadow this student for one day and chart the amount of time the student is involved in activities with large groups, small groups, peers, and independent assignments.

6. Teaching by topic is an effective tool for meeting the needs of a diverse group of students. Design a lesson for a particular grade level and determine the objectives that can be met for students functioning two years below and two years above the grade level for which the lesson was originally designed.

References

Barringer, C. & Gholson, B. (1979). Effects of type and combination of feedback upon conceptual learning by children: Implications for research in academic learning. *Review of Educational Research, 49,* 459–78.

Bennett, S.N. (1978). Recent research on teaching: A dream, a belief, and a model. *British Journal of Educational Psychology, 48,* 127–47.

Bloom, B.S. (1984). The 2 sigma problem: The search for methods of group instruction as effective as one-to-one tutoring. *Educational Researcher, 13,* 4–16.

Brophy, J.E. & Evertson, C.M. (1976). *Learning from teaching: A developmental perspective.* Boston: Allyn & Bacon.

Brown, T.J. (1986). *Teaching minorities more effectively: A model for educators.* Lanham, MD: University Press of America.

Budoff, M., Thormann, J. & Gras, A. (1984). *Microcomputers in special education.* Cambridge, MA: Brookline Books.

Campbell, B.J., Brady, M.P. & Linehan, S. (1991). Effects of peer-mediated instruction on the acquisition and generalization of written capitalization skills. *Journal of Learning Disabilities, 24,* 6–14.

Carlson, M.B., Litton, F.W. & Zinngraff, S.A. (1985). The effects of an intraclass peer tutoring program on the sight word recognition ability of students who are mildly mentally retarded. *Mental Retardation, 23*(2), 74–78.

Carnine, D. & Silbert, J. (1979). *Direct instruction: reading.* Columbus, OH: Merrill.

Cohen, P.A., Kulik, J.A. & Kulik, C.C. (1982). Educational outcomes of tutoring: A meta-analysis of findings. *American Educational Research Journal, 19,* 237–48.

Emmer, E.T., Evertson, C.M. & Anderson, L.M. (1980). Effective classroom management at the beginning of each school year. *Elementary School Journal, 80,* 219–31.

Evertson, C.M., Emmer, E.T., Clements, B.S., Sanford, J.P. & Worsham, M.E. (1984). *Classroom management for elementary teachers.* Englewood Cliffs, NJ: Prentice-Hall.

Ginott, H. (1972). *Teacher and child: A book for parents and teachers.* New York: Macmillan.

Greer, R.D. & Polirstok, S.R. (1982). Collateral gains and short-term maintenance in reading and on-task responses by some inner-city adolescents as a function of their use of social reinforcement while tutoring. *Journal of Applied Behavior Analysis, 15,* 123–39.

Gump, P.V. (1974). Operating environments in schools of open or traditional design. *School Review, 82,* 575–94.

Heron, T.E., Heward, W.L., Cook, N.L. & Hill, S. (1983). Evaluation of classwide peer tutoring systems: First graders teach each other sight words. *Education and Treatment of Children, 6,* 137–52.

Hughes, D.C. (1973). An experimental investigation of the effects of pupil responding and teacher reacting on pupil achievement. *American Educational Research Journal, 10,* 21–37.

Jenkins, J.J. & Jenkins, L.M. (1985). Peer tutoring in elementary and secondary programs. *Focus on Exceptional Children, 17*(6), 1–12.

Johnson, D. & Johnson, R. (1986). Integrating handicapped students into the mainstream. *Exceptional Children, 47,* 90–98.

King, R.T. (1982). Learning from a PAL. *The Reading Teacher, 35,* 682–85.

Maher, C.A. (1984). Handicapped adolescents as cross-age peer tutors: Program description and evaluation. *Exceptional Children, 51,* 56–63.

McCutcheon, G. (1980). How do elementary school teachers plan their courses? *Elementary School Journal, 81,* 4–23.

Niedermeyer, F.C. (1970). Effects of training on the instructional behaviors of student tutors. *Journal of Educational Research, 64,* 119–23.

Peterson, P.L., Marx, R.W. & Clark, C.M. (1978). Teacher planning, teacher behavior, and students' achievement. *American Educational Research Journal, 15,* 417–32.

Rieth, H.J., Polsgrove, L. & Semmel, M.I. (1981). Instructional variables that make a difference: Attention to task and beyond. *Exceptional Education Quarterly, 1,* 61–70.

Rosenberg, M.S., O'Shea, L. & O'Shea, D.J. (1991). *Student teacher to master teacher.* New York: Macmillan.

Rosenshine, B.V. (1980). How time is spent in elementary classrooms. In D.C. Denham & A. Lieberman (eds.), *Time to learn.* Washington, DC: National Institute of Education.

Sindelar, P.T. & Stoddard, K. (1991). Teaching reading to mildly disabled students in regular classes. In G. Stoner, M.R. Shinn, & H.M. Walker (eds.), *Interventions for achievement and behavior problems* (pp. 357–78). Eugene, OR: National Association of School Psychologists.

Smith, R.M., Neisworth, J.T. & Greer, J.G. (1978). *Evaluating educational environments.* Columbus, OH: Merrill.

Stainback, W., Stainback, S., Etscheidt, S. & Doud, J. (1986). A nonintrusive intervention for acting out behavior. *Teaching Exceptional Children, 19*(1), 38–41.

Stallings, J. (1980). Allocated academic learning time revisited or beyond time on task. *Educational Researcher, 9,* 11–16.

Stoddard, K. & Danforth, S. (in press). The BRIDGE Project: Collaboration for the needs of challenging students. In J. Paul, H. Rosselli, & D. Evans (eds.), *Restructuring Special Education.* New York: Harcourt Brace Jovanovich.

Valcante, G. & Stoddard, K. (1990, May). *Peer tutoring in natural community settings: Strategies for teacher training.* Paper presented at the American Association on Mental Retardation. Atlanta, Georgia.

Yates, J.R. (1988). Demography as it affects special education. In A. Ortiz & B. Ramirez (eds.), *Schools and culturally diverse exceptional students: Promising practices and future directions.* Reston, VA: Council for Exceptional Children.

Ysseldyke, J.E., Thurlow, M.L., Christensen, S.L. & Weiss, J. (1987). Time allocated to instruction of mentally retarded, learning disabled, emotionally disturbed, and nonhandicapped elementary students. *Journal of Special Education, 21,* 43–55.

Promoting Positive Behaviors

Mr. Dunbar is in his second year of teaching students with behavioral difficulties. He is quite frustrated with the inconsistency of his students' appropriate behaviors. His school has recently begun planning for school-wide restructuring. The aim is to ensure inclusion of all students in the school, with particular emphasis on students who currently have learning and/or behavioral disorders. Mr. Dunbar has mixed feelings about his school's plans to restructure. While excited about the spirit of inclusion that he hopes will characterize the entire school climate, he is somewhat fearful of what the restructured school will be like for students with learning and behavior difficulties. He is concerned because his students frequently engage in behaviors that do not endear them either to other teachers or to their peers who do not experience learning or behavioral problems.

Mr. Dunbar is convinced that if his students were to be fully integrated in school activities and classes they would not be successful academically or socially. After observing his colleagues and his own teacher behavior, Mr. Dunbar believes there is a core group of student behaviors that, if mastered, would increase their opportunities for school success—namely, those behaviors that end up on teachers' classroom rule charts: Staying on task; following directions; speaking and moving about the room with permission; keeping hands, feet, and objects to oneself; and respecting other students and adults. These are behaviors that enhance academic and social success in most classrooms. Moreover, Mr. Dunbar believes that if his students demonstrated these skills on a regular basis, they would fare better, not only in his class, but also in integrated settings.

Mr. Dunbar is well aware of times when teachers desire and expect certain behaviors of students that the students are incapable of performing. He firmly believes there should be a match between what teachers expect and what students can do. Essentially, teacher expectations need to be realistic and reflect student capability. He knows that students cannot be expected to perform behaviors or actions that are not in their repertoires. Accordingly, Mr. Dunbar confidently states that his students can perform each behavior he expects from them. He admits that he used to think his students didn't use positive behaviors because they didn't have the necessary skills. He thought they were so impulsive that they couldn't inhibit their verbal outbursts and didn't know the various ways people show respect for others. But Mr. Dunbar has observed them using these desirable behaviors. Just the other day, they wanted extra time in the gymnasium for free play. Mr. Dunbar told them that if they could make it through the morning without any classroom rule infraction, they could earn 30 minutes of gym time. That was an interesting morning. He watched as his students struggled to control their behaviors, but they all managed to comply. He smiled to himself as he overheard students reminding and encouraging each other to follow the posted class rules. He is now convinced that they do know how to use many appropriate behaviors. After giving it much thought, Mr. Dunbar has concluded that something is keeping his students from wanting to engage in the behaviors that he has posted around the room. He also believes that the frequency with which they engage in inappro-priate social behavior minimizes their academic and social success. Since he has observed them performing each of his desired social behaviors on occasion, the problem, as Mr. Dunbar sees it, is that they do not perform the behaviors consistently. He is now convinced that his students engage in appropriate behavior when it suits them. And more often than not, it doesn't.

With his school's restructuring movement underway, Mr. Dunbar wants his students to be successful both academically and socially. Therefore he is quite concerned about increasing positive behaviors among his students, with particular emphasis on those behaviors that teachers in his building perceive as facilitators of success in their classrooms.

*T*he challenges facing Mr. Dunbar as an educator are not unique. Many teachers and parents have voiced similar concerns, particularly when interacting with children and youth who exhibit learning and behavioral difficulties. As a result of these interactions, several questions are commonly posed regarding techniques for teaching and maintaining socially appropriate behavior. First, how do you motivate students to use behaviors that are socially appropriate? Second, what teaching approaches are commonly used to teach positive behaviors to children and youth? And third, once behaviors are learned, how do you get those behaviors to generalize, or be used in situations involving persons other than those responsible for skill instruction; how do appropriate behaviors generalize across myriad settings and remain over time?

The chapter will respond to these questions which are pertinent to proactive behavior modification efforts with children and youth. The emphasis is on the use of positive strategies for teaching appropriate behaviors. Various student contexts (home, school, and community) must be explicitly considered when planning, implementing, and evaluating behavioral change strategies. Thus, the foci of this discussion are (a) motivating students to perform desirable behaviors, (b) increasing desirable behaviors, and (c) promoting generalization and maintenance of newly learned socially appropriate behaviors in diverse student contexts.

Motivating Students to Perform Desirable Behaviors

Mr. Dunbar is convinced that his students are capable of performing the desired behaviors that compose his classroom rules. He relates a recent incident in which the students struggled, but managed to avoid violating the rules for an entire morning. Thus, based on his observations, they are capable of engaging in the appropriate behavior. Other teachers may not be so sure of their students' capabilities, particularly if they have not observed them being demonstrated in naturally-occurring situations. Those teachers will need to conduct an assessment of their students to determine if the behavior is one that students can perform readily or if it needs to be taught. Observation is a critical preliminary step for planning positive behavioral changes. Behavioral observation allows teachers to discern student proficiency on behaviors that students have learned. In effect, it assists in determining if students have learned the behavior, but fail to display it. When planning behavioral interventions, the first question to be asked is: Can the student perform the target behavior at will? Practitioners have an array of behavioral observation procedures from which to choose in determining student skill proficiency. As assessment techniques are discussed in detail in Chapter 9, they will not be addressed in this section. Instead, strategies for motivating students and teaching positive behaviors are presented here.

Let's assume that Mr. Dunbar is correct in his observations of his students—that his students have already learned the behaviors he expects. If he is also correct in noting that they don't perform the positive behaviors consistently, he, along with other teachers, is prompted to ask: What motivates students to use previously learned behaviors regularly? These questions must be addressed prior to implementing a program for positive influence on behavioral change. Once teachers have adequately assessed students, determined that they are physically capable of performing the behaviors, and know with confidence that the behaviors are in students' repertoires, the goal is to increase the frequency with which the positive behaviors are actually used.

In the earlier scenario, Mr. Dunbar observed his students following classroom rules and suggested that they can perform the behaviors he expects, but for some reason choose to do so sporadically, at best. This inconsistency is of great concern to Mr. Dunbar. His school is currently involved in developing strategies for restructuring to improve the education of *all* students, including his students who have behavioral and learning difficulties. He hopes to improve their quality of life by promoting the use of positive behaviors that will increase their chances for social success in school, home, and community settings.

In essence, Mr. Dunbar wants to change their behavior, from its current state of being undesirable and often ignored or punished by others, to being rewarded by teachers, parents, other adults, and peers. He realizes that, at times, his students do not use appropriate behaviors which they have already learned. Mr. Dunbar has pondered the notion many times that his students are capable of following rules, but are not motivated to do so. Mr. Dunbar, once again, has voiced a concern that is often heard throughout schools across the country. That is, what can teachers do to increase student motivation once skills have been acquired?

Research has been conducted on strategies for motivating students to perform academic tasks (Porter & Brophy, 1988). Many of the guiding principles are applicable when the task is a social or behavioral one. Various procedures can be used to increase motivation of children and youth in school settings; the techniques can also be used to increase motivation in settings outside of school. First, teachers should examine the quality of their relationships with their individual students. When the teacher–student relationship is positive and efforts are made to really "know" student likes and dislikes, matches can easily be made between instructional strategies and students' needs and preferences. Quite simply, if teachers frequently interact with their students and solicit their input on decisions that affect the students, students may be more motivated to learn the desired skill (Adelman & Taylor, 1983).

Suppose Mr. Dunbar discovered that, with the exception of what he observes in school, he knows very little about his students. Periodically he overhears them talking to each other about entertainment celebrities, whose names generally are unfamiliar to him. Or he hears snippets of conversations about events that occur in the students' community. For the most part, he has no idea what they're talking about. When Mr. Dunbar asks them to explain who or what they're talking about, they chide him and say that he wouldn't understand. He realizes that he really doesn't know what they do for recreation when they leave school. Mr. Dunbar is terribly disturbed by this, and decides to make an effort to get to know his students on dimensions beyond in-school academic and social behaviors.

Mr. Dunbar would be wise to attempt to gain genuine insight into his students, individually and as a group. He can structure a variety of opportunities to better understand his students, their perspectives, and the experiences they bring into the classroom. He can talk to them informally about their interests and his. Teachers can learn more about students when they show that they value the information. One technique is to have each student present information about an interest or talent that may not be obvious in school settings. For example, Mr. Dunbar might discover that one of his students is an excellent singer and has developed a singing or rap group in his neighborhood. Or he might discover that another student is looked up to by many children in the community because he discourages older children from bothering younger ones. Mr. Dunbar might also learn that one of his students can recite statistics on any past or present player in Major League baseball.

Mr. Dunbar could also carefully observe and participate in students' casual conversations more frequently to show interest and gain rapport with his students. Brief activities could be incorporated into the daily schedule to allow time for relationship building between Mr. Dunbar and his students and among the entire class. Figure 5.1 presents examples of brief activities that will help teachers learn individual student characteristics, while modeling the importance of finding out about each other. These examples illustrate ways in which teachers can discover aspects of their students' lives in school and other contexts. Positive teacher–student interactions must be developed before teachers can motivate students to perform appropriate behaviors. It is extremely difficult to discern

Figure 5.1 Relationship-Building Activities

Activity	Structure
Partner interviews	Class divides into dyads. Each dyad interviews each other on 3–4 questions (What do you like to do in your spare time? Who is your favorite entertainer? What do you most want others to know about you?)
	Each person reports to the class about the person interviewed.
Discovering similarities	Class is divided into dyads or triads. Each small group has 2 minutes to list all the ways in which they are alike.
Discovering differences	Class is divided into dyads or triads. Each small group has 2 minutes to list all the ways in which they differ.
News broadcast	Each person in the class will do a 2-minute newscast about self. (Person may include information about family, important events, interests, strengths, etc.)
Oral history	Each person in the class will tape record a family member talking about a family tradition or custom that is unique. Each day, one oral history will be shared with the class.
Wall of fame	Each person will bring or draw a picture of someone they admire. They will tell what they admire about the person. The pictures and a brief written report about the person will be posted on a classroom wall.
Teacher interview	Students can develop questions that they would like to ask the teacher. Teacher responds to a panel of students.
What's my line?	Students write an anonymous paragraph about themselves. One person reads each paragraph, while teacher and students attempt to determine who the paragraph identifies.
I believe . . .	Current event or issue is described on a card. Students select a card and either record or write their position on the issue with reason(s). Each student has 2–3 minutes to share their perspective with a partner, dyad, small group, or entire class.

motivators for individual students without understanding their likes, dislikes, and interests. When the teacher–student interaction is positive, teachers are privy to information about students that can be incorporated in motivational techniques. For example, suppose Mr. Dunbar discovers that his student, Jorge, enjoys drama and is quite creative. To entice Jorge to participate in class activities in which social skills are practiced, Mr. Dunbar could enlist Jorge's assistance in developing role-play scenarios for the class to perform.

After teachers have developed positive rapport with their students, several other strategies can be used to motivate them. One technique involves affording students with various opportunities for making meaningful decisions. Students must be provided with structured choices when learning to use target behaviors. Choices should be structured to facilitate student participation in practice activities (Adelman & Taylor, 1983; Mercer & Mercer, 1993).

Students can be presented with choices regarding many activities which are conducted in classrooms. According to Conrath (1988), the options offered to students must be genuine and sincere. Stated another way, students should not choose just for the sake of having choices. An example of providing genuine choice would involve Mr. Dunbar's presenting his students with several behaviors targeted for improving, and asking them to select the order in which the behaviors would be taught. He might also involve his students in decisions regarding establishing classroom rules and standards and identifying appropriate rewards and consequences. Curricular decisions could also be made with student involvement.

Students can help teachers determine student-preferred teaching methods. Grant and Sleeter (1989) identified three elements of teaching—content, context, and mode—that can be altered to accommodate student learning preferences. *Content* is the curricular materials that the teacher is expected to cover. The *context* is the setting in which the instruction occurs, and the *mode* is the manner in which the lessons are presented. Teachers can modify any, or all, of these elements to appease student learning styles and preferences. This information is particularly useful to teachers of students who are individually, culturally and/or linguistically diverse. Even though, for most teachers, the content is often predetermined and not under teacher control, there are aspects that can be altered.

Students can play a vital role in the process of identifying ways to enhance the existing curriculum. For example, if the objective is for students to demonstrate knowledge of inventions by famous Americans of all cultures, there are a number of ways in which students can do so. Once the lesson has been taught, students can decide among individual or group projects, oral reports, field trips to museums, simulated television interviews, cooperative learning activities, and so on. Thus, while the content in this situation was unalterable, the students would have had meaningful opportunities to influence the context and mode in which the lesson can be enhanced.

Relevant curricula are great motivators for learning.

In Mr. Dunbar's class, suppose he asks his students to think of a behavior that, when used, would help them avoid "getting in trouble in school." Much to Mr. Dunbar's surprise, the majority of his class states that they want to get along better with students in other classrooms. After further questioning, Mr. Dunbar finds out that his students want to be included in the nonacademic activities during lunch and after school. If Mr. Dunbar postpones his originally planned agenda to teach his students to initiate friendship with students from other classes, he will be changing the content and, probably, increasing their motivation to learn and use a meaningful skill. If he didn't heed their own needs assessment, he might teach the behavior of getting permission before talking, only to discover that they have no desire to learn or engage in that behavior. Other strategies for increasing student motivation follow.

Inciting Student Interest in Performing the Behavior

The need to learn or use the target behavior should be related in a way that is meaningful and relevant to students. It should be connected to events that occur in their everyday lives (Brophy, 1987). Only after learning about students' everyday lives can teachers ensure that the target behavior is perceived by students as meaningful. In Mr. Dunbar's class, if he knows that one of his students is preoccupied with thoughts of operating a convenience store, he can use store simulations to help students develop rationales for learning how to respect others, or how to follow directions. If other students hold primary responsibilities for taking care of younger siblings and relatives in nonschool settings, that information could be incorporated into lessons on the importance of keeping hands, feet, and objects to oneself. Students should be encouraged to provide the teacher with situations in settings outside of school in which the skill is needed.

Obtaining Student Commitment

There are several techniques to attain student commitment to learning and using target behaviors. A contract between teacher and student is one way to demonstrate the partnership involved with the target behavior (Deshler & Schumaker, 1986). Gain student support for involvement by having students suggest terms of the contract. For example, if Mr. Dunbar wants to garner student commitment to work on the skill of respecting others, and he assists them in establishing a rationale for learning the skill, he could discuss contracting as a way of showing that both parties are committed to working together on the desirable behavior. He could negotiate terms and conditions with students (the appropriate behavior to engage in, the rewards and the consequences, the duration of the contract, and the criteria for success). Students must see that Mr. Dunbar is committed to the partnership as well. He must be careful to deliver contingencies when and as they are identified in the contract.

Students could also be taught to petition to work on skills they see as relevant. Students could identify a skill they need, gain student signatures as an indication of commitment, and present it to the teacher. Student committees provide another forum for student involvement and commitment. Students could be divided into small groups to help with the planning that goes into teaching particular skills. For instance, for the skill of respecting others, students could easily assist with developing practice opportunities for students. Another committee might work closely with the teacher on identifying social reinforcers and making sure that they are varied, so students don't get bored with the social rewards.

Monitoring Progress and Providing Feedback

Motivation is enhanced when teachers continually monitor students and provide immediate and accurate feedback (Brophy, 1987). As when academic skills are taught, effective lessons contain certain components. A traditional academic lesson plan includes an advance organizer (or opening), the content (or body of the lesson), and a post organizer, or closing (Rosenberg, O'Shea, & O'Shea, 1991). Within the body of the lesson, the new concept or skill is demonstrated or modeled and the students are provided guided practice. Students are given structured activities to be completed under teacher supervision, often with teacher prompting and other forms of assistance. This step of guided practice is critical in academic lessons and in teaching desirable behaviors. According to the authors, it is only after guided practice activities can be completed with a 90% mastery level, should students be allowed to engage in activities independent of the teacher. Teachers can use traditional lesson formats when teaching positive behaviors. They must carefully monitor both guided and independent practice opportunities and provide immediate and accurate feedback.

If Mr. Dunbar were to teach a lesson on apologizing to others, he might develop a lesson plan similar to the one in Figure 5.2. Allowing students to have input can ensure meaningful participation and increase motivation. In the lesson plan of Figure 5.2, students make genuine decisions regarding their learning. For example, they determine the language in which the steps for apologizing will be written, and thus learned. Additionally, they brainstorm and create scenarios including the contexts in which they plan to use the target behavior. Motivation for using the skill of apologizing would be further enhanced by formulating a student committee. The committee could assist with evaluating the class overall on criteria attainment. The committee could also make recommendations based on their evaluations of when a new skill should be introduced. The committee may determine that instruction should be continued before progressing to another skill.

Setting Realistic Goals

Behavioral goals and evaluation criteria should be set at levels that are appropriate to student capabilities (Christenson, Ysseldyke, & Thurlow, 1989). According to Maag (1989), targeted goals should match student needs and abilities. The discussion in Chapter 9 of assessment provides several techniques that will help lead to an appropriate match between the two. To the greatest extent possible, students should be involved in their own goal setting and evaluation plans. They can be taught to use self-management techniques, which foster independence, and are discussed in more detail later in this chapter.

Using Powerful Reinforcers

Motivation is increased by ensuring that reinforcers are positive and appealing in value (Morgan & Jenson, 1988; Wang, 1987). Students and their family members can provide teachers with invaluable information on the power held by reinforcers. Teachers can solicit student feedback on their reinforcers of choice

Figure 5.2 Lesson Plan for Learning to Apologize to Others

Lesson plan component	Teacher behavior	Student behavior
Advance organizer	Tell students there are times when we say or do something that hurts someone. Give an example of a time you needed to apologize for something you said.	Students will discuss examples of times that they should have apologized, but didn't.
Content	Role-play with another adult how to apologize.	Observe teacher role-play.
	Have students label each step involved in the act of apologizing.	Decide the actions demonstrated by the teacher in the role-play.
	Write the steps (in the students' words) on the board.	Copy the steps to apologizing.
Guided practice	Divide class into dyads. Have each dyad brainstorm a scenario to practice apologizing. Give each dyad a tape recorder to describe the scenario leading up to apologizing. Have dyads practice the steps for apologizing.	Brainstorm a scenario. Dictate it into the tape recorder. Decide roles and practice the steps for apologizing.
	Monitor each dyad while they are practicing and prompt them with cues for incorrect steps. Provide each dyad with feedback on their role-play.	Discuss the dyad role-play with the teacher. Ask questions or make comments regarding what happened.
Independent practice	Have students continue practicing steps for apologizing using the taped scenarios as recorded by the other dyads. Observe the dyads and give specific feedback.	Using tapes recorded by other dyads, practice the steps for apologizing.
Post organizer	Review the steps for apologizing with students. Have students brainstorm a time when they're outside of school that they might need to use the skill. Inform students of tomorrow's activities.	Recite the steps for apologizing. Share with a partner a time (outside of school) when they will use the skill apologizing.

and parents can share information on what reinforcers hold the most value in home and community settings.

Structuring Success

Multiple opportunities should be structured for student success at levels that are challenging but appropriate. These opportunities in which students are successful are critical in increasing student motivation (Levin & Nolan, 1991). The self-efficacy theory (Bandura, 1977) holds that, for students to believe they can effect changes in their behavior, they must have opportunities to connect their behavior with positive outcomes. Thus, as students meet success on performing desirable behaviors, they are more likely to believe that they are capable of doing so again.

Teachers, like Mr. Dunbar, can use these along with other strategies to facilitate student motivation for increasing positive behaviors. Essentially, the teacher must make every effort to gain understanding about students' everyday lives and aspirations. With that information teachers can structure an array of opportunities, from which students can choose, that more closely resemble their own experiences.

Increasing Positive Behavior

The desire and effort to change the behavior of others is not new. Such attempts have been documented throughout human existence (Alberto & Troutman, 1990). Before discussing approaches for increasing positive behavior, it is fitting that the intent of these approaches be discussed. In school settings, teachers are often bent on getting students to comply with their commands. A myriad of strategies are used. Shores, Gunter, and Jack (1993) explored the nature of many teacher–student interactions. They characterized them as being either reciprocal or coercive in nature. *Reciprocal interactions* are those that occur between two persons, where parties feel mutually satisfied or rewarded. An interaction of this nature not only leaves both parties satisfied but also affects the possibility that the same responses will occur again. On the other hand, a *coercive interaction* is one in which one person in the interaction makes an aversive statement. In that case, the person who made the aversive statement either avoids the situation or does so only to get what is wanted.

It has been suggested that the coercion of students, by teachers, to engage in desirable behaviors might attribute to the growing numbers of students who avoid school settings by dropping out prior to graduation (Sidman, 1989). The focus of this book is on a proactive approach to student behavior management. In keeping with that theme, discussions on behavior management should be tempered with the caution that proactive orientations of managing behavior are preferred over those that are reactionary. Stated another way, establishing and developing positive teacher–student rapport and structuring opportunities that enhance student success are preferred over reacting to student behavior that is problematic. It is better to engage in teacher behavior that consistently fosters positive relationships with students than to intervene after a crisis or behavioral problem occurs. Moreover, teachers must also be able to recognize when behavioral interventions are coercive and elicit avoidance behaviors from students.

Myriad strategies have been developed expressly to modify or alter human behavior. In school settings, efforts to increase the frequency in which students display positive behaviors often emanate from the behavioral, social learning, and cognitive models. A description of each model follows, along with practical examples of each model's use in the classroom.

Behavioral Model

According to behavioral theory, all behavior—both appropriate and inappropriate—is learned. Behaviorists, believing that behavior is observable and measurable, are not concerned with internal reasons maladaptive behavior occurs (inner conflicts, etc.). Instead, the emphasis is on the events in the environment that serve to maintain the behavior. Experiments conducted on environmental stimuli led to what is now known as the behavioral model. Two types of conditioning (or learning) have been used to modify behavior—respondent conditioning and operant conditioning. Respondent (or classical) conditioning is a behavioral principle that refers to learning and is based on the work of Ivan Pavlov, the famous Russian physiologist.

Pavlov discovered that dogs salivated when presented with cues, such as a food dish, that mealtime was approaching. The food dish, which was associated with feeding, was considered a conditioned stimulus. He later paired a neutral object, that in isolation had no association with feeding (a bell), with meat powder, an unconditioned stimulus. The meat powder was unconditioned, in that it produced an involuntary response. Pavlov was successful in demonstrating learning by pairing the meat powder, an unconditioned stimulus, with a neutral stimulus to produce a learned, or conditioned, response (Coleman, 1992). Thus respondent conditioning, because it is learning that involves involuntary responses, has little utility in classroom instruction.

Operant conditioning, or learning, emanated from the work of Skinner (1953). Its principles are frequently used in school settings to manage behaviors. In essence, behaviorists believe that behavior is learned primarily through the manipulation of environmental events. A basic tenet of operant conditioning is that consequences of behavior determine whether the behavior is strengthened or diminished. According to this theory, behavior can be increased by carefully arranging behavioral consequences. Consequences are events that occur after students engage in a target behavior, and can be either positive (reinforcement) or negative (punishment) (Smith, Finn, & Dowdy, 1993).

For an example of operant conditioning, suppose Mr. Dunbar holds a class meeting with his students to determine what behavior they want to increase. They might decide to be nicer to each other in the classroom. Upon further discussion, Mr. Dunbar could pinpoint the students' chosen target behavior to "making friendly statements to peers." Mr. Dunbar could interview his students to ascertain meaningful social rewards for individual class members. That is, he could ask the students what leadership roles they would like to assume as a reward, or what group game or activity they would like to do. Similarly, Mr. Dunbar could interview his students to determine the unpleasant consequences to be delivered when students do not perform the target behavior or meet their criteria for success.

Each time he observed the students making friendly statements to peers, Mr. Dunbar would deliver the mutually agreed upon reward. On the other hand, if students made antagonistic statements to their peers, the social reward would not be delivered; instead unpleasant consequences would result. Initially the goal would be to create social "pay-offs" when students made friendly statements to their peers. It is hoped that the social rewards would then motivate the students to increase the frequency of friendly peer-directed statements.

Reinforcers

According to behavioral theory, appropriate behaviors are learned as a result of environmental events that reinforce or increase the frequency in which the behavior occurs. Reinforcement of behaviors is tantamount to the success of behavioral management programs. While there are many types of reinforcers, they generally serve to strengthen behavioral responses, or increase the chance that the behaviors will recur (Wood, 1992). If a student engages in a socially appropriate behavior that is followed by a consequence, and the student performs the behavior again, the consequence is a reinforcer.

Reinforcers can be positive or negative. A positive reinforcer involves presenting a desirable consequence following the use of appropriate behavior. While a positive reinforcer involves the presentation of a pleasant event, negative reinforcement entails withdrawing an unpleasant event. A negative reinforcer occurs when a negative event is removed following a desired behavior. A student fidgets with toys in her desk instead of completing an assignment. She looks up and sees the teacher standing next to her desk. As she dislikes working with the teacher standing next to her (negative event), she takes out her assignment and resumes work. The teacher then moves away from the student's desk. The teacher's presence was removed and the student increased the desired behavior.

It is critical that the reward selected by the student be one that is desirable and pleasant (Gearheart, Weishahn, & Gearheart, 1992). Rewards selected without student input may not strengthen behavior if students do not perceive them as positive, or pleasant. In the case of Mr. Dunbar, if he did not poll or interview his students on events that are positive to them, and uniformly rewarded all students with extra free time, a problem would be posed for some students. There may be students in the class who do not consider extra minutes of free time as a positive event; they may even find unstructured free time as an *unpleasant* event. Some students might prefer being allowed to perform a classroom responsibility over earning unstructured free time. Figure 5.3 presents examples of positive and negative reinforcement.

When determining reinforcement, the developmental needs of students must be considered. Primary reinforcers are rewards that are basic to survival (food, drink, sleep). The use of food as a reinforcer has been criticized in the past, and is rarely used as a sole means of behavior modification (Nelson & Rutherford, 1988). When used, these reinforcers are usually provided for younger students or students with severe behavioral difficulties (Kerr & Nelson, 1989) and should always be combined with another form of behavior modification. An occasion for combining reinforcers would be when students are unable to delay gratification. As soon as the appropriate behavior is demonstrated, the teacher would pair a primary or tangible reinforcer with a secondary reinforcer. The teacher would give the student an orange slice while smiling and saying, "We are all happy with the nice way you're waiting."

Tangible reinforcers include other nonedible reinforcers that are delivered to students when desired behaviors have been demonstrated (Kerr & Nelson, 1989). Examples of tangibles are stickers, pencils, and erasers. A behavior management program in which tangibles are used must be monitored carefully. Tangible reinforcers lose effectiveness if they continue to be used as rewards after students tire of them or find them no longer appealing. Tangibles are also less effective when they are not delivered immediately following the desired behavior (Mercer & Mercer, 1993).

Figure 5.3 Examples of Positive and Negative Reinforcement

Positive reinforcement

Student remains in seat during math instruction.	Teacher smiles and gives student a coupon allowing 10 minutes to sing into the tape recorder. (presentation of a desirable-event smile and coupon)	Student remains in seat during the next math instruction period.

Negative reinforcement

Teacher sits next to student while student completes math assignment.	Teacher moves away from student to another area in the classroom. (withdrawal of teacher presence—an unpleasant event)	Student completes the next math assignment without interruption.

Secondary reinforcers are rewards that are intangible and are paired with primary reinforcers; the intent is to gradually replace the primary reinforcer with a social reinforcer (Smith, Finn, & Dowdy, 1993). Social reinforcers are a part of many behavior management efforts. Verbal praise, for instance, is a social reinforcer that is commonly used to communicate to students that their behavior is socially desirable. Other secondary reinforcers include the use of positive notes and memos, hugs, and public displays of school work. As with primary reinforcers, students must also assist in deciding appropriate social rewards.

Token reinforcement is another technique used to teach appropriate social behaviors. When using this form of reinforcement, teachers give students tangible tokens or symbols of rewards immediately following the appropriate behavior. Tokens provide students with an alternative to immediate gratification. They are delivered immediately, but exchanged at a later time for the reward(s). Prior to implementing a token economy system, teacher and students should define and agree on the conditions for earning tokens as well as the exchange rate for rewards. Individual student characteristics should drive the development of token economy plans. Keeping in mind that students will vary on their preferred rewards, the plan should allow for individual diversity. Some classrooms actually set up "stores" to allow students to exchange their tokens for objects or opportunities they desire.

Remember Mr. Dunbar's class, presented at the beginning of the chapter. His students do not consistently remain in their seats. If he were to institute a token reinforcement system with his class, he might solicit their assistance in determining (a) what to use as tokens, (b) what the rewards will be (for individuals and group), and (c) how many tokens must be redeemed to earn the reward. Once these decisions are made, he would systematically observe students on the target behavior throughout the school day. At varied intervals, he would simultaneously give all students in their seats a token and verbally praise them for performing the appropriate behavior of sitting in their seats. Mr. Dunbar would be wise to initially structure frequent opportunities for success. He should also gradually lengthen the time between reward occasions. As with any reinforcer, care must be taken that the rewards continue to be pleasurable and maintain appeal for students.

Shaping

Another behavioral principle used to increase positive behavior is that of shaping. Some target behaviors are composed of several actions or subskills. For example, Mr. Dunbar is concerned that his students don't come to their small-group activities when he requests. Complying in this instance is composed of several actions or subskills. It means that students must (a) gather the needed materials, (b) go immediately to the assigned area, and (c) sit down quietly. If Mr. Dunbar expects students to comply with that request, they must successfully perform each of these actions.

Effective teachers monitor student understanding and give immediate feedback.

Some of Mr. Dunbar's students gather their materials when asked, but don't immediately go to the assigned area. It is not uncommon for them to wander around the room before going to their small groups. In other words, they perform some but not all of the behaviors that result in performance of the target skill. In this situation, Mr. Dunbar could use the behavioral principle of shaping to improve their compliance with his request. For shaping to be successful, a task analysis (see Gagne, 1985, for a detailed description), or sequenced list of requisite steps, should be conducted on the completed or terminal behavior to determine the steps necessary for successfully performing the desired behavior. Shaping refers to the procedure in which, initially, all behaviors that approximate (resemble) the target behavior are reinforced. The reinforcement of behaviors resembling the target behavior becomes more discriminating, as behaviors more closely approximate the target behavior. Gradual reinforcement continues on the approximated behaviors until the target behavior is performed correctly (Stephens, 1977).

If Mr. Dunbar wanted to use shaping to encourage student compliance, he would reinforce any behavior that resembles those he desires. For example, if a student, Raj, gathered his materials immediately, he would be reinforced. When Raj heads toward the small-group area, he would be reinforced. He would be further reinforced as he comes to the assigned area. Mr. Dunbar could gradually shift the reinforcement to ultimately occur only when the completed desired behavior is performed (gathering materials and coming to the assigned area in a timely manner).

Chaining

Chaining is another technique used to increase positive behaviors when the target behavior involves more than one step or subskill. Again, a task analysis must be conducted to determine the sequence of the behavior's subskills. Once that has been done, the desired behavior's first subskill is reinforced when it is performed. The first and second subskills are linked together to earn one reinforcement. This linking process continues until the last subskill has been demonstrated and reinforced. When all subskills have been taught in this manner, the student is capable of performing the terminal behavior (Center, 1989; Foxx, 1982).

If the target behavior of starting a math assignment were task analyzed, it might include the following sequence of subskills:

1. Get a piece of unlined paper from the counter.

2. Go to your desk.

3. Sit down.

4. Take out your math book.

5. Take out your pencil.

6. Open your book to the assigned page.

Figure 5.4 Reinforcement Schedule Used when Chaining

	Chaining
Step 1	reinforcement
Steps 1 & 2	reinforcement
Steps 1, 2 & 3	reinforcement
Steps 1, 2, 3 & 4	reinforcement
Steps 1, 2, 3, 4 & 5	reinforcement
Steps 1, 2, 3, 4, 5 & 6	reinforcement
Steps 1, 2, 3, 4, 5, 6 & 7	reinforcement

7.   Put your name on the paper.

8.   Read the directions.

The reinforcement would be delivered according to the sequence of activities displayed in Figure 5.4.

Fading

Another procedure designed to increase desirable behavior involves the use of prompts or cues. Often when students are unable to perform the target skill independently they require the assistance of others. They may need verbal or physical prompts to perform the terminal behavior. While students initially require verbal or physical prompts, practitioners must be cautioned regarding the extensive use of such assistance. At some point, the prompts or cues should gradually diminish to allow the student to perform the target behavior independently. To promote eventual independence, a fading process is implemented (Foxx, 1982). Fading is the gradual withdrawal of prompts used in teaching the target behavior. This procedure increases in effectiveness under certain conditions. Primarily, timing is crucial. If the prompting continues for extended periods of time, students rely on it and may not perform the desired behavior on their own; similarly, if prompting is withdrawn too soon, the desired behavior will not be performed (Alberto & Troutman, 1990).

Contingency Contracting

Contingency contracting is a procedure that lends itself to involving students actively in their own behavioral interventions (Salend, 1987) and to individualization (Hall & Hall, 1982). This procedure operates along the lines of the Premack principle (Premack, 1959). The Premack principle, or grandma's rule, simply states that a low-frequency behavior should be followed by a high-frequency behavior. A behavior that a child does not normally engage in (condition) should be followed up by a behavior that the child loves to engage in (reward). In this manner, if a child completes a dreaded assignment, he will be given time to do a desired activity (play a board game, paint a picture).

This procedure is implemented in several steps. First, the practitioner communicates with the student the rationale for learning the target behavior. Second, the practitioner and student determine the desired behavior. Third, the conditions in which the desired behavior should occur, and the contingencies for the behavior's occurring or not occurring are negotiated until mutual agreement is reached by the practitioner and student. Fourth, a contract is drawn up stipulating the conditions and contingencies. Fifth, the contract is read aloud and signed by the practitioner and the student and a witness to the agreement. A contingency contract for a student in Mr. Dunbar's class is presented in Figure 5.5.

Contingency contracts have been used quite successfully in a variety of settings for students with behavioral difficulties (Rutherford & Polsgrove, 1982). A critical element of contingency contracting is that of monitoring the occurrence of the target behavior. Center (1989) advised teachers to carefully monitor students on the desired behavior when possible. There are times when self-report has to be used. When students practice using target behaviors in settings outside of school, school personnel are not able to observe them. Student use of target behaviors in various contexts needs monitoring. While self-report is not the most favored method of monitoring, it can be facilitated by having the student report extensively on the situations in which the skill was practiced. Other individuals in that environment can also report on the student's skill performance.

Group contingencies can also be used to promote positive behavior. The steps used in developing individual contingency contracts can also be used to promote positive behavior among a group. If there are several students in the class who lack a certain skill, group contingencies can be established for the entire class. As an example, if most of Mr. Dunbar's students are breaking the rule of getting out of their seats without permission, he could discuss the problem with the class and define and demonstrate the target behavior. He could increase student motivation and participation by soliciting student input. His students can assist in determining the criterion for success and the group contingencies for meeting the preset criterion. Similarly, the group could also assist in determining group contingencies for failing to meet the preset criterion.

Group contingency plans should not be used unless students are capable of, and have experience, working cooperatively on common goals. If Mr. Dunbar's class is extremely antagonistic toward each other, he should teach and provide practice opportunities for them on group behaviors (cooperation, conflict resolution) prior to instituting group contingencies. Other concerns must be addressed before structuring group contingencies. First, the criterion for success should be set in such a way that student success is guaranteed initially. If Mr. Dunbar knows that his students get out of their seats without permission an

Figure 5.5 Example of a Contingency Contract

CONTRACT

Date <u>March 3, 1994</u>

I, <u>DeAndre</u>, will <u>start my math assignments</u>
Student   Target behavior

under the following conditions:

<u>no later than 5 minutes after Mr. Dunbar gives directions.</u>

In order to <u>start math assignments</u>, I must <u>1. Get paper from</u>
    Target behavior

<u>counter 2. Go back to my desk 3. Get out appropriate</u>
  (List steps for demonstrating target behavior)

<u>materials 4. Start math</u>

I am doing a good job if I

<u>Do each step no later than 5 minutes after Mr. Dunbar gives</u>

<u>directions.</u>
     (Evaluation criteria)

REWARDS

When I do a good job, I will earn

<u>10 minutes to listen to music with positive messages.</u>

I helped decide the terms of this contract and am in agreement with them.

<u>De Andre</u>   <u>Mrs. Townsend</u>
Student Signature   Teacher Signature

<u>Mrs. Thomas (Principal)</u>
Witness Signature

average of 10 times in one hour, he might set the criterion at 11 or 12 times (meaning that they would attain the positive reinforcement if persons in the class did not get out of their seats without permission more than 11 times in one hour). When his students have attained that criterion, Mr. Dunbar and his students could adjust the criteria for success.

Ethical and Legal Issues

A plethora of research exists documenting the effectiveness of the behavioral approach in increasing positive behavior (Gelfand & Hartmann, 1984; Nelson & Polsgrove, 1984; Reinert & Huang, 1987). There is no question that behavioral interventions can successfully increase positive behavior among students. Not all behavior modification practices, however, have been successful in effecting positive behavioral change (Nelson & Rutherford, 1988). Because some practices have been questionable, certain considerations must be addressed when designing and using these interventions.

Early on, a great deal of concern was directed at the use of behavior modification techniques in institutions, which spawned litigation. The *Wyatt v. Stickney* (1971) court case questioned persons' rights to appropriate treatment vis-à-vis the use of shock therapy. Litigation has also involved institutions using token economy systems that incorporated the withholding of individuals' basic needs. In this case, the basic needs of privacy and adequate space were used as reinforcers to effect behavioral change among the patients in an institution. While these issues generally involved persons living in institutions, concerns also exist regarding behavioral techniques implemented in school settings.

Specifically, ethical and legal issues have resulted in the identification of cautionary measures for teachers planning to use behavioral interventions (Nelson & Rutherford, 1988). The effectiveness of behavioral interventions is dependent upon the following conditions:

☐ Well-trained personnel. Behavioral interventions must be implemented by persons who are knowledgeable about the theoretical underpinnings. Furthermore, individuals must be proficient on the consistent use of techniques for manipulating those events that occur before and after desired behaviors (Nelson & Rutherford, 1988).

☐ Use of multiple interventions to effect behavioral change. Behavioral principles should not be used in isolation. It has been suggested that they increase in effectiveness when combined with other behavior change techniques. That is, positive reinforcers could be used along with observational learning, or modeling procedures (Nelson & Rutherford, 1988).

In addition, teachers must ensure that target behaviors are socially valid, or will improve students' quality of life (Wolf, 1978). Social validation of a potential target behavior takes the perspectives of several individuals into account. The teacher alone should not decide the behaviors on which a student needs to improve. Instead, various persons who are significant in students' lives should assist in making these decisions.

Ethical issues are raised when teachers alone decide the behaviors students need to change. The selected target behavior may improve the teacher's quality of life in the classroom, and may not necessarily impact that of the student. Suppose a behavior is selected for change because it is one that is a pet peeve or idiosyncrasy of the teacher. Assume that Mr. Dunbar has a hard time concentrating on what he's saying to the class if someone is doodling while he's talking. He may even believe that if students are not looking at him they are not paying attention. Thus, *he* decides that behavior needs to change.

Little does he know that, for one particular student, doodling helps her to concentrate and listen more attentively. Had Mr. Dunbar asked the student's other teachers, he would have discovered that they allow her to doodle when information is presented auditorily. In their experience, when not allowed to doodle she showed much less comprehension of the auditorily presented information. As you can see, in this scenario Mr. Dunbar would not have socially validated the target behavior. In Mr. Dunbar's case, changing that student's behavior of doodling while Mr. Dunbar is talking would do little to improve the student's quality of life. It might make Mr. Dunbar's life easier, but not the student's. Similar decisions and justifications must be made before developing behavioral modification plans.

Social Learning Model

Principles emanating from other theoretical approaches have influenced behavior change procedures. Many behavioral intervention programs in school settings are based on social learning theory (Bandura, 1973). Inherent in social learning theory is the notion that individuals learn behavior primarily by watching others. According to its proponents, this observational learning takes place as the target person observes the behavior of someone else (model) and the consequences of that person's behavior. In this manner, appropriate behavior is learned when the target student observes another student (for example) engaging in positive behavior and notes the positive reinforcement that follows demonstration of the behavior. The student who learns the behavior is likely to imitate the behavior as demonstrated by the model. Mercer and Mercer (1993) suggested the following guidelines for teachers desiring to implement modeling:

1. Select the behavior.
2. Select the model.

3. Give the model and the observer directions concerning their roles.

4. Reinforce the model for exhibiting the behavior.

5. Reinforce the observer for imitating the behavior.

When using observational learning or modeling, it is essential that the models be persons who perform the target behavior correctly. Additionally, research on the use of modeling to teach behaviors has shown that models must be selected carefully. Models are most effective if they are persons whom the target students hold in high esteem (Stephens, 1977). With that in mind, it would be futile for a teacher trying to teach her students to complete assignments to enlist the aid of a student model who is unpopular among the other students. If the teacher used that student to model the desired behavior and reinforced that student for displaying that behavior, the teacher's desired outcomes may not occur. It is unlikely that the other children would emulate the unpopular model's behavior. Observing the rewards earned by unpopular students may not, in and of themselves, motivate onlooking students to imitate the behavior.

Others have suggested that the model should be capable of performing the behavior appropriately, but should also at times be viewed as a coping model, or one who can be observed struggling to perform the desired behavior (Stephens, 1977). In essence, a coping model does not come across immediately as knowing how to perform the desired behavior, but appears more human as she or he attempts to display the behavior, in much the same way as someone who is initially learning the behavior.

Cognitive Model

Growing concerns with some of behavioral approach's limitations gave rise to other methods of positively influencing student behavior. This process influenced the development of the cognitive-behavioral model (Coleman, 1992). It was felt that an approach which connects both the behavioral and cognitive aspects of learning would increase effectiveness. The cognitive-behavioral modification approach (Meichenbaum, 1977) incorporates a nexus of cognitive and behavioral interventions. Carpenter and Apter (1988) defined cognitive-behavioral interventions as those that "actively employ the cognitive processes of the student in the intervention procedure" (p. 157). Most cognitive behavior modification approaches of teaching appropriate behaviors are designed to teach students to control their own behaviors and are characterized by four components (Lloyd, 1980). These approaches commonly include:

1. Modeling—students observe and listen to the self-talk of the person teaching the behavior

2. Verbalization—students employ a self-talk process to facilitate learning the behavior

3. Self-directed strategies—students implement the technique on themselves

4. Problem-solving strategies—students are taught a problem-solving framework that can be applied to various situations

Thus, cognitive-behavioral modification acknowledges the influence of cognition on student behavior (Coleman, 1992). In employing it, students are taught to think out loud when initially learning a desired behavior. They are gradually taught to whisper their self-thoughts, and ultimately use their inner voices or think to themselves. If Mr. Dunbar were to use a cognitive-behavioral modification approach to teach his students to avoid fighting when teased, the lesson might look like the one in Figure 5.6.

An area of cognitive-behavioral modification that gets considerable attention is self-management. Self-management (or monitoring) is defined as the procedures by which students systematically regulate their own behavior (Carpenter & Apter, 1988). It is composed of three aspects—self evaluation, self-reinforcement,

Figure 5.6 Cognitive-Behavioral Lesson Plan on Avoiding Fights

Element	Teacher behavior	Example
Cognitive modeling	Teacher presents a scenario to students in which someone says something negative about the teacher's clothing. Teacher demonstrates how to avoid a fight while verbalizing thought processes involved.	Teacher: I can tell I'm starting to get mad. What choices do I have so I can stay out of trouble? □ I can tell her to stop. (She probably won't though.) □ I can move away from her to another area. What should I do? I'll move away from her. How should I reward myself? I did a great job of getting away from her before I lost my temper!!!!
Teacher-guided practice	Have students practice the same scenario and talk out loud as teacher closely monitors.	Teacher will provide encouraging words and assist students with error correction if necessary.
Student-guided practice	Have students demonstrate the skill while whispering their thoughts.	Demonstrate for students how to self-reinforce or continue practicing when skill is not mastered.
Covert self-instruction	Have students practice the skill in various contexts while using inner thought processes (e.g., no talking out loud or whispering).	Teacher can observe student demonstration in school settings and have students and others in other settings report on student performance in contrived and naturally occurring situations.

Source: Adapted from Meichenbaum & Goodman (1977).

and self-monitoring. *Self-evaluation* occurs when students systematically observe their own behavior and compare it to a predetermined standard. Accordingly, they must be aware of their own behavioral performance and realistically assess the target behavior. When students can evaluate their own behaviors, they can be taught to self-reinforce. *Self-reinforcement* requires students to administer their own reinforcing consequences for meeting the predetermined standard. *Self-instruction* occurs when students use self-talk to facilitate the maintenance of the desired behavior (Alberto & Troutman, 1990).

The intent of interventions that incorporate self-regulation strategies is to facilitate student independence. Proactive efforts to effect behavioral change should encourage students to internally manage their behaviors. Some behavior management approaches, by design, encourage students to rely on others to inhibit their undesirable behaviors. In a similar manner, others are relied upon to facilitate desirable behaviors. Self-regulation strategies, in response to that concern, aim to gradually move target students from external to internal loci of control (Carpenter & Apter, 1988).

Promoting Generalization and Maintenance

Generalization and maintenance continue to concern people who utilize these approaches to facilitate positive behaviors (Schloss, Schloss, Wood, & Kiehl, 1986). The following illustrates a lack of generalization. Mr. Dunbar's class was having difficulty riding the bus to and from school without incident. Every day he received several bus write-ups about his students' behavior on the bus. In one week, Mr. Dunbar counted 25 incidents of wrestling on the bus. He was concerned greatly about the children's safety on the moving bus and decided to target the behavior of staying in the seat from the time students board the bus until they reach their drop-off point. For an entire month, Mr. Dunbar implemented the following behavior change procedures.

1. He talked to the students about their behavior on the bus and talked about the danger involved in wrestling on a moving bus, both for the driver and the students. He solicited their reasons for wanting to change the behavior.

2. He talked to their parents to inform them of his plans to target that behavior and solicited their input on its social validity and their suggestions for consequences at home if a student brought home a note from the driver that the child did not wrestle on the bus.

3. He talked to the bus drivers on the social validity of that target behavior and solicited their involvement in the behavior change procedures he wanted to employ. He wanted the bus drivers to sign and date statements for each child who did not wrestle on the bus. The child would show the statements to the parent to get a reward at home, and Mr. Dunbar

would get carbon copies of the signed statements from the bus drivers the following morning to post in the classroom, where he too would provide a reward.

4. Mr. Dunbar set aside 20 minutes each day to role-play and discuss appropriate bus behaviors. He modeled alternatives to wrestling on the bus. He taught games the students could play while seated. He allowed each student to practice the alternatives during the session and used tokens and verbal praise to reward students during the group time for demonstrating the alternatives.

5. He set up a reinforcement menu of student preferences for rewards. Each reward was a secondary reinforcer and was not a manipulative that Mr. Dunbar had to purchase (special privileges, free time, art time, gym time, activity with teacher). Students decided the point at which they would be allowed to exchange their tokens for a secondary reinforcer.

Mr. Dunbar and the children's families consistently and immediately delivered the rewards to students when they did not wrestle on the school bus. Mr. Dunbar was delighted that his students increased the frequency in which they appropriately involved themselves in alternative activities on the bus. He was able to tell this because the numbers of write-ups his students were getting at the end of the month were very few. He was ready to target a different behavior when he received ten write-ups on one particular day that involved most of his class. He was quite disappointed, and headed out to the bus to investigate. To his surprise, there was a new bus driver, as the regular driver was out ill.

This distressed Mr. Dunbar greatly. It made him realize that while his students learned alternatives to wrestling, and were perfectly capable of demonstrating those alternatives, they reverted to their old behaviors in the absence of the regular bus driver. Unfortunately, this scenario is familiar to many educators attempting to modify behaviors. These concerns are not limited to techniques with origins in behaviorism.

In this case, the problem is that generalization of the learned behaviors did not occur. There are three types of generalization—stimulus generalization, response generalization, and maintenance generalization (Stokes & Baer, 1977). *Stimulus generalization* refers to the transference of a learned behavior or skill across persons, events, and settings. *Response generalization* involves transferring learning across behaviors, and *maintenance generalization* is the durability of learning over time. Thus, since Mr. Dunbar's class behaved differently when another bus driver was present, stimulus generalization must be programmed in Mr. Dunbar's continued efforts to effect positive behavior change among his students. Generalization must be planned for when teaching positive behaviors to students. Kazdin (1980) offers several suggestions to teachers who want to program for generalization and maintenance of learned behaviors.

1. *Include the peer group in interventions.* Children's peers can influence each other's behaviors. Peer-mediated interventions provide viable strategies for increasing positive behaviors.

2. *Use natural contingencies.* Rewards for using desirable behaviors should not be artificial, but be a part of the naturally occurring situation. For example, the use of verbal praise is more natural than rewarding a student with store-bought items.

3. *Use multiple persons and settings.* Students should be allowed to practice the target behavior with a variety of persons and in different settings. Teachers and parents can work closely to coordinate efforts in arranging and rewarding practice and to note naturally occurring opportunities for students to use newly learned skills.

4. *Teach self-management skills.* Students should be taught to monitor, evaluate, and reinforce themselves on using positive behaviors.

5. *Provide ample practice opportunities.* Sufficient opportunities for practice must be structured so students can gain proficiency on target behaviors.

6. *Conduct periodic follow-up assessments after interventions.* After providing students with interventions, teachers should allow a time period (2 weeks, 4 weeks) to lapse and evaluate students on the target behavior. This will determine the extent to which the learned behavior is durable over time.

Conclusions

Generalization and maintenance concerns continue to plague educators, researchers, parents, and students. It is evident that these issues must be addressed in every phase of increasing positive behaviors. The planning, implementation, and evaluation of strategies aimed at promoting positive behaviors must deliberately incorporate techniques that foster generalizing and maintaining the target behavior. Moreover, school personnel must forge partnerships with students, parents, and families to ensure that acquired skills will be practiced and reinforced across settings, situations, and persons.

Mr. Dunbar and countless other teachers are constantly challenged to develop, implement, and evaluate proactive (instead of reactive) behavior management techniques that will generalize to contexts both in and out of school. In summary, teachers must be proficient at gaining student insight as a preliminary step in determining external student motivators for initial use. Deliberate steps must be taken to move students from the need and desire for external motivators toward ones that are more internal (intrinsic).

Classroom strategies for promoting increases in positive behavior commonly emanate from behavioral, social learning, and cognitive theoretical approaches.

Before using one or a combination of models' principles, teachers should consider several factors—individual student characteristics, social validity, and the multiple contexts in which students will use the behavior.

Discussion Questions and Activities

1. Interview a student who frequently engages in undesirable behaviors to determine the student's preferences for (a) a behavior to target,(b) choices for positive consequences, and (c) teaching strategies (role-plays, small group instruction). Based on the interview, discuss how you would motivate the student to engage in desirable behavior.

2. Define an undesirable behavior that is of concern. Develop a lesson plan for teaching an alternative to that behavior.

3. Describe the procedures used in developing individual contingency contracts.

4. Interview a family member of a child with behavioral or learning difficulties. Develop a plan for developing a teacher–family member partnership.

5. You've been asked to deliver a brief talk on ways to promote generalization and maintenance of positive behaviors. Outline your key points.

Reflective Questions

1. Prior to implementing behavior change strategies, have you motivated student(s) by using various methods to determine which skills students have mastered?

2. Prior to implementing behavior change strategies, have you motivated student(s) by examining quality of teacher–student relationships?

3. Prior to implementing behavior change strategies, have you motivated student(s) by structuring activities which foster positive relationships among all class members?

4. Prior to implementing behavior change strategies, have you motivated student(s) by piquing student interest in changing behaviors?

5. Prior to implementing behavior change strategies, have you motivated student(s) by soliciting student commitments to learn new skills?

6. When increasing positive behaviors, do you use positive methods first?

7. When increasing positive behaviors, do you use social reinforcers alone or with other reinforcers?

8. When increasing positive behaviors, do you use reinforcers selected by students?

9. Do you implement ethical and legal safeguards when increasing positive behaviors by understanding issues pertaining to use of behavioral change strategies?

10. Do you implement ethical and legal safeguards when increasing positive behaviors by soliciting input from students, family, and community members when selecting target behaviors and strategies?

11. Do you implement ethical and legal safeguards when increasing positive behaviors by determining student progress toward goal attainment in school, home, and community settings?

12. Do you implement ethical and legal safeguards when increasing positive behaviors by planning for generalization and maintenance with those who play significant roles in students' lives?

References

Adelman, H.S. & Taylor, L. (1983). Enhancing motivation for overcoming learning and behavior problems. *Journal of Learning Disabilities, 16,* 384–92.

Alberto, P. & Troutman, A.C. (1990). *Applied behavior analysis for teachers* (3rd ed.). New York: Merrill.

Baer, D.M., Wolf, M.M. & Risley, T.R. (1968). Some current dimensions of applied behavior analysis. *Journal of Applied Behavior Analysis, 1,* 91–97.

Bandura, A. (1973). *Aggression: A social learning analysis.* Englewood Cliffs, NJ: Prentice-Hall.

Bandura, A. (1977). *Social learning theory.* Englewood Cliffs, NJ: Prentice-Hall.

Brophy, J. (1987). Synthesis of research on strategies for motivating students to learn. *Educational Leadership, 45*(2), 40–48.

Carpenter, R.L. & Apter, S.J. (1988). Research integration of cognitive-emotional interventions for behavior disordered children and youth. In M.C. Wang, M.C. Reynolds, H.J. Walberg (eds.), *Handbook of special education: Research and practice* (Vol. 2). New York: Pergamon.

Center, D.B. (1989). *Curriculum and teaching strategies for students with behavioral disorders.* Englewood Cliffs, NJ: Prentice-Hall.

Christenson, S.L., Ysseldyke, J.E. & Thurlow, M.L. (1989). Critical instructional factors for students with mild handicaps: An integrative review. *Remedial and Special Education, 19*(6), 49–58.

Coleman, M.C. (1992). *Behavior disorders: Theory and practice* (2nd ed.). Boston: Allyn & Bacon.

Conrath, J. (1988). A new deal for at-risk students. *National Association for Secondary School Principals Bulletin, 72*(504), 36–40.

Deshler, D.D. & Schumaker, J.B. (1986). Learning strategies: An instructional alternative for low-achieving adolescents. *Exceptional Children, 52,* 583–90.

Foxx, R.M. (1982). *Increasing behaviors of severely retarded and autistic persons.* Champaign, IL: Research Press.

Gagne, R.M. (1985). *The conditions of learning and theory of instruction* (4th ed.). New York: Holt.

Gearheart, B.R., Weishahn, M.W. & Gearheart, C.J. (1992). *The exceptional student in the regular classroom* (5th ed.). New York: Merrill.

Gelfand, D.M. & Hartmann, D.P. (1984). *Child behavior analysis and therapy* (2nd ed.). New York: Pergamon.

Grant, C.A. & Sleeter, C.E. (1989). *Turning on learning: Five approaches for multicultural teaching plans for race, class, gender, and disability.* New York: Merrill.

Hall, R.V. & Hall, M.C. (1982). *How to negotiate a behavioral contract.* Lawrence, KS: H&H Enterprises.

Kauffman, J.M. (1989). *Characteristics of children's behavior disorders* (4th ed.). Columbus, OH: Merrill.

Kazdin, A. (1980). *Research design in clinical psychology.* New York: Harper & Row.

Kerr, M.M. & Nelson, C.M. (1989). *Strategies for managing behavior problems in the classroom* (2nd ed.). Columbus, OH: Merrill.

Levin, J. & Nolan, J.F. (1991). *Principles of classroom management: A hierarchical approach.* Englewood Cliffs, NJ: Prentice-Hall.

Lloyd, J. (1980). Academic instruction and cognitive behavior modification: The need for attack strategy training. *Exceptional Education Quarterly, 1,* 53–63.

Maag, J.W. (1989). Assessment in social skills training: Methodological and conceptual issues for research and practice. *Remedial and Special Education 10*(4), 6–17.

Meichenbaum, D. (1977). *Cognitive behavior-modification: An integrative approach.* New York: Plenum.

Meichenbaum, D.H. & Goodman, J. (1977). Training impulsive children to talk to themselves: A means of developing self-control. *Journal of Abnormal Psychology, 77,* 115–26.

Mercer, C.D. & Mercer, A.R. (1993). *Teaching students with learning problems.* (4th ed.). New York: Macmillan.

Merluzzi, T.V. & Biever, J. (1987). Role-playing procedures for the behavioral assessment of social skill: A validity study. *Behavioral Assessment, 9,* 361–77.

Morgan, D.P. & Jenson, W.R. (1988). *Teaching behaviorally disordered students.* Columbus, OH: Merrill.

Nelson, C. & Polsgrove, L. (1984). Behavior analysis in special education: White rabbit or white elephant? *Remedial and Special Education, 5*(4), 6–17.

Nelson, C.M. & Rutherford, R.B. (1988). Behavioral interventions with behaviorally disordered students. In M.C. Wang, M.C. Reynolds, H.J. Walberg (eds.), *Handbook of special education: Research and practice* (Vol. 2), pp. 125–53. New York: Pergamon.

Porter, A.C. & Brophy, J. (1988). Synthesis of research on good teaching: Insights from the work of the Institute for Research on Teaching. *Educational Leadership, 45*(8), 74–85.

Premack, D. (1959). Toward empirical behavior laws: Positive reinforcement. *Psychological Review, 66,* 219–33.

Reinert, H.R. & Huang, A. (1987). *Children in conflict,* (3rd ed.). Columbus, OH: Merrill.

Rosenberg, M.S., O'Shea, L. & O'Shea, D.J. (1991). *Student teacher to master teacher: A handbook for preservice and beginning teachers of students with mild and moderate handicaps.* New York: Macmillan.

Rutherford, R.B. & Polsgrove, L.J. (1982). Behavioral contracting with behaviorally disordered and delinquent children and youth: An analysis of the clinical and experimental literature. In R.B. Rutherford (ed.), *Monograph in behavioral disorders:*

Severe behavior disorders of children and youth. Reston, VA: Council for Children with Behavior Disorders.

Salend, S.J. (1987). Contingency management systems. *Academic Therapy, 22*(3), 245–53.

Schloss, P.J., Schloss, C.N., Wood, C.E. & Kiehl, R. (1986). A critical review of social skills research with behaviorally disordered students. *Behavioral Disorders, 12,* 1–14.

Shores, R.E., Gunter, P.L. & Jack, S.L. (1993). Classroom management strategies: Are they setting events for coercion? *Behavioral Disorders, 18,* 92–102.

Sidman, M. (1989). *Coercion and its fallout.* Boston, MA: Authors' Coop.

Skinner, B.F. (1953). *Science and human behavior.* New York: Free Press.

Smith, T.E.C., Finn, D.M. & Dowdy, C.A. (1993). *Teaching students with mild disabilities.* Fort Worth, TX: Harcourt Brace Jovanovich.

Stephens, T.M. (1977). *Teaching skills to children with learning and behavior disorders.* Columbus, OH: Merrill.

Stokes, T. & Baer, D. (1977) An implicit technology of generalization. *Journal of Applied Behavior Analysis, 10,* 349–367.

Wang, M.C. (1987). Toward achieving educational excellence for all students: Program design and instructional outcomes. *Remedial and Special Education, 8*(3), 25–34.

Wolf, M.M. (1978). Social validity: The case of subjective measurement, or how applied behavior analysis is finding its heart. *Journal of Applied Behavior Analysis, 11,* 203–214.

Wood, J.W. (1992). *Adapting instruction for mainstreamed and at-risk students* (2nd ed.). New York: Merrill.

Wyatt v. Stickney, 325, F. Supp. 781 (1971); Supp. 1341 (1971).

Chapter 6

Reducing Undesirable Behaviors

Mr. Salters and Ms. Lomax teach in a school that is quite interested in inclusion. Its faculty and staff want to try alternative arrangements that reflect their vision of what an inclusive classroom should look like. Therefore, it is piloting a classroom in which a teacher of students with behavioral disabilities is paired on a full-time basis with a general education teacher to co-teach 25 students. Seven of the students were labeled in the past as having a behavior disorder. The purpose of this arrangement is to improve the services delivered to all students in the classroom without categorizing students as being special learners. School personnel want to provide more individualized and small-group instruction to children who are typically ineligible for services for students with exceptionalities. With their approval, it was decided that Mr. Salters and Ms. Lomax would teach in the piloted classroom.

At the onset these two teachers, who were friends, were quite excited about sharing teaching responsibilities for their classroom. Everything went along well for the first month or so. After that they began to share, independently, with other teachers in the building, concerns about the arrangement. Mr. Salters is disturbed by events he observes in the classroom. He believes that the co-teaching arrangement is working fine in the area of academics. He and Ms. Lomax complement each other's skills and interest areas nicely. But in the area of behavior management, he is not at all pleased. In fact, he feels they differ so much philosophically that they are consistently at odds with each other's plans for modifying behavior.

Mr. Salters believes that when students display inappropriate behaviors there are several techniques for reducing those behaviors. He feels that he is fair because he is consistent in the way he handles misbehavior. He believes that all students in the classroom should abide by the same set of classroom rules. He says that all students, regardless of ethnicity, class, gender, and ability, must comply with the rules he developed for the classroom. They are the same rules that he, as a child, was expected to live by. His teachers did not vary rules to accommodate individuals or groups of students. Mr. Salters therefore delivers the same consequences for all students when rules are broken, based on the offense. If a student is out of his seat without permission, Mr. Salters takes away a privilege. He firmly believes that all students should be treated the same way—that the only factor that should determine the intervention is the inappropriate behavior.

Ms. Lomax also believes that several techniques are available to her, but varies in the way she reacts to offensive behavior. She feels very strongly that no hard-and-fast rules can be made about decreasing inappropriate behavior. She uses differing techniques for the same offense, depending on the student. For example, when Patrick gets out of his seat without permission, she has him sit at his desk without talking to the other students for 10 minutes. When Connie gets out of her seat, she loses 2 tokens that she earned for displaying appropriate behavior. Hence, Ms. Lomax bases her choice of technique on the child's characteristics. She has observed that Patrick enjoys socializing with the other students. Therefore, when he misbehaves, she removes his opportunities to talk to his friends. Connie, on the other hand, does not enjoy talking to the other students, but does want to earn enough tokens to get the job of student assistant. The student assistant helps the teachers for the entire day by passing out supplies, and performing record-keeping tasks.

Ms. Lomax admits that she is also influenced by other student and family characteristics. She tries to empathize with students who appear to have a difficult time adjusting to school standards when they differ drastically from their home environments. She is aware of the cultural differences between herself and some of the students. As a result, she selects strategies that are sensitive to cultural and individual differences. Mr. Salters complains that Ms. Lomax is too lenient and at times excuses those students from rule compliance because she is fearful that school rules and expectations may violate the students' mores and customs as practiced in their home and community settings.

Ms. Lomax says she does not rigidly enforce classroom rules with students like Antoine. Antoine shares major childcare responsibilities for his younger siblings with another relative. He is not accustomed to being told constantly what to do and how to do it. He shows resent-ment of the adults at school who attempt to control his behavior by threatening him into compliance. Ms. Lomax said she was so disappointed about what happened when Mr. Salters wanted Antoine to finish his math assignment. She believes that Antoine probably would have completed it eventually if Mr. Salters had not resorted to a verbal confrontation. Once it reached that level, Antoine was adamant about not doing it and Mr. Salters was determined that Antoine suffer the consequences. The entire class watched as the two engaged in a verbal match that resulted with Antoine clearly the victor. Antoine is skilled at calling names and talking about others in ways the other students find quite humorous.

Neither teacher feels the other is capable of selecting appropriate interventions to reduce behaviors. Mr. Salters is convinced that Ms. Lomax's consequences are not justifiable. When asked for an example, Mr. Salters said that two days ago Ms. Lomax asked the students in her reading group to go over to the round table to record a group language experience story. Marcus, a physically active student, started twirling around on the floor while the others joined his reading group at the designated area. Mr. Salters complained that Ms. Lomax's initial reaction was to call attention to Marcus by calling out his name, putting a check next to his name on the board, and telling him in a stern voice to go to his area for reading. Marcus continued to spin on the floor as if he didn't hear a word she said. Ms. Lomax went through several steps of threatening Marcus with consequences of missing recess, having a writing assignment, and so forth. Judging by the smile on his face, Marcus was getting some satisfaction from her distress. Ms. Lomax finally said to Marcus that she was going to ignore him, and began her reading instruction.

After observing these exchanges, Mr. Salters noted that there appeared to be neither rhyme nor reason to the interventions used by Ms. Lomax. He said that when students behave in unacceptable ways, Ms. Lomax may take a

privilege away for a minor rule infra put a child's name on the board (a m quence) for one that is more severe.

*T*he school in which Mr. Salters and Ms. Lomax teach is similar to many schools throughout the country. They are involved in restructuring the ways in which children are educated. One reason for school restructuring is to include children with disabilities and those experiencing school difficulty in general education settings (Sailor, 1991). While schools alter traditional school structures (service delivery options, calendars, grading systems, parent and community representation), many exciting changes are taking place. As exciting as these changes may be, teachers are presented with new dilemmas. One change includes being placed in roles in which they may have inadequate training and preparation. In this instance, Mr. Salters and Ms. Lomax have found that their teaching roles have expanded to include sharing a classroom and responsibilities with a teacher from another discipline. These teachers are expected to collaborate on planning, instructional delivery, behavior management, and evaluation.

It appears that the two teachers maintain different philosophies and, consequently, different classroom management practices. Mr. Salters is concerned about what happens in their classroom when students engage in undesirable behaviors. He noted that his colleague's choice of interventions lacks logic and appropriateness. Similarly, Ms. Lomax expressed concerns about his behavior reduction strategies. She believes that Mr. Salters, when reducing inappropriate behavior, does not acknowledge sociocultural influences on student behavior.

Both Mr. Salters and Ms. Lomax have complained about the other's approaches to decreasing undesirable behaviors. For teachers, reducing negative behaviors is no easy task. The frustrations felt by Mr. Salters and Ms. Lomax are understandable. This chapter discusses common practices for reducing behaviors. To respond to specific issues articulated by Mr. Salters and Ms. Lomax, information will be provided on (a) selecting behavior reduction strategies, and (b) responding to surface or minor behaviors.

Selecting Behavior Reduction Strategies

Matching Behaviors to Interventions

Throughout the course of a day, teachers are constantly involved in decision making. When students display inappropriate behaviors, those decisions become increasingly important, and may even be made with little advance notice or planning. The challenge involves assessing multifaceted aspects of a situation to determine whether to intervene, what strategy to use, and how to evaluate its effects. One issue expressed by the co-teachers is that of matching the behavior reduction strategy with the target behavior. The severity of the behavior should be considered when making this decision. This cannot be done without determining how intrusive, or imposing, a strategy will be for an individual. The aim is to employ interventions that are least intrusive (Simpson, 1988).

The Council for Children with Behavior Disorders (1990) defined intrusiveness as "any stimulus event deployed to stop or interrupt ongoing behavior" (p. 245). That is, any strategy used to intervene in student behavior is intrusive. According to Braaten (1987), behavioral interventions range hierarchically in levels of intrusiveness.

Interventions vary regarding the amount of contact teachers must have with students to inhibit inappropriate behaviors. For example, suppose a student disrupted the class routine by singing during a spelling test. If the teacher gave the student a nonverbal cue to discontinue the behavior (the teacher places a finger to her lips and says "Sh-h-h"), the teacher's behavior, albeit mild, is intrusive. The strategy used in this scenario is less intrusive than one in which the teacher engages the student in a conversation about how many times the student has been warned and then takes privileges away. An intervention that might be even more intrusive would involve the teacher delivering a verbal reprimand, removing the child from the instructional setting, and placing her in time-out.

Interventions for reducing inappropriate behaviors should not be chosen in a serendipitous manner, but should be logical. Dietz and Hummel (1978) pointed out that when selecting logical behavioral interventions, ethical, effective, and efficient concerns must be addressed. The ethical considerations involve ensuring the match between the behavior's severity and the intervening strategy. Effective interventions are those that prove successful, while efficient interventions require minimal time for planning and implementing.

Behaviors must also be selected in light of children's disabilities or known behavioral difficulties. Gallagher (1988) maintained that teachers must be knowledgeable about student characteristics, especially when learning or behavioral difficulties are experienced. That is, Yolanda, a child with behavior disorders, may display impulsive behaviors frequently. When a teacher is trying to reduce those impulsive behaviors, Yolanda must be taught alternative behaviors. It is unlikely that Yolanda will be taught to engage in more appropriate behavior immediately, as interventions require time for sufficient modeling, practicing, and reinforcing. The interventions for her may consist of several techniques—nonverbal prompting, reinforcing alternative behaviors, and teaching the child to self-monitor. On the other hand, Olga, who rarely engages in impulsive behavior, may simply be given a verbal reminder or reprimand when she displays impulsive behavior.

Mr. Salters and Ms. Lomax are in a position to share expertise as a special educator and a general educator. They admit that their preservice training programs prepared them differently. One teacher received extensive training in social and behavioral techniques for changing behavior. The other teacher's training program emphasized innovative techniques for effectively teaching academic subjects. Since time is built into the schedules for collaboration and planning, they could share information on student characteristics (disability, sociocultural, familial) that would facilitate more appropriate matches between the student and the intervention.

Sociocultural Considerations

In the opening scenario, Ms. Lomax voiced concern regarding Mr. Salters' lack of cultural sensitivity when intervening with the children in their classroom. She believes that decisions involving ways to reduce inappropriate behaviors must factor in students' cultural and familial backgrounds. Ms. Lomax also has valid concerns about influences on student behavior based on cultural and individual differences. The effects of cultural differences on students' school performance has been sufficiently documented in the literature (Fradd & Hallman, 1983; Gay, 1993; McIntyre, 1993; Ogbu, 1990). Incongruities between ethnic-minority children's home and school settings are increasingly evident. Differences between the two settings show up in communication styles, cognitive styles, role expectations, task structures, and behavioral expectations.

Cultural differences, in and of themselves, are not problematic. It is the way in which those differences are perceived that give rise to differential teaching practices for certain groups of students. A study by Guttentag (1972) found that white preschool children engaged in passive behavior 60% of the time. In comparison, their black counterparts were passive 25% of the time. Depending upon the values held by the teacher, the black children who displayed more active behaviors could have been perceived as having behavioral difficulties. If the teacher expects preschool children to maintain passive behaviors more than 25% of the time, those children who do not may be perceived differently. Evaluating all children against standards established monolithically does not account for ethnic, gender, ability, and class differences. Adopting uniform classroom expectations and standards for every child in a classroom without regard to individual and cultural diversity is harmful.

It must be pointed out, though, that there are classroom rules and standards that must be consistent for each person in that setting. Teachers need to determine those classwide behaviors by which everyone must live. In making that determination, they must consider all factors. For example, Mr. Salters has been perplexed lately. Several of his students refer to their friends in class using what appear to be derogatory names. He is extremely bothered when he hears them refer to each other as "my dog."

Even though the students on the other end of the name calling do not seem at all bothered, Mr. Salters is quite offended. He considers them in violation of their classroom rule to refrain from name calling or put-downs. Mr. Salters is not aware that, to those students, "my dog" is not name calling. His students view name calling to be deliberate acts intended to make others feel bad. In their lexicon, "my dog" had come to be a term of endearment. In fact, it was reserved for use among the best of friends. While Mr. Salters might discuss (and role-play) choosing the appropriate setting and audience to refer to friends in this manner, he should not perceive it as a violation of the classroom rule. Students should be discouraged from putting each other down when it truly occurs, but Mr. Salters needs to be cognizant of cultural factors that give rise to certain behaviors. This cultural awareness will facilitate more accurate teacher perceptions, and consequently teacher practices, with all children.

As society becomes increasingly diverse, so do the roles of the classroom teacher. Students arrive at school with suitcases, backpacks, duffle bags, gym bags, plastic and paper bags filled with previous experiences! In the past, their experiences varied little. Most students arrived with similar values, family structures, educational experiences, and communication patterns. More recently, however, student experiences are as varied as the containers in which they are held.

When determining behavioral strategies for children, contexts beyond the classroom and school must be considered. Students spend enormous amounts of time in home, community, and—often—work settings. Thus all those settings must be examined when attempting to reduce undesirable behaviors. There may be forces within those nonschool settings that maintain undesirable behaviors. Teachers often lament that their efforts become undone when the child goes home. Reducing behavior in school may not generalize to other settings without deliberately working with parents and families to assist in those efforts (Fox & Savelle, 1987).

Teachers must become aware of the mores and customs of the children in their classrooms. This provides an opportunity to strengthen relationships with parents, as they are invaluable in facilitating teacher understanding of their cultures. As "experts" on their cultures and their children, minority parents, who traditionally have been distrustful of schools, might be encouraged to share information with their children's teachers. Mr. Salters, who appears oblivious to cultural factors, might have asked the children's parents how the children refer to friends in home and community settings. He might also find out if the parents consider the terms problematic. If they are not bothered, he might ask their help in planning activities to practice deciding when it is appropriate to engage in that behavior.

Ethnic minority children do not perform commensurate with their majority peers in school settings (Ogbu, 1990). Several factors have been identified as contributing to ethnic minority children's lack of school success. In accommodating culturally and linguistically diverse students, several recommendations have been made. One suggestion was to create culturally congruent classrooms (Cazdin, 1988). A popular example of cultural congruence is that reported by Au

(1980) of Hawaiian children who were having reading difficulty. When the reading tasks involved the students' creating a "talk story," which they were accustomed to doing in their home settings, the students were more successful.

Other researchers have suggested using educationally appropriate techniques in classrooms. In line with this, teachers are asked to alter their practices to incorporate educational techniques that accommodate minority children's learning styles (Almanza & Mosley, 1980; Sleeter & Grant, 1994). As an example, techniques involving direct instruction, peer tutoring, and cooperative learning are included among those touted as improving educational performance among these children. These techniques were first recommended in the area of academics. They have since been used to increase social and behavioral skills.

Culturally different children prefer tasks that involve interaction and cooperation among peers over individual tasks. Knowing that, teachers can tailor instructional and practice opportunities to accommodate this student preference. These children may be motivated to reduce their undesirable behaviors if practice opportunities were arranged in which they could use peer-mediated strategies, or group-oriented management activities. For those children who prefer a sense of belonging and group competition, activities could be arranged to fashion team games and sports.

Teachers must be aware of cultural differences and alter their practices to affirm those differences (Gay, 1993). Students with cultural and/or linguistic differences should be accommodated in a variety of ways. The modification of curricula, teaching and management practices, communication, expectations, class structure, and roles are among the many ways in which cultural differences can be affirmed.

As you recall, Mr. Salters believes that once he has developed classroom expectations and rules every student in the classroom should live by those rules. In using a positive and proactive approach to behavior management, teachers must determine the school and societal expectations that promote the well-being of everyone. These expectations involving student governance *should* be universal and maintained in classrooms regardless of student characteristics (ethnicity, gender, social class, ability level). The safety of others is such an expectation held by school and our society. School personnel at times find themselves faced with the dilemma of balancing the rights of others with the target student's behavioral difficulties. A student who has behavior disorders still has to abide by certain rules in society and in school.

Acts that endanger the safety and well-being of others are not tolerated in school, nor in society. Kauffman (1984) suggested that the rights of others must be considered when practitioners are deciding the appropriateness of interventions for students with deviant behavior. Thus students must be taught that we live in a society that is diverse in terms of mores, customs, beliefs, and behaviors. While this diversity should be affirmed in all aspects, there are school and societal standards by which everyone has to abide because they involve the protection of everyone; violation of those standards can not be tolerated.

Behavioral expectations often differ among home, school, and community settings. The following scenario is frequently played out in schools: Caitlin hits Maya. Mr. Salters has repeatedly cautioned his students to refrain from retaliating when someone does something to them. He expects students to report the incident to the nearest school personnel. Mr. Salters' request, however logical it may seem, may oppose behaviors expected and demonstrated in community and home settings. In those settings, the expectation may be that one must fight to protect self or property. In reconciling these differences between home and school, teachers must first identify school and societal expectations that are at odds with their students' cultures. Subsequently, they must communicate these differences to the students. Finally, they should teach the alternative behaviors that school, along with society, expects of its citizens.

Socializing minority children to be successful in school is important when attempting to reduce behaviors. For black children, Perry (1993) noted that "To become competent adults, African American children have to successfully negotiate the demands of three distinct and conflicting roles: their role in mainstream society, their role as a racial minority, and their role within the Black culture" (p. 2). Thus, these children must experience biculturality to increase school success.

While certain behaviors may be functional for minority students in non-school settings, they may benefit from explicit instruction and practice in *code switching,* or engaging in behaviors expected or demanded by a particular setting. This will allow students to switch between home and school behaviors, when in the respective settings. Be aware, however, that when teaching behaviors that differ from those practiced in home and community settings the interaction must not devalue students' customs and traditions. It is helpful to engage parents and respected adult community leaders in sessions in which code-switching behaviors are initially taught.

The ability of minority students to code switch becomes increasingly important to their success in school settings. This author remembers an experience with a group of 12 black adolescent females who were experiencing conflicts in a predominately white school that was located quite a distance from their neighborhoods. Prior to my contact with them, they were involved in frequent acts of name calling and fighting. As there was no black teacher on the campus, I was asked to spend an hour per week with them to provide same-ethnicity, same-gender role modeling and to facilitate their processing of leadership strategies that would increase their school success. After establishing rapport with them, I was quite candid about assisting them to identify behavioral differences between their school and home settings; I explicitly involved them in practicing setting-appropriate behaviors.

Practice opportunities usually consisted of role-plays and verbal rehearsals. The students were maximally involved as they selected the target behaviors, developed the role-play scenarios, and selected their own reinforcers. At the end of the school year, the aspect of the program that pleased the students most was the candor with which we worked on strategies to increase their school success. They consistently commented that no one had ever shown them how to "act" in school to stay out of trouble. Without devaluing cultural mores, school personnel, whether culturally similar or culturally different from their students, can encourage student awareness of the necessity for maintaining various behavioral skills in their repertoires. Students must also be cognizant of the equally important skill of knowing when to use which.

Responding to Surface Behaviors

Students often display inappropriate behaviors that are not serious, but are thought of as surface behaviors. These surface behaviors are minor ones that don't require intense intervention, but could be problematic if no one intervenes. If managed successfully, minimally intrusive interventions can be used to quickly reduce the target behavior, or prevent the undesirable behavior from continuing. Long and Newman (1980) delineated techniques for addressing surface behaviors. Namely, they are planned ignoring, signal interference, proximity control, humor to defuse tension, support from routine, value appealing, and removing distracting objects.

Planned Ignoring

Students may engage in undesirable behaviors to gain the attention of the teacher. If this is reinforcing the student's behavior, it is wise for the teacher to ignore the student while the target behavior is displayed. Planned ignoring, also referred to as *extinction,* is successful in reducing the frequency of a target behavior if it is one that is mild in severity and is not apt to be imitated by other students in the classroom (Morgan & Jenson, 1988). When planned ignoring is used, it is important that, as soon as the student engages in the appropriate behavior, the teacher immediately reinforces it.

Suppose Ms. Lomax is reading a story to her students. She realizes that some of her students dislike sitting for extended periods, so she allows them to sit, stand, stretch, kneel, or squat. But they must remain in the story area. Midway through the story, she notices out of the corner of her eye that Justin is inching away from his area toward the back of the classroom while looking at her. She believes he is doing it to get her attention; normally, she tells him to stay in his area several times.

Ms. Lomax believes that her expectations are reasonable, as she consulted several of her students' parents to ensure cultural accommodations in her rules and expectations. Under these conditions, she would be wise to try planned ignoring with Justin. She will need to try it on several occasions and document the results to evaluate its effects.

Now, when Justin begins inching out of his area, Ms. Lomax pretends not to notice. She doesn't look in Justin's direction, but begins passing out tokens and saying "You're sitting very nicely, Marissa." "Darwin, I like the way you're stretching your legs right in your area." She systematically gives a token and verbal reinforcement to those students who are remaining in their areas. At first she can tell that Justin is observing what's going on. He continues to inch away from his area, while she rewards more students for staying in theirs. The other students appear delighted with their tokens and verbal praise and Justin begins to ease back to his area. Ms. Lomax discretely monitors Justin's behavior so that as soon as he returns to his area she can say "Justin, I'm glad to see you standing in your area" and reward him with a token. She would then continue the story.

Ms. Lomax might use the form in Figure 6.1 to document the effects of the behavior reduction strategy. After several observations she could share it with Justin's older sister, who has primary responsibility for his care. If it works with Justin in the classroom, his sister might be inclined to try it at home.

Signal Interference

Many times students move gradually from positive to inappropriate behavior. There may be advance signs that students are going to demonstrate undesirable behaviors. In these cases, recognizing those oncoming signs can prevent target behaviors from occurring. To do so requires teacher observation, student interviewing, and family consulting to pinpoint signs that inappropriate behavior is imminent.

Suppose a student, Jaylon, has identified the target behavior of staying on task as one upon which he wishes to work. Usually, before he goes completely off-task, he starts tapping his pencil on the desk. When this occurs, Mr. Salters verbally reprimands him and a confrontation ensues. Jaylon especially dislikes having teachers publicly confront him. To avoid embarrassment around his friends, Jaylon "talks back" and tells Mr. Salters what he will not do. Mr. Salters usually views Jaylon's behavior as threatening and noncompliant.

Mr. Salters and Jaylon could privately agree on a solution to this problem that has been upsetting both of them. They might jointly suggest that, when Mr. Salters suspects Jaylon is going off-task, he would remind Jaylon to resume work by using a discrete, nonverbal prompt. They might decide that Mr. Salters should gain eye contact with Jaylon, and point to his own watch. This strategy would avoid teacher–student confrontations and subtly remind Jaylon to continue his task. When Jaylon heeds the nonverbal prompt, Mr. Salters could deliver a social reinforcer (coupon for special activity with a classmate, a desired school responsibility).

Figure 6.1 Strategy Evaluation Form

Name _____

Target Behavior _____

	Date	Strategy	Duration of undesirable behavior	Comments

Proximity Control

The position of the teacher relative to target students can influence student behavior. When students begin demonstrating undesirable behaviors, a simple intervention is for the teacher to physically position herself near the students. This act alone, or when accompanied by putting a hand on the student's shoulder, is often sufficient for students to reduce the behavior. An advantage is that it can be implemented without a break in the learning activities. To illustrate, when Stephanie thinks that she is not within Ms. Lomax's view or hearing, she tends to be disruptive. When Ms. Lomax interviewed Stephanie to try to determine an intervention for her, she discovered that Stephanie tries to get away with more when she thinks Ms. Lomax cannot see or hear her. Now, when Ms. Lomax observes Stephanie acting out, she simply continues instruction while walking over to Stephanie. Ms. Lomax monitors Stephanie's behavior as she draws closer. She merely needs to go over and stand near Stephanie. Or, she may put a hand on Stephanie's shoulder while she continues instruction. Stephanie, upon realizing Ms. Lomax's presence, continues her work.

Using Humor to Defuse Tension

There are times when situations occur in the classroom that could be volatile. Humor is needed to dissipate the tension and allow the climate to get back to normal. For example, Justin comes into the classroom dancing and continues even after Ms. Lomax asks everyone to be seated. Instead of Ms. Lomax getting angry, she might say "And to think I've been paying for dance lessons every week when I could've been getting them free. How about showing me those moves during free time?" Instead of using coercive behavior to get Justin to sit down, Ms. Lomax used humor. She managed to use a proactive approach that avoided a potential confrontation when Justin did not comply with the directive.

Support from Routine

Providing students with consistent routines adds a sense of security. In addition, students like to have advance organizers that prepare them for what is expected. An advance organizer might involve the teacher telling students what their morning will be like. After lunch, the advance organizer would provide students with information on the structure of the activities. For some students it is important to be told of any changes in the routine ahead of time.

Value Appealing

Another technique that works well with minor behaviors is that of appealing to the student's values. When a student engages in an inappropriate behavior, the teacher can request that the student stop that behavior and engage in an appropriate alternative. For example, Brie frequently tattles on her peers. On several occasions Brie has expressed concern that the other students in the class dislike including her in their leisure activities. Ms. Lomax could appeal to Brie's longing to have friends among her classmates by encouraging her to report positive actions by her peers, instead of negative ones. Ms. Lomax could privately remind Brie that kids like to receive compliments, but try to avoid those who tell on them.

Removing Distracting Objects

To avoid students manipulating objects that hold high appeal during inappropriate times, teachers are encouraged to remove them from student reach or sight.

Doing this before instruction time can minimize interruptions due distracting objects. Another option is to rearrange the student's work area to be less distracting. For instance, if Carlos is working on an individual project that requires concentration, Mr. Salters would move him away from the students who are working on a group project.

Surface management techniques are well suited for minor inappropriate behaviors. They are proactive, in that they attempt to prevent negative behaviors from escalating into coercive events in the classroom. When deciding interventions, surface interventions should be considered first, as they are less intrusive means of reducing undesirable behaviors.

Approaches to Reducing Behaviors

Operant learning principles

Most procedures designed to decrease the frequency in which undesirable behaviors occur are based on operant learning principles. Operant learning theory is derived from the works of Skinner (1953). According to this theory, behavior is maintained by the events that occur after it is emitted. Moreover, it is believed that those subsequent events, or consequences, either strengthen or weaken behavior. Consequences determine whether the behavior increases or decreases in frequency. If the behavior increases, the consequences serve to reinforce the behavior. If the behavior decreases, the consequences serve to punish the behavior. Thus positive and negative reinforcement are events that, when applied, are followed by increases in target behaviors. Conversely, punishers or aversives are unpleasant events that are applied following undesirable behavior; they can also be pleasant events that are taken away following undesirable behavior (Walker & Shea, 1987). If the undesirable behavior decreases in frequency following the presentation of an aversive event or the withdrawal of a positive event, the consequence was a punisher. This is important, as consequences that teachers think of as reinforcement may actually be punishment.

Similarly, those that are thought of as punishment may actually be reinforcement. If a teacher requires a student to remain after school for 5 minutes when he arrives to class late, and the student continues to be late, the penalty is a reinforcement, it is not a punisher. If it were, the student would decrease the number of times he arrived late to class.

Mr. Salters and Ms. Lomax each believe that the other has limited proficiency in reducing inappropriate behaviors with their students. They question each other's awareness of effective behavior reduction strategies. This section describes for Mr. Salters and Ms. Lomax, and other teachers, commonly used approaches for decreasing inappropriate behaviors. These include differential reinforcement, aversives, time-out, overcorrection, and response cost.

Differential Reinforcement (DR)

A limitation of some behavior reduction procedures is that they focus attention on the maladaptive rather than the target behavior. Differential reinforcement (DR) is a behavior reduction technique that is responsive to that concern. With DR, the emphasis is on performing behaviors other than the inappropriate target behavior. It involves the selective reinforcement of appropriate behaviors. There are various forms of differential reinforcement and it is most effective when used on students exhibiting minor behavior difficulties (Nelson & Rutherford, 1988).

One form of differential reinforcement, differential reinforcement of low rates of behavior (DRL), is used when the goal is to reduce the frequency with which the target behavior occurs. (The goal is not to eliminate this behavior from the student's repertoire, merely to reduce it.) If you recall, Ms. Lomax has noticed that Brie tattles on other students about anything and everything. She tells so much the other students don't want to involve her in their activities. Now, Ms. Lomax doesn't mind Brie's telling her when someone is doing something that could be harmful to themselves or others. So, instead of wanting to totally eliminate the behavior, she wants to reduce the rate in which Brie tells on others.

Ms. Lomax might begin by identifying statements that are positive reports of children. She could model positive report statements and facilitate an activity where students could act as news reporters. After each instructional period, they could take turns reporting on one or more persons in the class. They might say "Jonathan completed his work" or "Brie has on a pretty necklace." After teaching the positive behavior, Ms. Lomax could specify gradual reductions in the number of times Brie tattles on others. If Brie averages 15 tattling occasions during the morning session, Ms. Lomax might begin by reinforcing Brie when she tattles on others fewer than 13 times. The following week, Brie could be reinforced for telling on others fewer than 10 times during the morning session. The criterion for success could be continually monitored and adjusted.

There are three forms of differential reinforcement, which operate under the principle that when students engage in other, appropriate behaviors, the opportunities for engaging in the target behavior are reduced. Thus the goal is for the student to engage in these more desirable behaviors to the greatest extent possible. Differential reinforcement of the omission of target behavior (DRO) is used to reinforce the students for not engaging in the target behavior during certain intervals of time (Webber & Scheuermann, 1991). Imagine a student in Mr. Salters' math lesson who blurts out answers before the other students can complete the calculations. Mr. Salters would identify other behaviors that the student could engage in when she finishes before the others. The behaviors might include reading a novel silently or making instructional math cards that others can use for drill and practice. Mr. Salters would then reinforce her when she engaged in behaviors other than blurting out answers.

Differential reinforcement of incompatible behavior is a procedure in which a behavior that competes with the target behavior must be identified. The student is then reinforced for engaging in the incompatible behavior over the target behavior. For instance, a student cannot be in her seat and roaming around the room at the same time. If the target behavior is being out of seat without permission, the teacher would reinforce the student for being in her seat during certain periods. Initially, the teacher might reinforce the student for being in her seat every 5 minutes when a timer goes off. The timer may gradually be set for longer periods or the intervals between reinforcement may be varied to eliminate the student's being able to predict the reinforcement schedule.

Differential reinforcement of alternative behavior (DRA) is used when there is an acceptable alternative to the target behavior. Once identified, that alternative is reinforced on a schedule that fits the teacher and student. Suppose Ms. Lomax had been working with Jonathan on controlling his temper. When he gets angry, he becomes disruptive by slamming books and other objects on the floor. In addition to the disruption to the class, Ms. Lomax is concerned that he may accidentally hit someone in the class who gets in the way of his temper tantrums. If she were to brainstorm with Jonathan some more appropriate and less disruptive ways of venting anger, they might generate a list of options that they could evaluate in terms of practicality.

Jonathan, an avid sports enthusiast, might suggest that an area in the room where he could be alone to cool off would be helpful. Putting their heads together, he and Ms. Lomax might come up with an idea that incorporates his interests in the solution. Suppose they fashioned a coach's bench in a corner of the room. A wall in that section might be decorated with athletic posters. The corner could also be equipped with a few nerf balls and basketball hoop, a water bottle, a timer, scorecards (to keep track of how many times student used this "cool off" area). It might also be equipped with sport magazines.

Having done that, suppose they could reach an agreement on Jonathan going to the "coach's bench" to cool off when he gets angry. They could also agree on how much time Jonathan might need to calm himself down, so that he knows he is expected to return to his tasks immediately afterward. For Jonathan, the alternative behavior to tantruming would be to go to the coach's bench. When he does so, Ms. Lomax would reinforce that alternative behavior.

Differential reinforcement is a positive behavior reduction procedure that does not emphasize the negative target behavior. According to Webber and Scheuermann (1991), the advantages of differential reinforcement are that it:

☐ *is a positive approach to reducing behaviors.* It forces teachers to focus on and reward appropriate behaviors.

☐ *allows for the avoidance of punishment and its side effects on children and youth.*

□ *facilitates generalization, as it can be used by multiple persons in multiple settings.*

□ *promotes positive teacher-student interactions because of the positive nature of consequences delivered by teachers.*

It must be cautioned, however, that differential reinforcement of incompatible behaviors and differential reinforcement of alternative behaviors may be ineffective if the student has historically been reinforced for engaging in the target behavior. That is, if the student has been reinforced for demonstrating that behavior for a long period of time, these forms of differential reinforcement may be unsuccessful (Polsgrove & Rieth, 1983). In that case, it is advisable to use another behavior reduction strategy or use differential reinforcement in combination with another strategy.

Aversives

Before further discussing behavior reduction strategies, the issue of aversives must be addressed. As this textbook espouses a positive approach to managing student behavior, it may appear antithetical to deal with the use of aversive procedures. However, in light of the concern among teachers and parents and families, this chapter would be remiss in not including such a discussion. The use of aversive procedures has been heavily debated among practitioners of students experiencing behavioral difficulties (Council for Children with Behavior Disorders, 1990; Horner, 1990; Wolery, Bailey, & Sugai, 1988). The presentation of aversive stimuli involves applying an unpleasant event when a student engages in undesirable behavior. The stimuli's aversiveness is relative to the person with whom it is applied. That is, the degree to which stimuli are unpleasant depends on the individual. For some students, having to complete assignments in an in-school suspension room might be very unpleasant. For others, it might be rewarding. The student might have friends who are also in the in-school suspension room and, if it isn't closely supervised, that setting could afford those students opportunities to socialize and reinforce the undesirable behaviors.

The use of aversives to reduce inappropriate student behavior has been widely debated (Tobin & Sugai, 1993). Most persons agree with the punitive effects of extreme physical aversives (electric shock, tasting unpleasant substances). However, the aversiveness of many commonly used procedures may not be as clear to practitioners. Behavior reduction procedures should always be employed in conjunction with other procedures (Kerr & Nelson, 1989). That is, reducing behavior with any level of aversiveness must always be used with other interventions. According to Wood and Braaten (1983), students should also be taught the behaviors that are more appropriate and acceptable than the target behavior. To that end, if a student's target behavior is name calling with her peers, the teacher would use a behavior reduction strategy and also teach the student alternative ways of talking to peers (complimenting, talking about common interests).

Some researchers have documented positive effects with the use of aversive procedures (Rutherford, 1978; Stainback et. al., 1979). Neel (1983) reported that aversive procedures facilitated learning by suppressing those behaviors that are undesirable and interfere with children's academic progress. It has been suggested, however, that positive results obtained with aversive procedures are short-lived. For example, a study conducted by Iwata and Lorentzson (1976) found that the students engaged in the target behavior 6 months after the aversive procedure was implemented. Aversive procedures also fail to teach desirable behaviors and may induce aggression among children. Children may get the message that "might makes right" (McGinnis, Sauerbry, & Nichols, 1985).

The concern expressed over the use of aversive interventions has given rise to procedures developed to guide their use. Worell and Nelson (1974) suggested that procedures that are aversive should only be used under certain circumstances. The behavior must be viewed in regard to (a) its interference with the rights of others, (b) its interference with the student's own learning, and (c) its potential for harm to persons or property. These guidelines are appropriate safeguards for teachers to use when implementing behavior reduction strategies in school settings and other contexts.

It is critical that teachers recognize and manage surface behaviors, discussed earlier in the chapter, before they escalate and become problematic. When surface management strategies are ineffective in reducing inappropriate behaviors, there are procedures that are commonly implemented to manage behavior. In accordance, time-out, overcorrection, and response cost will be discussed next.

Time-Out

Another procedure used to decrease undesirable behavior is time-out. A variety of forms of time-out are used when students engage in inappropriate behaviors. The premise is that most students are reinforced for engaging in these behaviors. It is assumed that if the reinforcement is removed, the behavior will decrease (Zabel, 1986). Time-out practices range from least to most aversive. According to Rutherford (1978), planned ignoring, mentioned earlier in this chapter, is the least aversive form of time-out. In ignoring, the teacher's attention is removed while the student engages in the target behavior. The physical removal of a student to a time-out area is the most aversive. In that instance, the student is physically secluded from the other students after engaging in the target behavior.

While the two aforementioned procedures are the extreme versions of time-out, there are several levels in between. Smith, Finn, and Dowdy (1993) listed the following among time-out procedures.

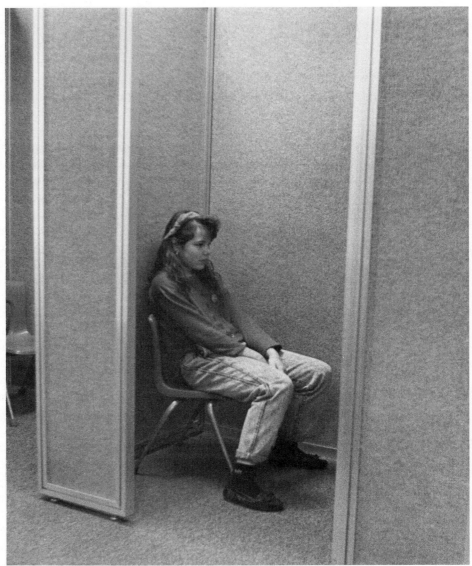

Guidelines must be followed carefully when using time-out procedures.

Time-out at desk.   The student, after engaging in the target behavior, remains at the desk and is not involved in class activities during the time-out period. The student may even be requested to put her head down on the desk. The other students are not allowed to interact with the target student. Hence, effectiveness is dependent upon the other students' withholding reinforcement. This intervention should be selected only if the target behavior is maintained by student attention. It is critical that, as soon as the target student engages in appropriate behavior, it be recognized with teacher and student praise and other forms of reinforcement. This step is especially critical to keep the student from constantly being viewed in a negative light by peers. For example, the student who is frequently reprimanded by the teacher may gain a notorious reputation among her peers.

In-class time-out area. The student, after engaging in the target behavior, is allowed to remain in the classroom but goes to a separate area. While in this area, the student may or may not be allowed to observe the learning activities of the other students in the classroom. If the student is not disruptive while in time-out, she should be allowed to observe the class activities. Not only does this keep the student involved in ongoing learning, but it also provides the student opportunities to observe her peers demonstrating appropriate behaviors.

Out-of-class time-out. The student is physically removed from the classroom and taken to another room. This form of time-out is to be used when the teacher cannot control the reinforcement that the student is receiving in the original setting. It may be that the other students continue to provide reinforcement for the inappropriate behavior, even after the teacher requests that they ignore the student's actions. There may be no area in the classroom that the student does not find reinforcing. When using this form of time-out, the teacher must be careful that the setting to which the student will go is not also going to provide reinforcement. Additionally, the teacher must be aware that, when the student leaves the room, he is not allowed to observe or participate in the classroom activities. Thus, upon returning to the classroom, the student must make up missed activities, or time-out will be used to escape or avoid unpleasant classroom tasks (Morgan & Jenson, 1988).

Time-out room. The student is physically removed from the classroom to a room in the building that has been designated as a time-out room. As this is the most aversive form of time-out, it is also the most suspect for unethical practices and abuse. State guidelines have been developed and school personnel have been urged to follow them closely when using this level of time-out. These guidelines address the room's size, lighting, and ventilation. An adult must carefully monitor the student in time-out. There are also guidelines to address the amount of time children and youth can be in time-out. It is recommended that students be in time-out for as little time as possible. Some teachers allow students to come out as soon as the student agrees to stop the target behavior. Others set a minimal time limit of a few minutes to 15 minutes, depending on developmental levels (Morgan & Jenson, 1988).

Time-out procedures have demonstrated effectiveness in reducing undesirable behaviors (Gast & Nelson, 1977; Polsgrove & Rieth, 1983; Rutherford, 1978; Rutherford & Nelson, 1982). The use of time-out procedures in reducing inappropriate behaviors is the most popular (Morgan & Jenson, 1988). Its popularity, however, does not prevent public and legal scrutiny. As a result, according to Gast and Nelson (1977), guidelines similar to the following have been developed for monitoring the use of time-out in school settings:

1. Time-out should begin with least aversive or milder levels. Once the decision is made to use time-out, begin with the mildest form—that of planned ignoring. After documenting its effectiveness, use the at-desk time-out procedure. Only move to the next levels if these are ineffective.

2. Time-out procedures should be clearly documented in terms of their effectiveness. Documentation should include description of procedure, duration, and its effect on the target behavior.

3. A list of behaviors must be developed. All behaviors that can, or would, result in time-out must be clearly communicated to students, families, administrators, and so on.

4. Written procedures must be developed. These procedures should clearly outline the manner in which students will be placed in time-out.

Even when Mr. Salters and Ms. Lomax carefully plan how they will use time-out with their students, they will continually face split-second decisions on its use. When a student demonstrates inappropriate behavior, they will have to make several determinations: (a) Is this a surface behavior in which the least intrusive strategies (planned ignoring, using humor, proximity control) can be used? (b) If not, is there an effective technique that is less aversive than time-out? (c) If not, is the target behavior one that the student knows will result in the use of time-out? (d) Which form of time-out will be least aversive and restrictive for that student? (e) What behaviors will be reinforced when the student is no longer in time-out?

Overcorrection

Overcorrection has been used by teachers to reduce aberrant student behavior. This procedure uses an instructional approach to behavior reduction. It involves students engaging in the appropriate behavior (Foxx & Azrin, 1973). Overcorrection can be accomplished by using either restitution or positive practice. Some students engage in behaviors that result in their negatively altering the environment. Candra gets upset because she does not get chosen to be a classroom special helper. She goes to her desk, rips up her assignment, and throws the tiny pieces of paper on the floor. If her teacher were implementing restitution overcorrection,

Candra would be requested to restore the environment to a condition that is better than it was. Candra would have to pick up the tiny pieces of paper on the floor and sweep the area, and redo her torn up assignment as restitution.

If the teacher chose to use positive practice overcorrection, Candra would be requested to practice walking over to the basket to turn in her assignment. She might also practice tearing scrap paper and putting it in the trash can to vent anger. The tenet of overcorrection is that inappropriate behaviors will be reduced by requiring students to restore their environments or by having them continuously repeat the appropriate behavior.

There have been limited numbers of studies using overcorrection techniques. While the results hold promise, Foxx (1982) developed the following principles to guide the use of overcorrection acts.

☐ They're directly related to the student's misbehavior.

☐ Like all effective punishment procedures, overcorrection is implemented immediately following the misbehavior.

☐ The overcorrection acts must be performed rapidly (pp. 96–99).

According to these authors, there are several advantages to using overcorrection. It is a one-to-one strategy, whereby the teacher must demonstrate the overcorrection act and closely monitor to ensure that it is performed accurately. Due to this component, the practice is instructional. It is intended to elicit effort from students. Reinforcement is withheld while the student is performing the overcorrection acts.

As is the case with time-out, there are legal ramifications involved in overcorrection practices. The time students spend overcorrecting should be closely monitored to guard against excessive practices and the usefulness of the overcorrection acts should also be monitored for functionality (Morgan & Jenson, 1988). In that regard, teachers should use this procedure on behaviors that are socially valid (as discussed in Chapter 7) and not request that students use overcorrection on behaviors that are not going to influence their quality of life.

Response Cost

Many teachers rely on a response cost procedure to decrease the frequency of undesirable behaviors. Response cost procedures involve withdrawing a reinforcer based on the student's engaging in inappropriate behavior. This procedure is frequently used in conjunction with a token economy system (Alberto & Troutman, 1990). An example of how it works would be that Andreia has been working on staying in her seat. The teacher sets a timer to go off during various times of the morning. She and Andreia agreed that every time Andreia is in her seat when the timer sounds, she will receive a Behavior Buck, which resembles a dollar bill. When Andreia has earned 10 Behavior Bucks, she will use them to "buy" 5 minutes of R and R. She will be allowed to relax quietly and do no school work. Andreia selected the reward because she says that she likes to have time to do nothing but daydream. In reaching an agreement, they also decided that when the timer goes off, if Andreia is out of her seat, she will return an already earned Behavior Buck.

Response cost procedures have been used to manage individual and group behaviors (Salend & Lamb, 1986). Their effectiveness is enhanced by ensuring (a) the amount of the fines match the severity of the inappropriate behavior—a harsh fine should not be leveled against a mild infraction; (b) teacher must give reinforcers that can be withdrawn—it is advised not to use edibles, as students can eat them prior to having them taken away; (c) students clearly understand the conditions of earning reinforcement and having it withdrawn; (d) students have opportunities to regain withdrawn reinforcers; and (e) the desirable behavior will be focused upon and reinforced as it occurs (Alberto & Troutman, 1990).

Conclusions

As you can see, reducing the behaviors of children and youth in school settings requires a significant amount of decision making. Teacher roles, in effecting changes in student behavior, are as diverse as the students who cross the classroom's threshold. Teachers must ensure that the behavioral expectations they hold for their students are not culturally monolithic. It is the teacher's responsibility to also identify societal norms by which all individuals are expected to abide. These societal norms should be those that, when violated, jeopardize the individual's quality of life (resulting in incarceration, expulsion from school).

Another role of the teacher in reducing undesirable behaviors is to become aware of cultural differences. Merely increasing one's awareness is insufficient to accommodate diverse learners. Knowing the customs, mores, and preferences of ethnic groups should influence teacher practices. While the focus should not be on negative behavior, a proactive approach to reducing behavior is advocated. Practitioners need to alter classroom structures and practices to prevent negative behaviors from occurring or escalating. Initially, surface or minor behaviors should be recognized and minor techniques implemented. It is only when those methods are ineffective that more intrusive procedures need be used.

When the decision to implement a behavior reduction strategy is made, the teacher has to determine which strategy, or combination of strategies, are appropriate based on student characteristics. Before effecting behavioral changes, it must be remembered that the school is not the only context in which the child interacts. To the greatest extent possible, teachers must develop interventions and communication systems that extend beyond the classroom and the school. Similarly, educators must reach out to the home and community settings to develop genuine relationships with those who play significant roles in children's lives.

Teachers need to enlist the support of community role-models to promote congruence between school, home, and community.

Discussion Questions and Activities

1. Your student, Anise, wants to reduce the number of arguments she gets into with her classmates. Show how you would work with her to develop a proactive behavior management plan.

2. Develop a case study of a teacher of students with learning and behavior problems who wants to use techniques for decreasing undesirable behaviors. The problem is that she is unaware of ethical considerations when implementing such procedures. Create the case study to illustrate some of these concerns, and facilitate a discussion based on your case study.

3. Demonstrate the use of a proactive strategy for reducing undesirable behaviors.

4. A local parent and family support group requested that you conduct a workshop on positive behavior management strategies that they can

implement at home. Plan (a) topics and subtopics to cover, (b) materials to be used, and (c) methods of evaluation.

5. Work with a group of students to develop a group plan to decrease an undesirable behavior. Immediately following the group meeting, tape record your reflections on the process. Share your notes and the plan with the class.

Reflective Questions

1. When working with students to decrease undesirable behaviors, do you employ behavior reduction strategies that are least intrusive to target student(s)?

2. When working with students to decrease undesirable behaviors, do you consider individual and cultural differences when selecting strategies?

3. When working with students to decrease undesirable behaviors, do you use techniques for responding to surface behaviors before implementing behavior change strategies?

4. When working with students to decrease undesirable behaviors, do you understand the advantages and disadvantages involved with using selected behavior reduction strategies?

5. When working with students to decrease undesirable behaviors, do you develop procedures for implementing selected behavior reduction strategies?

6. When working with students to decrease undesirable behaviors, do you solicit student, family, and community member input on procedures to be used in the classroom?

7. When working with students to decrease undesirable behaviors, do you inform all significant persons of student progress on decreasing undesirable behaviors?

References

Alberto, P. & Troutman, A. (1990). *Applied behavior analysis for teachers* (3rd ed.). New York: Merrill.

Almanza, H.P. & Mosley, W.J. (1980). Curriculum adaptations and modifications for culturally diverse handicapped children. *Exceptional Children, 46,*(8), 608–614.

Au, H.K. (1980). Participation structures in a reading lesson with Hawaiian children: Analysis of a culturally appropriate instructional event. *Anthropology and Education Quarterly, 11,* 91–115.

Braaten, S. (1987). *Use of punishment with exceptional children: A dilemma for educators.* Paper presented at the Eleventh Annual Conference on Severe Behavior Disorders of Children and Youth, Tempe, AZ.

Cazdin, C.B. (1988). *Classroom discourse.* Portsmouth, NH: Heinemann.

Council for Children with Behavior Disorders (1990). Position paper on use of behavior reduction strategies with children with behavioral disorders. *Behavioral Disorders, 15,* 243–60.

Dietz, S. & Hummel, J. (1978). *Discipline in the schools.* Englewood Cliffs, NJ: Educational Technology Publications.

Fox, J. & Savelle, S. (1987). Social interaction research in families of behaviorally disordered children: A critical review and forward look. *Behavioral Disorders, 12,* 276–91.

Foxx, R.M. (1982). *Decreasing behaviors of severely retarded and autistic persons.* Champaign, IL: Research Press.

Foxx, R.M. & Azrin, N.H. (1973). The elimination of autistic self-stimulatory behavior by overcorrection. *Journal of Applied Behavior Analysis, 6,* 1–14.

Fradd, S. & Hallman, C.L. (1983). Implications of and instruction of culturally and linguistically different students. *Learning Disability Quarterly, 6,* 468–78.

Gallagher, P.A. (1988). *Teaching students with behavior disorders* (2nd ed.). Denver: Love.

Gast, D.L. & Nelson, C.M. (1977). Legal and ethical considerations for the use of time-out in special education settings. *Journal of Special Education, 11,* 457–67.

Gay, G. (1993). Ethnic minorities and educational equality. In J. Banks & C. Banks (eds.), *Multicultural education: Issues and perspectives,* 2nd ed. Boston: Allyn & Bacon.

Guttentag, M. (1972). Negro-white differences in children's movement. *Perceptual and Motor Skills, 35,* 435–36.

Horner, R.H. (1990). Ideology, technology, and typical community settings: Use of severe aversive stimuli. *American Journal on Mental Retardation, 95,* 166–68.

Kauffman, J.M. (1984). Saving children in the age of Big Brother: Moral and ethical issues in the identification of deviance. *Behavioral Disorders, 10,* 60–70.

Kerr, M.M. & Nelson, C.M. (1989). *Strategies for managing behavior problems in the classroom* (3rd ed.). Columbus, OH: Merrill.

Long, N.J. & Newman, R. (1980). Managing surface behaviors of children in schools. In N.J. Long, W. Morse & R. Newman (eds.), *Conflict in the classroom: the education of emotionally disturbed children* (4th ed.). Belmont, CA: Wadsworth.

McGinnis, E., Sauerbry, L. & Nichols, P. (1985). Skill-streaming: Teaching social skills to children with behavioral disorders. *Teaching Exceptional Children, 11*(3), 160–67.

McIntyre, T. (1993). Reflections on the new definition for emotional or behavioral disorders: Who falls through the cracks and why. *Behavioral Disorders, 18*(2), 148–60.

Morgan, D.P. & Jenson, W.R. (1988). *Teaching behaviorally disordered students.* Columbus, OH: Merrill.

Neel, R. (1978). Research findings regarding the use of punishment procedures with severely behavior disordered children. In F. Wood & K.C. Lakin (eds.) *Punishment and aversive stimulation in special education.* Minneapolis, MN: University of Minnesota.

Nelson, C.M. & Rutherford, R.B. (1988). Behavioral interventions with behaviorally disordered students. In M.C. Wang, M.C. Reynolds, & H.J. Walberg (eds.), *Handbook of special education: Research and practice* (Vol. 2). New York: Pergamon.

Ogbu, J.U. (1990). Minority education in comparative perspective. *Journal of Negro Education, 59*(1), 45–57.

Perry, T. (1993). As cited in How racial and ethnic family and community characteristics affect children's achievement. *Research and Development Report.* March, 1993(3).

Polsgrove, L. & Rieth, H.J. (1983). Procedures for reducing children's inappropriate behavior in special education settings. *Exceptional Education Quarterly, 3,* 20–33.

Rutherford, R.B. Jr. (1978). Theory and research on the use of aversive procedures in the education of moderately behaviorally disordered and emotionally disturbed children and youth. In F.H. Wood & K.C. Lakin (eds.), *Punishment and aversive stimulation in special education: Legal, theoretical, and practical issues in their use with emotionally disturbed children and youth* (pp. 41–64).

Rutherford, R.B. & Nelson, C.M. (1982). Analysis of response-contingent timeout literature with behaviorally disordered students in classroom settings. In R.B. Rutherford, Jr. (ed.), *Severe behavior disorders of children and youth, Vol. 5* (pp. 79–105).

Sailor, W. (1991). Special education in the restructured school. *Remedial and Special Education, 12*(6), 8–22.

Salend, S. & Lamb, E. (1986). Effectiveness of a group-managed interdependent contingency system. *Learning Disability Quarterly, 9,* 268–73.

Simpson, R.L. (1988). Needs of parents whose children have learning and behavior problems. *Behavioral Disorders, 14,* 40–47.

Skinner, B.F. (1953). *Science and human behavior.* New York: Macmillan.

Sleeter, C.E., & Grant, C.A. (1994). *Making choices for multicultural education: Five approaches to race, class, and gender.* New York: Merrill.

Smith, T.C., Finn, D.M. & Dowdy, C.A. (1993). *Teaching students with mild disabilities.* Orlando, FL: Harcourt Brace Jovanovich.

Stainback, W., Stainback, S. & Derick, C. (1979). Controlling severe maladaptive behaviors. *Behavioral Disorders, 4,* 99–115.

Tobin, T.J. & Sugai, G. (1993). Intervention aversiveness: Educators' perceptions of the need for restrictions on aversive interventions. *Behavioral Disorders 18,*(2), 110–17.

Walker, J.E. & Shea, T.M. (1987). *Behavior management: A practical approach for educators* (5th ed.). New York: Merrill.

Webber, J. & Scheuermann, B. (1991). Accentuate the positive . . . eliminate the negative. *Teaching Exceptional Children, 24*(1), 13–19.

Wolery, M., Bailey, D.B. & Sugai, G.M. (1988). *Effective teaching: Principles and procedures of applied behavior analysis with exceptional students.* Boston: Allyn & Bacon.

Wood, F.H. & Braaten, S. (1983). Developing guidelines for the use of punishing interventions in the schools. *Exceptional Education Quarterly, 3,* 68–75.

Worell, J. & Nelson, C.M. (1974). *Managing instructional problems: A case study workbook.* New York: McGraw-Hill.

Zabel, M. (1986). Time-out use with behaviorally disordered students. *Behavioral Disorders, 12,* 15–21.

Chapter 7

Promoting Prosocial Skills

Ms. Edwards is faced with several firsts. She is in her first year of teaching children with exceptionalities. For the first time, her classroom is composed of children with differing cultural backgrounds. Looking ahead, she speculated that most of her students lack positive social and interpersonal skills. Ms. Edwards' preservice training focused on facilitating academic growth among students with special needs. She feels quite confident that she can effectively teach academic subjects. However, she is unsure of her ability to teach skills dealing with nonacademic subject matter, such as affect and social behaviors. She realizes that she has little experience teaching students to be socially competent.

During the initial months of school, Ms. Edwards observed and recorded many of her students' school behaviors. She also kept a journal in which she documented anecdotal comments from other students and school personnel regarding her students' behaviors. For example, Ms. Edwards found that typically, during a 20-minute period in the morning, her students were antagonistic toward each other. Seventy-six percent of the comments directed at peers were negative. It worsened in the afternoon when, during a 20-minute period, the negative comments occurred at least 89% of the time. Students rarely addressed each other by their given names, frequently referring to each other as "punk," "stupid," and "musclehead." Aggressive statements flew in all directions. For example, students commonly demanded that peers carry school supplies to them from the front of the class "or I'll mess you up." As a result of these verbal threats and insults, Ms. Edwards' students were unable to work or play together. The constant arguing interfered with activities planned to facilitate group cooperation.

Name calling and verbal threats increased when Ms. Edwards' students were mingled with other classes. In the cafeteria or school-wide assemblies and programs, her class was disruptive, joining forces to antagonize their peers from other classes.

School personnel often remarked to Ms. Edwards that her class lacked the ability to make friends and play appropriately with others. They reported that their students disliked being around Ms. Edwards' class. It seems that, on the playground, Ms. Edwards' class verbally threatens students to allow them to join in the other students' games of basketball and softball. Several parents have complained to the school principal that Ms. Edwards' students should not be allowed anywhere near their children. Based on these observations, Ms. Edwards has concluded that her students need social skill training and development.

As you recall, Ms. Edwards has had minimal training in teaching students to be socially competent. Therefore, she has several concerns. She is perplexed regarding ways to begin a social skill training program with students who have various needs. Ms. Edwards knows that her students' lack of prosocial skills will continue to place them at jeopardy in school and later, she suspects, in society. She does not question her students' need for effective academic interventions, but realizes they will be unsuccessful unless implemented soon.

Ms. Edwards has heard about several social skill training programs. She is reluctant to use any of the available programs until she addresses her training concerns. Because of her beliefs, she is emphatic about the use of techniques that are sensitive to her students' individual and cultural differences. She also recognizes the negativism her students exhibit in many of their behaviors. Presently much of the attention they get from others is negative as well. She wants to take a social skill training approach that focuses on positive (prosocial) behaviors.

*T*he current chapter has several purposes. It provides background information on social competence and rationales for implementing prosocial skill instruction in various settings. Ms. Edwards and other teachers are guided through requisite steps for effective prosocial skill instructional planning. An additional purpose is to inform teachers of commonly used prosocial skill instructional practices. Finally, the chapter presents strategies for promoting skill generalization and maintenance. Teacher practices that affirm individual and cultural differences are infused throughout the chapter.

Note that the intent of this chapter is not to discuss methods for reducing or eliminating negative social behaviors, as those were covered in Chapter 6. Instead, it will discuss practices that teach alternatives to inappropriate social behaviors, beginning with responses to the questions: What are social skills? and Why teach social skills? Subsequent to that discussion, the chapter is organized in the following sections: Prosocial skill training prerequisites, prosocial skill instructional practices, and generalization and maintenance strategies.

What Are Social Skills?

It is not uncommon for most teachers to want their students to be socially competent. What would be uncommon is if they all agreed upon what constitutes social competence. Coleman (1992) has suggested that social competence is broadly composed of social skills, affect and emotional factors, and self-management. The literature is replete with definitions of social skills (Reschly, 1985; Stephens, 1977; Hops & Greenwood, 1981; Gresham, 1981, 1986). Gresham (1988) pointed out that there are typically three categories of definitions. They either assume a perspective on how the target student is accepted by the peer group, are behavioral in nature, or address social validity.

According to Gresham, the peer acceptance definition determines social skill based on children's popularity among their peer groups. Peer acceptance is viewed as an outcome or indication of social skill development (Asher, Singleton, Tinsley, & Hymel, 1979). The extent to which children are accepted by their peers, or their social status, provides an indicator of social skill. Children who are judged as popular on social status indices are considered to have good social skills. Conversely, those who are unpopular are thought of as lacking age- and/or setting-appropriate social skills.

The behavioral definition of social skills considers not peer acceptance, but the child's behavior itself. One popular behavioral definition is that of Libet and Lewinsohn (1973). They viewed children with social skills as those who display behaviors that others positively or negatively reinforce; these children also inhibit behaviors that others tend to extinguish or punish. In this perspective, the determination of whether the child has social skills is dependent upon the reaction of others. When the child emits a behavior, do others reinforce that behavior? If so, then the child displayed a social skill. If the child's behavior incites others to punish or extinguish it, then it is not a social skill.

Gallagher (1988) defines social skills as "the ability to engage appropriately in interpersonal interactions and thereby gain social acceptance" (p. 146). Thus social skills can be thought of as those behaviors that engender favorable response by others. The extent to which a child has social skills is therefore relative to the persons with whom that child interacts. The teacher's perceptions of a child's social skill might differ from the perceptions of the child's family members or peer group. In effect, perceptions of persons in the home setting may differ from persons in the child's school setting. It is not uncommon for persons in the same settings to differ in their perceptions of a child's social skill. For example, there are times when the classroom teacher views a child's social behavior differently from lunchroom personnel or teachers of nonacademic subjects.

The social validity definition suggests that social skills are behaviors that indicate future success for children in that particular setting (Gresham, 1988). To illustrate, the behaviors demonstrated by children who are successful in a particular classroom might simply be an indicator of behaviors the teacher considers important for students to have acquired in order to "make it" or be successful in that classroom setting.

Other factors contribute to social competence. Recent attention has been given to the notion of reciprocal social interactions (Strain, Odom, & McConnell, 1984). Early social skill training approaches focused solely on teaching the child appropriate social skills. It was assumed that social skill deficits were due to deficiencies within the child. According to Strain and his colleagues, it is social reciprocity that indicates social skill. The interaction between the target child and others, not the target child's behavior alone, is the better indicator of social competence.

Why Teach Social Skills?

It is well understood that academic content is inherent in most school curricula. A primary goal of educators is to guide their students to academic competence. When the goal addresses the social domain, it is not as explicit. General and special educators don't always systematically teach students to be socially competent (Walker et al., 1983; Cartledge & Milburn, 1978; Gresham, 1981).

Early social skill training programs focused on academic instruction while merely establishing and enforcing behavioral limits (McGinnis, Sauerbry, & Nichols, 1985). Students were admonished for their inappropriate behaviors with no specific instruction on the socially appropriate alternatives to those deviant behaviors.

Cartledge and Milburn (1978) asserted that schools concentrate on improving academic competence or skills, and have neglected to emphasize the social skills instruction that leads to social competence. The authors reported that while

Peers will naturally reinforce positive social skills.

academic goals are usually expressed clearly, a "hidden curriculum" exists for social goals. Moreover, this hidden curriculum consists of the behaviors that teachers model for students, expect from students, and reinforce when performed by students.

Just as children must be carefully instructed on academic skills, the same holds true for social skills. It would be horrifying, for instance, to hear of a teacher berating a first-grader for not knowing how to multiply with regrouping. Such a scenario would not take place when the skill is academic. It is not uncommon, however, when the skill in question is a social one. A child running through the hallway might be told by the nearest adult that she should be walking instead of running and will be in serious trouble if she is seen doing that again. Even though the student is quite capable of walking, she may not have been shown the importance of walking in the hallway. She also may not have had demonstrations of appropriate hallway walking, or ample opportunities to practice that behavior. Yet, without any instruction, the child is expected to walk appropriately in the school corridors.

A movement is underway among educators. It promotes the inclusion of all students in general education settings. It has been proposed that general and special education no longer serve students separately, but become unified to better meet the needs of all students (Will, 1986; Wang, Reynolds, & Walberg, 1986, 1988). This merger, commonly called the Regular Education Initiative, has implications for social skill training for all students. Students with and without exceptionalities should be provided structured training on social skills. Previous efforts to include students with exceptionalities in general settings have been less than successful. The mainstreaming movement made several faulty assumptions about outcomes for students with exceptionalities when integrated in general education settings (Gresham, 1984; Gresham, 1983; Hollinger, 1987).

These authors maintained that the mainstreaming movement assumed that physically integrating children with disabilities into settings with children without disabilities would, in and of itself, increase social interactions among both populations. It was hoped that the opportunities for social interaction would ultimately increase; it was also believed that students with exceptionalities would be perceived more favorably by their peers. The intent was to provide role models for students with exceptionalities in less restrictive settings. Needless to say, for many of those students, their mainstreamed settings became "more restrictive" placements because neither they nor their peers were provided specific social skill training to promote interpersonal relationships (Gresham, 1981).

Gresham (1984) noted that the mainstreaming movement also neglected to consider students' levels of self-efficacy. Self-efficacy is composed of both efficacy expectations and outcome expectations (Bandura, 1977). Efficacy expectation is the student's own belief that she or he can perform the required behavior to achieve a certain outcome. The outcome expectation is the student's ability to estimate that a certain behavior will yield a particular outcome.

According to Gresham (1984), mainstreamed students are either reintegrated into a setting in which they have previously failed, or are integrated into a new setting. If the setting is a new one, they have not established a level of self-efficacy. He maintained that, without help, the probable outcome for these students is failure and the development of poor self-efficacy. Teaching students to use prosocial skills could increase their social success, and their levels of self-efficacy would rise concomitantly.

Social skill instruction, which facilitates peer relationships, also positively impacts post-school personal adjustment (Parker & Asher, 1987). Direct relationships were found to exist between poor peer interactions and drop-out tendencies. Poor peer interactions also correlate with propensities for juvenile and adult criminal activity.

Students with exceptionalities are typically less socially competent than their peers without exceptionalities (Bryan, Donahue, & Pearl, 1981; Kauffman, 1989). Social skill instruction is imperative for students with learning and behavioral difficulties. These students are typically referred for special education services as a result of perceived academic and/or social–behavioral deficits. It is often the social–behavioral deficits that preclude academic success and lead to more frequent referrals and, ultimately, identification of emotional impairments for these students (Ysseldyke & Algozzine, 1982). Thus, for some students, teaching them to be socially competent might allow them to remain in the general education setting.

Students who have not been labeled as having exceptionalities also need social skill training. Specifically, students who are at risk for learning or behavior problems are also in need of social skill instruction. It appears that even when these students are identified as at risk for dropping out, abusing substances, or becoming teen parents, schools do not automatically incorporate social skill training into their curricula. Much of the research with at-risk students has focused on academic interventions. These interventions often aim to improve reading, math, or language skill development (Slavin, Karweit, & Madden, 1989).

With such emphasis placed on improving academic outcomes, students who are at risk have received little training in social development. More often than not, social skill training in elementary and secondary classrooms has been used only with students who have identified exceptionalities (e.g., LaGreca & Messibov, 1981). Students' chances of receiving social skill training increase when they have a disability. As you can see, there is a compelling need to enhance prosocial skills among a number of student populations.

Social Skill Training Prerequisites

Ms. Edwards clearly recognizes her students' need to improve their social behaviors. She now has a better understanding of social skills and the rationale for training her students to be socially competent. She has decided to consistently provide her students with culturally sensitive social skill instruction and practice opportunities, while focusing on the positive aspects of their behaviors. There is only one problem—she doesn't know where to begin.

The following discussion details for Ms. Edwards and other teachers several social skill training prerequisites. More specifically, in planning for effective prosocial skill instruction, teachers must (a) identify target skills, (b) determine social validity, (c) motivate students, (d) select appropriate rewards, and (e) schedule time and place.

Identify Target Skills

Several steps must be taken prior to implementing social skill instruction. First, the skills which are targeted for instruction must be decided based upon perceptions of student deficits. Stated another way, a determination must be made as to which skills students need to develop or improve. Another decision facing the teacher is determining which skill to teach and when. These decisions often involve ethical issues that have not been resolved (Carpenter & Apter, 1988). Teachers must decide to teach certain social skills to alter student behavior. This becomes an ethical issue when a target skill is selected and its outcome is not going to make a difference in students' lives. Is the teacher altering student behavior, or teaching a skill, that is irrelevant in students' everyday lives in multiple contexts? It is critical that students be taught only those skills in which they are deficient, or they will not be motivated to perform them consistently (Snow & Farr, 1984).

In the case of Ms. Edwards' class, there are several behaviors upon which her students need to improve. For instance, Ms. Edwards might develop a list of behaviors like those illustrated in Figure 7.1. To accentuate appropriate behaviors, goals should be stated in positive ways. Instead of "making negative comments to others," state the behavior as a desired prosocial skill—"saying positive comments to others."

It may be tempting to address several skills simultaneously, however only one skill can be effectively targeted at a time. This selecting and specifying (pinpointing)

Figure 7.1 Potential Target Skill Summary

Class _____   Date _____

Prosocial skill	*Concern expressed by:*
1. Asking to join in	General Ed. teachers
2. Playing by group's rules	Ms. Edwards, Gen. Ed. teachers
3. Establishing friendships	Ms. Edwards, several parents
4. Resolving conflicts	Ms. Edwards, parents, Gen. Ed. teachers
5. Avoiding fights	Ms. Edwards, Gen. Ed. teachers, driver, parents

only one skill at a time will also increase student chance for success. Demonstrating success on one social skill can become a motivator by increasing student ambition and enthusiasm to learn and practice other prosocial behaviors.

Various techniques are recommended to assist in the teacher's decision-making process. Ms. Edwards has already identified several target skills through direct observation and recording procedures as noted in the opening scenario. She also maintained a journal documenting comments about her class made by others in the school. As several persons in the school setting expressed concern regarding many of her students' behaviors, Ms. Edwards needs to determine where to start.

To help make this decision, Ms. Edwards needs to prioritize the skills upon which her students need to improve. One method of prioritizing target skills would involve Ms. Edwards' compiling a list of prosocial skills upon which her students need instruction. In light of individual and cultural differences, it is critical that Ms. Edwards enlist the support and involvement of the students and their family members throughout the training process. Parents—and the students themselves—can provide valuable assistance on prioritizing skills to target for intervention.

Ms. Edwards can present families with a list of tentative skills that they can add to and rank order based on their perceptions of student needs and skill relevancy. Family members can report whether the child demonstrates the skill in the home or community setting. Students can assist by choosing which skills they desire to learn most. Having input from students not only enhances student motivation, but also increases the social validity of skill instruction (see Chapter 5 for a discussion of social validity). When planning, teachers should be mindful of the prosocial skills students believe will positively impact their quality of life. Once target students and others in their environments have been polled, the teacher can identify those target skills in which there is most agreement among school personnel, parents, and students.

Several assessment and observation practices are presented in detail in Chapter 9. Ms. Edwards could use some of those practices to aid in narrowing the list of prosocial skills that will be targeted for instruction. It must be cautioned, however, that when assessing social skills it is best to solicit input from several persons familiar with the child. Comparing their observations and other assessment data will determine the extent to which those individuals agree on the social skills that need addressing (Gresham, 1983). Those skills most agreed upon would be among the first targeted for intervention.

To further determine the order or priority for teaching prosocial skills, a task analysis could be conducted to list the steps necessary in performing the prosocial skill. Task analysis (Gagne, 1985) involves listing and sequencing the steps that enable an individual to demonstrate a particular skill. Some skills are prerequisites or subskills of others and should therefore be taught first. Completed prosocial skill demonstration is often dependent upon, and enabled by, the mastery of prerequisite skills. For example, the skill of establishing eye contact may be a prerequisite to introducing oneself if, in that culture, persons customarily look each other in the eye upon introducing themselves. In that case, the behavior of establishing eye contact would be taught and practiced before the skill of introducing oneself to others. In other cultures, establishing eye contact may not be practiced or perceived as necessary when making introductions.

Ms. Edwards should enlist the aid of her students' parents to provide additional information on their individual and cultural backgrounds. In the preceding example, the teacher might not have known how various ethnic group members introduce themselves unless students and their family members were consulted. Taking the effort to consult families can be rewarding for everyone involved. It affirms student diversity; the message transmitted is that diversity is valued and welcome in that setting. It also communicates a powerful message to the family members that there is a partnership between the teacher and family in meeting the needs of students.

Family members can be informed of the prosocial skill targeted for instruction. They can help task analyze its skill performance to ensure that instruction is not in conflict with student's cultural background. If Ms. Edwards selected the skill of introducing oneself for instruction first, she could ask several parents to record the steps they take when introducing themselves. Family members who are uncomfortable with writing the information could use a portable tape recorder provided by the teacher to list the steps or list them over the telephone. The point is that families should be given various levels of involvement, depending on their needs, in prosocial skill training. They must also have sincere opportunities to advise teachers on their children's individual and cultural mores and preferences.

Determine Social Validity

While there are various discussions of social validity throughout this book, it is important to reemphasize, as it pertains to prosocial skills. It is not enough for Ms. Edwards to select a skill upon which her students should improve. The skill may be one that she desires her students to acquire, but may not be one which the students or their family members find meaningful or socially valid. Schloss, Schloss, Wood, and Kiehl (1986) characterize social validity as having the capability to improve one's quality of life. To that end, when identifying target skills, the question must be asked Will the student's quality of life improve if this skill is learned? If the answer is no, the instructional time might be better spent on a skill that will reap positive outcomes (making or maintaining friends, holding jobs).

As you recall, Ms. Edwards is concerned about being sensitive to the individual and cultural differences between her students and herself. She needs to know how relevant potential target skills are. Carpenter and Apter (1988) suggested that teachers use a group format to solicit feedback on the practicality of the target skill. Ms. Edwards could engage the class in a group discussion on the behaviors they believe will have the most favorable outcomes. Someone in the group (or an adult) could list those socially valid behaviors that were discussed by the class. To further determine social validity, Ms. Edwards could interview her students' family members, community members, and other school personnel who come in contact with her students. Kazdin and Matson (1981) suggested asking persons in different settings what behaviors students need to demonstrate to be successful in that setting. For example, the bus driver can discuss behaviors that ensure student success on the school bus; they might be those social behaviors that allow students to remain on the bus without written violations or suspensions. General educators can list social behaviors that facilitate student success in their classrooms. Parents and other family members can list the behaviors they perceive necessary for getting along in their homes and communities.

Motivate Students

When the social skill to be taught has been identified and socially validated, the next step is to motivate students to want to acquire and use the prosocial skill. (Additional discussion of motivation is included in Chapter 5.) Motivating students can be accomplished in several ways. Students must see the relevance in learning social skills. According to Gresham (1988), some students have acquired social skills but don't use them. They have a performance deficit when they can perform certain social skills upon request, but don't use them in their everyday interactions. These students may not have associated positive outcomes with consistently performing the skill.

As Ms. Edwards' class is culturally mixed, she needs to enlist the support of family and community members to assist in motivating students. If the target skill is taking turns, Ms. Edwards could begin by providing a rationale for learning the skill. She could engage her class in a discussion of activities that friends enjoy doing together. In order to be motivated to want to make and keep friends, students must believe, for instance, that playing games and sports are much more enjoyable, and more gets accomplished, when people get along with each other. Her students could also brainstorm times when they have observed positive outcomes of others who maintained friendships.

Vocational social skills are also used to arouse student interest in skill acquisition. Students can often relate to skills that are needed to increase their chances of securing and maintaining employment. Ms. Edwards could invite representatives of minority-owned and other businesses to discuss skills facilitative of successful employment in their respective companies. High school and college coaches could also be invited to Ms. Edwards' class to discuss skills they look for and develop among their players. When providing students with a rationale for learning social skills, enlist persons with whom students positively identify. As in using models to demonstrate prosocial skills, it is recommended that they be persons whom the target students hold in high esteem (Stephens, 1977). For that reason, a teacher would enlist the support of persons in the home or community who are virtually certain to have positive effects on the students.

Ms. Edwards can capitalize on multiple opportunities to affirm her students' individual and cultural differences throughout prosocial skill training. She can use training techniques that empower them. As noted earlier in the chapter, she can involve her students in social skill training decisions. Ms. Edwards can communicate her concerns to the class. There are various ways in which prosocial skills can be learned. Ms. Edwards can allow her students to help determine the teaching approaches that maximize their learning. Her students can be allowed to (individually or in committees) evaluate their perceptions of different forms of prosocial instruction and practice activities. For example, skill demonstrations by role-play, direct instruction, peer demonstration, and peer coaching can be evaluated and discussed by students. Providing students with genuine choices increases their motivation for learning and raises self-esteem (Conrath, 1988). Thus it is imperative that Ms. Edwards solicit student input and involvement.

Another way to increase student motivation for social skill acquisition is to use fictional characters. One social skill curriculum revolved around "Critter," a socially inept character whose plight was used to encourage students to generate rationales for using prosocial skills (Walker, 1991). For each prosocial skill, a brief scenario is presented in which "Critter" is deficient in the skill that will be taught. The scenarios end with the main character experiencing observable negative consequences, as a result of his lack of prosocial skills. Students discuss the story and determine what skill was needed and what the outcome might have been if the character used the prosocial skill.

When discussing prosocial skills, keep in mind that even though students may not use prosocial skills consistently, they may be quite capable of discussing consequences associated with having or not having age- or setting-appropriate social skills. While the ultimate goal is for students to acquire prosocial skills, their being able to observe and discuss the benefits of learning the skill is an important step in their being receptive to skill instruction. Based on their observations of others who consistently use prosocial skills, target students may be able to verbalize the positive outcomes they vicariously observe of others' regular prosocial skill use. Hence, particularly in the early learning stages, students should be given many opportunities to observe the social rewards afforded to those who consistently behave in socially appropriate ways.

Select Appropriate Rewards

Social skill training and other behavior change programs typically use rewards to increase student motivation. The rewards vary according to stage of instruction, student interest, and abilities. During early instruction stages, rewards may be very frequent and tangible. Initially, it is extremely important for students to associate the use of prosocial skills with positive outcomes. As students progress, rewards should gradually move from tangible to social reinforcers. Tangible rewards consist of food, toys, markers, and other material objects. Examples of social reinforcers are opportunities to play a table game with others, verbal praise, and opportunities to run errands.

Rewards must be meaningful to students to increase their effectiveness. One technique for determining meaningful rewards is to observe and note student response to school privileges, as well as to tangible rewards. Students who are interested in art might attempt to use social skills if the rewards consist of markers or extra art time to plan and supervise the completion of a classroom mural. If a student continually asks to perform a classroom job, that job could become a reward for using prosocial skills. Ms. Edwards, in seeking relevant rewards, could also interview her students to find out what they consider rewards. Students could individually develop a reward menu for Ms. Edwards and their family members to use when appropriate social skills are displayed in school, home, and community settings.

Schedule Time and Place

Additional factors need to be planned prior to implementing prosocial skill instruction. Prosocial skill training should occur throughout the time children spend in their home, school, and community settings. That is, teachers and others should take advantage of natural opportunities to teach, provide practice, and reinforce positive behaviors. It is far better to capitalize on naturally occurring, as opposed to contrived, situations and dilemmas to ensure relevancy in skill rationale and instruction.

Even though prosocial skill training should be infused throughout the time children spend in the different environments, there should be time designated to provide deliberate instruction. Thus the classroom teacher and students should together determine scheduled prosocial skill training time periods. The designated times should be posted on the daily schedule and followed consistently. Students must see that the teacher is committed to prosocial skills. The time allotted for, and frequency of, this instruction varies according to developmental levels of students and extent of student need. Ms. Edwards would be wise to schedule 20–30 minutes of instruction per day for her students.

It is in the best interest of the teacher to garner support prior to prosocial skill implementation from those who have the greatest contact with the target students. School administrators and family members should be informed of the approach to be used in promoting prosocial skills. In that regard, Ms. Edwards could apprise her principal of the training techniques she will use and discuss the need to arrange ample, meaningful practice opportunities. The principal could also reinforce students who are faced with situations in which prosocial skills are needed and used.

In working with her students' parents, Mrs. Edwards could exchange information about the prosocial skills upon which students are currently instructed, based on the input from students, other teachers, and family members. Mrs. Edwards would work with parents on viable ways to encourage the scheduling of prosocial skill practice in home and community settings, along with discussions of the child's prosocial skill use in naturally occurring situations.

Social skill training in school settings is frequently conducted in small groups. When group instruction is used to promote prosocial skills, it is recommended that the groups be kept small. Ideally, a group should be comprised of 4 to 5 students depending on developmental levels and needs. Groups can consist of more students, but it must be cautioned that the group size be manageable to increase student opportunities for active involvement. Every student in the group should have adequate opportunities to participate in the activities and be observed for immediate feedback on skill performance.

In addition to selecting a time, there should be an appropriate area of the room designated for prosocial skill instruction. The area should be large enough to accommodate students' needs for personal space, physical movement, and the demands of the instructional activities. The area should be large enough to allow students to work in pairs or small groups, conduct role-plays, and hold group discussions. There should be wall space or bulletin and chalk boards for visuals. Group seating should be arranged to facilitate discussion. All students should be seated in such a way that they can view everyone else in the group. Circle and horseshoe formations are popular for group instruction because the physical arrangement is conducive to verbal exchanges among group members.

Prosocial skill instruction does not just happen. It takes a considerable amount of planning to create environments that are supportive of prosocial skill use. Prior to implementing prosocial skill training approaches, teachers must carefully consider target skills, social validity, student motivation, rewards, and time and place schedules.

Prosocial Skill Instructional Practices

When the prerequisites to social skill instruction have been addressed, the decision must be made regarding which instructional practice to use to enhance students' acquisition, generalization, and maintenance of prosocial skills. This section will describe prosocial skill instruction. It is organized according to a social skill training strategy classification (Gresham, 1982). According to Gresham, these strategies involve either (a) the manipulation of antecedents, (b) the manipulation of consequences, or (c) modeling. While practices have been classified in this manner, it must be recognized that some incorporate more than one instructional practice and overlapping is apparent. In those cases, the following practices are classified based on their most salient characteristics.

Manipulation of Antecedents

Strategies involving the manipulation of antecedents are characterized by the teacher's structuring events for target students to preclude inappropriate social behaviors. To illustrate, antecedent events are manipulated when the peers of target students make initiations toward the target students. It is believed that if target students' peers are instructed on ways verbally to invite target students to join in their activities, this could result in increased opportunities for target students to interact socially with their peers (Gresham, 1982). A word of caution is warranted regarding the use of techniques involving peer confederates (Brady et al., 1984) that teach peer groups to make social initiations with target students. These and similar procedures must be implemented by individuals who are cognizant of ethical concerns that have arisen.

Direct instruction, cognitive, and peer-mediated approaches are among the many instructional practices that involve the manipulation of antecedents.

Direct instruction.   Early social skill training efforts with children and youth with exceptionalities were based on a child-deficit model (Strain et al., 1984). It was assumed that the target child was not socially competent because of the child's social skill deficiencies. With this approach, social skills were taught to students apart from their peers and others who played significant roles in their lives. If a student was perceived as deficient in the skill of introducing herself, she would have been taught the steps to perform that skill in a context apart from other students. Direct instruction techniques were typically used in goal attainment.

Direct instruction is a set of teacher behaviors that include skill discussion, modeling, and practice (Hollinger, 1987). LaGreca and Mesibov (1981) used direct instruction techniques to teach conversational and joining-in skills to students with learning disabilities. Their findings indicated that the program was effective because it resulted in greater interactions between target students and their peers. It was also effective in improving the target students' interpersonal communication skills. Several studies have yielded promising results; direct instruction techniques have facilitated the acquisition of prosocial skills among children and youth (Goldstein, Sprafkin, Gershaw, & Klein, 1980; La Nunziata, Hill, & Krause, 1981).

Criticism has also been leveled against techniques that focused only on the target child. Primary reasons for the criticism have been that social interactions involve more than one person and intervening with the target child only fails to promote generalization and maintenance.

As you may recall, Ms. Edwards' class is extremely antagonistic toward each other. Ms. Edwards wants to replace the negative comments her students direct at each other with positive or friendly comments. If she were to implement a direct instruction approach with her students on the skill of complimenting others, she might engage in the following activities:

1. Discuss importance of making friendly comments to others.

2. Verbalize and model the steps for complimenting students.

3. Have students repeat each of the steps.

4. Help students put the steps in their own language (to facilitate memory).

5. Provide role-play opportunities for students to practice.

6. Verbally coach students on the steps.

7. Provide corrective feedback.

One social skill curriculum, skillstreaming (McGinnis & Goldstein, 1984; Goldstein et al., 1980) espouses a structured learning approach to teach prosocial skills to children and adolescents in a group format. It incorporates the principles of direct instruction and has an extensive research base supporting its social skill training methods.

Behavior rehearsal, another component of direct instruction, is also typically used to teach prosocial skills. It combines modeling and role-playing techniques. A suggested format for teachers to implement behavior rehearsal includes:

1. Set up a sequence of responses for students to observe. It is important to make certain that the behaviors they will observe are the desired ones.

2. Instruct students in advance as to which responses are to be noted by them.

3. Enact the behavior or have it performed by someone who will do it correctly.

4. Provide verbal descriptions for the behavior as it is occurring.

5. Reward those who are engaged in the activity as they are performing it, being sure that the observers see or hear the reinforcement.

6. Have students who have observed rehearse the activity, permitting students to provide verbal descriptions.

7. Repeat rehearsals as needed and have students engage in the actual behavior under authentic circumstances when possible. (Stephens, 1977, p. 321)

Cognitive approach. There has been a great deal of interest in the cognitive development of students with learning and behavior problems. Several approaches attempt to engage student cognition in interventions developed to facilitate student self-control. One curriculum, *The Self-Control Curriculum* (Fagan & Long, 1979), was developed to teach students to manage themselves and not rely on external controls. It is based on the psychoeducational approach (Knoblock, 1983) in which its success is dependent upon the teacher–student relationship. There are eight skill clusters inherent in the curriculum; four focus on cognitive development and four focus on affective development. The skill clusters are selection, storage, sequencing and ordering, anticipating consequences, appreciating feelings, managing frustration, inhibition and delay, and relaxation.

Verbal mediation techniques are often used to teach students systematically to be aware of their own behaviors. The *Think Aloud* program (Camp & Bash, 1981) incorporates strategies that allow students verbally to guide themselves through appropriate behaviors. In the case of Ms. Edwards, she might teach her students the following strategy for making friendly comments to others:

1. Decide to say something friendly.
   "Is there something that we both have in common?"
   > **Ex: "I see you like football."**
   "Is there something you like about the person?"
   > **Ex: "I really like that baseball cap."**

2. Say it with a friendly look.

3. Rate yourself.
   "How did I do?"

Peer-mediated approach.   Social skill instruction that only involves target students is remiss in not including peer groups in its training efforts. The peer group is powerful in affecting student behavior (McConnell, 1987). In light of the notion that the peer group of the target student can facilitate social skill training, several researchers have included components that also target the peer group.

While direct instruction techniques have demonstrated benefits in social skill acquisition, other areas have not been as promising. Several study results have failed to generalize to other settings, or prove durable over time (Shores, 1987). When direct instruction is provided to target students alone, other concerns have been expressed. Strain and colleagues (1984) discussed the notion of social reciprocity that is missing when it is assumed that only the target student has the deficit. When skills are taught to students in that isolated context, social reciprocity, or the acknowledgment that interactions involve more than one person, is not taken into consideration.

Another advantage to enlisting the involvement of the peer group is that newly acquired social skills can be "entrapped" (McConnell, 1987). The analogy of a tennis match is used by Hops and Greenwood (1981) to illustrate the manner in which social skills can be reinforced or extinguished by one's peers. The target student makes a social initiation or volleys to another person. When the initiation is socially appropriate, the other person is more likely to respond with a socially appropriate comment, and this exchange continues. However, when the target student emits a socially inappropriate initiation or response, the interaction is terminated or becomes a negative one.

A peer-mediated intervention was implemented with socially neglected children (Middleton, Zollinger, & Keene, 1986). Peer facilitators were used to involve target students in social activities. The unpopular children were paired with peer facilitators who were coached on social skill instruction. Subsequent to the study, the unpopular children were viewed more favorably than before the intervention. In another study, children with learning disabilities who were socially neglected were paired with popular children on different activities (Fox, 1989). The greatest gains, even after program completion, were evidenced by the students with learning disabilities who were paired with their peers who did not have learning disabilities on activities developed to discover mutual interests other than academics. Based on results obtained in the study, teachers may consider pairing students with similar interests to complete nonacademic tasks before structuring academic ones.

Based on results from a previous study, one social skill training package was revised and developed to strengthen its peer mediation component to impact generalization (Walker, McConnell, & Clarke, 1983). The modified intervention included components of direct instruction, individual and group contingency management, and coaching techniques. The techniques were effective in increasing the children's time on task and the time they spent engaging in social interactions on the playground. The authors were concerned with the issue of maintenance, as these positive effects were not evident at the time of follow-up. Another concern regarding social skill training packages is that of using group designs when various components are combined. It becomes increasingly difficult to determine the components that singly, or in combination, are most effective (Gresham, 1981). There are many implications for teachers to consistently document social skill training components and the effects of their use over time.

Peer-tutoring techniques have also been implemented to alter social behaviors. Peer tutoring is a procedure that has been primarily used as an academic intervention and has evidenced positive gains in those skills (Delquadri, Greenwood, Whorton, Carta, & Hall, 1986). Typically, students are paired and assigned either the role of tutor or tutee to teach or learn the skill (Franca, Kerr, Reitz, & Lambert, 1990).

Studies involving students with exceptionalities in tutoring situations have been conducted. Unsurprisingly, it has long been determined that the tutee benefits from academic tutoring arrangements. However, the social benefits received by tutors and tutees have been questionable. When anecdotal data were used to determine if students with behavior disorders benefited from serving as tutors to students with severe and multiple impairments, they reported perceptions of having benefited from tutoring others (Scruggs, Mastropieri, Tolfa Veit, & Osguthorpe, 1986). The students tutored on language and social skill activities.

Tutor effects were also investigated when students with behavior disorders tutored each other on fractions (Franca et al., 1990). Several social benefits were observed. The frequency with which the students interacted positively increased—even in the gym, a different setting than the one in which the tutoring sessions took place. Subsequent to the tutoring program, the social status of the tutors was raised; the social status of the tutees, however, was lowered. It is cautioned that, when the goal is to increase peer acceptance, target students should be instructed to assume the tutoring role as well as the tutee role.

Peer-mediated interventions appear to hold promise in teaching children and youth to be socially competent. Notwithstanding, there are concerns that must be addressed by those who implement interventions in which target students' peers are employed as behavior change agents. One needs to assess carefully any effects experienced by the peers involved in the training (see Strain, Cooke, & Apolloni, 1978, for ethical considerations).

Greenwood, Carta, and Kamps (1990) delineated other caveats in peer-mediated interventions. Teachers were advised to closely monitor target student and peer sessions. The quality of their interactions depends upon teachers' systematic monitoring of those interactions. Peer training is another issue. The researchers discussed the need for peers to be sufficiently trained before assisting target students with behavior change procedures. Peers should also be apprised of potential effects they might have prior to their agreement to participate. Specifically, they should be well informed regarding their influence on target students.

Manipulation of Consequences

Strategies involving the manipulation of consequences are also popular among classroom teachers. These strategies consist of the altering of events that occur after the target social behavior has occurred. These strategies include reinforcement, self-regulation, and peer confrontation.

Reinforcement.   When the target student engages in the appropriate social skill, and the teacher, family member, or peer group provides reinforcement, the consequences have been manipulated. When students do not use prosocial skills, they may have few positive social interactions. When they demonstrate appropriate skills and their peers react favorably, that consequence can be reinforcing.

Teachers must forge partnerships with families and community members to provide consistency in the reinforcement of prosocial skills across settings. Reinforcement techniques are discussed more completely in Chapter 5.

Self-regulation. There is a burgeoning research base documenting the efficacy of students employing self-regulatory procedures (Carr & Punzo, 1993; Lloyd, Bateman, Landrum, & Hallahan, 1989; Nelson, Smith, & Dodd, 1991). Self-monitoring, self-evaluation, and self-reinforcement comprise self-management skills (Carpenter & Apter, 1988). In self-evaluation, students are taught to judge their behavior periodically and systematically against a predetermined standard ideally set by students, teacher, and family members, when appropriate. Students are initially provided a prompt to observe and evaluate their own behavior. Ms. Edwards might have a brief evaluation form taped to her students' desks. After a conversation, they could complete the form and discuss their evaluations with Ms. Edwards or a peer. The use of the self-evaluation forms could also be shared with their family members. Families might be interested in instituting periodic self-evaluation systems with their children.

Students can be taught to reinforce themselves after using prosocial skills. Students could develop a list of social reinforcers that they can supply (a smile, telling yourself that you've done a good job, give yourself a few extra minutes to do something pleasurable). Upon meeting the predetermined standard in the evaluation phase of self-regulation, they would consistently reward themselves with one of their selected reinforcers.

Peer confrontation. One technique used to maximize peer involvement in social skill training is that of peer confrontation. A study was conducted that incorporated peer confrontation procedures (Sandler, Arnold, Gable, & Strain, 1987). Peers were trained to respond to target students following an inappropriate social behavior. For example, when target students engaged in undesirable behaviors, the teacher directed their peers to address the following:

> Subject _____ seems to be having a problem. Who can tell Subject _____ what the problem is?
>
> Can you tell Subject _____ why that is a problem?
>
> Who can tell Subject _____ what he needs to do to solve the problem? (Sandler, Arnold, Gable, & Strain, 1987)

The results attested to the strength of peer pressure on inhibiting negative social behaviors. Target students' peers were taught to employ peer confrontation procedures when the target students engaged in socially inappropriate behaviors. Even when the peer confrontation procedures were no longer practiced, there was evidence that the target student may have continued to be influenced positively by the presence of the peers.

Modeling

Social learning.   Another strategy, modeling, is employed when persons, other than the target students, demonstrate prosocial skills and consequences. The modeling of prosocial skills can be videotaped or live. While there are sundry social skill training methods from which to choose, their principles emanate primarily from the social learning theory (Bandura, 1977). Social learning theorists believe that behavior is acquired through one's own experience and through the vicarious observations of others. It is believed that individuals being observed serve as models to the target students.

Teachers should not select models haphazardly. According to social learning theorists, models should be similar to the target students in terms of age and gender. Models should also be viewed favorably by the target students (Bandura, 1977). Enlisting the assistance of models who are disliked by the target student will not facilitate observational learning. Behaviors of the target students can be inhibited or uninhibited depending upon the absence or presence of conse-quences delivered to the model (Center, 1989). For example, if the target student observes a model performing a prosocial skill and the student is verbally reinforced and given classroom privileges, the target student will be inclined to perform the behavior. However, when the model in a similar situation displays prohibited behavior, and the consequence is a punishing one, the target student's behavior is inhibited.

A caveat, according to this theory, is that failure to deliver consequences can either inhibit or uninhibit the behavior of target students. This occurs either when the model performs a prosocial skill that goes unrewarded or when the model performs a prohibited skill that bears no consequence. Thus, it becomes critical to student learning that appropriate consequences be delivered immediately following the behavior.

Ms. Edwards, in the scenario at the beginning of the chapter, should observe student interactions in the school to determine appropriate models for her students. As her class is culturally diverse, she could enlist same-gender and -ethnicity models when possible and arrange opportunities for her students to observe them demonstrating prosocial skills. For instance, Ms. Edwards has a male student who is of Asian American ethnicity; he is new to the school and wants to meet new students, but he is uncomfortable. Once the student selects the target behavior, Ms. Edwards, realizing the importance for the student, could seek a similar student in her class (or another) to aid in the social skill instruction. If she is successful in getting a student from another class to assist, a time could be worked out to allow the other student to role-play how to introduce oneself to others. Students must not only observe the skill being demonstrated but also the positive consequences resulting from the models' use of prosocial skills.

Students do not learn simply by watching the behavior of others. There are several processes that compose observational learning. Center (1989) noted that, in order for observational learning to occur, the target student must first attend to the model. It was suggested that several characteristics of the model affect the extent to which observational learning is facilitated. When the model is someone with whom target students can and do identify, more attention is given.

After gaining attention, Gresham (1982) characterized the next process as that of retention, or memory. It is necessary for students to not only attend to the model but also recall the observed information. The third process of observational learning is reproduction. Imitation is needed to perform the behavioral responses that were observed and remembered. Merely remembering behavioral responses does little good if the person is physically unable to perform the behavior. When teaching social skills, teachers must assess students to determine their physical abilities and developmental levels to perform the target skill.

Program for Generalization and Maintenance

Children and youth with exceptionalities can and do acquire prosocial skills with training involving various techniques and practices, many of which embrace social learning principles. Several studies have documented the acquisition of these skills (LaGreca & Messibov, 1981; Walker et al., 1983). But, irrespective of the evidence of skill acquisition, many social skill training approaches continue to undergo criticism. Once the skills are acquired, few interventions have facilitated transfer of learning and durable results. The issue of generalization and maintenance continues to plague researchers, practitioners, target students, and their families. Baer, Wolf, and Risley (1968) identified three components of generalization. Stimulus generalization occurs when the learning is transferred across a variety of peoples, events, and settings. Response generalization takes place when the learning transfers across behaviors, and maintenance generalization occurs when learning is durable over time. This section focuses on generalization and maintenance strategies, assessment, structured practice opportunities, and the family/community member-mediated approach.

Strategies

To promote generalization and maintenance, Kazdin (1980) proposed the use of several techniques in social skill training. The peer group was recommended to prompt target students on prosocial skills. The use of natural contingencies is favored over unnatural ones. The stimuli used to invoke the desired behaviors should be expanded to include various situations. Stated another way, it is suggested that a variety of persons and settings should be used in social skill training. Training students in self-management strategies was also proposed to promote maintenance. Many social skill training programs fail to address issues of generalization and maintenance (Schloss et al., 1986).

Assessment of Generalization and Maintenance

When planning and implementing social skill training, it is critical that teachers assess the generalization and maintenance of learned skills. Generalization assessments should determine whether students are using the skills in settings other than the one in which they were taught, or with persons other than those involved in the training. Maintenance assessments would determine if students are using the prosocial skills after a lapse in time since the skills were taught. An interval of 2 weeks is the minimum amount of time between training completion and follow-up. Another follow-up assessment could be conducted when 4 weeks have lapsed. Periodic follow-up assessments should be conducted thereafter. Refer to Chapter 9 for assessment and observation procedures.

Structured Practice Opportunities

When students are taught academic skills, they are often provided continual practice opportunities during initial instruction phases. Long after the skill has been taught, they should continue to receive opportunities to practice those academic skills to enhance generalization and maintenance. In a similar vein, practice opportunities are vital components of social skill acquisition, generalization, and maintenance. Naturally occurring opportunities in which students can practice prosocial skills don't always present themselves in a consistent or timely fashion.

If students have difficulty ignoring the teasing of others on the bus, the teacher, who does not accompany students on the bus, must simulate that setting to teach the prosocial skill consistently in the classroom. Thus it is often necessary to role-play, or artificially produce stimuli which will invoke student use of prosocial skills, to provide students with reinforcement or corrective feedback. Stephens (1977) advocated the use of role-playing in training students on social competence. Role-play situations were characterized as occasions in which students either assume their own roles in uncharacteristic settings or assume uncharacteristic roles in typical settings. In the example of the students with difficulty on the bus, the students would assume their own roles in a setting that differs from the one in which the student needs to use the prosocial skill most.

Involving Family and Community in Prosocial Skills Training

Many educators and researchers have begun acknowledging the power held by parents and families in effecting behavioral change among children and youth. The teacher–family–community member relationship is crucial in discussing generalization and maintenance of prosocial skill instruction. Coleman (1992) advised educators "(1) that their role with parents is a consultative one, and

Role plays and skits can be excellent approaches for teacher social skills.

(2) that parents should be viewed as individuals, not as a homogeneous group" (p. 220). She noted that family members must be perceived as experts with enlightening information and opinions about their children. This helps families feel respected and valued and enhances the spirit of cooperation between the school and the family. This assurance provided to family members is even more critical when there are cultural differences.

Minority parents in particular may distrust or be uncomfortable with school personnel. Additionally, these parents often report feeling alienated from schools when they were children. When teachers are aware of the reasons families are reluctant to become involved in their children's education, they look for barriers to family involvement and do not assume the families don't care about their children's education. Instead, efforts are made to eliminate factors that prohibit family involvement in social skill training.

Family involvement has been advocated for all students and is associated with students' academic and social gains. When the students are culturally different, it becomes even more critical in enhancing school success (Comer, 1987). In establishing a relationship with culturally different family and community members, teachers should solicit information from them to better understand individual and cultural differences. As an example, information obtained on family traditions—celebrations of weddings, births, and holidays—can be enlightening to the teacher. The teacher can more accurately arrange role-play scenarios to simulate meaningful events that take place in target students' home and community settings.

According to Simpson (1988), families have differing needs and educators must be aware of this. One student's family may want to reinforce at home behaviors practiced in the school setting. Another student's family member may choose to assist the teacher in the actual social skill training sessions with role-plays in which prosocial skills are modeled. Family involvement can be categorized as a continuum; it ranges from passive family participation (receiving notes sent home) to active family participation (parent workshops) (Cervone & O'Leary, 1982). It may, however, be necessary to train or assist family members in assuming their desired roles.

Training on target students' social behaviors has typically been implemented apart from their family members. One study was conducted in which at-risk students and their normally achieving peers were trained simultaneously with their parents on prosocial skills. Parents were trained to teach, arrange practice opportunities, and provide feedback on student use of the prosocial skill in home and in community settings (Walker, 1991). After the training, the at-risk students approximated the normally achieving students on most of the measures.

When parents are employed as behavior change agents, skill generalization and maintenance are facilitated. Simpson (1982) stated "It seems logical that when parents are trained to manage maladaptive behavior in the environment in which the response is manifested, the greatest degree of success and generalization will be realized" (p. 149).

Ms. Edwards is now ready to plan, implement, and evaluate culturally sensitive prosocial skill training with her students. She realizes that there are many different approaches to enhancing prosocial skills among children and youth that will extend into their various contexts. She is also aware of the many decisions that face her as a teacher in this regard. She knows that when faced with these decisions—selecting socially-valid target behaviors, training techniques, and practice opportunities—it is ultimately those individual and cultural qualities that students bring to the learning situation that will assist her decision making.

Discussion Questions and Activities

1. Discuss the process of planning prosocial skill instruction. Include factors to be considered and their rationales.

2. Observe a student in two different settings (school, community). List the behaviors you assume increase student success in each setting. Interview an adult in each setting to determine the setting-specific behaviors that facilitate success. Compare your observations with those of the other adults. Discuss the similarities and differences.

3. Tape record a message to a new student's family to explain your social skill instructional procedures and to begin developing a teacher–family partnership.

4. Meet individually with two students in the same class to develop a menu of social reinforcers. Compare the two students' choices.

5. Develop (a) a lesson plan to teach students in your class to invite new students to join their activities, and (b) a plan to assess generalization and maintenance.

Reflective Questions

1. When teaching prosocial skills do you enlist students and significant others in identifying target skills?

2. When teaching prosocial skills do you prioritize potential target skills and teach those that will affect student quality of life?

3. When teaching prosocial skills do you engage parents and community members in arranging opportunities for students to practice in various settings?

4. When teaching prosocial skills do you use innovative techniques to motivate students to use newly learned social skills?

5. When teaching prosocial skills do you employ meaningful reward systems when students demonstrate acquired social skills?

6. When teaching prosocial skills do you designate a time and place to practice prosocial skills?

7. When teaching prosocial skills do you use naturally occurring situations as opportunities to promote social skills?

8. When teaching prosocial skills do you involve students' peers or family members in social skill instruction?

9. When teaching prosocial skills do you match the social skill instructional approach with student characteristics and preferences?

10. When teaching prosocial skills do you assess generalization of learned social skills to other settings and persons?

11. When teaching prosocial skills do you assess maintenance of learned social skills (over time)?

References

Asher, S.R., Singleton, L.C., Tinsley, R.R. & Hymel, S. (1979). A reliable sociometric measure for preschool children. *Developmental Psychology, 15,* 443–44.

Baer, D.M., Wolf, M.M. & Risley, T.R. (1968). Some current dimensions of applied behavior analysis. *Journal of Applied Behavior Analysis, 1,* 91–97.

Bandura, A. (1977). *Social learning theory.* Englewood Cliffs, NJ: Prentice-Hall.

Brady, M.P., McEvoy, M.A., Gunter, P., Shores, R.E. & Fox, J.J. (1984). Considerations for socially integrated school environments for severely handicapped students. *Education and Training of the Mentally Retarded, 19*(4), 246–54.

Bryan, T., Donahue, M. & Pearl, R. (1981). Learning disabled children's peer interactions during a small-group problem-solving task. *Learning Disability Quarterly, 4*(1), 13–22.

Camp, B.W. & Bash, M.A. (1981). *Think aloud.* Champaign, IL: Research Press.

Carpenter, R.L. & Apter, S.J. (1988). Research integration of cognitive-emotional interventions for behaviorally disordered children and youth. In M.C. Wang, M.C. Reynolds & H.J. Walberg (eds.), *Handbook of special education research and practice,* Vol. 2. (pp. 155-69). Oxford: Pergamon.

Carr, S. & Punzo, R.P. (1993). The effects of self-monitoring of academic accuracy and productivity on the performance of students with behavioral disorders. *Behavioral Disorders, 18*(4), 241–50.

Cartledge, G. & Milburn, J.F. (1978). The case for teaching social skills in the classroom: A review. *Review of Educational Research, 48,* 133–56.

Center, D.B. (1989). *Curriculum and teaching strategies for students with behavioral disorders.* Englewood Cliffs, NJ: Prentice-Hall.

Cervone, B.T. & O'Leary, K. (1982). A conceptual framework for parent involvement. *Educational Leadership, 40*(2), 48–49.

Coleman, M.C. (1992). *Behavior disorders: Theory and practice.* Boston, MA: Allyn & Bacon.

Comer, J.P. (1987). New Haven's school–community connection. *Educational Leadership, 44*(6), 13–16.

Conrath, J. (1988). A new deal for at-risk students. *National Association for Secondary School Principals Bulletin, 72*(504), 36–40.

Delquadri, J., Greenwood, C.R., Whorton, D., Carta, J.J. & Hall, R.V. (1986). Classwide peer tutoring. *Exceptional Children, 52*(6), 535–42.

Fagan, S.A. & Long, N.J. (1979). A psychoeducational curriculum approach to teaching self-control. *Behavioral Disorders, 4,* 68–82.

Fox, C.L. (1989). Peer acceptance of learning disabled children in the regular classroom. *Exceptional Children, 56*(1), 50–59.

Franca, V.M., Kerr, M.M., Reitz, A.L. & Lambert, D. (1990). Peer tutoring among behaviorally disordered students: Academic and social benefits to tutor and tutee. *Education and Treatment of Children, 13*(2), 109–128.

Gagne, R.M. (1985). *The conditions of learning and theory of instruction* (4th ed.). New York: Holt.

Gallagher, P.S. (1988). *Teaching students with behavior disorders.* Denver: Love.

Gast, D.L. & Nelson, C.M. (1977). Legal and ethical considerations for the use of timeout in special education settings. *Journal of Special Education, 11,* 457–67.

Goldstein, A.P., Sprafkin, R.P., Gershaw, N.J. & Klein, P. (1980). *Skillstreaming the adolescent.* Champaign, IL: Research Press.

Greenwood, C.R., Carta, J.J. & Kamps, D. (1990). Teacher-mediated versus peer-mediated instruction: A review of educational advantages and disadvantages. In H.C. Foot, M.J. Morgan & R.H. Shute (eds.), *Children helping children* (pp. 177–205). New York: Wiley.

Gresham, F.M. (1981). Social skills training with handicapped children: A review. *Review of Educational Research, 51,* 139–76.

Gresham, F.M. (1982). Misguided mainstreaming: The case for social skills training with handicapped children. *Exceptional Children, 48,* 422–33.

Gresham, F.M. (1983). Social skill assessment as a component of mainstreaming placement decisions. *Exceptional Children, 49,* 331–36.

Gresham, F.M. (1984). Social skills and self-efficacy for exceptional children. *Exceptional Children, 51*(3), 252–61.

Gresham, F.M. (1986). Conceptual issues in the assessment of social competence in children. In P.S. Strain, M.J. Guralnick & H.M. Walker (Eds.), *Children's social behavior: Development, assessment, and modification* (pp. 143–79). Orlando, FL: Academic Press.

Gresham, F.M. (1988). Social competence and motivational characteristics. In M.C. Wang, M.C. Reynolds & H.J. Walberg (eds.), *Handbook of special education: Research and practice* (Vol. 2) (pp. 283–302). New York: Pergamon.

Hollinger, J.D. (1987). Social skills for behaviorally disordered children as preparation for mainstreaming: Theory, practice, and new directions. *Remedial and Special Education, 8*(4), 17–27.

Hops, H. & Greenwood, C.R. (1981). Social skills deficits. In E. Mash & L. Terdal (eds.), *Behavioral assessment of childhood disorders* (pp. 347–94). New York: Guilford.

Hops, H. & Greenwood, C.R. (1988). Social skills deficits. In E.J. Mash & L.G. Terdal (eds.), *Behavioral assessment of childhood disorders,* (2nd ed.) (pp. 263–314). New York: Guilford.

Kauffman, J.M. (1989). *Characteristics of behavior disorders of children and youth.* Columbus: Merrill.

Kazdin, A.E. (1980). *Research design in clinical psychology.* New York: Harper & Row.

Knoblock, P. (1983). *Teaching emotionally disturbed children.* Boston: Houghton Mifflin.

LaGreca, A.M. & Mesibov, G. (1981). Facilitating interpersonal functioning with peers in learning disabled children. *Journal of Learning Disabilities, 14,* 197–99.

LaNunziata, L.J. Jr., Hill, D.S. & Krause, L.A. (1981). Teaching social skills in classrooms for behaviorally disordered students. *Behavioral Disorders, 6,* 238–46.

Libet, J.M. & Lewinsohn, P.M. (1973). Concept of social skills with special reference to the behavior of depressed persons. *Journal of Consulting and Clinical Psychology, 40,* 304–312.

Lloyd, J.W., Bateman, D.F., Landrum, T.J. & Hallahan, D.P. (1989). Self-recording of attention versus productivity. *Journal of Applied Behavior Analysis, 19,* 417–23.

McConnell, S.R. (1987). Entrapment effects and the generalization and maintenance of social skills training for elementary school students with behavioral disorders. *Behavioral Disorders, 12,* 252–63.

McGinnis, E. & Goldstein, A.P. (1984). *Skillstreaming the elementary school child.* Champaign, IL: Research Press.

McGinnis, E., Sauerbry, L. & Nichols, P. (1985). Skillstreaming: Teaching social skills to children with behavioral disorders. *Teaching Exceptional Children, 11*(3), 160–67.

Middleton, H., Zollinger, J. & Keene, R. (1986). Popular peers as change agents for the socially neglected child in the classroom. *Journal of School Psychology, 24*, 343–50.

Nelson, J.R., Smith, D.J. & Dodd, J.M. (1991). A review of self-management outcome research conducted with students who exhibit behavioral disorders. *Behavioral Disorders, 16*, 169–79.

Oden, S. & Asher, F.R. (1977). Coaching children in social skills for friendship making. *Child Development, 48*, 495–506.

Parker, J.G. & Asher, S.R. (1987). Peer relations and later personal adjustment: Are low-accepted children at risk? *Psychological Bulletin, 102*, 357–89.

Reschly, D.J. (1985). Mildly handicapped learning characteristics: Implications for classification, placement, and instruction. In M. Wang & M. Reynolds (eds.), *Research of selected issues in the education of handicapped children*. Washington, DC: United States Department of Education.

Sandler, A.G., Arnold, L.B., Gable, R.A. & Strain, P.S. (1987). Effects of peer pressure on disruptive behavior of behaviorally disordered classmates. *Behavioral Disorders, 16*(1), 9–22.

Schloss, P.J., Schloss, C.N., Wood, C.E. & Kiehl, W.S. (1986). A critical review of social skills research with behaviorally disordered students. *Behavioral Disorders, 12*, 1–4.

Scruggs, T.E., Mastropieri, M., Tolfa Veit, D. & Osguthorpe, R.T. (1986). Behaviorally disordered students as tutors: Effects on social behavior. *Behavioral Disorders, 12*(1), 36–44.

Shores, R.E. (1987). Overview of research on social interaction: A historical and personal perspective. *Behavioral Disorders, (13)* 233–41.

Simpson, R.L. (1982). *Conferencing parents of exceptional children*. Rockville, MD: Aspen Systems Corporation.

Simpson, R.L. (1988). Needs of parents whose children have learning and behavior problems. *Behavioral Disorders, 14*, 40–47.

Slavin, R.E., Karweit, N.L. & Madden, N.A. (eds.). (1989). *Effective programs for students at risk*. Needham Heights, MA: Allyn & Bacon.

Snow, R.E. & Farr, M.J. (1984). *Aptitude, learning, and instruction, Vol. 3: Cognitive and affective process analysis*. Hillsdale, NJ: Erlbaum.

Stephens, T.M. (1977). *Teaching skills to children with learning and behavior disorders*. Columbus: Merrill.

Strain, P., Cooke, T. & Apolloni, T. (1978). The role of peers in modifying classmates' social behavior: A review. *Bureau Memorandum, 19*, 15–16.

Strain, P., Odom, S. & McConnell, S. (1984). Promoting social reciprocity of exceptional children: Identification, target behavior selection, and intervention. *Remedial and Special Education, 5*, 21–28.

Walker, B.L. (1991). *The effects of parent-involved and supported leadership and social skill training with at-risk and normally achieving and developing students*. Doctoral dissertation, University of Kansas, 1991.

Walker, H.M., McConnell, S. & Clarke, J.Y. (1983). *Social skills training in school settings: A model for the social integration of handicapped children into less restrictive settings*. Paper presented at XV International Conference on Behavioral Science: Childhood Disorders—Behavioral–Developmental Approaches, Banff, Alberta, Canada.

Walker, H.M., McConnell, S., Holmes, D., Todis, B., Walker, J. & Golden, N. (1983). *ACCEPTS: A curriculum for children's effective peer and teacher skills.* Austin, TX: PRO-ED.

Wang, M.C., Reynolds, M. & Walberg, H.J. (1986). Rethinking special education. *Educational Leadership, 44*(1), 26–31.

Wang, M., Reynolds, M. & Walberg, H. (1988). Integrating the children of the second system. *Phi Delta Kappan,* 248–51.

Will, M.C. (1986). Educating children with learning problems: A shared responsibility. *Exceptional Children, 52,* 411–15.

Ysseldyke, J.E. & Algozzine, B. (1982). *Critical issues in special and remedial education.* Boston, MA: Houghton Mifflin.

Chapter 8

Involving the Group

Mr. Blakely, a fourth-grade general education teacher for 12 years, feels he is very effective with about 30% of his students. These students love to learn, approaching each activity with zeal and endless energy. He feels confident about reaching these students. For another 40% he believes learning is occurring about half the time. Simple rote activities are easily accomplished, but as the students move into higher cognitive processing activities they seem lost. He just doesn't have time to work with these students to ensure that they understand basic concepts before advancing to higher processing skills. But his real concern is the "bottom" 30% of the class. These students are definitely "losing out" in his classroom. He just doesn't have time to meet their diverse needs through individual assignments. He knows that most of their disruptive behavior is due either to their home environment or to their lack of success in his general education classroom. He thinks that if he could get these "challenging" students into an exceptional education classroom their needs would be met, because the exceptional education teacher has more time to work one on one,

and has the special skills needed to work with these "difficult" students.

The target students in Mr. Blakely's class would be reassigned to Ms. Daniels' exceptional education classroom. Ms. Daniels has been an exceptional education teacher at Sommerville elementary school for over 10 years. Her expertise lies in her ability to design individual assignments for each of her students. Her classroom is very structured, with appropriate rewards and consequences interjected throughout the day. The schedule is similar from day to day. Ms. Daniels' students know her expectations and follow the structured routine. As students enter the room, each one picks up a folder and begins an individual assignment or activity. Ms. Daniels circulates around the room, providing reinforcement for appropriate behavior and assistance to any students needing academic instruction or help. Mr. Blakely feels certain that his "challenging" students would receive a program suited to their diverse individual needs once they entered Ms. Daniels' exceptional education classroom.

*T*he case study of Mr. Blakely and Ms. Daniels highlights how general and exceptional education teachers can inadvertently sabotage the development of social skills and prohibit the utilization of a very effective teaching tool, teacher-facilitated student group work. Teachers often assert that if they had fewer students in their classroom they could effectively meet the needs of all their students. In addition, teachers believe the primary reason exceptional education teachers are more effective for special needs students is the small class size in the exceptional education classroom (Stoddard & Frye, 1993). The contention is that the exceptional education teacher has the time to work individually with each student in a one to one tutoring session.

Neither Mr. Blakely nor Ms. Daniels considered the fact that in a very individualized setting the students had little if any opportunity to learn to work in groups. The less opportunity these students have to work in group activities, the less chance they would ever have of being successful in the larger group of general education or, on a larger scale, successful in life. These teachers mistakenly believe that meeting the individual needs of a student means that the student works individually on assignments or works one on one with the teacher or teacher's assistant. This chapter focuses on the use of teacher-facilitated/ student-led groups as an effective management technique and as a means for increasing academic skill development. In addition, it presents the following types of group settings:

☐ Class meetings

☐ Nonacademic groupings

☐ Skill-specific groupings

☐ Dyads

☐ Cross-age tutoring

☐ Cooperative learning groups

Specific techniques used within group settings—such as group contingencies—are also highlighted.

The Practice of Grouping Students

Successful academic and social outcomes when using student groups requires considerable planning and monitoring on the part of the teacher (Valcante & Stoddard, 1990). The teacher must determine the purpose of the group both academically and socially. The practice of student grouping with teacher direction is common. In both exceptional and general education classrooms, students are often grouped by ability for reading and mathematics instruction. Student-led groups, with teacher facilitation, are often *not* implemented—especially in classrooms with disruptive students. Teachers repeatedly complain that the disruptive students can't "handle" working in student groups. Thus the students continue to work in isolation and never practice the important skills enhanced through group activities. This may be due to the practice of grouping students haphazardly with instructions to complete a project in 3 days. This often results in counterproductive outcomes in both the academic and social domain.

The benefits of student group activities include an increase in overt social behaviors such as listening to others, appropriate reactions to others' comments, and appropriate body space (Coleman & Webber, 1988). Less obvious affective social skills and attitudes strengthened through group activities are interdependence on others, responsibility to others, increased self-esteem, and a sense of belonging (Brown, Foster, Hummel, & Lazerson, 1988).

Academic gains can also be realized when using teacher-facilitated/student-directed group activities. Academic gains are due in large part to the opportunity for children to be actively engaged in learning for a larger proportion of time than in the traditional teacher-directed learning model (Greenwood et al., 1987). Students need to receive many opportunities to practice new learning material (Rosenshine & Stevens, 1986). When teachers attempt to individualize learning for a student, the student often receives very brief (3-minute) "snapshots" of learning. In the implementation of group work, a student could receive 30 minutes of the same guided practice. This 27-minute increase would enable the student to receive ten times the amount of guided practice as the time allocated in the traditional learning model.

Many different types of student groupings can be designed, depending on the purpose of the group and the type of learning process and outcomes. For any group activity to be successful, all group members must benefit and membership in the group must be viewed as a positive action for each member (Rosenberg, O'Shea, & O'Shea, 1991). A teacher must plan carefully to ensure these two outcomes occur as a result of the grouping. This requires that the teacher be knowledgeable of each student's areas of strength and weakness and group accordingly depending on the lesson. Furthermore, the teacher must constantly monitor the groups and make adjustments to the groups as needed for optimum development for all group members. For example, a student may possess aptitude in mathematics and could be viewed as a leader for a particular learning group. The same student may be struggling with reading and the composition of the group may need to be altered.

Types of Teacher-Facilitated/ Student-Led Work Groups

Class Meetings

Class meetings are designed as a forum for the entire class to discuss general classroom procedures or classroom problems. Topics for the meeting can be brought up by the students or the teacher. The primary focus of the class meeting is on group dynamics within the classroom, not on improving academic achievement. But the outcome of the meeting may enable students to learn more efficiently through a redesign of a class procedure. The real purpose of class meetings is to build a sense of community within the class. A class meeting can be especially beneficial for those classes that meet for one session a day. Considerable change has taken place in our schools within the last 10 years, and one of those changes is that students lack a sense of identity to a group. The class meeting can provide the student with the security of a group.

Opponents of class meetings emphasize that time spent on nonacademic procedures results in decreased academic performance (Rosenshine & Stevens, 1986). The investigations cited by Rosenshine and Stevens do not measure the effects of activities such as group meetings on the less tangible but critical variables of self-esteem or ability to work with others. A balance must be reached in our design of education curriculum to ensure the mastery both of basic academic and basic life skills.

The class meeting can be a quick 15-minute session or a full 60-minute classroom period. The purpose of the class meeting must be clearly stated and it should not be used as a quick "filler" at the end of a class period. Topics for the meeting are submitted so an agenda can be drawn up by a student. It is best to provide for an open agenda in the last few minutes of the scheduled time. Rules for discussion and responses to points of discussion should be clearly stated. The teacher facilitates discussion and assists the student leader to ensure the rules for discussion are followed. The role of the teacher may change depending on how much direction the class needs. A teacher may realize a class needs a great deal of direction in the beginning, but the astute teacher constantly changes the amount of direction versus facilitation with an ultimate goal of a class meeting that is student-led and teacher-facilitated. Lessons on valuing diversity, developing empathy towards others and developing a sense of responsibility for the class community are a few of the less tangible but significant benefits of class meetings.

Nonacademic Grouping

These groups can be developed based on the interests of the children or random selection based on a specific characteristic such as birth month. These groups should be developed specifically for completing logistical activities and only for short periods of time such as lunch or bus time. The student composition of nonacademic groups is left primarily to random selection. This provides a good opportunity for students to practice appropriate social skills. However, the possibility of problems resulting is increased through the random selection of group members (Morsink, 1984). This practice of nonacademic grouping enables the teacher to determine if the effective group skills of the students are generalizing to other settings.

Skill-Specific Groups

The practice of skill-specific grouping is a popular teaching technique implemented in many general and exceptional education classrooms. The method is based on the premise that instruction or practice of skills is more efficient—hence more effective—if all students participating in the activity are functioning at or near the same ability level. These groups can be teacher-directed, student-led, or a combination of both teacher direction and teacher facilitation. A hierarchy of skills to be mastered is designed by the teacher (or commercially prepared). As each student moves through the hierarchy of skills, the teacher constantly monitors the progress of each student and the overall progress of the group. It is critical that the students are not placed in a group and then left in the same group regardless of progress. A criticism of skill-specific grouping is the negative connotation of a particular group's being perceived as "the dummies of the class." Teachers perceive skill-specific grouping as a means for efficiently moving students through a curriculum (Stoddard & Frye, 1993), but as educators they must constantly weigh the value of moving efficiently through lessons against the impact skill-specific grouping has on the self-concept of students. Teachers may inadvertently escalate behavior problems through student assignment in the above manner. Skill-specific grouping should be used in conjunction with other learning settings to ensure that students do not confine their own learning ability due to the ability of the preselected group (Gearheart, Weishahn, & Gearheart, 1988).

Peer Dyads

Involving a student's peer to assist the target student to be successful in school has been implemented through various formats since the inception of formal educational practices. Research has clearly demonstrated the effectiveness of peer dyads (Carlson, Litton, & Zingraff, 1985; Scruggs & Richter, 1985; King, 1982) as a method for teaching academic content and a means for enhancing appropriate behavior in the general or exceptional education classroom. Peer tutoring groups can take many forms. The typical peer tutoring forum consists of a more capable student assisting a less capable student. Tutoring can also involve a team of three members (one tutor and two tutees) or a grouping of as many as six students of heterogeneous ability.

An equally effective but less often-used format is the utilization of a student with learning/academic problems in the role of tutor (Dineen, Clark, & Risley, 1977). If this format is utilized, it is imperative that the student functioning as the "tutor" have knowledge of the information to be learned. This can easily be accomplished through the use of cross-age tutoring (more comprehensively explained later in this section). The less able student can also function as the tutor through careful planning. The teacher can set the situation for the tutor to use flashcards with the answer to the flashcards written on the side of the card facing the tutor. This technique allows students of varying ability levels to be viewed as leaders in the class. Heron, Heward, Cook, and Hill (1983) contend that the most successful dyads are those in which there is active participation by both members of the group in a tutor-tutee interaction mode. In addition, those practice areas that have a predeveloped correct-answer key enable students of equal abilities to pair into a learning group. A correct-answer key can prevent arguments of over-zealous partners who are certain their incorrect answer is correct.

The practice of peer grouping can improve the academic and social skills of the tutor as well as the tutee (Cohen, Kulik, & Kulik, 1982; Greer & Polirstok, 1982; Maher, 1984). Campbell, Brady, and Linehan (1991) noted substantial skill improvement for peer tutors as a result of teaching a language-arts skill to their partner. Additionally, the authors found that students tutored by another member of their class scored higher than those students independently studying the same information.

Peer tutoring enables a student to practice appropriate social skills (Jenkins & Jenkins, 1985), which can also improve a student's social standing within the class. As Stoddard and Valcante (1991) found, peer tutoring can provide a structure for social interaction between students who do not normally socialize. If the expectation of the peer tutoring experience is to increase interaction between two students, the dyad must meet for a consistent period of time over a continuing period of time. Those peer tutoring sessions resulting in quick mastery of information will be successful for teaching the prescribed content, but the limited interactions of the tutor and tutee will not promote the development of a relationship between partners.

The success of a peer tutoring program relies on a clear understanding of the expectations and procedures for the tutoring session. It is critical that peer tutors are trained in the skill of tutoring. Niedermeyer (1970) found increased mastery of content when tutors were given structured training. This training includes teaching the tutor a structured plan for each session, providing practice in appropriate feedback, developing a practical means for evaluating the progress of each session, teaching the tutor appropriate specific academic and social praise for correct responses, and what to do when conflicts develop between the dyad. The initial training may slow the start of the tutoring sessions but it is imperative that the tutor and tutee are cognizant of the responsibilities and are capable of completing the assigned task. The teacher models appropriate behaviors through-out the teaching day, but the structure of the session and the important social interaction skills required of both partners need to be demonstrated by the teacher (Stoddard & Valcante, 1991).

The tutor has to be committed to the tutoring session and approach each session with the same enthusiasm a classroom teacher needs to approach each lesson. Those programs where a contingency plan was designed for the positive learning and interaction of the tutor–tutee group also report higher success rates (Delquardi, Greenwood, Whorton, Carta, & Hall, 1986). A point system can be implemented for those tutoring groups who finish the daily assignments or reach mastery of material. Valcante and Stoddard (1990) also found that providing social and intrinsic reinforcement to the dyad when the two successfully function as a team enhances the standing of both members of the dyad. The reinforcement of both "team" members encourages a sense of unity between the two students and reduces any negative feelings or roles of one student being viewed as the "helper" and the less capable student being perceived as "needy."

The use of peer tutors for teaching appropriate social skills is not as readily implemented as the use of dyads for attaining academic information. In teaching social skills, the peer assists the target student throughout the day. For example, the target student may need help with impulsively calling out during the day. The student knows this is not allowed in the classroom and would like to stop but has a difficult time controlling the impulsive habit. The teacher, tutor, and tutee can decide on a one-word verbal cue or a physical cue like a hand signal. This cue would be the reminder for the target student to stop. In addition, the teacher can give the dyad a social reward if the number of call-outs decreases and the number of hand-raises increases. The social reward should be activities that the pair reciprocally participate in, such as board games or computer time. The development of pairs such as the above-mentioned dyad result in minimum time devoted by the teacher to the skill. The most successful dyads are those in which the tutor is a relatively popular member of the class who has been noticed by the teacher to demonstrate empathy towards others.

Stoddard and Pike (1990) reported that the implementation of the peer program reduced teacher disruption time taken to monitor behavior and increased the positive social interaction of peers who normally did not interact. In addition, Stoddard and Pike found that the target student was viewed more positively by other members of the class due to the relationship that developed between the two students in the dyad.

The academic and social benefits of peer tutoring has been clearly demonstrated in various settings and with a myriad of groups. The implementation of this as a daily practice in general and exceptional education classrooms has not been realized. Trained peer-tutoring groups are an effective means in which students practice to master skills previously taught by the teacher. Immediate feedback, increased time on task, and a substantial amount of time engaged in practice are three of the main variables that makes peer tutoring such an efficient technique to use with students who have a wide range of abilities.

Cross-Age Tutoring

Cross-age tutoring is a subset of tutoring that pairs students of different ages or grade levels to work on a specific academic skill. Another purpose for the dyad can

Research has clearly demonstrated that older students tutoring younger ones is an effective strategy for teaching academic content and enhancing appropriate behavior.

be one of a mentor (tutor) to an unmotivated student (tutee). The goal of this model is for the two to develop a friendship built on trust. Academic skills can be practiced, but the primary goal of the program is to provide the target student with a "friend," someone who builds the student's self-concept through discussions and activities during the planned peer time. Researchers (Juel, 1991; Stoddard & Pike, 1990) report success with the use of cross-age tutors incorporating college-age athletes and elementary-age students. The student athletes were placed in the school settings to provide academic tutoring, but a profoundly positive effect on the self-concept of the target students was also noted for both investigations. Cross-age peer tutors could be implemented across grade levels *or* school levels, as noted in Table 8.1.

An advantage of cross-age tutoring over peer tutoring is that, in most cases, the older student is more capable academically so the concern of incorrect information being relayed is reduced. The above activities do not require the tutor to have a background in any specific area. It does require the tutor to know the math facts being studied. Stoddard and Pike (1991) noted that three of the older students participating in the cross-age tutoring program did not have mastery of higher-level multiplication facts and adjustments needed to be made as to the information being studied with several of the dyads.

Table 8.1 Cross-Age Tutor Groups

Tutor	Tutees	Activity
High school	Middle	Prepare eighth-graders for high school setting
High school	Older elementary	Tutor math facts
High school	Younger elementary	Read books
		Tutor math facts
		Listen to reading
Older elementary school	Younger elementary	Tutor math facts
		Read books
		Listen to reading
Middle school	Older elementary	Prepare fifth-graders for middle school

Cross-age peer tutoring has resulted in increased student self-concept, improved attitudes about individuals with disabilities, enhanced social relationships, and decreases in negative behavior. Placing students in the position of a teacher reinforces academic skills, builds self-concept, and encourages appropriate behavior (Brown et al., 1988).

Cooperative Learning Strategies

In cooperative learning groups the goal is that "we sink or swim together." This philosophical orientation has proven to be an effective management tool in the private business sector (Peters & Waterman, 1982) and is now being implemented throughout the education system from preschool to institutes of higher education. Despite the popularity of the cooperative philosophy, teachers at all levels of education are slow to implement cooperative learning groups. The resistance (Harris & Aldridge, 1983) is due to concerns about accountability, giving up control of the classroom, watering down the curriculum, perceived lack of administrator and parent support, and fear that ultimately less learning will occur.

The research on cooperative learning has resulted in primarily positive results with some conflicting findings. Johnson, Maruyama, Johnson, Nelson, and Skon's (1981) meta-analysis of various learning settings indicated that cooperative learning strategies resulted in higher gains both in academic achievement and the affective domain than traditional learning settings. However, Tateyama-Sniezek (1990) concluded from her meta-analysis of 12 cooperative learning studies that despite the positive aspects in such areas as social development and self-esteem, significant gains in academic achievement were not found. Many teachers, administrators, parents, and students (Walberg & Wang, 1987) contend the important lifelong skills practiced in cooperative learning in the area of social

Cooperative learning groups help students learn how to get along with groups of people as well as to consider diverse solutions to problems.

skills, social interaction, and self-concept are as significant as other academic curricula and thus support continued implementation of the strategy.

Teachers (Augustine, Gruber, & Hanson, 1990) reporting success with cooperative learning find that certain basic practices are critical in implementation if cooperative learning is to extend beyond the traditional practice of "group" work (Stoddard & Pike, 1990). Table 8.2 focuses on several of the critical

Table 8.2 Implementation of Components of Cooperative Learning

Specify instructional objectives	Both academic and collaborative	
Determine group size	2 to 6 students	
	3 students may be best for a new group	
Assign students to group	heterogeneous group if possible	
Arrange the room for group work	chairs should be in a circular format for each group	
	provide adequate spacing among the groups	
Plan materials to promote interdependence		
Determine role assignments	coordinator	checker
	recorder	research runner
	includer	encourager
	observer	
Explain the academic task		
Determine grading system for project and explain to class		
Determine rules for the teams		
Teacher monitors the groups		
Evaluation of the groups	teacher provides feedback	
	self/group evaluation	

components of cooperative learning strategies (Johnson, Johnson, Holubec, & Roy, 1984).

In specifying *instructional objectives* the teacher must determine what objectives are to be accomplished for the lesson. The objectives may include academic as well as collaborative objectives to enhance the communication skills of each student.

The *group size* is determined by the activity or needs of the student. Johnson and colleagues (1984) purport that beginning cooperative learning groups are better able to function when the numbers of the group are relatively small (such as three students). As the group size enlarges, so does the need for more sophisticated communication skills for each group member. Teachers must be sure that the students are able to function successfully as small teams before moving to larger teams.

The task of *assigning students to particular groups* is an essential component of a successful working group. The teacher must be knowledgeable of each student's ability concerning the particular task and the unique personalities of the students. A team with members of various ability levels provides the students within the group a unique challenge to practice very important lifelong communication skills. Groups may be changed as the need arises. By changing group membership, students will be given the opportunity to interact with more diverse levels of students.

A concern reported by many teachers and students (Stoddard & Pike, 1990) is that the more capable students do all the work and the less able or willing students "coast on the coat tails" of the higher achievers. The astute teacher needs to monitor very closely and alleviate this problem through the establishment of a debriefing session where students have the opportunity to express their concerns about nonproductive group members. Other means for reducing the anxiety of group members who believe a nonproductive member is within their ranks is the establishment of two grades: one grade for the group on the process of utilizing the cooperative learning components and a separate grade for the group project. In addition, the teacher can give individual grades for each clearly delineated part of the project. Through this method the students are encouraged to practice cooperative learning strategies but do not feel unsuccessful if a particular group member does not cooperate despite the other group members' best efforts.

A learning environment needs to be planned and organized for learning groups to complete assignments efficiently. An effective *room arrangement* reduces distractions and heightens time on task. The students within the group should be facing each other in a circular format. The circle enables all individuals to be viewed and heard equally. In addition, sufficient spacing among the circle groups will provide a sense of belonging to a particular group and reduce the need for students constantly to interrupt students in other working groups.

The learning *material to be covered for the lesson* must be carefully planned by the teacher. In planning, the teacher must set the goal of interdependence among group members. This may require the teacher to give certain pieces of information to certain team members who must then teach the other team members, or the teacher may have fewer resources available so the students must collaborate to be successful. The need to structure the lessons to encourage collaboration diminishes as the communication skills of the students develop and collaboration occurs naturally.

Role assignments of various tasks to different group members are an effective means for allowing students to gain a new view of the learning situation. A specific role assignment enables the less able student to have a task that is not beyond capability but is equally important to the success of the process or the final product. A student who tends to monopolize the conversation could be assigned the task of "observer." In this job the student could not add comments, but observes the lesson and takes notes on how the group is working as a team. The student with a negative attitude could be assigned the role of "encourager." In this role the student's task is to provide the other group members with words of encouragement. The less capable student may be assigned the role of "research runner." This student would be responsible for getting research books or needed materials for the other members of the group to complete an activity—a very important role, but one that does not require a great deal of reading or writing. Teachers can design new roles as the need arises. Roles can also change within and between groups. Through a change in role assignment a student can practice the many different responsibilities for completing a project.

As in any lesson, the teacher must provide clear direction or *explanation of the academic task.* The objectives of the task, final goals, and final products must be communicated, and the teacher should ask for student feedback to ensure comprehension of the assignment.

The sophistication of the students' collaborative skills and the nature of the activity determine the *type of grading system* that should be utilized for the project. A concern of many teachers and students is that a student's unwillingness to complete an assignment will affect a hard-working student's grade. Through the use of individual accountability and monitoring of the group, a teacher will ensure that fair workloads are being completed and each student is mastering the information to be learned.

Rules for the working group and the class as a whole can be determined by the teacher or by the students and the teacher. As in most classroom rules, the number should be few and stated clearly. Expected communication skills are necessary in the rules for cooperative groups and may include such statements as "learn from logic not group pressure," "majority does not rule," "use each other's name," or "stay with your own working group." These rules are also reminders of effective communication skills that enhance cooperative efforts.

The difficult task for the teacher is effective *monitoring of the groups.* The teacher needs to be constantly circulating and assisting students throughout the room. The goal of the teacher is to facilitate learning and provide as much direction as necessary for learning to occur. In the initial implementation of cooperative strategies, students will need more guidance, cues, and instruction not only on the information to be learned but also on how to work as a group. The teacher cannot participate in the group process of a team, however the student assigned as "observer" can keep the teacher posted on the progress of the group, both in the area of academic content and interactions of the group. The teacher can provide the necessary modeling and reinforcement of effective communication skills. It may also be necessary for the teacher to provide brief summaries during the working session and to conduct an end-of-the-lesson summary to ensure that students have an understanding of critical aspects of the lesson.

An *evaluation of each group* or a time for reflection on the cooperative process that took place in each group is critical if students are to develop the skills of collaboration. During evaluation the teacher and students provide feedback to each other and to the teacher on what was learned and how the activity affected the process of their own learning. During the evaluative time, use such questions as:

- ☐ Did you learn something today?
- ☐ Did you help or hurt the group and how?
- ☐ Did any group member hurt you and how?

☐ What could you do differently next time?

☐ What would you like other group members to do differently next time?

Questions like the ones above assist in the process of evaluating cooperative lessons. This component of cooperative learning allows each student's concerns to be valued and addressed. Students will initially have a difficult time discussing the above questions and considerable facilitating by the teacher will be necessary.

The above components will assist teachers in setting up truly collaborative learning situations. Through effective utilization of the components of cooperative learning, many of the concerns of teachers and students about the problems of workload and ownership will be significantly reduced.

The effectiveness of cooperative learning strategies can be enhanced by adapting various aspects of the strategy (Slavin, Madden, & Stevens, 1990). The following techniques are variations of cooperative learning strategies (Manning & Lucking, 1991). A case study for adapting each strategy is illustrated after each description. An advantage of cooperative learning strategies is that many adaptations can be made to fit the needs of various age levels and the varying needs of same-level students.

Student Teams–Achievement Divisions (STAD)

This strategy involves four students of various ability levels teaming together to help each other master material (Slavin, 1978). Students are required to take individual quizzes for mastery of knowledge. In addition, the students earn bonuses for team efforts.

> Mr. Blakely's fourth-grade classroom divides into teams of four students. Mr. Blakely determines the members of each group, basing his decision on a desired mix of differing genders, ethnic background, and ability levels. The assignment for the students is to master the meaning of a list of vocabulary words. Mr. Blakely gives the students the words, a dictionary, and flashcards. Two students are assigned the roles of writer (of the note cards) and two students are assigned the roles of researcher (looking up the words in the dictionary). The students earn bonus points every time Mr. Blakely hears a positive comment about an individual's mastering a word. These bonus points can be used as extra credit during the grading period.

Cooperative Integrated Reading and Composition (CIRC)

This program was created to enhance the reading and writing skills of intermediate-grade students (Madden, Slavin, & Stevens, 1986). Students are assigned to teams and the teacher works directly with one team while the other teams works collaboratively on reading and writing activities such as vocabulary development, story predictions, story summaries, and decoding skills. When all team members believe they are ready for the quiz, a preassessment is completed to determine their readiness and to diagnose any weak areas. A quiz follows the preassessment and reinforcers are provided for those teams working collaboratively and reaching mastery.

> The students in Mr. Blakely's class use CIRC during their language-arts period. After placing each student on a team, Mr. Blakely gives the class assignment to all the teams. The assignment entails the students' reviewing vocabulary, reading a story, reviewing highlights of the story, and writing a different ending for the story. A written comprehension quiz is individually completed by each student when the team members believe they are ready. Mr. Blakely spends time with each team checking their review of vocabulary, reviewing the selected highlights from the story, and listening to the student's choices of story endings. The role assignments for this cooperative lesson include a discussion leader, a vocabulary voicer, a summarizer of summaries, a writer, an encourager, a timekeeper, and an observer. The observer would write down all positive and negative statements by the students. The students would receive one bonus point for every positive statement that goes beyond the number of negative statements.

Jigsaw

Six students are assigned to each team to learn new academic material. In each team a student is assigned to learn part of the academic material. After reading the assigned section, the student meets with members from other teams who have been assigned to read and learn the identical information for their own group. After the students review the information, they return to their own groups, where they are now assigned the title of "expert" for that particular piece of information. The experts must then teach their expertise to the members of their original team (Aronson, Blaney, Stephan, Sikes, & Snapp, 1978).

> In Mr. Lawrence's science class each student has been assigned to a team. Mary, Ken, Steve, and Lucy are on one team and each has been assigned an approximately three-page section of the American history text to read and outline. Mr. Lawrence gives them approximately 20 minutes to complete this activity. Once the group has read and outlined the section, each student goes with team members from the other groups who have read and outlined the same sections. This new group become the "experts" for those particular pages in the text. The "experts" discuss their outlines and determine highlights from the section that would be important for other students to study, then design a story that compares American life today with that of the early Americans. Mr. Lawrence gives this group the rest of the period to finish the activity. The next day, the original groups get together. Mary, Ken, Steve, and Lucy are now

back together again. Their assignment requires each "expert" to share their story and discuss the highlights with their original team members. In addition, Mr. Lawrence assigns each team member a role of timekeeper, includer, recorder, and summarizer.

Team Assisted Individualization (TAI)

This strategy is designed to utilize cooperative and individualized learning in mathematics in the intermediate grades (Slavin, Madden, & Leavey, 1984). Each student takes a mathematics test to determine placement for activities. Then students begin the math activities and self-pace through the mathematics problems. Each team member of the four-person team assists the others and checks each team member's work. When students are ready they take the unit test; the tests are then scored by student checkers. The teacher facilitates and evaluates student progress. Teams are reinforced for mastery of material.

Mr. Blakely gives a pretest on division, including single-digit and double-digit division problems. Team members are assigned in mixed ability groups based on Mr. Blakely's diagnosis from the pretest. Students work in teams on the division problems, both computation and word problems. As students complete a packet of material at their level, a unit test is given and graded by students assigned the role of checker. The checker would have a master key for grading all papers. Mr. Blakely would give team bonus points for those teams progressing into new levels not previously mastered. Bonus points would be used to encourage progress, not to determine which student is farthest along in the division problems.

Teams-Games-Tournament (TGT)

Teams of four students each are assigned to master material selected by the teacher. Student progress is measured in a tournament format in which students compete against other teams with similar ability levels. Points are awarded for team winners and reinforcers are earned for those teams working collaboratively.

Students in Mr. Lawrence's seventh-grade science class would divide into teams of four members based on their ability (as determined by Mr. Lawrence). Role assignments would be given out by Mr. Lawrence and would include a researcher, a writer, an includer, and an encourager. Each student would be responsible for knowing the characteristics and functions of various types of bacteria as found in the handout and in the text. The group would provide the means for studying the information. The student's knowledge of the bacteria would be assessed during the weekly tournament game with questions by Mr. Lawrence. Students winning the tournament would receive bonus points, and points would also be earned for those groups working collaboratively with quiet, positive voice tones.

Cooperative learning strategies have proven effective as a means for teaching students lifelong social interaction skills, increasing self-esteem, and providing acceptance in the classroom for a more diverse population of students (Johnson et al., 1981). Although academic gains have not been as widespread for cooperative strategies (Cotton & Cook, 1982; McGlynn, 1982; Tateyama-Sniezek, 1990), the variety of practices encompassing cooperative strategies in combination with other instructional practices has proven to be promising for various ability levels of students (Slavin et al., 1990). As students end formal schooling and enter society as productive citizens and leaders in society, the communication and collaborative skills emphasized in cooperative learning will be crucial to their success in the workforce and in life (Peters & Waterman, 1982; Walberg & Wang, 1987).

The effectiveness of cooperative learning as a strategy for increasing academic achievement and social skills is enhanced with the inclusion of reinforcement for group collaborative group efforts (DeVries & Slavin, 1978; Madden et al., 1986; Slavin, 1978; Slavin, Leavey, & Madden, 1984). The practice of group contingency can be applied to a variety of learning settings involving student groups.

Group Contingencies

Group contingency can be used for any general or exceptional education class as either a positive reward or loss of reward. The contingencies can be applied independently, dependently, or interdependently (Litow & Pumroy, 1975). Each contingency is more effective if implemented based on the needs (age and interest level) of the group. Independent contingency is applied once the rules of the group are set. Students individually earn the reward as they meet the rules of the group. Independent contingencies are noncompetitive and do not use peers as a means for encouragement of appropriate behavior. Dependent contingencies are designed to allow one student to earn the reward for the entire class. This strategy is helpful if the student is capable of meeting the expectations and needs encouragement. This technique should not be used as a punishment for the class if the student does not meet the required expectation. Interdependent contingencies require all members of the class to earn the reward for the class. The procedure is similar to dependent, but in this strategy each student in the class is responsible for earning or losing the reward for the other students in the classroom. Caution again must be used in implementing this strategy. If a particular student continues to prevent the class from receiving the reward, the student will be ostracized and the student's inappropriate behavior may escalate. Group contingencies are most effective when rewards are given for appropriate behavior rather than being taken away for inappropriate behavior.

Conclusions

The effectiveness of, and need for, group efforts has been realized in the workforce and in our society. If teachers are providing education for lifelong learning, then more efforts must be made toward the practice of collaborative work among students. In addition, as our culture becomes more diverse it is imperative that students be taught to value diversity and respect differences. This can only be accomplished when students are allowed to work together to view different opinions, values, and abilities. Mr. Blakely and Ms. Daniels could effectively work together in a collaborative venture that would allow both the general and exceptional education students to learn from and with each other. Although Ms. Daniels is very effective in her teaching methods, her students are not able to practice the important lifelong skills of communication and collaboration. Mr. Blakely does not have the time to meet individually with each child to ensure mastery of content. Perhaps Mr. Blakely and Ms. Daniels could design a program that allows the students to work in different types of group settings. The individual meeting time that Mr. Blakely never can arrange could be spent more effectively and efficiently in group activities where students are learning from each other and about each other. Then students would not only have the academic knowledge necessary for lifelong learning, but they would also possess the skills necessary to work collaboratively in a diverse society.

Discussion Questions and Activities

1. Class meetings have been determined to be an effective means for enhancing social skills and structuring a positive classroom structure. Design an outline for an initial class meeting to take place the first or second day of the new school year. Share these outlines with other preservice teachers to determine what topics can be used as initial "ice breakers" for students.

2. The advantages and disadvantages of skill-specific grouping are noted in this chapter. Interview four teachers to determine their rationale for using (or not using) skill-specific grouping. Develop a position statement that details your philosophical position concerning the practice of skill-specific grouping.

3. The use of peer dyads is highlighted in this chapter. Identify the essential elements of effective peer dyads.

4. The training of peer tutors has been recognized as critical for the success of a peer tutoring program. Develop a training manual for peer tutors in your particular grade level. Be sure to include the following components:

   □ Commitment by the peer tutors

☐ Importance of teamwork

☐ Time schedules for each session

☐ Appropriate methods for feedback

☐ Methods for dealing with conflicts

☐ Methods for measuring progress

5. Develop a lesson plan incorporating cooperative learning strategies as noted in this chapter. Include the components below in the lesson plan. Share these lesson plans with other students and critique the plans for inclusion of the components:

☐ Instructional objectives

☐ Assigning students to groups

☐ Room arrangement

☐ Material to be covered

☐ Determining group size

☐ Role assignments

☐ Explanation of the academic task

☐ Determination of grading system

☐ Rules for the working group

☐ Monitoring the groups

☐ Evaluation/processing of each group

6. Based on the readings in the chapter, develop a response to a parent who believes that the use of cooperative learning strategies waters down the curriculum and hinders the advanced development of the very bright child.

References

Aronson, E., Blaney, N., Stephan, C., Sikes, J. & Snapp, M. (1978). *The jigsaw classroom.* Beverly Hills: Sage.

Augustine, D.K., Gruber, K.D. & Hanson, L.R. (1990). Cooperation works! *Educational Leadership, 47* (4), 4–7.

Brown, S.I., Foster, H.L., Hummel, J.W. & Lazerson, D.B. (1988). The effectiveness of cross-age tutoring with truant high school students with learning disabilities. *Journal of Learning Disabilities, 21* (4), 249–52.

Campbell, B.J., Brady, M.P. & Linehan, S. (1991). Effects of peer-mediated instruction on the acquisition and generalization of written capitalization skills. *Journal of Learning Disabilities, 24,* 6–14.

Carlson, M.B., Litton, F.W. & Zingraff, S.A. (1985). The effects of an intraclass peer tutoring program on the sight word recognition ability of students who are mildly mentally retarded. *Mental Retardation, 23* (2), 74–78.

Cohen, P.A., Kulik, J.A. & Kulik, C.C. (1982). Educational outcomes of tutoring: A meta-analysis of findings. *American Educational Research Journal, 19,* 237–48.

Coleman, M. & Webber, J. (1988). Behavior problems? Try groups! *Academic Therapy, 23*(3), 265–75.

Cotton, J.L. & Cook, M.S. (1982). Meta-analyses and the effect of various reward systems: Some different conclusions from Johnson, Maruyama, Johnson and Nelson. *Psychological Bulletin, 92,* 178–83.

Delquardi, J., Greenwood, C.R., Whorton, D., Carta, J.J. & Hall, R.V. (1986). Classwide peer tutoring. *Exceptional Children, 52,* 535–542.

DeVries, D.L. & Slavin, R.E. (1978). Teams-Games-Tournament: Review of ten classroom experiments. *Journal of Research and Development in Education, 12,* 28–38.

Dineen, J.P., Clark, H.B. & Risley, T.R. (1977). Peer tutoring among elementary students: Educational benefits to the tutor. *Journal of Applied Behavior Analysis, 10,* 231–38.

Gearheart, B.R., Weishahn, M.W. & Gerheart, C.J. (1988). *The exceptional student in the regular classroom* (4th ed.). Columbus: Merrill.

Greenwood, C.R., Dinwiddie, G., Bailey, V., Carta, J.J., Dorsey, D., Kohler, F.W., Nelson, C., Rotholz, D. & Schulte, D. (1987). Field replication of classwide peer tutoring. *Journal of Applied Behavior Analysis, 20,* 151–60.

Greer, R.D. & Polirstok, S.R. (1982). Collateral gains and short-term maintenance in reading and on-task responses by some inner-city adolescents as a function of their use of social reinforcement while tutoring. *Journal of Applied Behavior Analysis, 15,* 123–39.

Harris, J. & Aldridge, J. (1983). Ten reasons why peer tutoring won't work. *Academic Therapy, 19* (1), 43–46.

Heron, T.E., Heward, W.L., Cook, N.L. & Hill, S. (1983). Evaluation of classwide peer tutoring systems: First graders teach each other sight words. *Education and Treatment of Children, 6,* 137–52.

Jenkins, J.J. & Jenkins, L.M. (1985). Peer tutoring in elementary and secondary programs. *Focus on Exceptional Children, 17* (6), 1–12.

Johnson, D.W., Johnson, R.T., Holubec, E.J. & Roy, P. (1984). *Circles of learning: Cooperation in the classroom.* Alexandria, VA: Association for Supervision and Curriculum Development.

Johnson, D.W., Maruyama, G., Johnson, R., Nelson, D. & Skon, L. (1981). Effects of cooperative, competitive, and individualistic goal structures on achievement: A meta-analysis. *Psychological Bulletin, 89,* 47–62.

Juel, C. (1991). Cross-age tutoring between student athletes and at-risk children. *The Reading Teacher, 45*(3), 178–86.

King, R.T. (1982). Learning from a PAL. *The Reading Teacher,* 35, 682–85.

Litow, L. & Pumroy, D.K. (1975). A brief review of classroom group-oriented contingencies. *Journal of Applied Behavioral Analysis, 8,* 341–47.

Madden, N.A., Slavin, R.E., & Stevens, R.J. (1986). *Cooperative integrated reading and composition: Teacher's manual.* Baltimore: Johns Hopkins University, Center for Research on Elementary and Middle Schools.

Maher, C.A. (1984). Handicapped adolescents as cross-age peer tutors: Program description and evaluation. *Exceptional Children, 51,* 56–63.

Manning, M.E. & Lucking, R. (1991). The what, why, and how of cooperative learning. *The Social Studies, 82* (3), 120–24.

McGlynn, R.P. (1982). A comment on the meta-analysis of goal structures. *Psychological Bulletin, 92,* 184–85.

Morsink, C.V. (1984). *Teaching special needs students in regular classrooms.* Boston: Little, Brown.

Niedermeyer, F.C. (1970). Effects of training on the instructional behaviors of student tutors. *Journal of Educational Research, 64,* 119–23.

Peters, T.J. & Waterman, R.H. (1982). *In search of excellence: Lessons from America's best companies.* New York: Harper & Row.

Rosenberg, M.S., O'Shea, L.J. & O'Shea, D.J. (1991). *Student teacher to master teacher: A handbook for preservice and beginning teachers of students with mild to moderate handicaps.* New York: Macmillan.

Rosenshine, B. & Stevens, R. (1986). Teaching functions. In M.C. Wittrock (ed.), *Handbook of research on teaching* (pp. 376–91.) New York: Macmillan.

Scruggs, T.E. & Richter, L. (1985). Tutoring learning disabled students: A critical review. *Learning Disability Quarterly, 8,* 286–89.

Slavin, R.E. (1978). Student teams and achievement divisions. *Journal of Research and Development in Education, 12,* 39–49.

Slavin, R.E., Leavey, M. & Madden, N.A. (1984). Combining cooperative learning and individualized instruction: Effects on student mathematics achievement, attitudes, and behaviors. *Elementary School Journal, 84,* 409–22.

Slavin, R.E., Madden, N.A. & Leavey, M. (1984). Effects of team assisted individualization on the mathematics achievement of academically handicapped and nonhandicapped students. *Journal of Educational Psychology, 116,* 227–83.

Slavin, R.E., Madden, N.A. & Stevens, R.J. (1990). Cooperative learning models for the 3 R's. *Educational Leadership, 47*(4), 22–28.

Stoddard, K. & Frye, B.J. (1993). *Intern exchange: Implementing the cooperative consultation model at the teacher training level.* Unpublished manuscript.

Stoddard, K. & Pike, C. (1990, March). *Reducing stress: Teaching can be enjoyable.* Paper presented at the Kentucky Council for Exceptional Children, Lexington, Ky.

Stoddard, K. & Valcante, G. (1991, April). *"Classroom buddies": Methods and effects of mainstreaming on special needs preschoolers and kindergarten regular education students.* Paper presented at the National Council for Exceptional Children Conference, Atlanta, GA.

Tateyama-Sniezek, K.M. (1990). Cooperative learning: Does it improve the academic achievement of students with handicaps? *Exceptional Children, 56* (5), 426–37.

Valcante, G. & Stoddard, K. (1990, May). *Peer tutoring in natural community settings: Strategies for teacher training.* Paper presented at the American Association on Mental Retardation, Atlanta, GA.

Walberg, H.J. & Wang, M.C. (1987). Effective educational practices and provisions for individual differences. In M.C. Wang, M.J. Reynolds & H.J. Walberg (eds.), *Handbook of special education: Research and practice, Vol. 1. Learner characteristics and adaptive education.* Toronto: Pergamon.

Chapter 9

Assessing Individual Children

By November of the first year Ms. Bateman taught fourth grade at Brady Elementary, she felt her class had settled into a routine and most students were progressing nicely. There were a few students, however, who puzzled and concerned her. She feared she was not meeting their needs very well. Her efforts to individualize instruction had left her feeling inadequate and unskilled in dealing with some of her students' problems. Hoping to get some help in working with a few of her students, Ms. Bateman scheduled a meeting with the Teacher Assistance Team, one of the special services teams at Brady.

There are 26 students enrolled in Ms. Bateman's fourth-grade class, including two children who have been identified as eligible to receive special education services and several other students who have special needs, although they have not yet been formally identified as exceptional children. The other fourth grade class has 28 students, but none of them has been identified as a student with disabilities. At Brady, teachers can indicate a preference for a larger class with fewer children who have special needs or a smaller class with more children who have special needs.

All children at Brady are educated in the regular classroom except those with severe or profound disabilities. For students in the regular classroom setting, special education services are provided by two special education teachers who work collaboratively with the other teachers. Usually the special education teachers provide indirect services through consultation or through technical assistance regarding specialized programs or techniques. Upon request, the special education teachers also co-teach classes with general education teachers. Because two children in Ms. Bateman's class have been identified as having disabilities, the special education teachers collaborate frequently with Ms. Bateman about programming and behavior management for both the two target students and the entire class.

At the beginning of the year, the special education teacher who functions in a resource role visited Ms. Bateman's class frequently. With his help, Ms. Bateman implemented a class structure based upon predictable, predetermined schedules and consequences. A general class schedule is posted on her front bulletin board and individual schedules are posted on students' desks and in Ms. Bateman's planning book. The individual schedules outline specific children's schedule variations. Each day begins with a brief class meeting to review the day's schedule, reinforce classroom procedures, and to discuss any unfinished business from the previous day. The morning is devoted to language arts, reading, and math, except

Wednesdays when the children have physical education. During this time, Ms. Bateman assigns the students to small groups. Groups have assigned tasks, and the students may help each other while Ms. Bateman rotates among the groups, teaching and monitoring progress.

When content lends itself to cooperative learning activities, Ms. Bateman prefers to use small, cooperative learning groups for instruction. Every third or fourth week, Ms. Bateman has changed membership in the groups to avoid cliques and to balance academic achievement levels. At this point she thinks most children enjoy the group work and work well together.

At the beginning of the year, Ms. Bateman also spent at least an hour a day for several weeks teaching and reviewing routines for going to the rest room, going to and from the cafeteria, getting ready for the bus, paying for lunch, getting supplies, and dealing with a variety of other transitions within the classroom. She enlisted the class in establishing consequences for following—or not following—the rules. This time now seems to have been spent productively because her class seems to operate almost automatically. The children know what is expected and how they get their own needs met. They know how to earn rewards and what will happen when they don't follow the rules.

When problems arise, the class discusses them. Impromptu meetings are held when a problem is interfering with the ongoing activities in the classroom. Students are encouraged to resolve problems among themselves, and, if necessary, Ms. Bateman acts as a mediator. At the end of each day the class meeting includes a summary of the day's highlights; students may raise issues or concerns. The most frequent topic has been the class rule specifying that children "treat others with respect and kindness."

When problems are not resolved through routine classroom procedures or classroom problem-solving discussions, teachers may seek assistance from either the teacher assistance team or the child study team. The Teacher Assistance Team (TAT) was instituted for the primary purpose of helping teachers plan and implement interventions that will either provide extra support (so children do not have to move to more restrictive settings) or be diagnostically useful first steps in the referral process to special education. This team consists of the assistant principal and elected teachers on the faculty. Currently there are two special education teachers, a general education teacher from the lower elementary grades, and a general education teacher from the upper elementary grades. Since this team has been in operation, referrals to special education have been reduced by over 50%. Meetings are held weekly on Monday afternoons. Members of the team and teachers who are presenting to the team are provided substitute teachers during the team meetings.

The Child Study Team (CST) has as its primary purpose the coordination of all procedures related to the identification, evaluation, and placement of students with disabilities. This team is responsible for planning and reviewing assessment data, overseeing the creation of the IEP, and monitoring re-evaluations and IEP revisions in accord with the provisions of IDEA (the Individuals with Disabilities Education Act). Permanent members of this team are the guidance counselor, an elected general education teacher, and one of the special education teachers (who is also on the teacher assistance team). An administrator attends all initial placement meetings and the school psychologist attends as many of the meetings as she can. Temporary members include the parent(s) and the teacher(s) of the child being discussed.

Teams of teachers working together provide valuable support and technical assistance to each other.

In this chapter, we will follow the assessment process of four of Ms. Bateman's students. For each student we will give a brief background synopsis, a synopsis of the special services team meeting, the type of information gathered through the assessment techniques or instruments, and the outcome recommendations. At the end of the chapter there are brief synopses about each of the assessment tools and procedures. Also included are guidelines and general information about the assessment process for persons who are working in settings that do not have school-based assessment teams.

The Referral Process:
Challenges and Opportunities

To initiate the assessment process, Ms. Bateman notified the chairperson of the teacher assistance team that she wanted to be included on the agenda. Ms. Bateman was asked to complete a brief referral form (Figure 9.1), and shortly

Figure 9.1 Teacher Assistance Referral Form

Brady Elementary
Request for Teacher Assistance Team (TAT)

To: Teacher assistance team facilitator

From _____

Please place the following item on the TAT agenda. Thank you.

Name of student(s) to discuss: _____

Situation: _____

_____

_____

Please check below if you would like to specifically invite any of these staff:

___ principal   ___ assistant principal ___ guidance counselor ___ psychologist

___ special education teacher ___ social worker ___ behavior management resources

date _____

thereafter she received a notice specifying when the team meeting would be held and a list of topics on the agenda. She assumed there would be an informal discussion about her class and afterwards someone would come and help her. The meeting, however, was not what she expected. Discussion was focused and participants were informed. Ms. Bateman actually felt a bit intimidated and unprepared. Everybody else seemed to know what they were talking about, so she was uncomfortable admitting her lack of preparation. She was also surprised by how much work they expected from her. She thought they would come in and solve her problems, but the team members clearly expected her to solve her own problems with assistance from them.

At the end of the team discussion, Ms. Bateman agreed that she needed to gather additional information about the children she had discussed. The team thought these data would help clarify questions and concerns about each child. The team also specified the best methods to gather the needed information. They had available a variety of techniques, both formal and informal, and standardized, norm-referenced instruments as well as criterion-referenced measures—but their approach was more than just testing. Their process consisted of collecting information that would help specify and verify problems and make decisions about students (Salvia & Ysseldyke, 1991). Because Brady Elementary tries to include all children in general education classes, their focus tended to be on accommodations that would support success within the classroom, rather than referral to another class or program. By the end of the meeting, Ms. Bateman felt both intrigued and apprehensive. It was clear to her that she would learn more about assessment procedures, but she really did not feel prepared to function in that role. She was discouraged by her efforts to remedy the problems, and really wanted relief.

While the structure of the specific referral procedures at Brady Elementary was set by the administration, it is in accord with guidelines established by the school district, and with state and federal laws. IDEA specifies a number of conditions that must be met related to assessment. The first has to do with *parental involvement.* School systems are clearly expected to encourage and enable the active and meaningful involvement of parents in decisions regarding their children. Before a child can participate in any individualized assessment activity, parents must consent. (See Table 9.1 for a list of parent and child rights specified in IDEA.) IDEA also specifies functions that must be performed by a *multidisciplinary committee.* Most districts have established school-based committees function as coordinators to carry out the duties specified by law. IDEA specifies that the following persons must be present for the IEP meeting: a person from the educational program who can commit resources (an administrator); the student's teacher; one or both of the child's parents; the student when appropriate; and, at the first IEP meeting, a member of the evaluation team or someone who can interpret the evaluation procedures.

At Brady *prereferral teams* were established to help teachers and students before formal entry into special education. Similar teacher teams are being established in many schools; they may be called by different names such as educational management teams or school instructional teams (Strickland & Turnbull, 1990), teacher assistance teams (Chalfant, Pysh, & Moultrie, 1979), school consultation committees (McGlothlin, 1981), and a preintervention team (Graden, Casey, & Christenson, 1985). These teams were developed in response to the growing body of research suggesting that most children referred for evaluation were placed in special education programs (Algozzine, Christenson, & Ysseldyke, 1982). For example, Sevick and Ysseldyke (1986) found that 92% of children who were referred for possible evaluation were tested and 75% of the children tested were placed. Pugach and Johnson (1989) hypothesized that existing structures require teachers publicly to defend their reasons for referring children, thereby forcing teachers prematurely to decide that a child needs services. Since the team members are largely colleagues of the referring teacher, they are inclined to support the teacher's appraisal. "No mechanism exists for a reinterpretation of the teacher's initial perception of the situation, although such early perceptions may not represent an accurate reflection of the actual problem. The problem as it is initially conceptualized by the referring teacher may be concretized prematurely" (Pugach & Johnson, 1989, p. 218).

Additionally, studies have reported that, until prereferral teams were instituted, teachers in general education programs made few substantive educational

Table 9.1 Procedural Safeguards Specified in IDEA

Right to due process
1. A due process hearing may be initiated by either parents or public agency when there are differences of opinion that cannot be otherwise resolved. The due process hearing is an impartial forum for discussing the issues.
2. Any party may:
    (a) have representation by counsel or be advised by an expert in the field,
    (b) present evidence,
    (c) cross-examine witness(es),
    (d) prohibit introduction of evidence that has not been shared with other party at least 5 days prior to presentation,
    (e) obtain written verbatim record of proceedings, and
    (f) obtain written findings.
3. The educational agency must assume the cost of the hearing.

Independent educational evaluation
1. Parents may obtain an outside evaluation at the public agency's expense if they are dissatisfied with the evaluation done by the public agency.
2. School system must consider the outside evaluation in its deliberations.

Notification of action and meetings
1. School systems are obligated to provide parents with the following notices:
    (a) full listing of due process safeguards,
    (b) description of action taken,
    (c) rationale for action and evidence used in decision making, and
    (d) description of other factors that were considered.
2. These notices must be in parent's primary language.
3. Parents have the right to be fully informed of and to attend meetings that have to do with evaluation.

Consent
1. Parental consent is required before:
    (a) initial evaluation, and
    (b) initial placement.
2. Although consent is not required for continuation in special education, notice must be given if changes in placement are proposed.

Confidentiality of educational records
1. Access to records is limited to persons who have official business and who have been approved for such.
2. A list must be available of all persons who have access.
3. Parents may review records and request that they be destroyed when agency no longer needs information.
4. Parents may request that information be explained and they may request the records be amended to correct inaccurate information.

Withdrawal of consent
Parents have the right to withdraw consent for evaluation or placement.

modifications before referring students (Ammer, 1984; Munson, 1986; Pugach, 1985; Zigmond, Levin, & Laurie, 1985). Furthermore, despite legal preference, special education programs are often perceived as responsible for the education of exceptional children (Strickland & Turnbull, 1990). General education teachers report perceiving themselves as lacking necessary time, skills, or resources to deal with exceptional children, hence they are often willing—even eager—to relinquish responsibility for them (Gartner & Lipsky, 1987). In some states, funding formulas have also supported the provision of services in segregated settings because school districts receive more money for children placed in self-contained settings or pull-out programs than for children in general education settings (Blackman, 1989).

Pre-referral teams work with classroom teachers to keep challenging students in general education settings. Reports indicate that these teams can be productive settings that promote professional sharing, support, and training; however, they can consume considerable amounts of time and require considerable paperwork. As in the case of Ms. Bateman, they can also be intimidating if productive channels of communication are not established among members of the team and the general school faculty (Harrington & Gibson, 1986). In schools where these teams have functioned effectively, referrals to special education have been reduced (Morsink, Thomas, & Correa, 1991).

Case One: Kisha   Ms. Bateman's first referral was Kisha, a bright, verbal child who is younger than most of the children in the class. Kisha has difficulty paying attention and completing tasks; she is easily distracted and very active. To Ms. Bateman, it seems that Kisha is always out of her seat, talking with her neighbors, and wiggling. Kisha frequently forgets her papers, books, jackets, and lunch. Ms. Bateman is often frustrated when working with her because Kisha demands so much attention and has difficulty following through on instructions and completing her work. Academically, Kisha is average to slightly above average. Homework completion is inconsistent; she turns in her work about half the time. Kisha's tests and quizzes range from outstanding to below average, with no consistent pattern. Although Kisha is presently at grade level according to the district's yearly achievement tests, Ms. Bateman worries that she will fall behind because of her lack of self-discipline and organization. She wonders whether Kisha might have an attention deficit disorder that could benefit from medication.

The team meeting started with Ms. Bateman's describing Kisha and her difficulties. Team members asked a lot of specific questions that Ms. Bateman had never really considered. What happens when . . . ? How does Kisha feel when you do . . . ? How frequently does . . . happen? Ms. Bateman was taken aback. She had come to them for help, but they were asking her questions she felt compelled to answer even though she had never really thought about them. The discussion helped her realize how little she really knew about Kisha. She told the team that she felt she needed to learn a lot more about Kisha before she was really prepared to talk about interventions, and team members suggested that Ms. Bateman collect direct observations, complete a behavior checklist, review Kisha's records, and talk with her parents.

Observations. After some discussion about what was feasible and what would be most useful, the team decided that Ms. Bateman should collect the following observational data:

- ☐ Duration of time on task
- ☐ Frequency of out-of-seat behavior
- ☐ Frequency of forgetting homework, books, jackets, and lunch
- ☐ Ratio of assignments given and assignments completed
- ☐ Grades on assignments completed

The team recommended that Ms. Bateman start with the frequency counts so she could further define the nature of Kisha's problems and identify her successes. Ms. Bateman created a chart that divided the day by periods (Figure 9.2). She attached a watch to a clipboard where she kept the chart and carried them throughout the day. For two weeks, every time Kisha exhibited one of the problematic behaviors listed on the chart, Ms. Bateman tallied or noted it. When she noticed that Kisha was working on task, Ms. Bateman timed the duration and noted it.

At the end of each week, Ms. Bateman compiled the data by adding the total tallies for each problematic behavior during each period. Since she had followed her schedule fairly closely, she did not compute a rate for the data. Had the amount of time for each period varied considerably, she would have computed a ratio of frequency divided by time. Furthermore, she considered the first data gathering rudimentary—simply intended to help her better define the problem.

Inspection of her data indicated that social studies was Kisha's best period and language arts her most problematic. Tuesday (Figure 9.2) was fairly typical. Altogether Kisha appeared to be working on task 43 minutes of the 120. She was out of her seat ten times; she did one of the four assignments and did not do well on it; and she did not bring in her homework. Compared to her performance in social studies, this was noteworthy; however, Ms. Bateman did not have a ready explanation for these differences in performance.

At the suggestion of one of the TAT members, she collected more data that might help her sort out why Kisha was having trouble. She decided to collect A-B-C observations each time she noticed that Kisha was distracted (Figure 9.3). A-B-C observations are anecdotal observations that are recorded in three columns: *antecedent* (what happened prior to child's behavior), *behavior* (of target child), and *consequence* (what happened after child's actions). These observations

Figure 9.2 Example of Data Recording Form

Brady Elementary
Data Recording Form

Name: _Kisha_   Date _Tues_ Day _2_

Purpose of Observation _____

	Period 1	Period 2	Period 3	Period 4	Period 5	Period 6
Subject	Lang Arts	Soc. St.	Math	Science	PE	Art
Time	8:30-10:30	10:45-11:15	11:20-12	12:30-1:15	1:20-2:00	2:05-2:50
Time on task	10 35 6 22 4 83	all	5 362 1 55	30	—	—
Out of Seat	₸₸₸ ₸₸₸	/	////	//	—	₸₸₸ /
Assignments Given	4	2	3	2	—	/
Assignments Completed	/	2	½	/	—	/
Assignment Grade	poorly done	A	Inc.	B	did well!	did well even tho
Other:						Out of seat.
Other:	No HW		No HW			
Other:						

Comments:

Figure 9.3 Example of Behavioral Observation—
Student A-B-C Observation Form

BEHAVIORAL OBSERVATION - STUDENT

STUDENT: __Kisha__   GRADE: __4__   DATE: __12/5__

TEACHER: __7. Bateman__ SCHOOL: __Brady__

ANTECEDENT	BEHAVIOR	CONSEQUENCE
8:35 I assigned pp. 82 & 83 in wkbk	K took out book & started leafing thru it	8:45 - I ? if she knew what to do
she shook her head. I told her pp. again	she worked a few minutes & started gazing out window	8:57 I walked by pointed to next problem — gave reminder
reminder	she returned to work (3 min) then gazed out	9:05 - I ? if something was wrong & ? if she understood work
my ?	she nodded yes & showed me her work - 2/8 wrong	I pointed out her errors
my correction	she corrected & resumed work	I stood close by & watched
me-close	K worked (10 min !)	I moved away to answer Ben's ?
I moved	K watched me started working for st. in her desk	I returned & ? how she was doing -
my ?	K went back to work	

RECOMMENDATIONS: _As long as I stood close to Kisha, she worked — but she was easily distracted when no one was watching_

INDIVIDUAL BEHAVIOR PROGRAM NECESSARY: Y   N

SIGNATURE: _____

helped her form hypotheses about the classroom conditions that exist when Kisha has difficulty and the classroom conditions that maintain Kisha's behavior. Figure 9.3 is a brief excerpt from one of the observation sheets. As can be seen on this sheet, Kisha had difficulty working independently. When Ms. Bateman was standing close by, Kisha worked. When Ms. Bateman was paying attention to others, Kisha looked out the window and made errors in work she seemed to understand.

Ms. Bateman then decided to collect data in social studies, the class in which Kisha seemed most involved, to determine what differences might exist that would explain Kisha's behavior. To the extent possible, Ms. Bateman collected data during language arts and social studies for one week. She kept her clipboard and her watch with her at all times during these periods. For this one week, during both Language Arts and Social Studies, Ms. Bateman recorded the beginning and ending times of the class and made quick notes so she could reconstruct an A-B-C chart. She jotted down duration of problematic behavior as well. Whenever Kisha spontaneously returned to work, Ms. Bateman noted the conditions. At the end of each day, she transferred her notes to an A-B-C sheet and wrote more comprehensive notes. At the end of the week, she reviewed the data to see if there were patterns. It appeared that Kisha did best in situations where she was busy and engaged, and did poorly when she had quiet seatwork or had to listen to the teacher. In social studies, the class had been building topographical maps in cooperative groups. Kisha's job had been to read directions to the group as they tried to complete their map. In language arts, the class had been expected to complete seatwork or listen to Ms. Bateman's lectures.

While these data seemed to indicate that Kisha has difficulty when she is assigned seatwork and listening to lectures, the data do not clarify why Kisha has these problems. Without some notions of what is causing the problem, it is difficult to select possible interventions; consequently, additional data were gathered about Kisha's intellectual and achievement level, as well as her medical and social/emotional history.

Developmental history. Ms. Bateman scheduled a conference with Kisha's parents to find out more about her behavior at home, her development prior to school, and her medical history. She used an outline for gathering developmental histories recommended by the guidance counselor (Table 9.2). Ms. Bateman started the interview by asking for factual information such as how many brothers and sisters Kisha has, their names, ages, others in the home, and so on (information in the Identifying Information section that was not in Kisha's chart). These questions prompted Kisha's mom to talk about their life as a family. Ms. Bateman jotted short notes, but mostly she listened carefully. She used the outline in Table 9.2 so that she would be certain to cover all important topics, but conducted the interview in a comfortable, supportive, conversational

Table 9.2 Case History Information

Identifying Information
Child: name, address, telephone, date of birth, school, grade
Parents: father's name and occupation; mother's name and occupation
Family: sibling's names and ages; others in the home
Clinic: date of interview; referral agency; name of examiner

Birth History
Pregnancy: length, condition of mother, unusual factors
Birth conditions: mature or premature; duration of labor, weight, unusual circumstances
Conditions following birth

Physical and Developmental Data
Health history: accidents, high fevers, other illnesses
Parents' health: habit of eating and sleeping, energy and activity level
Developmental history: age of sitting, walking, first words, first sentences, language
   difficulties, motor difficulties

Social and Personal Factors
Friends
Sibling relationships
Hobbies, interests, recreational activities
Home and parent attitudes
Acceptance of responsibility
Attitude toward learning problem

Educational Factors
School experiences: skipped or repeated grades, moving, change of teachers
Preschool education: kindergarten, nursery school
Special help previously received
Teachers' reports
Child's attitude toward school

atmosphere. Kisha's mother reported that Kisha had not had any unusual medical problems, and that Kisha had progressed through the developmental steps within the normal time frames (walking at 16 months, jumping at 2½ years). Her mother reported that Kisha was "always into everything from age 3 to 7, but has calmed down a lot in the last few years." The parents reported that they were generally happy with Kisha's achievement level, but said she was also disorganized at home and needed consistent reminding to pick up her possessions. The parents gave permission for Ms. Bateman to contact Kisha's pediatrician for more detailed information. The physician said he saw Kisha only a few times a year for routine checkups and ordinary childhood illnesses. He reported that Kisha had been born prematurely, but she had quickly caught up with her age mates with respect to developmental milestones. He said he had no idea that she exhibited any signs of attention deficit, and suggested that Ms. Bateman might complete a behavior checklist to see how her perceptions of Kisha compare with other teachers' views of children with and without attention problems.

Cognitive ability.   District level ability testing had been conducted in the third grade, and the special education teacher administered a screening tool to Kisha to further determine her ability level. In accord with the law, when the assessment procedure involves administering an individual academic, social, or behavioral instrument, the parents were notified by Ms. Bateman of her wish to assess their child and the reason for the assessment. The district administered the cognitive abilities test (Thorndike & Hagen, 1993) to all third-graders at Brady Elementary. Kisha scored at the 80th percentile on the verbal battery, the 75th percentile on the quantitative battery, and the 93rd percentile on the nonverbal battery. After obtaining her parents permission, the special education teacher administered the Slosson Intelligence Test—Revised (SIT) (Slosson, 1990). It is a short screening test used to obtain estimates of cognitive ability. Since Kisha scored in the above-average range on both measures, further testing was not recommended.

Behavior checklist.   To compare Kisha with other groups of children, Ms. Bateman, Kisha, and her parents completed the behavior rating scales from the Behavior Rating Profile (BRP-2) (Brown & Hamill, 1990). The BRP-2 is a set of behavior rating forms. One is completed by the parents, one by the teacher(s), and a three-part scale is completed by the student. Parents are presented with statements such as "My child _____ complains about doing assigned chores or lies to avoid punishment or responsibility." Parents indicated whether the statement is very much like their child, like their child, not much like their child, or not at all like their child. The teacher form is similar in format, but the content pertains more to school. For example, the teacher form includes items such as "The student _____ tattles on classmates and doesn't follow directions." Both the parent and the teacher forms include 30 items. The student rating form contains 60 questions, some about home ("My parents bug me a lot"), some about school ("My teacher often gets angry with me"), and some about peers ("I don't have enough friends"). Ratings are compared to the performance of the 1362 children in the standardization sample, all of whom were enrolled in general education programs.

As can be seen from the BRP of Figure 9.4, Kisha's ratings of her relationship with peers fell below 7—as did her mother's and teacher's ratings. Scores below 7 are considered to differ significantly from the norm and are cause for concern.

Outcomes and recommendations.   When all the data were collected, the team met again to discuss how to serve Kisha in the classroom. Ms. Bateman had studied the data as they were collected and was now convinced there were a number of adaptations she could make in her classroom that might help Kisha.

Figure 9.4 Example of Behavior Rating Sheet

B R P

BEHAVIOR RATING PROFILE SHEET

LINDA L. BROWN & DONALD D. HAMMILL

Name _Kisha_

Parent's Name _____

Address _____

School _Brady_

Teacher (Grade) _Bateman_ (_4_)

Examiner _____

Referred by _____

(Scaled Scores: Mean = 10, Standard deviation = 3)

COMMENTS:

Date Tested _____ YEAR _____ MONTH

Date of Birth _____ YEAR _____ MONTH

Age _____ YEARS _____ MONTHS

BRP Scales	Raw Scores	Scaled Scores
Student Rating Scales		
Home Scale	15	10
School Scale	12	8
Peer Scale	4	5
Teacher Rating Scale		
Teacher # 1	44	6
Teacher # 2		
Teacher # 3		
Parent Rating Scale		
Mother	45	45
Father		
Other		
Sociogram		
Question # 1		
Question # 2		
Question # 3		

© Copyright 1978, Linda L. Brown & Donald D. Hammill

Additional copies of this form are available from PRO-ED, 333 Perry Brooks Building, Austin, Texas 78701

When she went to the teacher assistance team this time, she felt empowered and ready to participate in improving Kisha's educational program.

Together Ms. Bateman and members of the team outlined the following plan:

1. Ms. Bateman would set up a contract with Kisha that specified goals to increase the number of finished work assignments and improve in-seat and on-task behavior.

2. Ms. Bateman would teach Kisha to monitor her own behavior. First, Ms. Bateman and Kisha would both collect data and Kisha would earn a privilege of her choice if the data corresponded.

3. Kisha would be given the option of moving to a study carrel when she was having difficulty concentrating. The study carrels were equipped with headphones that could be used to block out classroom sounds. They also had a clock so that Kisha could keep track of how long she took to complete assignments.

4. Notes would be sent home about her progress, in an effort to involve her family in a positive rather than punishing way.

Case Two: Max　From her experience in presenting Kisha to the teacher assistance team, Ms. Bateman better understood how the team could help her. When she later presented Max, she knew what questions she wanted to ask and had a clearer vision of the kind of help she wanted. Ms. Bateman sees Max as a bright, likable boy who seems well adjusted around her, but has had a history of unpredictable eruptions in school. Academically, he does average work and there seem to be no concerns. Behaviorally, although Ms. Bateman has had no problems with him, he has gotten into fights on the playground and has been suspended from school for fighting on the bus. Previous teachers report liking him, but not knowing him well. His family seems highly supportive of the school and very concerned about Max's doing well. As far as Ms. Bateman knows, there are no stressors in his life that would cause him to have the social problems he has. While Ms. Bateman believes there must be a problem, she does not know what it is.

This time, when Ms. Bateman consulted with the teacher assistance team, she wanted information about what type of data to collect and how best to collect it. Together Ms. Bateman and the team decided that they needed more information about *when* Max got into trouble—what precipitated the problem, what followed the problem, and how Max saw the situation. Ms. Bateman developed a critical incident report form that she agreed to complete after each incident (Figure 9.5). After several such episodes, data from these forms might help them understand what is triggering the outbursts.

One of the team members suggested that she do peer ratings. Since no one seemed to know Max well, Ms. Bateman thought this an intriguing idea.

Figure 9.5 Example of Critical Incident Report Form

Observation of: _____   Observer: _____

Date: _____ Time: _____ Place: _____ *Activity: _____ * Problematic behavior: How long did it last? _____ min./ hr. Describe:	What happened to the child or in child's proximity immediately before the behavior occured?	How was the difficulty resolved? (How was the behavior stopped?)
Date: _____ Time: _____ Place: _____ *Activity: _____ * Problematic behavior: How long did it last? _____ min./ hr. Describe:	What happened to the child or in child's proximity immediately before the behavior occured?	How was the difficulty resolved? (How was the behavior stopped?)
Date: _____ Time: _____ Place: _____ *Activity: _____ * Problematic behavior: How long did it last? _____ min./ hr. Describe:	What happened to the child or in child's proximity immediately before the behavior occured?	How was the difficulty resolved? (How was the behavior stopped?)

*Activity: Reading, art, lunch, etc. In the next slot specify
    1. if the activity is directed and controlled by the teacher,
    2. if the teacher is present and available but not directing the activity, or
    3. if the teacher is not present.

Moreover, it would give her valuable information about all the students in her class. Ms. Bateman's colleague shared two different sociometric strategies, both described in the training manual for the Iowa Assessment Model in Behavioral Disorders (Wood, Smith, & Grimes, 1985). One of the approaches involves students rating their classmates on a global like–dislike scale. The other contains specific stems. Respondents rate classmates on the specific stems. After some deliberation, Ms. Bateman decided to use both strategies because they provided complimentary information. She modified the forms presented in the Iowa Model to fit her own needs. She reasoned that data from the instrument depicted in Figure 9.6 would tell her how well all students in her class were regarded by their classmates. Data from the instrument in Figure 9.7 would provide clues regarding why some children were popular and others unpopular.

Figure 9.6 Illustration of the Peer Nomination Technique

	Would like to have him/her as one of my best friends	Would like to have him/her in my group but not as a close friend	Would like to be with him/her once in a while but not often nor for a long time	Would rather not have anything to do with him/her	Dislike him/her
1. Jeff					
2. Ola					
3. David					
4. Mike					
5. Sharon					
6. Kofi					
7. Sun Le					

Ms. Bateman and the TAT also decided that she would gather some informal data from Max. One of the team members suggested she try storywriting, a process in which the teacher writes an interpretive narrative of a particular event. Usually it is a sequential story of events, including suspected emotional states of participants and the events or activities the teacher suspects influenced the events. The teacher must recognize that these are her impressions and note such in the writing. Phrases like "I felt the child was extremely angry" instead of "the child was extremely angry" are used to portray the interpretive nature of the story. While one is free to write about possible feelings and theorize about causes and solutions in interpretive storywriting, one must also use care and professional judgment because the stories may be examined by other professionals and by the parents.

Outcomes and recommendations. After the discussion with the teacher assistance team, Ms. Bateman began collecting data. It took several months for her to have the type of data she felt she needed because Max's outbursts were infrequent. After reviewing four such outbursts and data from the peer nomination and storywriting, Ms. Bateman decided that Max's problems stemmed from poor social skills. His peers said he bragged about being able to do things that he really could not do. They also said that he messed up games when he joined in. After several such comments, Ms. Bateman made a point of observing Max in groups. She noticed that he tended to dominate conversations, expected other children to follow his lead, and neither listened carefully to what they said nor

Figure 9.7 Illustration of the Peer Rating Technique

DIRECTIONS: The purpose of this activity is to find out which people in the class do certain things more than others. You will see 16 phrases listed down the left of the page with the names of people in our class listed across the page. Select the three students who are most like the phrase, then select the three students who are least like the phrase. Put a "+" under the students who are most like the phrase. Put a "−" under the students who are least like the phrase.

	Jeff	Ola	David	Mike	Sharon	Kofi	Sun Le
1. Says nice things to others							
2. Is friendly to others							
3. Listens to others							
4. Helps others							
5. Cooperates with others							
6. Shares with others							
7. Pays attention in class							
8. Understands others							
9. Is considerate of others' feelings							
10. Is fun to talk to							
11. Is liked by others							
12. Is happy when others are successful							
13. Plays games fairly							
14. Contributes to class teams							
15. Is easy to work with							
16. Is trustworthy							

attended to their wishes. His outbursts all occurred after another student goaded him about something he was unable to do. It seemed Max was unable to tolerate the everyday teasing that kids often engage in. Thus they tended to tease him even more.

The team concurred with Ms. Bateman that social skills instruction might benefit Max as well as other children. After some discussion, Ms. Bateman decided to institute a daily 15–20 minute social skills activity based upon *Skillstreaming the Elementary School Child* (McGinnis & Goldstein, 1984). She felt it was appropriate to involve the entire class in this program because Max clearly was not the only child who might benefit from the activities.

Case Three: Harold   Harold is older than his classmates, and he has already been identified as having emotional and behavioral disabilities. He is currently eligible for special education services within the regular classroom; however, Ms. Bateman is beginning to wonder if he does not need to be in a more restrictive setting.

Harold and his family are well known to most of the school's faculty. Harold is the fourth-born child in a family of six children. All his older brothers and sisters have had behavior problems at school, and all tested within low academic ranges. Harold's mother is drug dependent, and has been convicted of prostitution. She has left the family for months at a time on several occasions; she is currently out of the home and her children do not know where she is or how to contact her. The father owns a small store and provides adequately for the family when he is sober. However, he drinks heavily, and sometimes goes on binges that are frightening to the children. Given these circumstances, the older children are often left to care for the younger ones. Harold rarely talks about his family at school. On the few occasions when he joins in, he mentions his older sister with some affection.

Harold has come to school with bruises. When he came with bruises on his face the first time this year, Ms. Bateman asked Harold how he got the bruise. Harold replied "I fell down" and would not elaborate. Ms. Bateman was concerned about possible abuse, but she had no clear evidence, so she consulted with her principal. Ms. Bateman thought she should report her concerns to the child protection services, but was not certain how to proceed. Her principal told her that others had been through the same routine and that each time it happened he feared for Harold. The principal thinks the father abuses Harold whenever questions are raised, but everyone in the family covers up the abuse so well that it is impossible to establish any evidence. On several occasions Harold has implied that his father caused the bruises, but no one in the family, including Harold, will acknowledge abuse when investigators visit the home.

Ms. Bateman is very concerned about how best to help Harold. She knows that whenever abuse is suspected, teachers are required by law to report their concerns; yet if the investigation results in more abuse but no help, she questions whether it is really the right course of action. She does not want to break the law; neither does she want this child to be abused anymore. This dilemma is making her wish Harold were with a more experienced teacher and in a more restrictive setting.

In addition to her concerns about abuse, Ms. Bateman is discouraged by Harold's lack of progress with his reading and math skills. He is approximately a year and a half behind his classmates in most academic activities, he rarely participates in group discussions, and he does not turn in his assignments. When Ms. Bateman works individually with him he completes his work, but at other times, he seems to have no confidence in his abilities. When his classmates attempt to help him, he wants them to give him the answer but will not work with them or accept tutorial help. Harold's handwriting is very difficult to read, and his oral reading is slow, cautious, and delivered with little expression. He does have good comprehension for what he reads, however. Harold comes to school many days so sleepy he cannot stay awake. When questioned Harold will not say why he is so sleepy.

Harold has few friends; most of the children seem to be afraid of him. Ms. Bateman is also uncomfortable around him sometimes. His manner is gruff, he often scowls, and his third-grade teacher remarked "He's like a time bomb waiting to explode." Early in the school year, Harold got into an altercation with another boy on the playground. They found a baseball. Since they could not find its owner, they decided they could keep it but the boys argued about who should get it. The other boy challenged Harold, saying he saw the ball first and that it should be his. Harold picked up the baseball bat and swung it at the other boy. The teacher on playground duty saw him, and shouted at him to drop the bat. He did, but he went through the rest of the day angry and sullen.

Ms. Bateman wonders if Harold would be better served in a more restrictive setting. She currently gives him special independent assignments, she takes care to place him in groups with other children who are very patient and willing to work with him, and she tutors him independently 3 days a week. She has placed fewer demands on him than the other children, and tolerates some behavior from him that she does not tolerate from other children. While believing that each child is an individual, she sometimes wonders how fair the differential treatment is. She also wonders if she might be doing something else to help Harold be more successful at school.

Ms. Bateman took her concerns to the Teacher Assistance Team before going to the Child Study Team because she wanted to make certain that she had done all that she could before consideration of a change in placement by the Child Study Team. Even though she thought a more restrictive setting might be needed, she was reluctant to share her concerns with the family. She also wanted another forum in which to explore what to do regarding the suspected abuse.

The Teacher Assistance Team was familiar with Harold's case and listened carefully to the program he was currently receiving. Given the information and the degree of Ms. Bateman's concern, the team agreed that it was time for a careful examination of Harold's academic progress and social/emotional development. They began by focusing on Harold's reported lack of emotional and social progress over the last few years. If the team planned to discuss a change of placement into a more restrictive environment, the father would need to be informed and referral would need to be made to the Child Study Team. Before taking such action, the Teacher Assistance Team recommended that Ms. Bateman carefully review information from the school folder and past psychological records. They also requested that the special education teacher on the team visit the classroom and observe.

Observational reports.   Ms. Seng, the special education teacher who visited the classroom, gathered observational data using a momentary time sampling technique. She chose this technique because it enabled her to collect data on several different behaviors during the same session. In momentary time sampling, the observer records the behavior that is occurring when the predetermined interval occurs. In Ms. Seng's case, at every 10-second interval Ms. Seng coded and recorded Harold's behavior. Ms. Seng knew this system well and could keep up the pace of recording a behavior every 10 seconds. She used the recording code listed at the bottom of Figure 9.8. In some instances, she noted specific behaviors in the comments column on the form. After establishing that Harold's problems were most prominent during language arts, Ms. Seng took data for 20 minutes each day for two weeks using a time sampling method.

At the end of two weeks, Ms. Seng compiled the data and charted it using a bar graph. Although graphing seemed like a lot of work, the visual picture helped make sense of the data and made it easier for Ms. Seng to show others what she had found. As can be seen in Figure 9.9, Harold's two most prevalent off-task behaviors were putting his head down and making disruptive noises. For the purpose of graphing, she decided to aggregate the less frequent behaviors into a category called "other off-task behaviors." Included in this category were: talking out, verbal and physical aggression, "strange" (catch-all for problematic behavior not specifically coded), profanity, and teacher interventions.

Ms. Seng found that on most days, Harold was off task for more than half the observation period. The graph provided Ms. Bateman a visual representation that enabled comparison of on-task behaviors with inappropriate behaviors.

Referral reports.   Ms. Bateman also reviewed the reports written when Harold was sent to the office over the past year. She found that Harold had been referred to the office ten times. Four referrals were from the lunchroom; two times were for noncompliance, once was for yelling, and once was for threatening a student from another class. He had been referred three times by his bus driver for yelling, including once for yelling a profanity at a passing motorist. He had been referred twice by teachers on playground duty for bullying other children, and once for throwing the girls' jumprope on the roof. In looking at the dates, she found that four of the referrals were during one particular week this year.

Review of records.   Ms. Bateman also reviewed Harold's school and psychological records. With Harold currently receiving special education services, she

Figure 9.8 Time Sample Form

Brady Elementary
Twenty Minute Time Sample Form

Date __9/10__   Name __Harold S.__
Beginning Time: __9:20__   Observer: __MRS. Seng__
End Time: __9:40__
Purpose of Observation: __Record off task behaviors in Lang. Arts.__

This form is designed to assist in the collection of time samples with 10 second intervals.
Type of data: ___ whole interval ___ partial interval __✓__ momentary time sample

Minutes/ Seconds	10	20	30	40	50	60	Comments
1.	+	+	H	H	H	H	
2.	H	N	N	N	+	+	
3.	T	T	+	+	+	+	
4.	+	N	S	S	S	T	chewing on
5.	T	N	N	+	+	+	shirt
6.	+	+	N	N	T	T	
7.	IA	T	VA	TI	+	+	Tapped students
8.	+	+	+	+	+	N	head.
9.	N	T	T	VA	VA	P	argued c
10.	VA	PA	PA	PA	TI	P	hit other kid—
11.	TI	+	+	+	+	+	teacher stopped
12.	+	+	+	+	+	+	
13.	+	+	+	H	H	H	
14.	H	H	H	H	N	N	
15.	N	TI	H	H	H	H	
16.	H	H	H	H	H	H	Teacher: "Head
17.	TI	+	+	+	+	+	up, please"
18.	+	+	+	H	H	H	↓
19.	H	TI	+	+	+	+	same
20.	+	+	N	N	+	+	

Key for Behavior Codes

Code __+__ Meaning: __On task__   Code __PA__ Meaning: __Physical Aggression__
Code __H__ Meaning: __Head down__   Code __VA__ Meaning: __Verbal Aggression__
Code __T__ Meaning: __Talking out__   Code __S__ Meaning: __Strange Behavior__
Code __N__ Meaning: __Noises__   Code __P__ Meaning: __Profanity__
Code __IA__ Meaning: __Inappropriate Interactions__   Code __TI__ Meaning: __Teacher Intervention__

Figure 9.9 Harold's Off-Task Behaviors for Reading, PE, Recess, and Language Arts

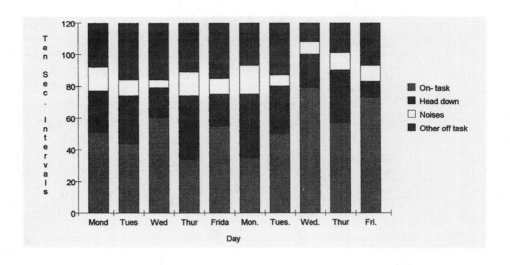

found achievement tests and cognitive functioning tests from an updated staffing review that was a year and a half old. She found that Harold's intelligence test scores on the Wechsler Intelligence Scale for Children III were within the "average" range, with an obtained score of 89. Harold had been given the Test of Education Achievement—Comprehensive Form (Kaufman & Kaufman, 1985). He earned a percentile rank of 15 on the Reading Composite and a percentile rank of 5 on the Math Composite.

His third-grade teacher had been asked to complete a behavior rating scale, the Comprehensive Behavior Rating Scale for Children (CBRSC) (Neeper, Lahey, & Frick, 1990). The CBRSC measures school functioning for children aged 6 to 14 years old in nine areas: inattention-disorganization, reading problems, cognitive deficits, oppositional conduct disorders, motor hyperactivity, anxiety, sluggish tempo, daydreaming, and social competence. On the CBRSC the teacher rates behavioral characteristics of the child as occurring in a range from "not at all" to "very much." Scores from the CBRSC indicated Harold was low in the areas of reading problems, oppositional conduct disorders, anxiety, and social competence.

Recommendations and outcomes. When the teacher assistance team met again to determine whether to proceed with a referral to the child study team, they found several interesting patterns. They found that over 50% of the critical incidence reports occurred on Mondays. They speculated that when Harold is tired, he may be less able to control himself; therefore, they decided to institute a system in which Harold reported to the school clinic for a few hours of rest on days that he was tired and having difficulty staying awake.

They also found that multiple critical incident reports were filed around the time Ms. Bateman had seen the bruises on Harold, a finding that renewed their concerns about child abuse. After some discussion, they decided to call Protective Services again and speak directly to the person who would do the investigation, detailing specifically their concerns and fears. During the discussion, the point was made that sometimes Protective Services did not investigate as fully and carefully as others might like because the referrals are so general that workers don't know what to look for. In this instance, if the worker is carefully informed about the history and past fears, Protective Services might be more sensitive to Harold's vulnerable situation.

The data also suggested that Harold was more likely to act inappropriately during less structured activities. The teacher who specialized in working with students who have emotional and behavior disabilities would also work with Ms. Bateman in developing interventions to increase Harold's social skills, including a contract that required Harold to monitor himself during recess. Ms. Seng would return the next month to collect data measuring the effects of this intervention.

The teacher assistance team also suggested that Ms. Bateman give Harold a comprehensive criterion-referenced academic test. They suggested the Brigance Inventory of Basic Skills (Brigance, 1983). They felt this would help Ms. Bateman to pinpoint areas of academic ability. Finally, the team decided to monitor Harold for one more month before referring him to the child study team.

Case Four: Donna   Donna is a quiet, pretty girl in Ms. Bateman's class who is repeating the fourth grade. At times, she is so withdrawn she almost disappears. Donna's academic work is inconsistent. Although she sometimes appears to understand the topic and demonstrates satisfactory achievement, at other times she appears "out of it." Ms. Bateman has been puzzled at her inability to get to know Donna. While most of the children have been open and forthright about themselves and their families, Donna has not. On several occasions Ms. Bateman has had casual conversations with a group of girls that included Donna. Most of the girls volunteered a great deal about their personal lives—what they like to do in their spare time, what members of their family do, and what they do with their friends. Donna has never volunteered any information. Once she left the group and joined another activity, but other times she just remained silent. Ms. Bateman also noticed that Donna did not have any close friends. Yet, despite her aloofness, she did not seem to be disliked by the other children. Ms. Bateman wonders whether she should be more insistent about Donna's academic work, whether she should focus on helping Donna make more friends, and whether Donna may need counseling.

Before going to the teacher assistance team, Ms. Bateman reviewed Donna's school records. She found that Donna is part of a military family and has been in four different schools since kindergarten. She also found an incident report about a troubling event in the third grade. The third-grade teacher was standing outside the open door of the classroom talking with the school psychologist when the room erupted in laughter and noise. The teacher immediately looked into the room and told the class to quiet down. A couple of the children said that, on a dare, Donna had exposed herself to several boys. Both the boys and Donna denied it. The boys and Donna maintained their stories and the teacher felt she never quite understood what had occurred. After reading the account of the incident, Ms. Bateman had concerns about sexual acting out and the possibility of sexual abuse.

After hearing Ms. Bateman's synopsis of her concerns about Donna, the teacher assistance team decided that individual evaluation was needed in order to better understand Donna's view of school and her life. Such an evaluation could be done by the child study team, so Ms. Bateman referred Donna to them.

Child study team.   The child study team functioned somewhat differently from the teacher assistance team. This team briefly reviewed the referral, concurred with the reasons for referral, and began planning their work. They decided that a thorough social/emotional evaluation was necessary and scheduled time with the school psychologist. The school guidance counselor agreed to meet with the family to discuss Donna's development and behavior at home and in the community. Ms. Bateman was assigned the task of calling Donna's parents to schedule an interview with both the guidance counselor and Ms. Bateman. The interview was to obtain permission to administer individual tests to Donna. After acquiring the proper parental permission forms allowing individual assessment for the purpose of determining need for special services, the team would begin compiling information.

After the meeting with the child study team and before collecting the information, Ms. Bateman and the school guidance counselor met with Donna. They discussed their concerns about her withdrawn behavior and told her that over the next few weeks several people would be meeting with her and her family to gather information to see what the school may be able to do to help. They told Donna that if she had any questions about the meetings or procedures to come to them and ask.

The psychologist's evaluation.   The psychologist administered both self-report measures and a projective instrument in an effort to learn more about Donna's views. Self-report tools are paper-and-pencil measures that require the respondent to react to written statements about their view of themselves. The self-concept instrument that the psychologist used was the Piers Harris Self-Concept Measure (Piers & Harris, 1969). The Piers Harris Self-Concept measure is a self-report instrument that measures the way children feel about themselves. In addition, it measures the way children may feel in certain other areas: behavior, intellectual and school status, physical appearance and attributes, anxiety, popularity, and happiness and satisfaction. The test was designed with a third-grade reading level. It contains 80 statements to which the student answers yes or no. The test can be easily administered and scored by a teacher, but it is suggested that a psychologist be involved in the interpretation. Item content is obvious, so children are able to respond in accord with the way they want to be perceived.

On the Piers Harris Self-Concept Scale, Donna scored at the 18th percentile, indicating a low self-concept. In addition, the test identified low self-concept in the areas of intellectual and school status, anxiety, and physical appearance and attributes.

While self-report procedures enable the respondent to present a desired picture of self, projective testing is more covert. In responding to items, the child is not aware of what self-picture is being portrayed. Because the interpretation of these measures can be complex, only qualified and trained psychologists are licensed to administer them. The underlying assumption of projective testing is that, when presented vague stimuli and asked to respond, people will project their emotions and feelings onto the stimulus; thus their responses represent important, sometimes unconscious, feelings, values, and beliefs. In most cases the response is verbal, such as with the Rorschach Ink Blot Test (Rorschach, 1942). With the Rorschach, the responses reflect the perceptions a person may have when expressing what he sees in an ink blot. In other cases the response is graphic, such as the Human Figure Drawing Test (Koppitz, 1968) or the House Tree Person Test (Buck & Jolles, 1966).

In Donna's case, the school psychologist administered the Human Figure Drawing (Koppitz, 1968), the Children's Apperception Test—CAT (Bellack & Bellack, 1949/74), and the Rorschach Ink Blot (Rorschach, 1942). In the first test, Donna was dissatisfied with her first effort, saying "the body's not right." Both her first and second drawings were executed with less detail than one would expect from a child of her age. Her figures were small, and all wore an artificially happy face. She was not interested in discussing her drawings (Figure 9.10). Her stories on the CAT reflected anger toward parental figures and conflict about this anger. For example, in response to the card depicting bears sleeping, she replied,

> The three bears were hibernating, but they woke up because they were hungry. The papa went out and got stung by bees. The mother went out and fell into a trap. The baby fell on top of the mother so the baby was not hurt. Then they went back to their cave and lived happily ever after.

Figure 9.10 Two of Donna's Responses to Koppitz's (1968) Human Figure Drawing

1st effort

2nd effort

On the Rorschach her responses reflected the sadness and alienation she is feeling that is causing her anger. All her responses reflected good reality testing, but they also reflected the isolation and unhappiness she is experiencing. Most of her responses focused on small, recognizable sections of the ink blots, and in many cases these responses were cold or dangerous animals such as a fish, crab, wolf, and bear. She never mentioned a person, and most of her responses were sparse. Her efforts to defend against her anger and unhappiness are requiring a good deal of her psychic energy which may, at least in part, explain her withdrawal and social isolation.

Clinical interviews with child and family.   Clinical interviews are conducted to determine characteristics and patterns of behavior for individuals or groups (such as families). Interviews may cover a variety of areas. In certain instances, the interview technique may be based on a certain model of assessment or treatment (Olson, Russel, & Sprenkle, 1989). In many cases where interviews are given, the results are interpretive.

The school social worker conducted interviews with the parents, with Donna alone, and with all members of the family. In her interview, Donna stated that "the other kids don't like me because I'm so big." She also stated that she has never made many friends because "we just move anyway." In the interview she was quite verbal about her family life, although she stated that she felt awkward talking about them. She mentioned quite fondly instances of visiting her grandmother and of a vacation she took with her mother a few years ago. When asked if there was anyone in the family she did not like so well, she answered there was a cousin but would not go into details. Asked about leisure activities or hobbies, she stated she didn't have any and that most of the time she just watches TV.

In the parent and family interviews, it was quite evident that the father is the head of the household. The father answered the majority of the questions for the family. Unless asked questions directly, the mother or children did not volunteer information. In instances where they did answer, the mother and children would periodically glance over to the father. In the interview with the parents, the mother felt that she and Donna had a good relationship most of the time. The parents expressed some concern that Donna had not made a friend at the present school and stated that she had two particularly close friends at the last base. They also stated that they have been going through some particularly hard times financially. They had "gotten into some credit difficulties" and were just now beginning to have a little extra money. They stated that their free time had mostly been spent watching television for the last few years because they had no money to do anything else.

Recommendations and outcomes.   The child study team met to discuss the information compiled by Ms. Bateman, the school psychologist, and the school social worker. Donna's parents participated in this discussion. After reviewing the data, members of the team concurred that Ms. Bateman's concerns were related to Donna's lack of self-esteem and her inability to form meaningful relationships with peers. They discussed several options for dealing with Donna's needs. The parents seemed to prefer individual counseling that could be obtained at the base.

The guidance counselor offered to assist the family in obtaining information about, and access to, therapists on the base. She had a good working relationship with several mental health and financial counselors. She also volunteered to check on Donna regularly to be certain that the plan was succeeding. The Child Study Team decided neither further assessment nor referral for special education services was necessary at that time, but they agreed to review Donna's progress in three months.

After the meeting, Ms. Bateman met with the guidance counselor to discuss planning for Donna. Together they decided that Ms. Bateman's most helpful contribution, in addition to what she was already doing, would be the sensitive introduction of stories and classroom discussion about children's anger at their parents, dealing with strong, controlling people, and expressing oneself in appropriate versus inappropriate ways. They decided that, as with Harold, the Skillstreaming Program (McGinnis & Goldstein) might be helpful.

Sharing Assessment Data with Others

Ms. Bateman was dismayed by her discomfort in sharing information about the children in her class with their families. She was afraid that if she was honest and direct, the families would become defensive; yet she felt it was important that they have a realistic picture of how their child was performing at school. She approached the guidance counselor with the question "Do you know any particularly good ways for me to relay information about my students to their families?" The counselor was delighted by her question because she wanted to encourage more proactive approaches to teacher-family conferences. She had often been asked to mediate conflicts between families and teachers. It seemed to her that some teachers seemed to feel they should tell families how to deal with their own children. Families experienced such directive behavior as judgmental and took offense. In response, they attacked the teacher and the interaction between family and teacher disintegrated into blaming the other person. To help teachers in her school become more skillful in establishing positive, proactive alliances with families, the counselor had been searching for some appropriate structures. Recently, she had found two that appealed to her and she was eager for someone in her school to see how well they worked.

The first, the McGill Action Planning System (MAPS) (Forest & Lusthaus, 1990), is actually a curriculum tool designed to be a positive planning tool. To the extent possible, MAPS involves all persons who are important in the child's life and who are involved with the child on a regular basis. Nobody is involved who does not *know* the child, thus everyone present is invested in the child. Prior to the meeting, an agenda is set and shared so that everyone can come prepared. Participants arrive, having thought about the questions. The process ensures that everyone's opinions are aired.

The discussion always starts with the questions *What is your dream for (child)?*

What do you want for (child)'s future? Responses to this question set a positive tone for planning as well as establishing from the start what various people's hopes and aspirations are.

The second questions *What is your nightmare about (child)'s future? What don't you want to happen in the future?* clarify the fears and worries members of the group

Good diagnostic procedures help to clarify who the child is, not just what deficits she might have.

may have. Addressing these can often help the discussion proceed to a more productive level.

The third questions *Who is (child)? What are child's gifts, strengths, etc.?* are designed to elicit a global picture of the child. In traditional conferences, the focus is often only on the characteristics of the child that are problematic, and the child's talents can be overlooked. When this happens, participants may leave with an even more dismal, negative view of the child. In the MAPS approach, this question ensures a more balanced discussion.

By the time the group has discussed the first three sets of questions, participants' hidden agendas—their often-unspoken hopes and fears—have been voiced and a balanced view of the child has been established. Such discussion enables constructive, cooperative planning for the future, thus the fourth question is designed to start that process: *What does (child) need in order to be successful?* Responses to this question are framed positively but also help to clarify what can and cannot be done by different people. It is also during the discussion of this question that assessment data may again be shared and discussed. These data can be helpful in examining expectations.

The fifth question *What must be done?* sets in motion concrete, immediate planning. Before the meeting is over, a typical day is planned and special arrangements are made. Duties are assigned and a timeline set.

The other system the guidance counselor shared was a student-led system. It was developed as a strategy for teaching children to evaluate themselves and for giving parents feedback about their child's progress in school (Table 9.3). When used as in Table 9.3, it is also a useful assessment tool that enables the teacher to observe the interaction between parent and student and provides windows into the child's view of herself. This approach could also be used as a way of discussing assessment data. Children who have been monitoring their own behavior and have been working with a contract are particularly appropriate candidates for this type of conference. The possible agenda for the student-led conference could be:

☐ Discussion of why monitoring or the contract were started

☐ Explanation of the procedure and student's role

☐ Data sharing and discussion of progress

Table 9.3 lists guidelines for this type of conference.

The process of sharing assessment data and convincing others to support the findings and recommendations is critical to its usefulness. No matter how clear the assessment data, if the family, the child, and other relevant people do not understand or agree with the data, the data are useless. Because of the importance of this process, it is essential that school staff plan it with care.

Table 9.3 Student-Led Parent—Teacher Conferences

☐ A student-led parent–teacher conference provides an opportunity for students to evaluate their progress and lead a reporting conference.

☐ You may have four conferences taking place simultaneously. Set up a sitting area in each corner of the classroom. During conferences that include visits to various centres, the student leads the parent around the room as well.

☐ The conference is approximately 30 minutes long.

☐ Your role in such a conference is supporter and observer; however, if the conference is to constitute an informal report to parents, you will want to be a more active participant. You may also wish, or be required to, complete an evaluation of the student's work to accompany the one completed by the student and the parent.

☐ Give parents an opportunity to schedule a separate parent–teacher conference if they wish to discuss a sensitive matter without the student present.

☐ Students benefit by:
   —having the conference focus on their strengths and accomplishments.
   —accepting greater responsibility for reporting on their progress to their parents.
   —taking increased responsibility and ownership for their own learning.
   —assuming greater accountability for the work they produce.
   —increasing their skills of organizing, communicating, managing time, problem-solving, decision-making, self-evaluating, and goal-setting.
   —having increased communication/interaction time with their parents.
   —having an opportunity to teach their parents and, in the process, demonstrate their understanding of skills and concepts.

☐ You benefit by:
   —having a greater opportunity to teach skills in a real-life context.
   —having increased parent interest, participation, and support.
   —having an opportunity to observe parent–child interaction.
   —using less time in total for conferences, while increasing the time each parent has to view the student's work.
   —having students show significant academic and behavioral growth as they begin to take more responsibility for their own learning.
   —having the student serve as translator for ESL parents, thereby freeing more of the multicultural worker's time for a parent–teacher conference if necessary.

☐ Parents benefit by:
   —having longer conferences.
   —having increased communication/interaction with their children.
   —seeing their children as self-confident, enthusiastic learners.
   —recognizing the importance of encouraging their children.
   —celebrating their children's accomplishments with them.
   —experiencing a more relaxed atmosphere than that of the traditional parent–teacher conference.

Source: reprinted with permission of: Evaluation Techniques and Resources Book II © 1992 B.C. Primary Teachers' Association

Overview of the Assessment Process

The four cases described in this chapter illustrate a variety of the issues teachers encounter during the assessment process, but they all involve team decision making. Since not all schools have established school-based teacher assistance teams, teachers also need to be able to manage the assessment process independently. However, as illustrated in the preceding cases, people have differing views of children, and it is very important that teachers involve others in the assessment process whether or not prereferral teams exist. Figure 9.11 illustrates the steps in the decision-making process. As it shows, the process is a lengthy one for several good reasons. This step-by-step process allows for careful deliberation about why a child is having difficulties and it allows time for personnel to change their minds about a child. It requires that teachers take time to implement and evaluate interventions in the general education classroom before they refer the child for additional services. It requires that a number of people be involved in the process, and it necessitates the use of a variety of assessment procedures. In an area so riddled with conflict, there is likely to be consensus among raters and instruments only about those students who have serious disabilities.

Whether working with a team or independently, teachers must remember that problems with the assessment process abound. Without careful planning and monitoring of the process, the system detailed in Figure 9.11 may result in poor to inadequate services. The process can be unnecessarily cumbersome, and students in need of immediate services can be neglected. Some students may not receive services because they do not meet the predetermined qualifications, and other students may be labeled inappropriately because of bias in the instruments or the assessors. Because of the potential problems, school professionals need to be especially sensitive to children and their families during this stressful process.

For teachers wishing to start a prereferral or teacher assistance team, Morsink and colleagues (1991) list ten dimensions that must be present if the team is to work, regardless of the specific model to be implemented.

1. *Legitimacy and autonomy.* Teams need a legal basis for existing, but they also need to be valued by the school administration and faculty. If the team is seen as just one more meeting requiring paperwork, it has a major barrier to overcome before it can be judged successful. If, however, the administration perceives the team as being an effective tool for solving problems, and if teachers believe they are both helping others and learning themselves, the team will be valued and legitimate.

2. *Purpose and objectives.* To function well, team members and faculty at large need a clear understanding of the purpose of the team as well as the tasks and procedures that will be used by the team.

Figure 9.11 Steps in Assessing and Planning Interventions for Challenging Behaviors

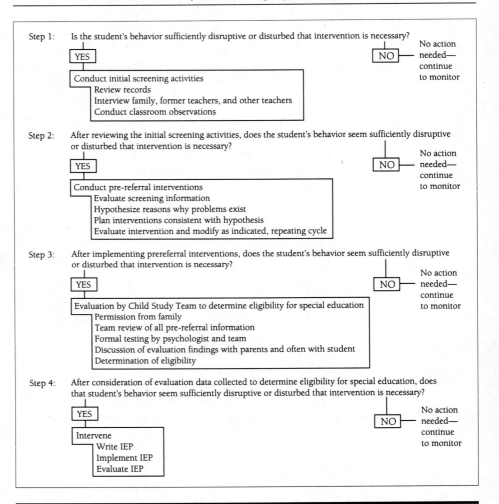

Step 1: Is the student's behavior sufficiently disruptive or disturbed that intervention is necessary?

YES — NO — No action needed—continue to monitor

Conduct initial screening activities
- Review records
- Interview family, former teachers, and other teachers
- Conduct classroom observations

Step 2: After reviewing the initial screening activities, does the student's behavior seem sufficiently disruptive or disturbed that intervention is necessary?

YES — NO — No action needed—continue to monitor

Conduct pre-referral interventions
- Evaluate screening information
- Hypothesize reasons why problems exist
- Plan interventions consistent with hypothesis
- Evaluate intervention and modify as indicated, repeating cycle

Step 3: After implementing prereferral interventions, does the student's behavior seem sufficiently disruptive or disturbed that intervention is necessary?

YES — NO — No action needed—continue to monitor

Evaluation by Child Study Team to determine eligibility for special education
- Permission from family
- Team review of all pre-referral information
- Formal testing by psychologist and team
- Discussion of evaluation findings with parents and often with student
- Determination of eligibility

Step 4: After consideration of evaluation data collected to determine eligibility for special education, does that student's behavior seem sufficiently disruptive or disturbed that intervention is necessary?

YES — NO — No action needed—continue to monitor

Intervene
- Write IEP
- Implement IEP
- Evaluate IEP

3. *Competence of team members and clarity of their roles.* Team members need to possess expertise in their own field in order to work on a team where they are expected to share expertise. In addition to their own professional skills, team members need to understand their role, its responsibilities, and its limits. Likewise, others on the team need to share similar understandings and expectations.

4. *Sharing knowledge and skills with others.* Too often teams get into trouble because members are protecting their own turf. They have relevant skills and knowledge that they do not share with others. Ultimately, effective teams are ones where members trust each other sufficiently to share professional knowledge and to teach skills to others so that optimal services are provided. For example, a school psychologist with experience and knowledge in assessing affective issues in children might insist that a teacher wait until the psychologist could test the child or the psychologist could teach a skilled special education teacher interview and semi-projective techniques (sentence completion/draw a person) that might yield information similar to what the psychologist would obtain, but in a shorter time.

5. *Awareness of the individuality of team members.* People's needs and sources of motivation change as they grow and develop; therefore, groups need to be able to respond to the changing needs of members.

6. *Process of team building.* People need to learn to work together—thus most groups evolve over time. Many authors have talked about the "storming, norming, performing" cycles that happen in groups as they become more productive.

7. *Attention to factors that impact on team building.* Teams that establish a cooperative climate tend to promote social support, positive interpersonal relationships, professional self-esteem, and achievement.

8. *Leadership styles.* The behavior of the group leader significantly impacts the way a group functions. Authoritarian leaders tend to squelch discussion and free information exchange, but decisions get made. Democratic leaders involve everyone and usually elicit support and help from participants, but the process may take time. Laissez-faire leaders neither direct nor take responsibility. Typically, little is accomplished with such a leader.

9. *Implementation procedures.* For the team to work optimally, everyone needs to participate, care needs to be given in reaching consensus, and attention needs to be given to all the factors that impact decisions.

10. *Commitment to common goals.* When members share a common goal, there is a source of motivation to draw upon when problems are encountered; however, when members have different goals, teams can get bogged down in discussions that have little to do with the effective functioning of the team.

Morsink and her colleagues (1991) outlined the "rules of the game" for effective leadership. Increasingly, teachers are leading teams and expected to generate enthusiasm and motivation among members of the team.

Rules of the Game for Effective Leaders

Always do right. This will gratify some people and astonish the rest. Since right is defined differently by different groups, leaders must understand the values of the group and be a model. Leaders are judged more strenuously than others, thus leaders must exemplify the values of the group.

Rose-colored glasses never come in bifocals. Stated differently, all wrongs cannot be righted with the stroke of a sword. Leaders must think about the whole group when making decisions. Sometimes group members may not agree with decisions because they do not have all the information the leader has. Leaders may need to protect some group members or adjust decisions to

fit political realities. In the long run, such decisions may benefit the group.

If you mess up, 'fess up! Good leaders try to anticipate errors and plan how to avoid making them, but when they make an error, they admit it and learn from their mistakes.

Criticism is a compliment. Criticism can help people grow. Successful leaders learn how accept criticism and learn from it.

If you yell at the umpire, you get thrown out of the game. Successful leaders work out their differences with authority figures privately. Publicly they support the commonly agreed upon position.

Brief Summary of Assessment Tools

As was seen in the four cases in Ms. Bateman's class, there are many different assessment strategies and tools that may be helpful when trying to understand a child, a class, or a family. Some of the more commonly used are reviewed in this section.

Self-Report Instruments

Self-report instruments are paper-and-pencil measures that require the child to respond to a set of questions about self. These measures were popular when phenomenology and ego psychology dominated therapeutic practice, but as behaviorism gained influence clinicians lost interest in them because children gave "inaccurate" responses and because children could engage in "impression management"; that is, they could report what they want others to think about them rather than what they actually think about themselves. Recently, however, this technique has enjoyed a resurgence of popularity as clinicians have acknowledged the concept of multiple realities.

These instruments may be read to nonreaders, although most measures suggest that children under age 8 may not have developed the cognitive ability to respond to the items. Older children typically respond with simple answers: true/false, yes/no, frequently/sometimes/rarely, or a Likert rating. Younger children are sometimes asked to select a happy face (agreement) or sad face (disagreement).

Self-concept measures are the most commonly used self-report. Among the better known instruments are the Coopersmith Self-Esteem Inventory (Coopersmith, 1967), Nowicki-Strickland Locus of Control Scale for Children (Nowicki & Strickland, 1973), Piers Harris Children's Self-Concept Scale (Piers & Harris, 1969), Revised Children's Manifest Anxiety Scale (What I Think and Feel) (Reynolds & Richmond, 1978), and the Self-Perception Profile for Children (Harter, 1985).

Behavioral Observations

Behavioral observations are commonly used by teachers, clinicians, and researchers to gain data about the child in his natural environment and these data may be used to validate data gathered through other techniques. They are flexible, easily adapted, and inexpensive. Observations may be done by the teacher or by an outside observer. Observers may use a multitude of techniques that range from simple counting to complex categorization of observations using pre-established coding systems. Data are gathered in a variety of ways including tallies on a clipboard, mechanical counters, and computers.

Critical incident reports are accounts of specific events that occur—often crises or puzzling events about which the teacher wants to have a record.

Antecedent-behavior-consequence (A-B-C) observations are organized observations that record the antecedent (what happened before an event) in one column, the child's behavior (the event) in a second column, and the consequence (what happened after the event) in a third column.

Setting analyses are descriptions of the classroom environment that provide information about class size, utilization of space, available equipment and materials, use of time, and type of classroom structure.

Direct measures of target behaviors are quantifiable accounts of how often or for how long a target behavior was observed. Table 9.4 summarizes some of the more frequently used approaches to gathering quantifiable data.

Time sampling is another procedure for acquiring complex data across settings or over extended time periods. Time sampling involves dividing the observation time into equal or variable time intervals and recording whether specific predefined behaviors occur during these preselected units of time. Three common types of time sampling are: whole-interval time sampling, partial-interval time sampling, and momentary time sampling. In whole-interval time sampling, behavior is recorded if it occurs throughout the interval; in partial-interval time sampling, behavior must occur only during a part of the interval, and in momentary time sampling, the recorded behavior is occurring at the moment of observation.

Table 9.4 Direct Observation Strategies

Type of Measure	Considerations
Simple frequency count *Jose was out of his seat five times today during our 30-minute class.*	Provides meaningful comparison data, but time unit must be kept constant.
Percent/rate of occurrences (no. of occurences/no. of opportunities for the event to occur) *Maria turned in her homework on 60% of the days during the grading period.*	Easy to understand. Equalizes unequal opportunities to respond across time. Need approximately 20 opportunities to respond. Appropriate for naturally occurring events.
Duration of occurrence (total amount of time event occurred) *Greg was out of the class for 41 minutes today.*	Provides total amount of time event lasted, but does not tell how often it occurs nor what the average time of duration is.
Duration per occurrence *Jessica was sent to time-out 12 times during the month for an average of 18 minutes.*	Provides information about how often the behavior occurs and for how long. (Can also provide total duration information.)
Latency (elapsed time from presentation of stimulus to the start of the response) *Alexis took 3.5 minutes to get started on his work once the directions were given.*	Appropriate for compliance monitoring.

Behavior Checklists

Behavior checklists are lists of problem and prosocial behaviors commonly seen in children. Raters, typically teachers and parents, indicate whether, or how frequently, the child being rated demonstrates the behavior. Most checklists yield scores on several factor analytically derived dimensions. The two commonly seen dimensions are aggression and withdrawal/anxiety. Checklists are used (a) to determine severity of a problem (how do a particular child's problems compare to the normative sample), (b) to measure pre- to post-behavioral improvement, and (c) as research tools, to describe the characteristics of a given population.

Initially behavior checklists were designed to provide an objective rating of another person's behavior; however, the research literature has been consistent in reporting biases in ratings (Cairns & Green, 1979; Epanchin & Rennells, 1989). Raters appear to rate the same child consistently across both time and instruments; however the same child is not consistently rated by different raters (Epanchin, 1991). Inconsistencies in behavioral ratings are probably due to childrens' differing behaviors across settings (for example, reading and recess) and variations in instructions given to raters (Have you seen this behavior in the last 6 weeks? versus Is this behavior typical of this child?). Miller (1977) suggests that after raters have completed a behavior checklist, clinicians should use the tool in a structured interview (You checked that your son steals. Can you tell me more about that?). By using checklists in this manner, clinicians are able to obtain better information about raters' biases.

There are a number of measures commercially available. In addition to the ones already mentioned in this chapter, those commonly used include: Child Behavior Checklist (Achenbach & Edelbrock, 1980), Conners Parent Rating Form and Conners Teacher Rating Form (Conners, 1982a, 1982b), Revised Behavior Problem Checklist (Quay & Peterson, 1984), and Walker Problem Behavior Identification Checklist (Walker, 1983).

Projective Tests

Projective tests are only administered by trained, licensed clinicians, usually clinical psychologists. There are several different formats for projective testing, some more structured than others, but all are based on the assumption that people will project personally significant issues onto vague, ambiguous stimuli. In this method, children are presented stimuli such as ink blots, incomplete sentences, or pictures of people or animals involved in activities but without obvious affect. Children are asked to respond with a story or with associations to the stimuli. These measures have scoring systems, although most believe their value lies in their clinical utility rather than in their scores. In the hands of experienced, well-trained clinicians, these instruments can provide rich information about the areas that most trouble a child—information that is particularly useful for clinical work.

Clinical Interviews/Developmental Histories

Clinical interviews are probably the most frequently used technique for gathering assessment data. While they are used for a variety of purposes, the two most common uses appear to be gathering developmental and social histories from parents and assessing the child's view of problems. Unstructured interviews are often used in clinical settings to assess areas of the child's particular concern, whereas structured interviews are used more frequently for research. Both may provide useful diagnostic data. Topics typically covered in clinical interviews include: the interviewee's perception or understanding of the current problem, descriptions of current level of functioning and some gauge of how longstanding and severe the problems are, a chronology of medical and family events that may be associated with current problems, and a description of family strengths. As with behavior checklists, research has reported that many parents' memories do not provide accurate accounts of actual facts—rather descriptions of how the parent remembered an event—and these recollections are often colored by the affect and biases of the parent. As part of the New York Longitudinal Study, Chess,

Thomas, and Birch (1966) gathered developmental information at regular intervals about children in their sample. Later, they compared parents' recollections of events with notes taken during the regular interviews about the children's development over the years. In 12 of the 33 cases examined, researchers found significant distortions in parental recall. This is not meant to imply that parental accounts are not valuable. On the contrary, parental views of the problem, biased or not, are essential pieces of the diagnostic picture.

Conclusions

In this chapter we have reviewed the cases of four children in Ms. Bateman's class. In each case the children were assessed and discussed by a team. The team then developed strategies to collect more specific information. The information was collected from a variety of sources and with a variety of techniques: review of the records, observational data collected by the teacher in the form of anecdotal records, time samples, and teacher-developed checklists, commercial instruments, and psychological testing. Once the information was gathered, the team developed plans to monitor and review the child's behavior or to obtain more complete information.

Earlier chapters of this book presented strategies for implementation in the classroom. Most children will respond positively to these structures and techniques, but a few will need individualized interventions. Once the process of individualization begins, teachers repeat cycles of assess, plan, implement, evaluate, until a strategy is clearly effective. When a child starts responding positively to an intervention, progress needs to be monitored to ensure continuous progress. This chapter has reviewed issues that are likely to be encountered during this process. Selected assessment techniques have also been described, but the discussion was not comprehensive. There are many more instruments and techniques that may be employed to assess and monitor programs. Interested readers are encouraged to refer to texts on assessment procedures and tools.

Discussion Questions and Activities

1. With permission of the family and teacher, select some measures described in the chapter and use them with a child you know well. Did the data you obtained fit your perception of the child? After having used the instrument, what do you think of it?

2. Attend a teacher assistance team or a child study team meeting in a local school. Observe the behavior of each participant carefully. What did each person do to contribute to the discussion? Did anyone interfere with the process? How?

3. Interview parents of a child who has been evaluated for eligibility in a special education program. Ask what was done, how the parents felt, and what impressed them positively or negatively. What could have been done to help or improve the process?

4. Attend a parent conference and take notes on the topics discussed. Also record who speaks, for how long, and the topic about which the person spoke. Do your findings fit your expectations?

5. Collect different types of observational data on children in a classroom. Analyze carefully what you learned and how it could have been more helpful.

6. Think about ethical dilemmas associated with the assessment process. These could include the child abuse issue raised in this chapter or confidentiality concerns. Interview an experienced teacher to see if the teacher has dealt with such issues. Discuss with your class how you would and should respond to these situations.

Reflective Questions

1. When troubled by an individual child's behavior, do you routinely implement and evaluate several different strategies or interventions in your classroom before referring?

2. Do you regularly share opinions and concerns about students with colleagues and are your concerns discussed openly and compassionately?

3. Does the individual assessment process in your school reflect a sincere commitment to understanding a child or is it a bureaucratic process focusing on whether the child qualifies?

4. Do you take the time to research the instruments being used to assess students in your classroom? Do you know how carefully they have been standardized and how valid they are?

5. Do you take baseline data or keep anecdotal records so that you know how intense and frequent, or of what duration, problem behaviors are?

6. Have you developed systems to monitor individual children's behavioral progress?

7. Do you read reports written about students in your class both carefully and critically? If you think information is inaccurate, do you register your opinions?

8. Do you gather information about the student in various settings with various people?

9. Are families part of the team or are they subtle scapegoats?

10. Do staff on your assessment teams take the time to obtain comprehensive pictures of the children and their families?

11. Do teachers know the children's interests, hobbies, family circumstances, and special talents? Are children more than a disability?

12. Do staff know what and how the child being studied thinks about his problems?

13. Do staff know what the child and the family want for help? What will they view as helpful?

14. Are records kept confidential?

15. Are parents' rights explained clearly?

16. Is jargon used during the parent–school conferences?

17. Are parents vastly outnumbered by school people during conferences?

18. Do persons involved in the assessment process believe that none of us have the only right answer and that we are striving to understand the needs and views of all relevant persons in the case?

19. Are developmental issues carefully considered? Do people discuss whether the problems a child is having are developmental, reactive, or long-standing?

20. Would you trust your own child to the process at your school?

References

Achenbach, T. (1981). *The Child Behavior Checklist for ages 4–16.* Burlington, VT: University Associates in Psychiatry.

Achenbach, T. & Edelbrock, C. (1980). *Teacher's Report Form.* Burlington, VT: University Associates in Psychiatry.

Algozzine, B., Christenson, S. & Ysseldyke, J. (1982). Probabilities associated with referral-to-placement process. *Teacher Education and Special Education, 5,* 19–23.

Ammer, J. (1984). The mechanics of mainstreaming: Considering the regular educator's perspective. *Remedial and Special Education, 5,* 15–20.

Bellack, A. & Bellack, S. (1974). *The Children's Apperception Test.* New York: CPS Company. (Original work published in 1949.)

Blackman, H. (1989). Special education placement: Is it what you know or where you live? *Exceptional Children, 55,* 459–62.

Brigance, A. (1983). *Comprehensive Inventory of Basic Skills.* North Billerica: Curriculum Associates.

Brown, L. & Hamill, D. (1990). *Behavior Rating Profile.* Austin: PRO-ED.

Buck, J. & Jolles, I. (1966). *House–Tree–Person.* Los Angeles: Western Psychological Services.

Cairns, R. & Green, J. (1979). How to assess personality and social patterns: Observations or ratings? In R. Cairns (ed.), *The analysis of social interactions: Methods, issues, and illustrations.* Hillsdale, NJ: Erlbaum.

Chalfant, J., Pysh, M. & Moultrie, R. (1979). Teacher assistance teams: A model for within-building problem solving. *Learning Disability Quarterly, 2,* 85–96.

Chess, S., Thomas, A. & Birch, H. (1966). Distortions in developmental reporting made by parents of behaviorally disturbed children. *Journal of the American Academy of Child Psychiatry, 5,* 226–34.

Conners, K. (1982a). *Conners Parent Rating Scale (CPRS).* Toronto: Multihealth Systems.

Conners, K. (1982b). *Conners Teacher Rating Scale (CTRS).* Toronto: Multihealth Systems.

Coopersmith, S. (1967). *Coopersmith Self-esteem Inventory.* San Francisco: Freeman.

Epanchin, B. (1991). Assessment of social and emotional problems. In J. Paul and B. Epanchin (eds.), *Educating emotionally disturbed children and youth* (307–49). New York: Macmillan.

Epanchin, B. & Rennells, M. (1989). Parents' and teachers' sensitivity to unhappiness reported by undercontrolled children. *Behavior Disorders, 14,* 166–74.

Forest, M. & Lusthaus, E. (1990). Everyone belongs with the MAPS Action Planning System. *Teaching Exceptional Children, 22* (2), 32–35.

Gartner, A. & Lipsky, D. (1987). Beyond special education: Toward a quality system for all students. *Harvard Educational Review, 57,* 367–94.

Graden, J., Casey, A. & Christenson, S. (1985). Implementing a pre-referral system: Part II. The data. *Exceptional Children, 51,* 487–96.

Harrington, R. & Gibson, E. (1986). Preassessment procedures for learning disabled children: Are they effective? *Journal of Learning Disabilities, 19,* 538–41.

Harter, S. (1985). *Self-perception profile for children.* Available from the author, Psychology Department, University of Denver, Denver, CO.

Kaufman, A. & Kaufman, N. (1985). *Kaufman Test of Educational Achievement— Comprehensive Form.* American Guidance. Circle Pines, MN.

Koppitz, E. (1968). *Psychological evaluation of children's human figure drawing.* New York: Grune & Stratton.

Koppitz, E. (1983). Projective drawings with children and adolescents. *School Psychology Review, 12,* 421–27.

McCarney, S. (1989). *Attention Deficit Disorders Evaluation Scale (ADDES).* Columbia, MO: Hawthorne.

McGinnis, E. & Goldstein, A. (1984). *Skillstreaming the elementary school child.* Champaign, IL: Research Press.

McGlothlin, J. (1981). The school consultation committee: An approach to implementing a teacher consultation model. *Behavioral Disorders, 6,* 101–107.

Miller, L. (1977). *Louisville Behavior Checklist Manual.* Los Angeles: Western Psychological Services.

Morsink, C., Thomas, C. & Correa, V. (1991). *Interactive teaming: Consultation and collaboration in special programs.* New York: MacMillan.

Munson, S. (1986). Regular education teacher modification for mainstreaming mildly handicapped students. *Journal of Special Education, 20,* 489–502.

Neeper, R., Lahey, B. & Frick, P. (1990). *Comprehensive Behavior Rating Scale for Children.* San Antonio: The Psychological Corporation.

Nowicki, S. & Strickland, B. (1973). A locus of control scale for children. *Journal of Consulting and Clinical Psychology, 40,* 148–54.

Olson, D., Russel, C. & Sprenkle, D. (1989). *Circumplex model: Systemic assessment and treatment of families.* New York: Haworth.

Piers, E. & Harris, D. (1969). *Children's Self-Concept Scale (The way I feel about myself).* Nashville: Counselor Recordings and Tests.

Pugach, M. (1985). The limitations of federal special education policy: The role of classroom teachers in determining who is handicapped. *Journal of Special Education, 19,* 123–37.

Pugach, M. & Johnson, M. (1989). Prereferral interventions: Progress, problems, and challenges. *Exceptional Children, 56,* 217–26.

Quay, H. & Peterson, D. (1984). *Revised Behavior Problem Checklist.* P.O. Box 248074, Coral Gables, FL 33124.

Reynolds, C. & Richmond, B. (1978). What I think and feel: A revised measure of children's manifest anxiety. *Journal of Abnormal Child Psychology, 6,* 271–80.

Rorschach, H. (1942). *Psychodiagnostics.* New York: Grune & Stratton.

Salvia, J. & Ysseldyke, J. (1991). *Assessment in special education* (4th ed.). Boston: Houghton Mifflin.

Sevick, B. & Ysseldyke, J. (1986). An analysis of teachers; prereferral interventions for students exhibiting behavioral problems. *Behavioral Disorders, 11,* 109–117.

Slosson, R. (1990). *Slosson Intelligence Test—Revised.* East Aurora, NY: Slosson.

Strickland, B. & Turnbull, A. (1990). *Developing and implementing Individualized Educational Programs,* (3rd ed.). Columbus: Merrill.

Thorndike, R. & Hagen, E. (1993). *Cognitive Abilities Test—Form 5.* Chicago: Riverside.

Walker, H. (1983). *Walker Problem Behavior Identification Checklist (WPBIC)—* Revised. Los Angeles: Western Psychological Services.

Wood, F., Smith, C. & Grimes, J. (1985). *The Iowa assessment model in behavioral disorders: A training model.* Des Moines: State Department of Public Instruction, The State of Iowa.

Zigmond, N., Levin, E. & Laurie, T. (1985). Managing the mainstream: An analysis of teacher attitudes and student performance in mainstream high school programs. *Journal of Learning Disabilities, 18,* 535–41.

Chapter 10

Student—Teacher Dialogue: A Cooperative Search for Understanding and Connection

Sixth-grader Jason stormed off the court, furious that his team had lost the game. As he stomped away, he muttered, "If they'd only passed the ball to me. I'd have made the goal. Stupid, f---ing Fred!" Meanwhile Fred and the other team members were congratulating the winners and reassuring themselves that they had played a good game and been worthy opponents.

Shortly after the game ended, the school bell rang, beckoning everyone back to classes. Everyone but Jason lined up affably. Jason, however, was walking around the periphery of the playing field, still fuming and muttering under his breath. He seemed not to hear the bell or to realize that his class was entering the school building.

Having witnessed the entire episode, Ms. Stallings was considering her options. Her first decision had to do with getting Jason into the building. She could take her class inside and give them an assignment, then go after Jason; she could notify the office and ask them to retrieve Jason; she could ignore him, assuming he would return when he realized the class had gone in; or she could shout to him, publicly calling attention to his temper outburst.

Ms. Stallings' Options

Her decisions are not finished once Jason is back inside her classroom because she still has to determine how to respond to his outburst. These decisions can promote Jason's social-emotional development and relationships within the class and with her, or they can ostracize and alienate Jason from both her and the class. Among Ms. Stallings' options are the following.

1. *Punishment.* She could get Jason's attention by shouting orders to him and by punishing him for his bad sportsmanship. If she is annoyed by his childish behavior and impatient with his lack of control, this is likely to be the response she will prefer. She might reason, "After all, 11- and 12-year-old boys certainly should know how to control themselves and be good sports." This response may result in quick compliance, but it is unlikely that it will contribute to a long-term solution of the problem. It may, however, contribute to Jason's frustration. Punishment may stop the immediate behavior, but it rarely solves the problem. In this case Jason is not hurting someone else; he is merely being an immature child. Punishment in his eyes may be unfair, because to him the disappointment of losing is real and important. Thus punishment may only serve to add to Jason's frustration.

   This response is a common one when schoolteachers are pressed to find ways to get large groups of children to comply with their directions. Students' response to punishment can serve as a negative reinforcement to teachers: the obnoxious behavior stops when the teacher punishes, so this can be a seductive technique for teachers. Unfortunately, teachers often benefit more than students.

2. *Cajoling, consoling or reassuring.* Ms. Stallings could send her class into the building, give them an immediate assignment, and then find Jason and try to cajole him into a better humor with a comment like "Oh, come on. It's not such a big deal. You tried and so did your teammates. Everyone loses sometimes." If Ms. Stallings believes Jason is over-reacting and making a big issue of a small problem, she may be tempted to use this option. Although her intentions might be to help Jason get over his disappointment quickly, consoling and reassuring are likely to convey indifference or criticism that could hamper communication between Jason and Ms. Stallings. If Jason perceives Ms. Stallings as not understanding, he is likely to be even more upset and disappointed. Responses such as "Oh, come on. It's not such a big deal" can be interpreted as meaning "Your feelings are not important" or "Your activities are no big deal." Statements like "You tried and so did your teammates. Everyone loses sometimes" minimize the disappointment and hurt. He has both the hurt of the game and the frustration of not being understood.

3. *Confrontation.* Once she had her class in the building and busy with work, she could find Jason and point out to him that being a good sport is a problem for him, and that he needs to work on this. She could easily think of other times when he has acted similarly to this present situation. Maybe she needs to set this as a goal for him. If Ms. Stallings views her role as both teacher and counselor, she might select this option. In effect, she would be assuming the responsibility of teaching Jason to look at his own problems. While teachers are often called on to function in this capacity, whether they want to or not, this role can be problematic if teachers do not feel comfortable and exercise caution in using the technique. It can quickly become a tool for control and hostility and it can open up topics for discussion that teachers are unprepared to deal with. Done with care and compassion, however, this response can build relationships and promote students' social and emotional development.

4. *Contracting.* Ms. Stallings could negotiate an individualized contract with Jason in which he might agree to control his behavior in exchange for a reward he selects. This approach can be an effective one, but it needs to follow a discussion in which motivation to change is explored. Contracts are probably best used in conjunction with other interventions. Furthermore, they are only used when the teacher is willing and able to follow through and monitor the contract. Contracts are appealing because they spell out expectations and consequences and they are a concrete way of involving children in solving their own problems, but they should not be entered into lightly. Contracts are discussed in greater detail in Chapter 5.

5. *Teach deficit social skills.* She could assume that Jason reacted as he did because he lacks better social skills. He may not have learned how to deal with winning and losing. He may not have sufficient self-control to hide or control his disappointment. He may need to be taught how to deal with issues of winning and losing. If Ms. Stallings selects this option, she may use a book, a movie, a news story about a famous athlete, or some role-plays. In class the entire group could work on such issues. Jason is probably not the only student who has problems losing. This technique was discussed in greater depth in Chapter 7.

6. *Ignoring.* She could ignore the entire incident and thereby provide Jason with the space and time to cool off. Especially if this reaction is not typical of Jason, he might just be having a bad day. Not making a major issue of his outburst might lessen his embarrassment. In effect, this is also punishment. It can be effective in not reinforcing or perpetuating problem behavior, but it does not teach what to do. Many children just become angrier when given the silent treatment.

7. *Empathetic relationship building.* Ms. Stallings might empathize with him about how hard it is to lose, especially when you have worked very hard. Maybe understanding and friendship will be more helpful than teaching, preaching, confronting, or punishing. Counselors maintain that this response is the one most likely to open communication and create a context for meaningful, trusting dialogue.

8. *Prevention of contagion.* She must also be concerned about how to prevent the other children from being drawn into Jason's anger. If the muttering continues, other students may become involved and greater problems could result: Jason could get in a fight with another boy, or the other kids might start teasing and belittling Jason. Their reactions could just fuel his disappointment and anger.

Consequences of Ms. Stallings' Decisions

Teachers face such decisions daily in schools across our continent. The consequences of such decisions significantly impact both the student's behavior as well as the teacher-student relationship; therefore such decisions need to be carefully considered. Deciding what to do, however, is not a simple task. Classrooms are complex environments and children are complex beings who bring diverse experience and perceptions to bear on the classroom each day. Teachers, faced with making hundreds of decisions, find ways to make sense of the continual hustle and bustle of the classroom by devising personal theories (Ross, Cornett, & McCutcheon, 1992). In a sense, these theories act to organize the "reality" of the classroom into manageable schemes and provide teachers with rationales for action and direction. Many factors impact teachers' personal theories: values, experience, school culture, community, students' personal theories, parental attitudes, for example. Each of these influences impacts the moment of decision making, and the nature of the teacher/student relationship that ultimately determines the potential for growth, change, and learning.

Ms. Stallings was not faced with making a decision about a child she did not know, but a child with whom she had an established relationship and history. Jason's behavior could only be interpreted in light of Ms. Stallings' perceptions of him and the nature of the relationship they shared. Ms. Stallings remembered other times Jason had difficulties with losing. She could guess how far he might go in acting out his disappointment. She may have had a sense of how he might respond to the various options and could therefore rule out certain responses based on her experience with Jason.

Ms. Stallings was also aware that Jason's behavior had an impact on the rest of the class and considered the possible ramifications in her decision making process. She and Jason were members of an interrelated group. Their relationship did not occur in isolation, but within the context of other lives and relationships that were intricately connected and in which certain agreements about behavior and relationship had been established. The group norms and standards that had been established within the classroom had to be taken into account, as did the rules and standards of the greater school community.

Ms. Stallings' personal values also colored her decision making and set the tone of her interaction with Jason (Witherell & Noddings, 1991). If, for instance, she valued the honest expression of emotion, she might have seen Jason's behavior more positively. In this view, Ms. Stallings might actually welcome Jason's behavior as an opportunity for insight and growth. On the other hand, if she viewed Jason's behavior as acting "spoiled" or "babyish," she might have been annoyed by his response. A third possibility might be that Ms. Stallings viewed Jason's behavior as a symptom of his low self-esteem, and the importance he placed on winning may have saddened her. Whatever the view Ms. Stallings may have of Jason's behavior, it would be conveyed to the child through voice and expression, and would substantially impact the dynamics of interaction and the possible outcomes.

Finally, Ms. Stallings' conceptualization of her own role, as well as those of her students, influenced her actions. Her answers to the following questions guided her decision making: Did she feel it was her job to counsel students, or simply to teach them? Did she view herself as "teacher," "counselor," "enforcer," "manager," or "mother hen"? And how did she view the students, as "charges," as her "babies," as "crazies," as "achievers," or as "survivors"? The various theories of child development and behavior also imply teacher/student roles and may strongly influence teacher beliefs. The metaphors teachers use to conceptualize student and teacher roles guide practice and impact the moment (Tobin & LaMaster, 1992).

The Relationship Between Decision Making, Core Beliefs, and Personal Theories

With so many factors influencing the nature of teacher/student relationship and possible courses of action, how do teachers actually make decisions? Are teachers consciously aware of their own values, beliefs, and theories and the ways these impact students, or do they believe they are "technicians" that implement the strategies of experts in a detached and unbiased manner? As teachers are moving into new identities as decision makers, a growing interest in reflective practice has emerged. Teachers who interact daily with students whose behaviors are challenging need to understand not only the impact of their beliefs, theories, and behavior on students, but also the impact students' beliefs, theories, and behavior have on them. And then, teachers need to try to understand how this all comes together within the complex environments of schools.

Teachers' Core Beliefs and Theories

The teachers' lounge in many schools is often a place of lively conversation. Freed from the isolation of the classroom, teachers unite into a protected haven where they exchange stories, opinions, and theories with their colleagues. Often teachers discuss incidents that have recently taken place in the classroom, interactions with administrators, or aspects of school policy that they have strong feelings about. Sometimes they talk about students; how a certain child "drives them crazy," or how much another student has "improved." Teachers have strong opinions and beliefs about children, teaching, and the effectiveness of schools. These beliefs and values are evident in their stories and conversations, and can be detected by examining their language. Ayers (1992) suggests that probing teachers' stories provides a door to understanding the meaning of teaching:

> . . . Our stories are never neutral or value-free. Because they are always em-
> bedded in space and time and people, they are necessarily infused with
> values, forever political, ideological, and social. Our stories occur in cultural
> contexts, and we not only tell our stories, but in a powerful way our stories
> tell us. Interrogating our stories, then—questioning and probing our
> collective and personal myths—is an important pathway into exploring the
> meaning of teaching. (p. 35)

Students who pose "behavior problems" for teachers often challenge teachers' beliefs and theories, as well as those of the school at large. With these students, it is particularly important for teachers to understand the meaning they are attributing to student behavior. If teachers do not understand how their own biases, values, and beliefs impact their relationship with students, they may be blind to their contribution to the "problem behaviors" they perceive. In addition, teachers who do not critically examine their own practice, often remain limited in the number and manner of choices they perceive as responses to students' behaviors.

Bruner (1986) describes how the manner in which we "construct" another's character has a tremendous impact on our interpersonal relationship. In our narrative thought and in our stories about students, Bruner suggests that we merge character, setting, and action into the *dramatis personae* of fiction and of life. He states that we make choices between alternative "construals" that greatly influence how we act and react with others:

> . . . And those constructions are by no means arbitrary. . . . They also reflect
> our beliefs about how people fit into society. The alternate ways in which we
> can construe people, moreover, often run into conflict with each other, and
> the conflict leaves us puzzled. Indeed, the act of construing another person is
> almost inevitably problematic. For all that, the choice of one construal rather
> than another virtually always has real consequences for how we deal with oth-

ers. Our construal of character, indeed, is our first and perhaps most important step in dealing with another. (p. 39)

Two elements of Bruner's account are particularly important for teachers of students who are experiencing conflict in the classroom or at home: construal of character and choice over construal.

Construal of character. Often students who pose behavioral challenges send "mixed messages" that particularly stress and confuse us. We may, for example, alternate between viewing a student as a "victim" and a "victimizer." The courses of action, the nature of interaction, and the relationship that result from these opposite images may be similarly opposite. Teachers often experience frustration, confusion, and even feelings of betrayal when a student acts in ways that contradict their image of the student. When a child who seems to be working hard and making great strides to improve suddenly reverts to old antisocial behaviors, teachers can feel hurt, disappointed, and manipulated or betrayed, when in fact the child's change in behavior may have little to do with the teacher. It is important that teachers continually reflect on and critically examine their reactions to students, lest they adopt defensive postures. One of the most commonly seen defensive postures that teachers assume is choosing the worst possible construal of a student's character in an effort to avoid their own personal disappointment. When this happens, teachers are viewing students as problems and may thereby contribute to students' living up to that image.

Control over construal. Bruner (1986) suggests that we have choices in the way we construe others. He allows for the possibility of changing the way we envision a child. There are many dimensions to children. We can consciously choose ways of seeing them that are more conducive to the development of a positive, therapeutic relationship. This does not refer to superficial positive statements about a person; rather, it refers to finding and enjoying the positive qualities in a child as a means of forming an authentic relationship. The possibility of choice reminds us that children are far more multifaceted than our descriptions of them sometimes suggest. We often "reduce" children in our thoughts to simple patterns of behavior dictated by our labels or construals. In so doing, we run the risk of responding to children in a superficial way and failing to appreciate aspects of their being that run counter to our labels.

Bruner's ideas empower teachers. They focus on issues that teachers have control over. Teachers can change themselves, but they cannot force or make others change. An experienced teacher expressed this very well:

> Throughout the 20 years I have been teaching I have continually met and heard about troubled students, angry students, special needs students, dysfunctional students, high incidence students, low incidence students, behavior disordered students. The descriptors change as our jargon evolves and the

catalysts vary with the times, but "problem kids" are a constant in our profession. What is becoming clear to me is that *kids don't change*, it is teachers who
must adjust their own reactions and attitudes. Herein lies the power of our
profession to empower the next generation. I think I have known this inher-
ently for a long time. (Personal communication from Mary Petovello, teacher
in Terrace, British Columbia, August 1993)

This does not imply that students *cannot* change. On the contrary, when teachers
change, students also are likely to change. The choice to change, however, is
ultimately determined by each individual. Teachers can build relationships and
they can create situations that motivate change, but ultimately personal change is
within the control of the individual.

Exploring Metaphors of Teaching and Learning

As teachers begin to realize that their own beliefs and values are important
influences on classroom dynamics, they come to understand that being an
effective teacher involves ongoing critical reflection. Examining, and in some
cases changing, the metaphors used to describe teacher and student roles is a
useful way to explore the images that guide practice. If, for example, we write a
narrative describing a child, or describe her or him to another, we can critically
examine our depiction of the child and change it. It is important to recognize that
we have a choice in how we view children. Tobin and LaMaster (1992) suggest
that, by consciously changing guiding metaphors, teachers can change their
beliefs about their roles in the classroom, and in so doing directly impact the
nature and quality of the relationships with students.

Tobin and LaMaster (1992) report a very interesting study that they
undertook with a science teacher named Sarah who was having considerable
difficulty in the classroom. When the study commenced, Sarah was experiencing
such severe "management" problems that she was losing confidence in herself as
a teacher. The researchers worked with Sarah to investigate her own beliefs
through journal writing, conversation, and interview. They observed Sarah
teaching many times and constructed vignettes based on their observations.
Sarah's students and peer teachers were also interviewed to grasp their perceptions of Sarah.

Throughout the course of the study, Sarah identified metaphors for her
teaching role. She explored these metaphors by writing her beliefs about each
role. As she began to focus on her beliefs, she came to realize that she held
contradictory images and opposing sets of beliefs. She envisioned herself as a
manager who managed by being a comedian. She examined her beliefs that if she
could make students laugh they would like her and do what she wanted.
Responsibility, in the comedian metaphor, is solely on the teacher to perform in
order to captivate her audience. Faced with the disappointment of her manage-

ment skills, Sarah became preoccupied with classroom management and she began to see her students' behavior in a negative light.

Sarah also saw her role as that of "assessor." She was uncomfortable with this role and associated it with the metaphor of "rewarder and punisher." Because she wanted to be fair, she was torn between being consistent and efficient in assigning grades and keeping records, and in challenging all students to equal work. In her perception, some students tried hard and failed, while others passed with little effort. It troubled Sarah that many of the failing students regarded her as unfair.

The primary purpose of the study was to look at how teachers change. The primary focus of intervention was to help Sarah change her metaphors for teaching. Sarah reconceptualized her metaphor for classroom management from comedian to social director. As "social director" Sarah envisioned herself inviting students to a learning event worth attending. It was the students' responsibility to accept the invitation and learn. In this metaphor, responsibility for learning is shared by teacher and students. The researchers report that "when Sarah adopted the new metaphor, changes were observed in the classroom immediately" (Tobin & LaMaster, 1992, p. 127).

Sarah also came to change her metaphor of assessor from punisher and rewarder to "a window into the student's mind." This metaphor was suggested by a member of the research team. As Sarah adopted this metaphor, she formulated new beliefs over time that resonated with this image. Again, the change in metaphor produced almost immediate results in the classroom. Change was confirmed by observers, students, and Sarah's colleagues. As Sarah reflected on the changes she was experiencing in the classroom she explored her emerging beliefs. One important result of Sarah's reflection was that she came to believe that "the teacher's expectations about behavior are likely to be self-fulfilling" (Tobin & LaMaster, 1992, p. 131).

Based on their study with Sarah, Tobin and LaMaster conclude that it is possible to help teachers change sets of beliefs about their teaching roles and thereby change behavior. By helping Sarah create a new conceptualization (metaphor) for her role, Sarah was also able to change related teaching behaviors simultaneously. As they describe their findings,

> Teaching can be defined in terms of roles undertaken by teachers. And just as metaphors are at the basis of all (or most) concepts, so the metaphors used to make sense of the main teaching roles can be the focus for reflection and change. The power associated with changing these metaphors is that changes in metaphors lead to reconceptualized roles and associated beliefs. Further, a focus on metaphors at this level of generality enables teachers to consider whether or not there are significant conflicts between the way they conceptualize and what they believe about their role of facilitator of learning. (Tobin & LaMaster, 1992, p. 134)

As teachers reflect upon their interactions and relationships with students, it is important that they endeavor to understand their guiding images and metaphors. Bruner's insights on the importance of how we construe another's character and Tobin and LaMasters' conclusions about the importance of metaphors in practice lead to the realization that *simply learning and utilizing "effective methods" for "classroom management" is insufficient.* If a teacher views her students as "troublemakers" and herself as the "enforcer," her classroom will mirror her beliefs. Positive action within a classroom where teacher and students are conceptualized in antagonistic roles is severely constrained.

Working Within the Context of Relationship

Decisions concerning how to respond to students' behaviors can only be made within the context of relationship. The probability that Jason would respond favorably to any of the options Ms. Stallings considered would be heavily influenced by the nature of their teacher/student relationship. Establishing positive relationships with children who are experiencing emotional or behavioral difficulties can be extremely challenging, especially if the child acts in an aggressive manner. Issues surrounding control and power, if not critically examined and reflected upon, can sabotage the best efforts of creating positive, encouraging relationships.

Barth (1986) describes aggression in children as being contagious. He describes a cycle that, counter to intentions, results in caregiver and child teaching each other to be more aggressive. In one such scenario, an adult responds to a student's aggressive behavior with loud and threatening behavior. If the child complies, the adult "learns" that control reduces aggression, at least in the immediate situation. If the child does not comply, the adult "learns" to fight harder. In this type of power struggle there are no winners. Teachers who attempt to control their students by "outpowering" them preclude the possibilities of building trusting relations that foster cooperation. Unfortunately, as was pointed out in Chapter 2, the disappointing findings reported by Knitzer, Steinberg, and Fleisch (1990) in *At the Schoolhouse Door* suggest that for the most part we are responding to children who are experiencing emotional difficulties by imposing exorbitant amounts of control. In general education settings, Poplin and Weeres (1992) also found a similar concern with control and a lack of authentic relationships.

Spence (1978) describes the detrimental effects on relationship that stem from a belief that it is necessary and possible to control others.

> Those men and women that [sic] attempt to control the behavior of others end by hating the human species for its recalcitrance and apathy and by hating themselves for their own weakness. Attempts at behavior control create

pathogenic contexts that drastically cripple the cooperative, learning, and productive capacities of mankind. (p. 285)

One of the fundamental challenges of establishing therapeutic relationships with students who act in aggressive ways is to interrupt rather than perpetuate the cycle of control. This is difficult to do within the context of schools where teachers are generally expected to "control" their students. Those students who are eventually labeled as behavior disordered often tend to be the students who, in Barth's terms, have learned to "fight harder" during their years in school, and whose behaviors challenge the metaphors of control that many teachers and administrators adhere to.

The Language of Relationship

One way to interrupt the cycle of control is to stop participating in it. Rather than using language to *tell* students what to do and how to act, we can invite children to enter into dialogue. We can use language to talk *with* students about their feelings, behavior, and meanings. This deceptively simple suggestion to change the way we use language in schools is by no means a simple or easy solution. It requires an openness to listen to what students have to say, and also a genuine willingness to enter into the child's view. Nel Noddings (1992) describes the teacher's responsibility to both see students and see "with" students.

> The teacher-student relation is, of necessity, unequal. Teachers have special responsibilities that students cannot assume. Martin Buber (1965) wrote that teachers must practice "inclusion"; teachers must, that is, take on a dual perspective: their own and that of their students. They must try to see the world as their students see it in order to move them from a less to a more satisfactory view. Good teachers do not reject what students see and feel but, rather, work with what is presently seen and felt to build a stronger position for each student. To do this effectively requires the creation and maintenance of a trusting relationship. (p. 107)

Noddings goes on to say that when teachers practice inclusion, they free students to pursue their own growth, rather than constraining them to meet the personal and professional needs of the teacher. In other words, when teachers are genuinely willing to respect the integrity of students' views, by necessity they relinquish the goal of imposing their own.

Noddings (1992) explains that children who have experienced this type of inclusive care at home respond naturally to teachers' efforts of inclusion, but if teachers' behavior is unfamiliar, students may have difficulty recognizing or responding to care. For example, if a child's parents justify abusive behavior by telling the child it is for her own good, she will have difficulty trusting a teacher's efforts to work in her behalf. This requires the teacher to work harder to

Positive regard between students and teachers promotes constructive dialogue.

understand the student's view. Noddings states, "This puts an even greater burden on teachers to listen, to receive, to respond to what is really there" (p. 108).

Teachers can learn to "see with" students by engaging them in dialogue. Dialogue, Noddings (1992) stresses, is open-ended and cannot genuinely occur if the outcome is predetermined. When teachers engage students in conversation to persuade them to comply with a decision that is already made, this is not dialogue. Rather, *dialogue is a cooperative search for meaning.* It allows us to connect with each other, to know each other, and to understand each other's needs. Dialogue allows us to talk about what we do and provides opportunities to question. Dialogue provides the foundation for caring relationships. It is the language of cooperation, not control.

Students who have experienced excessive amounts of control in school or at home may not know how to engage in dialogue at first, and may resist sincere invitations to share in a search for mutual understanding. These students may have come to expect that their opinions and views will not be valued. What teachers do when students do not respond to their attempts to engage them in genuine dialogue is very important. If teachers respond with anger, coercion, or rejection, students perceive an underlying message of control and distrust the words of encouragement. However, if students' decisions are honored and respected, especially when they do not conform to our wishes, then the message of action and the message of words are consistent and the potential to establish trust is greatly enhanced.

The options Ms. Stallings perceives as she views Jason's behavior can only be approached within the agreements that have been established about how language is used in the classroom. If language is habitually used in the classroom in negotiation, in exploring meaning, and in coming to understanding, then Jason and Ms. Stallings will have an established avenue for exploring behavior through dialogue. If genuine dialogue is not fostered within the classroom, it will be unlikely that talking to Jason about his behavior will be beneficial, especially at a time when he is already angry. The options left to teachers who are unable to establish trusting relationships with students through dialogue almost always rely on some form of control.

Context and Culture

Behavior, communication, and relationship do not take place in a vacuum, but within particular times and places. When considering the nature of relationship and communication within schools and classrooms, one must consider the contextual and cultural dimensions without which meaning cannot be determined. Hall (1981) tells us that the complexities of human experience are structured and made meaningful through a highly selective screen that is influenced by activity, situation, status, experience, and culture.

> The rules governing what one perceives and is blind to in the course of living are not simple; at least five categories of events must be taken into account. These are: the subject or activity, the situation, one's status in the social system, past experience and culture. (p. 85)

In order to enhance genuine communication and understanding in schools, it is important for teachers to try to understand the cultural meanings and biases students bring to the classroom. In this way, teachers can try to grasp how and what students perceive. Hall (1981) reminds us that it is difficult to try to understand perspectives that are different from our own, especially in our fast-paced world. However, failure to do so can lead to children feeling alienated in the classroom.

Bruner (1986) suggests that schools should be places where children learn about culture and are given opportunities to talk about and influence classroom culture. He suggests one of the primary functions of schools should be to create a forum for discussing various cultural meanings and their impact on the classroom. Bruner suggests this should be an ongoing process in which students are encouraged to voice their own perspectives and beliefs. In Bruner's view, culture is not a fixed set of rules, but an everchanging agreement about meaning that takes place in various groups such as schools, families, and ethnic groups.

Leaning on Bruner's depiction of culture, we could talk about classrooms as places where certain agreements are negotiated between members about meaning. This is influenced by the greater school culture, which has its own meanings, and school culture is influenced by community culture, and so on. Trying to understand what a specific behavior "means" and what to "do" about it, can only be considered within the agreements that have been negotiated within the classroom, the school, the home, and the community. Behavior, and the possible responses to behavior, have different meanings in different times and places.

In Bruner's vision of schools as forums for negotiating meaning, we see a metaphor for schooling where power is shared, not imposed. Interpersonal reasoning, the ability to "talk appreciatively" to one another, even when we are very different, is of critical importance for achieving satisfying friendships, marriages, business relationships, and—ultimately—world peace (Noddings, 1991). Bruner (1986) sums it up beautifully:

> It is not just that the child must make his knowledge his own, but that he must make it his own within a community of those who share his sense of belonging to a culture. It is this that leads me to emphasize not only discovery and invention but [also] the importance of negotiating and sharing—in a word, of joint culture creating as an object of schooling and as an appropriate step en route to becoming a member of the adult society in which one lives out one's life. (p. 127)

Students each bring their own unique culture and meaning to the classroom. If that meaning can be expressed and is valued, students can hold a share in the continual negotiation of class and school culture. When students come from culturally diverse backgrounds, as Hall (1981) has pointed out, it takes time and great effort to genuinely understand each other and then to work towards establishing mutual understandings and agreements. When this does not happen, it leads to alienation. Children who have been labeled as "behaviorally disordered" challenge the norms of school culture. Often teachers and administrators try to impose their own views on these students, rather than inviting students to explain their own meanings and participate in negotiating new meanings.

In the case of Ms. Stallings and Jason, they may have attributed very different meanings to "losing," as well as to Jason's response to losing. However, within the context of the classroom new meanings can be negotiated if teachers and students are willing to enter into respectful dialogue. Classrooms hold endless opportu-

---

🔲 *Conflict Negotiation Skills*

Check understanding. Paraphrase or restate your understanding of the other person's position and clearly explain your view.

Don't presume knowledge of others. Explain your own views only. Don't try to tell others what you think they think.

Focus on needs, feelings, and interests. Instead of repeating the obvious conflict, delve into your own underlying beliefs and issues.

Search for negotiable points. When differences occur, there are usually some issues that are negotiable and some that are not. Don't get stuck on the non-negotiables.

Know your own style. Self-knowledge is power, and knowing how you respond in disagreements gives you the ability to reposition yourself.

Know how you deal with your own anger. Understanding your own triggers helps you control yourself. Giving in to anger rarely helps in solving a problem.

Try to see the issue from the other person's perspective. Understanding the other person's perspective helps one be more flexible in finding solutions.

Reframe the problematic issues. Approaching the problem from different perspectives can create new ways of thinking about the problem and lead to acceptable solutions.

Criticize what people say, not who they are. Criticism should be directed at ideas and statements, not at people. Personalizing conflict is not constructive.

Seek win-win solutions, not compromises. Find solutions where all parties get what they need, not a little bit of something that they need. Creative, persistent negotiation can lead to win-win conclusions.

Source: Adapted from Scherer (1992).

---

nities for entering into negotiation. When teachers and administrators take the initiative to settle conflicts for children according to their own meanings, they seriously impede opportunities for children to learn some of the most important lessons of all.

Ms. Stallings' Decision

As Ms. Stallings watched the episode develop, she admitted to herself how annoying she sometimes found Jason. He was so intense and so demanding! It seemed he always had to be the best and be in control and he could never just smile and let things roll off his back. In contrast, Ms. Stallings was very uncomfortable with conflict, and Jason's intensity often created conflict in the classroom. This incident was less threatening to Ms. Stallings because she was not directly involved. Furthermore, it was a beautiful, warm day and the other students seemed reasonably calm and cooperative. She therefore decided it was time she and Jason worked out a better way to deal with such problems. Ms. Stallings recognized that Jason's intensity motivated him to try to be better. Such powerful motivation needed direction and focus, not punishment and squelching. She wrote the following note to her principal:

> Dear Ms. Ortiz,
> Jason Blackmon is having a minor temper tantrum on the playground. I want to handle the problem, but I want back-up from the office if I need it. I am taking my students into our room and I will get them started on their work, then I plan to go back outside to talk to Jason. Please watch the front of the building just to make certain he does not run away (I don't think he will). Also, please monitor my class over the PA system or send an adult to monitor as soon as possible.

The outside of the note was addressed to Ms. Ortiz with instructions that the note should be opened by anyone staffing the office. Ms. Ortiz had made it clear to teachers that she was there to help when necessary, so Ms. Stallings was comfortable asking for help under the circumstances. Furthermore, she was concerned about leaving a classroom of students unattended. If something should happen while she was out of the room, she and the school would have liability problems.

Ms. Stallings went inside with her class, told them she had an errand to run, and gave them several options: pleasure reading, working on homework, quiet game playing, or simply resting. The one absolute requirement was they remain in their seats and or in chairs at a center, and that they stay quiet so as not to disturb the classrooms across the hall and next door. She also told them that Ms. Ortiz would be checking on them, and heard the monitoring PA system click on.

As she walked toward the playground, she saw Jason coming down the hall, still upset. When he saw Ms. Stallings, he started explaining that he did not hear the bell.

Ms. Stallings responded, "I know. I saw you. You seemed upset. Why don't you tell me what happened." As she talked, she moved to a quiet nook between lockers in the hallway.

Jason followed, replying, "I was open a lot, but they wouldn't pass the ball to me. I'm good. I could have made more goals. We could have won!"

Ms. Stallings did not share Jason's self-assessment. She knew he could shoot the ball, but he did not get himself into the play so that other kids could pass to him. However, she said, "You really wanted to win."

He replied, "Yeah, and I think we could have won if I could have shot more."

"It sounds as if you really wanted your team to be the best and you don't feel you did all you could have done."

"Right. I never win. I never get the trophies. I'm never the best! This time I thought I could be." With that revelation, he started crying.

His tears made Ms. Stallings feel inadequate. For a moment, she wasn't sure what to do, then she remembered her goal: to help Jason take more responsibility for his behavior and learn some new ways of coping with his intense feelings. She replied, "You're so disappointed! Do you suppose that's why you didn't hear the bell?"

He nodded his head affirmatively.

She replied, "Does that kind of thing happen often? You're so involved in your own thoughts that you don't hear things or forget things?"

He nodded affirmatively and began crying harder. Ms. Stallings again felt very uncomfortable. What if someone walked down the hall and saw them. What would they think? How would Jason feel if a classmate came out and saw him in tears? She wanted to cajole him to stop crying but, remembering principles of communication, she was silent for a moment, then said, "Sounds like you're feeling awful—not successful, not as good as you want to be."

He nodded affirmatively, wiped his tears, and replied, "I want to be the best in something. Everybody in my family is good but me. My brother has a shelf full of trophies for swimming."

Ms. Stallings asked, "How old is your brother?" and Jason replied, "Fourteen." She observed, "It's really hard when you have a brother who does everything so well. Brothers often compare themselves. Do you and your brother?"

By this point, Jason seemed to be calmer and more willing to talk. "My parents compare us. I want to be as good as he is."

"He has had three years more than you to win trophies. You're really a good student and you have a great penalty shot. Do you think you might expect too much of yourself?"

"Well, maybe sometimes, but. . . ." He hesitated. Ms. Stallings observed, "It seems to me you expect yourself to be the best most of the time and when you aren't, you get mad—like today." He nodded affirmatively, but said nothing. She continued, "Do you want to work on that?" He nodded again.

At that point, Ms. Stallings was concerned about the rest of her class. She suggested to Jason that they return to class and continue this conversation later in the day. She told him that, if he wanted, they could develop a plan that might help him control himself. He seemed agreeable, and they walked down the hall to their classroom.

Ms. Stallings thought her relationship with Jason had improved in that one encounter. She felt more positively about him, and she sensed the feeling was mutual. As they entered the room, however, Allen commented, under his breath but loud enough for others to hear, "Here comes the cry baby—waa, waa, waa." Several kids sitting close by started laughing. Ms. Stallings was furious. She quickly turned to Jason, whispering, "Ignore them. I'll take care of this." She winked privately at him, but otherwise seemed not to react.

Jason took his seat and she picked up her plan book and studied it a minute. She then put it down and asked the class, "Do you think it is good to want to win?" A few heads nodded. "Do you think it is good to want to be the best?" More heads nodded. She continued, "Today on the playground we had an excellent game between two well-matched teams. As always has to happen, one team won and one team lost. One of the players who lost was upset because he wanted to be the best. He wanted his team to win. Was that wrong?" A few shook their heads no. "As we walked in the room, I heard an unkind comment about that student who wanted to win. Someone accused him of being a cry-baby because he wanted to win. I have trouble with such unkind behavior. We spend a lot of time together in the class. If we are to be happy in here, I think we need to be honest with each other and we need to be kind to each other." With that, she started the lesson. Nothing else was said until the end of the day, when she called both Jason and Allen to the back of the room. She turned to Allen and asked him if he had anything to say to Jason. Allen nodded and apologized. Jason reciprocated, "I understand. I shouldn't have lost my temper." All three shook hands at Ms. Stallings' suggestion.

Interpersonal Communication Skills

The conversation with Jason would probably not have gone very well had Ms. Stallings not possessed some important communication skills. She listened empathetically to Jason, and she communicated clearly and unambivalently to the class. Effective communication such as Ms. Stallings demonstrated requires considerable knowledge and skill.

A number of systems have been developed that help guide teachers in their dialogues with students. The systems can be excellent guides in determining what to say next or how to start the process, *if the teacher has positive regard for the student and if the teacher is comfortable and focused on helpful issues.* Ms. Stallings was sensitive to her own feelings and concerned about finding positive alliances with her students. In her solution, no one was embarrassed, and honest, fair values were advanced. In such a context, the following strategies can be very helpful. However, none of these strategies are effective when used by an angry, hostile teacher who only goes through the motions of the techniques.

Systems for Communication

Most communication systems emphasize the importance of empathetic listening to others as a fundamental for good communication. Carl Rogers (1961) maintained that the *major barrier* to interpersonal communication comes from our very natural tendency to judge—to approve or disapprove of others. Rogers

Children bring many conflicts to school. They need help in dealing with these problems if they are to be free to learn.

developed a therapeutic system based on empathetic listening, maintaining that empathetic listening enables others to examine themselves and to grow. Rogers believed that having our feelings heard, understood, and reflected back to us helps us feel accepted and understood. This understanding provides us with a view into ourselves and enables us to change and to grow (Rogers, 1951). Dr. Elton Mayo suggested that "one friend, one person who is truly understanding, who takes the trouble to listen to us as we consider our problems, can change our whole outlook on the world" (quoted in Nichols & Stevens, 1957).

Behaviors that promote effective communication with others include: *warm, welcoming behaviors* such as smiles and other nonverbal behaviors; *nonjudgmental reactions,* as seen when helpers invest in or focus on others' strengths, not their problems; *empathy,* or trying to see the situation from the other person's perspective; and *respect,* faith in others' ability to solve problems (Gazda, Asbury, Balzer, Childers, & Walters, 1991). Conversely, behaviors that inhibit

Table 10.1 Communication Inhibitors

Detective	(attends to facts and drills the other person about details instead of attending to feelings). The detective controls the flow of conversation, which puts the other person on the defensive.
Magician	(denies the existence of the problem). This is disrespectful because it denies the validity of the person's experience and perception.
Foreman	(keeps the other person busy and thereby avoids the problem).
Hangman	(shows the other person how past actions have contributed to the current problem). This makes the other person feel guilty and punished.
Swami	(knows and predicts exactly what's going to happen and thereby relieves self of responsibility).
Labeler or sign painter	(has a label for every problem and names the problem, but goes no farther).
Drill sergeant	(gives orders and expects they'll be obeyed). Because they believe they know just what the other person should do, drill sergeants don't give explanations, listen to feelings, or explain their commands; they just direct.
Guru	(dispenses proverbs and cliches as though the sole possessors of wisdom). Guru's words are too impersonal, general, and trite to be helpful.
Historian	(digs up old personal stories—golden oldies).
Florist	(is uncomfortable talking about anything unpleasant so gushes flowery phrases to keep other person's problems at safe distance).

Source: Adapted from Gazda, Asbury, Balzer, Childers & Walters (1991).

communication or alienate others include the ones listed by Gazda and others (1991) in Table 10.1 and by Gordon (1974) in Table 10.2. In both tables the problematic responses reflect the speaker's self-absorption and inability to connect empathetically with others. Bolton (1979) suggests that some of these roadblocks are not destructive at all times, but at high-risk times (that is, at times when the other person is under considerable stress). Some of these responses may not create obvious problems in communication, but they do create distance.

Instead of using one of these potentially problematic responses to a person who is in conflict, empathetic listening is recommended. Also called "active listening" (Gordon, 1974) or "reflective listening" (Bolton, 1979), this entails careful attention to the person in conflict and demonstration of empathetic understanding through verbal and nonverbal attention and through statements that demonstrate the person has been heard *and* understood. In the dialogue between Ms. Stallings and Jason, Ms. Stallings demonstrated on several occasions that she had heard and understood Jason's problem. Statements such as "sounds like you're feeling awful . . . not successful . . . not as good as you want to be" are reflective; they indicate that the listener heard both the affect and the content of the speaker. Such statements help the speaker understand his inner turmoil, which in turn enables the speaker to move toward constructive action (Carkhuff, 1973).

Table 10.2 Gordon's Roadblocks to Communication

The first four may prompt a child to get to work and stop daydreaming, and they might redirect the child's attention, but it is unlikely that they will be effective in starting a trusting, open dialogue.

Ordering, commanding, directing. (Don't waste any more time. Get to work!)

Warning, threatening. (If you don't get to work, you'll lose all your points during this period.)

Advising, offering solutions or suggestions. (You need to pay better attention in class—then you won't miss so many questions.)

Teaching, lecturing, giving logical arguments. (Remember, if you want to be in Ms. Simpson's class, you must do well in this class. You need to finish these fractions and you still have grammar to complete. If you don't get to work, you won't have time.)

The next four responses may well cause a frustrated child to become even angrier and they certainly will not promote open, trusting dialogue.

Moralizing, preaching, giving "shoulds" and "oughts." (When you have a problem, you need to leave it at the door. Put it out of your mind. You ought to focus on what we are doing. You shouldn't worry about your problems at home.)

Judging, criticizing, disagreeing, blaming. (Your mother shouldn't have filled out this form. She doesn't know how to do it. Can she even read?)

Name calling, stereotyping, labeling. (You're lazy! All boys your age get that way, but you'll never succeed if you don't get off your backside!)

Interpreting, analyzing, diagnosing. (I've got your number. You're just trying to get out of doing this work. I know you don't like it, but you have to do it!)

The final four responses block communication because they are distancing. The speaker is acting as if in a superior role.

Praising, agreeing, giving positive evaluations. (You've got such a good brain. I know you can solve this problem.)

Reassuring, sympathizing, consoling, supporting. (When you get a little older, you'll realize that this really is not such a big deal. This is such a typical adolescent problem.)

Questioning, probing, interrogating, cross-examining. (What did you say when that happened? Why did you say that? Has that ever happened before?)

Withdrawing, distracting, being sarcastic, humoring, diverting. (Let's get back to work. Boy, who took your smile this morning. I don't care if you blow your entire year!)

Source: Gordon (1974).

Gordon's I-Messages

In his system of effective communication, Gordon (1974) emphasizes the importance of determining who has the problem. He suggests that if the child has the problem (is the person who is upset), then the teacher uses active or reflective listening. If, however, it is the teacher who is upset, the teacher needs to be more assertive in expressing feelings. This too requires skill, because confrontations and accusations usually result in defensive responses. Gordon devised the "I-message" as an effective strategy for asserting oneself while not making the other person defensive. An I-message consists of three parts: a description of the behavior that is causing the problem, a description of that behavior's effect on the speaker, and identification of the speaker's feelings that result from the behavior. For example, Ms. Stallings could have said to Allen, "When you made fun of Jason, I got upset and then it seemed to me that your teasing embarrassed Jason. I was worried that he would get upset again. When one person in our class is upset, the whole class gets distracted." Statements such as this don't attack, but they do clearly identify the problem and put the other person in the position of responding constructively. Had Ms. Stallings turned to Allen and criticized him "You shouldn't speak like that to someone in this class," Allen might have been quiet, but he might also have been angry at being publicly criticized. Guilt might even exacerbate his anger.

Life Space Interviewing

Originally developed by Fritz Redl (1959) and his colleagues for use in a residential treatment center for aggressive boys, this technique has been used in psychoeducational settings for well over 30 years. Redl developed the intervention when he realized that the aggressive boys he was working with could not wait for therapy to talk over problems; however the boys did seem to be receptive to talk and self-reflection shortly after a crisis happened. A day or two later, even several hours later, the boys had pushed the conflict out of their minds, and it was too late for self-reflection. Bringing up the problem days later was like bringing up a new problem, and it often actually caused new eruptions. Wood and Long (1991) quote a student who graphically illustrates how hard it can be for some of these children to talk about their problems: "Talking about my past is like picking up a dead dog out of the road that's been hit by a car" (p. 104).

The life space interview is based upon therapeutic tools that are used in the life space of the child in conflict. Problems are discussed in the here and now, not when the therapy hour arrives. Primarily intended for "clinical exploitation of life events" and "emotional first aid," the life space interview helps children gain new insights into their problems and learn new ways of coping. The purposes of the life space interview are to help children become aware of their maladaptive attitudes, recognize their distortions of social interactions, learn new problem-solving skills, maintain control when upset, and deal with frustrations before they become overwhelming.

Prior to implementing the use of life space interviews in their program, DeMagistris and Imber (1980) studied typical classroom discussions and found that teachers often told children what they did wrong, conveying the sense of being criticized. Teachers rarely tried to understand children's views of an incident and discussions were rarely private. Often the teacher and student ended in a stand-off with the child being punished for inappropriate behavior.

In a life space interview, teachers adhere to certain therapeutic principles. When deciding whether to conduct a life space interview, Morse (1980) identifies several factors that should be considered:

1. *Is there sufficient time to discuss the problem?* Interruptions and a sense of being rushed do not contribute to establishing open, trusting communication.

2. *Does the child appear to be receptive to such a discussion?* One does not try to engage a child in self-reflection when the child is furious. At that point talk needs to be focused on getting calm and getting control.

3. *Is the teacher in the right frame of mind?* When teachers are still angry with a child, they are in no frame of mind to convey warmth, empathy, and concern—nor are they likely to be very receptive to what the student has to say. Teachers need to be relatively calm when they undertake an LSI.

4. *Is the setting appropriate?* Self-disclosure should be done in a setting that protects a person's privacy. In the case with Jason and Ms. Stallings, had a group of children walked down the hall as Jason began to cry, more harm than good might have resulted.

5. *Is the issue under discussion in an LSI closely related to other issues the child is currently working on?* Children are developing organisms, and most have many areas in which there is room for improvement. Pointing out *all* areas of improvement only serves to make a child feel inadequate. Teachers and families need to select the issues about which they are most concerned and focus on those. After these issues improve, there is time to work on new issues. Trying to do everything at once will overwhelm and antagonize the child.

6. *Is the issue one that the child is psychologically ready to understand?* Helping children gain insights into themselves and their behavior is somewhat like peeling layers off an onion. As one aspect of a problem is understood, related components become apparent. Problems take a long time to develop, thus they take time and patience to be understood. As noted in 5 above, teachers need to set priorities and then work slowly on helping the child understand the issue. Moving too quickly can also antagonize and hurt the child.

Once a teacher has decided to conduct a life space interview, Morse (1980) suggests seven steps to follow:

1. *Find out how the child perceived the event/problem.* People see events differently. Before any progress can be made in solving the problem, teachers

need to know what the child is thinking and how the child perceives the problem.

2. *Find out if the child thinks this kind of problem happens often.* If the child sees the problem as a fluke event that rarely happens, the child is not likely to be motivated to work on the problem. If, however, the child thinks this kind of problem happens frequently, the child is likely to be concerned about how to solve the problem.

3. *Share your view of the event/problem.* In a nonjudgmental manner the teacher needs to let the child know how she perceived the event or the problem. This is not done in the spirit of the teacher is right and the child wrong, rather to present a different way of viewing the problem. If the child values the relationship with the teacher, the child is likely to consider and value the teacher's perspective.

4. *Convey a sense of acceptance and try to avoid making child defensive.* The teacher strives to create an atmosphere in which the child experiences the right to be heard (that her feelings are valued).

5. *Help the child think of the consequences of behavior.* As a means of teaching children to problem solve, the teacher helps them consider the consequences or implications of their actions. This places children in the role of evaluating themselves and their own behavior.

6. *Search for reasons why the child might want to change (sources of motivation).* Plans to change only work when children are invested in them. The child has to want something in order to work on changing; thus before agreeing upon a plan for change teachers need to understand why the child might be willing to change.

7. *Develop a plan to deal with the problem, if possible.* These plans need to be realistic and attainable or the child will experience even further failure and despair.

Naslund (1985) conducted a longitudinal study in which she reported the outcome of her study of 1404 LSIs—every LSI conducted at Rose School during one academic year. (Rose School is a school in Washington, D.C., for children who have severe emotional and behavioral disabilities between the ages of 6 and 13.) She found that students who were developmentally older, had been in the program longer, and had above-average IQs responded best to the technique. Her results also suggested that peer-related crises were the most frequent reason for undertaking an LSI, while classroom work was the least frequent cause. Finally, she found that children who had participated in LSIs showed an increase in their classroom work, a decrease in their loss of self-control, and an increase in their requests for LSIs—indicating their wish to talk about problems as ways of handling stress.

Conclusions

Effective communication with children involves entering into dialogue with them, allowing them to tell their stories, and genuinely "hearing" what they say. This can only take place when teachers are sensitive to others and reflective about their own thoughts, values, beliefs, etc. That is, unless teachers are willing and able to establish and engage in mutually respectful relationships with students, they can use all the right words but the message may run counter to what they "say." When communication fails, it is easy to attribute the failure solely to the student's social and emotional "problems" or to the constraints placed on teachers by school policy or standards. While this attribution often relieves teachers of the responsibility to examine their own relationships and practices, it seriously limits possibilities for growth and change, not only for their students, but also for themselves.

Throughout this chapter we have explored some of the dimensions that impact teachers' communication and decision making as a means of stressing the complexity of effective and therapeutic student–teacher relationships. We have looked at aspects of teaching that require teachers both to examine themselves, their roles, their language, and their beliefs and to understand their students' perceptions of roles, language, and beliefs. We believe that teachers need to understand the enormity of the challenge and to give themselves room to learn and change.

Teachers must realize that reflection on their own teaching and their relationships with students may uncover aspects of themselves that create discomfort, as well as areas of teaching and communication in which they feel inadequate. If teachers expect themselves to be perfect, if they are unable to accept that they do not always know what to do, and if they are unduly harsh on themselves when things go "wrong," reflection will become a painful process they may want to avoid. However, if teachers can view the classroom as a place where everyone learns, look at their students as their "teachers," and view problems as opportunities to understand their students and themselves better, then they may be more willing to examine their own practices continually as a natural part of an ongoing process.

Discussion Questions and Activities

1. Observe in a classroom and describe as specifically as possible a conflict that arises. Try to portray various perspectives in describing the event as fairly as possible. After describing the event carefully, brainstorm alternative explanations as well as possible responses for the problem.

Consider the implications of each response, then share your list with class-mates and encourage their additions. Once your list is as complete as possible, answer the question In your opinion, is there one explanation and response that is clearly better, and why or why not?

2. Describe two children that you know—preferably that you teach. Use as many adjectives as possible in describing each child. Fold the descriptions up and put them away for several days, then re-examine them. What types of construals have you given each child? Can you think of other possible construals?

3. Describe your "power" in your classroom. How did you get it and how do you maintain it? Would you like to be more powerful? Why or why not? When your class gets loud and unruly, how do you feel? What do you do? Can you think of other, more desirable responses?

4. Practice using I-messages in response to the following situations:
You are giving directions to your entire class about how to complete a social-studies project. Two kids are whispering to each other, oblivious to your instructions. Several other children sitting close to them seem more interested in the whispered conversation than in your directions.

Jason is a very bright sophomore boy in your tenth-grade social-studies class. The class has been working in cooperative learning groups to complete a project on ancient Greece. Jason's group has developed a very impressive, creative project. In the process of checking on each group's progress, you make a suggestion to Jason's group. He rolls his eyes, as if to imply that your suggestion was ridiculous and reflected a lack of under-standing on your part.

Alexis never turns in his homework, but he does very well (often the best) on all his tests and in-class assignments. You have an established grading procedure that allows 30% of the total grade for homework. Since Alexis has not done his homework, he cannot get a good grade in your system, and this worries you.

One of your colleagues asked to have a child with emotional and be-havioral difficulties placed in her classroom. You concurred, but now you are disturbed because the child is failing. You believe her expectations for this child are unrealistic.

5. Tape record yourself in dialogue with a child and analyze your dialogue. How did you do?

Reflective Questions

1. Do you continually assess your reactions to students, monitoring when your own biases and personal conflicts might be affecting your judgment?

2. Do you know your students' hobbies, interests, and preferences regarding friends and activities?

3. Do your students believe you care about them? Do your students trust that you know what is in their best interest? How do you know? Why do you think you do?

4. What do you think your responsibilities are to your students?

5. Describe the type of relationship you think you should have with your students.

6. Which students in your class annoy you most and why? What can you do to change your feelings, independent of actions the student might take?

7. Which students in your class appeal to you the most and why? Do you like these students because of who they are or because they meet your needs?

8. Are your feelings about students, both positive and negative, evident to other students?

9. What role(s) do you play in your classroom? How do you know? What data support your response?

10. Monitor your dialogues with your students. Do you know what you want to accomplish when you enter into a dialogue with an upset student?

11. Do you give students time to respond thoughtfully?

12. Have you been able to establish a sense of trust and safety?

13. Do you avoid value judgments and counteraggression?

14. Are you careful not to intrude into the student's private "space," psychologically and physically?

15. Do you convey a sense of confidence and ability to deal with and solve problems?

16. Do you use time lines to help students organize their thoughts about events?

17. Do you assist students in clarifying issues and seeing cause and effect?

18. Do you convey support and alliance through your body language and attitude? Do you avoid excessive touching?

19. Do you use concrete words when talking to an upset student? Is your language clear and easily understood? Do you maximize student talk and minimize your own talk?

20. How have you achieved your authority in your classroom and in your school? Is your power based in genuine ability to help or gained through your ability to punish and limit?

References

Ayers, W. (1992). Teachers' stories: Autobiography and inquiry. In W. Ross, J. Cornett, & G. McCutcheon (eds.), *Teacher personal theorizing: Connecting curriculum practice, theory, and research* (35–49). Albany: State University of New York Press.

Barth, R. (1986). *Social and cognitive treatment of children.* San Francisco: Jossey-Bass.

Bolton, R. (1979). *People skills.* New York: Simon & Schuster.

Bruner, J. (1986). *Actual minds, possible worlds.* Cambridge: Harvard University Press.

Buber, M. (1965). Education. In M. Buber (ed.), *Between man and man* (pp. 83–103). New York: Macmillan.

Carkhuff, R. (1973). *The art of helping: A guide for developing helping skills for parents, teachers, and counselors.* Amherst, MA: Human Resource Development Press.

DeMagistris, R. & Imber, S. (1980). The effects of life space interviewing on academic and social performance of behaviorally disordered children. *Behavior Disorders, 6,* 12–25.

Gazda, G.M., Asbury, F.R., Balzer, F.J., Childers, W.C. & Walters, R.P. (1991). *Human relations development: A manual for educators* (4th ed.). Boston: Allyn & Bacon.

Gordon, T. (1974). *Teacher effectiveness training.* New York: McKay.

Hall, E. (1981). *Beyond culture.* New York: Anchor Books/Doubleday.

Knitzer, J., Steinberg, Z. & Fleisch, B. (1990). *At the schoolhouse door: An examination of programs and policies for children with behavioral and emotional problems.* New York: Bank Street College of Education.

Morse, W. (1980). Worksheet on life space interviewing. In N. Long, W. Morse & R. Newman (eds.), *Conflict in the classroom: The education of emotionally disturbed children,* (4th ed.) (267–70). Belmont, CA: Wadsworth.

Naslund, S. (1985). Life space interviewing: A psychoeducational interviewing model for teaching pupil insights and measuring program effectiveness. *The Pointer, 31,* 12–15.

Nichols, R. & Stevens, L. (1957). *Are you listening?* New York: McGraw-Hill.

Noddings, N. (1991). Stories in dialogue: Caring and interpersonal reasoning. In C. Witherell & N. Noddings (eds.), *Stories lives tell: Narrative and dialogue in education.* New York: Teachers College Press, Columbia University.

Noddings, N. (1992). *The challenge to care in schools: an alternative approach to education.* New York: Teachers College Press, Columbia University.

Poplin, M. & Weeres, J. (1992). *Voices from the inside: A report on schooling from inside the classroom.* Claremont, CA: Institute for Education in Transformation.

Redl, F. (1959). The life space interview in the school setting. *American Journal of Orthopsychiatry, 33,* 717–19.

Rogers, C. (1951). *Client-centered therapy.* Boston: Houghton Mifflin.

Rogers, C. (1961). *On becoming a person: A therapist's view of psychotherapy.* Boston: Houghton Mifflin.

Ross, W., Cornett, J. & McCutcheon, G. (1992). *Teacher personal theorizing: Connecting curriculum practice, theory, and research.* Albany, NY: SUNY Press.

Scherer, M. (1992). Solving conflicts—not just for children. *Educational Leadership, 50,* 14–18.

Spence, L. (1978). *The politics of social knowledge.* University Park, PA: The State University of Pennsylvania Press.

Tappan, M. (1991). Stories told and lessons learned: Toward a narrative approach to moral development and moral education. In C. Wetherell & N. Noddings (eds.), *Stories lives tell: Narrative and dialogue in education.* New York: Teachers College Press, Columbia University.

Tobin, K. & LaMaster, S. (1992). An interpretation of high school science teaching based on metaphors and beliefs for specific roles. In W. Ross, J. Cornett, & G. McCutcheon (eds.), *Teacher personal theorizing: Connecting curriculum practice, theory, and research* (115–36). Albany: SUNY Press.

Witherell, C. & Noddings, N. (1991). *Stories lives tell: Narrative and dialogue in education.* New York: Teachers College Press, Columbia University.

Wood, M. & Long, N. (1991). *Life space intervention: Talking with children and youth in crisis.* Austin, TX: PRO-ED.

Chapter 11

Crisis Management

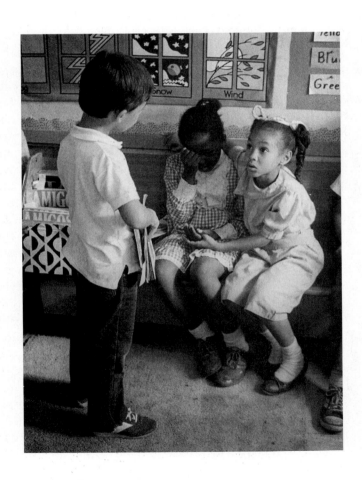

Seth is a 16-year-old sophomore in high school. He is the youngest of three boys. One of his brothers is in a juvenile detention center and the other is serving time in the county jail. Seth, much like his brothers, becomes uncontrollable when angered. His teachers have described him as a time bomb waiting to explode. He loves to tease people, but gets upset when others tease him. He dislikes school, his teachers, and most of the students. In school, he prefers to keep to himself. He says that the students act too silly and that's the reason he likes to hang out with older guys who have either finished or quit school.

Seth is very worried about his mother. She recently remarried, and he suspects that his stepfather physically and verbally abuses her. Seth has never seen him harming her physically, but has often returned home to find his mother crying and with bruises she wouldn't explain. Seth continues to warn his stepfather to keep his hands off her, which always leads to an argument between the two of them. His stepfather frequently threatens to put him out of the house. Seth says the only reason he continues to live there is for his mother's protection. He believes that if he moves out, his stepfather will seriously injure her.

The other day Seth returned home from school and noticed that his mother's eyes were swollen; she had obviously been crying. She told Seth she just wasn't feeling well, but Seth didn't believe her. He was convinced that the swollen eyes resulted from his stepfather's hitting her. When he confronted his stepfather, they started fighting. Seth ran from the house and spent the night at his cousin's.

In his first-hour class the next day, Seth sauntered in as the teacher said good morning. Seth grumpily muttered "Yeah, right!" He went to his desk and slammed his books down. Seth continued to make loud noises during class. Another student headed up the aisle to sharpen his pencil. Seth extended his leg across the aisle and the student accidentally stepped on Seth's foot. Seth threatened to "beat the s--t" out of him if he came past one more time. The student told Seth that he would walk up the aisle whenever he pleased. Seth was furious! He leaped from his seat, grabbed the student by the collar of his shirt, and backed him into the wall. Seth swung his fist back, and the teacher ran up just as he was about to hit the other student.

*S*eth's emotions are highly volatile. He is losing control of his behavior and is in a state of crisis. Similar scenarios involving students in crisis occur all too often in public school settings. These crises interfere with both learning and safety. Students in crises jeopardize the well-being of other students, teachers, and themselves.

This chapter presents proactive crisis management techniques for children and youth. In crisis management, a discussion of preventive strategies should precede the presentation of techniques deliberately planned to reduce crises and promote problem-solving skills. Throughout life, stress-producing events are inevitable. Students must become aware that it is impossible to stave off all stressful situations. While many events can be controlled, some cannot. Having acknowledged this, the emphasis in crisis management should be on the ability to control how one reacts to stressful or anxiety-producing events. Ultimately, educators are challenged to use potential crises as opportunities for instruction. Actual and simulated events can be used to model and practice strategies for recognizing potential crises and engaging in socially acceptable techniques for anxiety reduction.

It is critical that students and teachers practice preventive techniques. Both teacher and student behaviors can be altered to de-escalate situations before they become so intense that they result in a crisis. There are, however, occasions when teachers may be unable to foresee a crisis. Under those circumstances, strategies should be employed that encourage students to look realistically at what occurred and to facilitate student ownership of crisis behavior. An important aspect of crisis management is that students become cognizant of their feelings and learn to manage their impulses while under duress. Consequently this chapter will also address techniques that may appear reactive because they are implemented in response to a crisis. Even though those techniques are used following crises, they proactively facilitate alternatives to inappropriate behaviors for preventing and managing future crises in home, school, or community settings.

Proactive Crisis Prevention Strategies

There are two types of crises: developmental and accidental (Caplan, 1964). A developmental crisis occurs during milestones in children's lives (starting school for the first time, losing a tooth for the first time, entering adolescence). On the other hand, an accidental crisis results from a loss of coping skills when individuals are faced with increased demands.

This section will focus on the prevention of accidental crises in school settings. While schools are the settings discussed here, teachers can arm students with crisis prevention and management strategies that will serve them in their home and community as well. At times, it is impossible to separate events that contribute to crises from the various environments in which students spend significant amounts of time. Boundaries blur regarding events and settings that

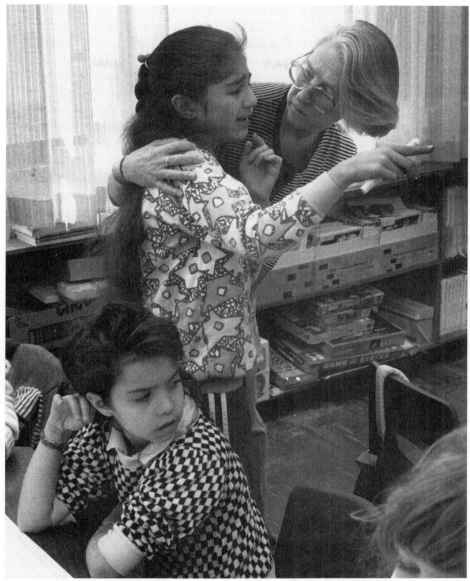

Teachers help children solve problems through care, support, and empathetic listening when a child is upset.

precipitate crises. This is demonstrated in Seth's behavior. While his crisis manifested in the classroom, it probably had little to do with school. Seth was troubled when he entered the classroom. His anxiety likely stemmed from his concern about his mother and his inability to do something about it. These feelings may have been compounded by his most recent altercation with his stepfather. Had his teacher been aware of his mood, the teacher might have been able to help Seth manage his anxiety, thus avoiding his confrontation with another student.

There are no situations that result in crises for all individuals. While everyone experiences anxiety-producing events, few if any of these events send all persons experiencing them into crisis. Whether an event becomes a crisis is individual-specific. It is critical that persons working with children and youth understand the relativity of crises. According to Greenstone and Leviton (1987), "Crises occur when unusual stress in a person's life renders her unable to cope with the world by utilizing those personal mechanisms normally available to her" (p. 40). This stress can be produced by situations in which that reaction is expected; stress can also be produced by situations in which the reaction is unexpected. Some events are associated with stress and considered more anxiety-producing than others. An example of an anxiety-producing event is the sudden death of a loved one. Adults perceive this event as stressful and it is likely to produce high levels of anxiety in children and youth. An example of an event that adults might not associate with anxiety is an adolescent who is worried about her friends' impressions of her. Her family may be unable to purchase the trendy, expensive athletic clothing that has become popular in her peer group. When she and three friends decide to dress alike for an upcoming school function, that adolescent may become anxious. Knowing that she cannot buy the outfit (and rapidly running out of excuses), she may be stressed more than her normal coping strategies can handle.

A teacher observing this may be tempted to suggest that she not upset herself over something as trivial as wearing name-brand clothing. The teacher might even advise the student to wear what she has and to forget about it. The teacher might moralize further by insisting that it is a person's character that matters more than her clothing. As illustrated here, teachers aren't always aware of events that children and youth perceive as stressful. The tendency may be to downplay the significance of events occurring in children's lives if teachers don't view them as stressful.

Wood and Long (1991) suggested that "Once an adult learns to see a crisis through the eyes of the student, greater empathy, support, realistic problem solving, and behavioral self-control can occur" (p. xii). Teachers, in working with children and youth who have problems resulting from contemporary societal pressures, must be reminded that even when the child's concerns appear unfounded or senseless they are real and may be traumatic to that particular child. Furthermore, events that produce stress in children are unique to each individual. The diversity in classrooms impels teachers to define anxiety from the individual child's perspective.

This realization will assist teachers in determining events that precede crises among their students. If teachers can discern events that trouble students, they are able to predict and consequently plan instruction for potential crises. It is apparent that Seth's teacher was oblivious to signs that there were troubling events occurring to him outside the school setting. Therefore, strategies for addressing those conflicts were not implemented.

Increasing numbers of public school students experience stressful situations on a daily basis. School experiences may or may not be as stressful as their experiences in other settings. Home and community settings may contribute greatly to students' stress levels. Being unable to "check their stressors at the door," these students may use school as a place for acting out conflicts arising elsewhere. As a result, public school educators must structure classroom experiences that acknowledge and accommodate students who experience in- or out-of-school conflicts.

The nature of conflicts that occur among children and youth must be understood. Conflicts are not necessarily negative. They provide "teachable moments," in which meaningful opportunities to model and teach socially acceptable responses can be structured. Seth, as you recall, is troubled by what's happening at home among his mother, stepfather, and himself. Having just had a fight with his stepfather, school is providing an outlet for his pent-up feelings of anger and frustration. Had his teacher behaved differently when Seth entered the classroom, the situation might not have escalated as it did.

The following discussion delineates alternative teacher behavior that can prevent students from being in crises. To further aid teachers in understanding conflicts among students, Long (1974) depicted the "conflict cycle." It emphasizes the cyclical nature of conflicts and the environment's roles in creating and maintaining stressors in children's lives. The conflict cycle consists of a series of events in children's lives that perpetuate stress. Children experience stressful incidents, display behavior that reacts to the incidents, get negative reactions from others, and experience additional stress resulting from those reactions. When the incidents are not resolved, a crisis results.

The resulting crisis does not affect the student alone. Long (1974) suggested that, just as teachers influence student behavior, the students affect teacher behaviors. Long noted that when students behave in negative ways, the teacher may alter her behavior in response. Doing so may cause the teacher to engage in behavior that is uncharacteristic. The usually mild-mannered, even-tempered teacher may raise her voice or become confrontational. Long reported when that happens a power struggle may ensue between teacher and student.

Interventions with children experiencing conflict should be designed to break the conflict cycle. To break the cycle, teachers must first have insight about their students. This insight needs to go beyond what is traditionally considered as getting to know one's students. It must go deeper than knowing what they like to do in their spare time or to what careers they aspire. It means that teachers must get involved with students on interpersonal levels (Glasser, 1972). In essence, teachers must be perceptive of student behavior under normal circumstances to know when students are behaving differently. They must be careful observers of each student in the classroom and solicit information from others who are most familiar with the child's patterns of behavior. Cultural and individual differences of students dictate a need for teachers to interpret behavioral and communication styles accurately. It is beneficial to gather perceptions of teachers who have positive relationships with the student. Another way to get feedback on teacher perceptions is to tell the student the perception of her behavior and ask if it is accurate. To illustrate, if the teacher suspects that Seth is not himself, she might say "Seth, I'm not sure, but it looks like something is bothering you. . . ."

If Seth's teacher is aware of his behavior on a day-to-day basis, when he acts differently she will be ready for changes in his temperament or demeanor. If they occur, the teacher can deliberately alter classroom events or interactions to support crisis management. The aim is to develop a relationship with students that will lead to insight into their behavior. Only then will it be known if Seth is undergoing stress and needing intervention.

Teacher-Student Interactions

Ideally, teachers should have positive relationships with their students before attempts are made to assist them in managing crises. This presents a new challenge for educators, as classrooms are more diverse than ever before. Diversity is obvious in ethnicity, social class, linguistics, and ability. What may be less apparent in the diversity among the members of any particular ethnic group. For instance, childrearing patterns, cultural orientations, and extent of dominant culture identification are variations that occur among members of the same ethnic group. Because of differences observed both among and within ethnic groups, techniques must affirm individual as well as cultural differences.

Techniques are available for developing relationships between teachers and students who are culturally or individually different. Teachers must begin on the first day developing sincere relationships with students. Maintaining open and honest lines of communication undergirds positive interpersonal relationships. The following relationship-building skills facilitate open and honest communication between teacher and students.

Empathic listening. As discussed in Chapter 10, it is imperative that teachers encourage students to talk to them about whatever is on their minds. Students must feel that what they say is important. To communicate this, teachers need to use body language that puts students at ease while listening and talking to them. To determine what others find comfortable requires an astute observer. Notice the distance maintained by the student when talking to the teacher; the student may be uncomfortable if the teacher is too close physically. Take cues from the student. If, as the teacher walks toward the student, the student begins to back off, it is a sign that the student is uncomfortable with the teacher's physical proximity. Another technique is to ask directly if the student likes the seating arrangement, or even if standing is preferred. Soliciting and honoring student requests communicates the teacher's willingness to accommodate various student styles.

Most people have been taught to use eye contact as a way of communicating interest in what the speaker is saying. This listening technique may violate some children's cultural or individual preferences. Teachers need to be sure that looking the student in the eye does not cause student discomfort. Teachers should make every attempt to understand the student's views. Even when the teacher disagrees with the student's perspectives, he or she must communicate respect. Suppose Seth talks to his teacher about his stepfather. If the teacher is an empathic listener, the conversation might go like this:

Seth: *My stepfather is so mean to my mom and me that I won't be happy until I get back at him.*

Teacher: *Seth, I can understand your feeling angry at your stepfather. Help me understand what you mean about "getting back at him."*

Seth: *Well, I feel like having some gang bangers beat him up real bad because that's what he deserves.*

[*The teacher does not want to appear supportive of Seth's having his stepfather beaten up, but does want to support his feelings of anger and powerlessness.*]

Teacher: *That situation must be really hard to deal with. I can tell you're angry about the way your stepfather has treated you and your mom. I think you also believe that he should be punished for what he's done. Is that right?*

Seth: *Yeah, I'm tired of letting him think he can do whatever and get away with it.*

Teacher: *I can see how you can be angry enough to want revenge. I would like for us to talk more about what to do with the anger you feel.*

[*Seth's teacher validates Seth's feelings of anger, but also encourages him to explore those feelings. The teacher would listen to Seth and encourage the brainstorming of other options for addressing the problem.*]

Trustworthiness.   Another message teachers must communicate is that they can be trusted by students. Activities can be structured to promote teacher–student interdependence. Interdependence is demonstrated when two or more individuals have common goals and rely on each other to fulfill their responsibility toward goal attainment (Johnson & Johnson, 1983). To facilitate interdependence the teacher and student must first identify mutual goals, delegate activities, and provide each other with feedback.

If Seth's teacher had gotten to know his background, she would know that he loves watching movies. Any money he gets, he spends on either movie tickets or video rentals. He especially likes classic movies and enjoys telling their plots when anyone asks about one. His teacher wants her students to be able to write a book report discussing the characters, plot, and symbolism evident in the book. She wants the assignment to be motivating and doubts if having to read a book and write about it will be exciting to her students. Therefore, she decides to have the class write about their favorite movie before requiring a book report. She could enlist Seth's assistance in modeling this skill for the class. The teacher and Seth jointly plan an activity for the class on movie reports. If Seth agrees to this teacher–student collaboration project, several objectives will be accomplished. In addition to being motivating for Seth, it will allow the teacher to structure an opportunity for interdependence and the mutual demonstration of trust between the two.

The teacher might share her concerns with Seth about wanting to motivate the class to write a movie report. She could also tell Seth that she would like him to work with her to increase motivation because she is well aware of his interest in movies and his skill in detailing movie characters, settings, and plots. She could ask him if he would be comfortable working with her to model reporting a movie. If Seth agrees, the teacher could work with him to ensure that the major points are covered before he models the technique to be learned. Afterward, the teacher and Seth would provide each other feedback on their efforts to motivate the class to report on movies.

Teachers must also develop another kind of trust among their students. It is imperative that students know the teacher will protect (not disclose to others) information students have shared. When students self-disclose, they must feel assured that the disclosure will not be part of conversations among teachers and others who play no role in the disclosure. Moreover, even when other parties are involved, the teacher must fully inform them of the nature of the confidentiality agreement. Teachers then must use their professional judgment to determine if information needs to be shared to protect the student. For example, if a student confided to a teacher that she had recently been contemplating suicide, it would be unethical for the teacher to withhold that information from those who may be concerned with seeking help.

Reciprocity.   Relationships between teachers and students should be reciprocal and mutually rewarding. Teachers are often viewed in helping roles in the classroom. They are the ones who help students learn and provide class structure and routine. Teachers should structure opportunities in which students play helping roles in the classroom. All class members need to feel that they are contributing worth to the class, just as they need to do in their families. In this regard, both students and teachers have meaningful opportunities to contribute to the class.

Froyen (1993) discusses the notion of covenant management in classrooms. It centers on the development of social–emotional aspects of relationships in the process of facilitating student learning. Froyen proposes the establishment of a climate in which caring exists. Caring occurs among teachers and students and supports students who are willing to engage in risk-taking behavior. This willingness is necessary if students are to be prepared for the many challenges confronting them.

Classroom Environment

While classroom structure has been discussed in detail in Chapter 4, a few details specific to crisis prevention are presented here. The classroom environment should be assessed to determine if there are aspects that exacerbate crises. Aspects of the classroom environment that may be suspect are:

- ☐ *Physical space.* The classroom arrangement should accommodate a variety of learning, working, and communication styles and preferences. For example, areas should be structured for students to work alone or in small groups. The same holds for areas allowing student socialization and privacy. Areas for group activities should be designated, along with areas for private activity (music, art, leisure reading, journal writing). Having designated areas provides students with alternatives to inappropriate behaviors.

- ☐ *Traffic patterns.* Patterns for traffic flow should be established with students and need to be well supervised. Students should help determine the rules by which they will be governed.

- ☐ *Instructional programming.* Student characteristics should influence instructional formats. Stated another way, curricular decisions should be made based on characteristics such as interests, skills, motivation.

- ☐ *Locus of control.* Activities should be structured to provide students with choices when possible. Doing so models the importance of individuals' making decisions regarding aspects of their lives.

- ☐ *Management style.* The teacher's management style should not be characterized by power, but should facilitate the involvement of students in their own academic and social management.

Proactive Crisis Management

Aggressive and violent acts are witnessed in schools with alarming regularity (Guetzloe, 1993). Students' inability to cope with stressful events may attribute to this rising tide of school violence. Teachers must make every effort to teach students techniques that will prevent their anxiety from escalating to out-of-control behaviors. While preventive efforts should be the major focus of crisis management procedures, advance plans must also be in place for managing crises when they do arise.

Teachers must assess classroom events and determine if, and to what extent, the situation warrants intervention. Once the decision is made to intervene, an intervention must be selected that accommodates cultural and individual needs. According to Long (1974), the intervention should be designed to break the cycle of stressors on the student. Swanson and Rinert (1979) suggested evaluating several aspects of the classroom environment to identify modifications needed to reduce student stress levels.

☐ Demands and expectations in setting

☐ Student ability to respond to demands

☐ Student–peer relationships

☐ Student–teacher relationships

☐ Student self-concept

☐ Student motivation for the crisis behavior

Teachers need to continually assess these factors and to program activities that ensure matches between student attributes and environmental characteristics. Crises are not sudden, spontaneous events. They develop gradually and occur following an upsetting event or combination of events in students' lives. To that end, students undergo crises in three phases. As students experience anxiety resulting from home, school, and community conflicts, teachers must recognize each phase—pre-crisis, crisis, and post-crisis—and teach students effective strategies to manage their own anxieties.

Pre-Crisis Phase

One of the first steps in crisis management is recognizing the three phases. Just recognizing phases of crises that individuals go through may be a challenging task. There are no common behaviors that are unique to each particular phase. In the opening scenario, Seth entered the classroom in an observably grumpy mood. All students in the pre-crisis phase may not be as overtly upset as Seth. Each phase may manifest itself differently in individual students. Some children may display acting-out behaviors, while others may exhibit withdrawn behaviors (Center, 1989). Many variables influence student behavior during any crisis phase. The variables include, but are not limited to, cultural experiences, family customs, observations of others' reactions to stress, communication style, and individual preferences.

Several strategies can be implemented during the pre-crisis phase to prevent the full development of a crisis. This phase usually involves a change in students'

Figure 11.1 Defense Mechanisms: Anxiety Types

Anxiety Type	Arises when
Reality anxiety	environmental events threaten person
Neurotic anxiety	id impulses threaten ego regulations
Moral anxiety	behavior to be engaged in threatens the superego or moral development

moods and/or behaviors. The nature of the change may vary from student to student, making it imperative that teachers alert themselves to the various behaviors of their students before crises occur.

As stated earlier, student populations have become increasingly diverse (Banks & Banks, 1993). This diversity is apparent along lines of ethnicity, social class, ability, communication, linguistic, religion, work, and socialization styles and preferences. In recognizing pre-crisis indicators for each student, teachers must factor in cultural and individual diversity. It is no longer safe to assume that teachers "know" their students well enough to single-handedly identify crisis predictors. To recognize impending crises and intervene effectively, the teacher needs to involve others in the process.

Persons who play significant roles in the lives of students should be enlisted to help gain insight into students' moods and behaviors. These people include the student, family members, community members, and peers. When it is determined that the student is in a pre-crisis phase, intervention can take on several forms. The goal at this point is to prevent additional crisis development (Wimberley, 1985). Popular strategies to prohibit crises are presented here. The ones to be discussed are rooted in psychodynamic, psychoeducational, and cognitive theoretical models.

The psychodynamic model is derived from Sigmund Freud's psychoanalytic theory (Coleman, 1992). Freud, a physician and psychologist, postulated that interactions occur among the id, the ego, and the superego to produce behavior. The *id* is considered the pleasure center that seeks immediate gratification. The *superego* is compared to one's conscience because it focuses on right versus wrong. While the id and the superego are at two extremes, the *ego* mediates among the pleasure-oriented id, the conscience-oriented superego and reality (Newcomer, 1993; Wicks-Nelson & Israel, 1984). The reader can refer to Fine (1973) for detailed descriptions of the psychodynamic model.

The following are basic principles of the psychodynamic model:

☐ Defense mechanisms are formulated by individuals to relieve anxiety (Figure 11.1).

☐ Children undergo five stages of psychosexual development.

Figure 11.2 A-B-C Model for Rational Thinking

A (Activating event)	B (Belief)	C (Consequence)
	Irrational thinking:	
No date for the prom	"No one asked me to the prom because no one likes me."	anxiety
	Rational thinking: "It would have been nice to have a date for the prom, but I can still have a good time without one."	confidence

☐ Children are unaware of their intrapsychic conflicts.

☐ Intervention involves providing children with insight to their conflicts.

☐ Conflict among the id, ego, and superego produces three anxiety types.

The psychoanalytic model of working with children in crisis in the classroom has been criticized for its lack of utility in that setting (Fagan, Long, & Stevens, 1975). It is also criticized for its emphasis on the unconscious and, thus, its lack of access for scientific investigations on its effects. Moreover the psychoanalytic approach promotes classroom conformity over child development. Interventions espoused by psychoanalysts require time and training that is extensively beyond the realm of classroom teachers.

The psychodynamic approach to crisis prevention attempted to modify the psychoanalysis model to be more applicable in school settings. According to Rezmierski and Kotre (1974), the psychodynamic approach to working with children should facilitate emotional expression among children while accommodating the crises they experience. A basic principle of this approach is that children are unaware of their internal conflicts, and intervention should therefore provide students with the insight needed to resolve them.

In helping children become insightful about their thought processes and their behaviors, cognitive approaches have been implemented. These emanated from psychodynamic approaches for preventing and managing crises and often entail cognitive restructuring. Cognitive restructuring is a process in which the teacher guides the students in identifying erroneous beliefs or thoughts they may hold and assists them in developing more appropriate thoughts and beliefs.

Rational emotive therapy (RET), developed by Albert Ellis in 1955, is a method designed to correct individuals' distorted thinking patterns (Ellis, 1962; 1973). RET theory holds that conflict occurs as a result of the relationship between belief systems and behaviors. Moreover, it is believed that the assessments persons make of the events in their lives are problematic. To encourage rational thinking in children, Ellis developed an A-B-C model that demonstrates the relationship of events, beliefs, and consequences, as presented in Figure 11.2.

When Seth was in his pre-crisis phase, his teacher might have used rational emotive education (REE) to prevent his out-of-control behavior. Ideally, it could be implemented daily with small groups as a group crisis-prevention technique. Waters (1982) identified ten irrational beliefs commonly held among children:

1. It's awful if others don't like me.
2. I'm bad if I make a mistake.
3. Everything should go my way; I should always get what I want.
4. Things should come easy to me.
5. The world should be fair and bad people must be punished.
6. I shouldn't show my feelings.
7. Adults should be perfect.
8. There's only one right answer.
9. I must win.
10. I shouldn't have to wait for anything. (p. 52)

Goals have been identified for using rational emotive therapy and rational emotive education for children and adolescents. The goals are to:

1. Correctly identify emotions.
2. Develop emotional vocabulary.
3. Distinguish between helpful and hurtful feelings.
4. Differentiate between feelings and thoughts.
5. Tune into self-talk.
6. Make the connection between self-talk and feelings.
7. Learn rational coping statements. (Waters, 1982, p. 1)

Life space interviewing (LSI) (Redl, 1959) is another technique that has been used in crisis prevention and management. It is discussed in detail in Chapter 10 and will be mentioned briefly here. It is predicated on the empathic relationship that the teacher develops with students. LSI proponents believe that when working with children and youth, therapy should be conducted in the event's naturally occurring setting at the time the event occurs. This intervention primarily focuses on applying emotional first aid and the clinical exploitation of life events (Clarizio & McCoy, 1983). Clinical exploitation of life events in crisis management will be described later in the chapter. The pre-crisis phase is an opportune time for teachers to engage in emotional first aid. Principles for emotional first aid (Redl, 1971) are discussed with suggested activities.

1. *Drain off frustration and hostility.* Students who have low frustration tolerances may be in crisis as a result of their inability to tolerate feelings of frustration. These students may need additional preparation for events that could result in their being in a crisis situation. If Seth was looking forward to going on a field trip that needed to be canceled, his teacher could tell Seth privately that the trip had to be canceled and the reason for it. She

could also involve Seth in a project to assist in making the arrangements for the next field trip. The teacher could initiate the conversation with "I know how disappointed you must be. . . . " This allows an opening for Seth to discuss his feelings.

2. *Provide emotional support for managing feelings of panic, fury, and guilt.* When children are feeling anxious and under stress, they are likely to need assistance in managing those feelings. Being available to talk out their feelings shows support; it also helps them to make sense of what they are feeling. Seth's teacher, after noticing his unpleasant disposition, could say "Seth, you don't seem quite yourself this morning. Give me a minute to get everyone started on an activity and I'll be glad to listen."

3. *Maintain communication when the teacher–student relationship is threatened.* When teachers intervene in student behaviors, they risk damaging the teacher–student relationship. Students may view their teachers negatively when they make attempts to reduce inappropriate behaviors. It is imperative that teachers make every effort to salvage the relationship when students are upset about their intervening. Even when students come across as wanting to sever the relationship, teachers must continue to keep the lines of communication open. One method is to assure students that an episode of inappropriate behavior does not alter the relationship. Students are often embarrassed by their inappropriate behavior and may need reassurance that such an episode will not be held against them. In addition, it is comforting to students to know that they have opportunities to start fresh each day.

4. *Regulate social and behavioral traffic.* For some students, crises can be prevented when teachers remind them of classroom rules and regulations. Alert teachers can gauge the level of teacher-directed management individual students need to prevent crises. For some students, having an adult in the vicinity is enough. For others, it may be necessary verbally to remind students of the rules. Seth's teacher could have applied this principle when he was griping about the student who walked down the aisle where Seth's leg was extended. The teacher could have talked to Seth privately and reminded him to take advantage of the area in the room designed for students who feel the need to be alone for a while.

5. *Umpire disputes.* Teachers at times are needed to mediate internal and external conflicts that arise. For example, if students are involved in playing a board game and one accuses the other of cheating, the teacher may need to listen to both sides and help them sort out the appropriate action. Conflicts may also occur within a student who is torn between doing something that she knows is wrong in order to fit in with her peers. Seth's

Figure 11.3 Activities for Managing Frustration

Activity	Description
Experiencing obstacles	Teacher gives student a task to complete and induces frustration by creating physical, temporal, or interpersonal obstacles blocking student's ability to complete the task.
Experiencing conflicts	Teacher creates dilemmas for students by giving them a directive and interfering with their compliance. For example, the teacher might tell a student to work without talking to anyone. The teacher then persistently asks questions that encourage the students to talk instead of working as directed.

teacher could have used any of the mentioned emotional first-aid techniques to try to prevent the crisis that later developed.

The psychoeducational approach to preventing behaviors leading to crises is developed from principles in the fields of psychology and education. Prior to its development, it was acknowledged that psychologists focused on affect and emotions, while educators focused on cognition (Fagan, Long, & Stephens, 1975). The two distinct disciplines failed to recognize the intersection of affect and cognition. The self-control curriculum (Fagan et al., 1975) provides teachers with a curriculum designed for children with impulsive behaviors. These children demonstrate inability to control their behaviors. In developing the self-control curriculum, the authors identified and designed activities based on eight components of self-control:

- □ *Selection*—accurate perception of incoming information

- □ *Storage*—retaining received information

- □ *Sequencing and ordering*—organizing actions based on planned order

- □ *Anticipating consequences*—relating actions to expected outcomes

- □ *Appreciating feelings*—identifying and constructively using affective experiences

- □ *Managing frustration*—coping with stress-producing obstacles

- □ *Inhibition and delay*—restraining tendencies for action

- □ *Relaxation*—reducing internal stress and tension (Fagen et al., 1975)

The curriculum includes various activities in each of the components that allow students to practice the desired skill. As an example, the activities for managing frustration are highlighted in Figure 11.3. When using these and similar activities, teachers must be careful to preface them with a thorough discussion of the purposes. Moreover, these activities should be concluded with examples of real-life situations from which similar feelings of frustration are produced (Long, 1976).

Crisis Phase

Seth's teacher did not prevent him from having a crisis in school. The scenario ended as Seth was about to hit another student. In characterizing school crises, Wimberley (1985) noted the following characteristics: "(a) the student's behavior is out of control, (b) the student demonstrates behavior that is potentially self-injurious, (c) the student's behavior is potentially harmful to others in the school environment" (p. 23). Teachers often have to assess the situation quickly to determine if intervention is necessary. Many behaviors demonstrated by students that result from stress and anxiety may be effectively managed with the

Effective teachers prevent problems from escalating into crises through understanding students' behavioral cues.

use of the previously mentioned crisis prevention strategies. Due to the stressors facing children and the frequency with which aggressive acts are modeled in the media, there may be occasions when crisis prevention is difficult, or worse.

Teachers should model and maintain positive attitudes regarding crises. They should encourage students to take advantage of the problem-solving opportunities inherent in crises. Effective crisis intervention utilizes five components, according to Greenstone & Leviton (1987). They are immediacy, control, assessment, disposition, and follow-up. The authors noted that the teacher must intervene as soon as it is determined that a crisis is occurring. In addition to ensuring the safety of everyone present, the goal is to relieve the students' anxiety. The teacher, having noticed Seth about to hit the other student, could have directed the other student to another area of the room and calmly requested that Seth go to the area where he can be alone and calm down before discussing the incident.

The student, having lost control, needs the teacher calmly to take charge. The teacher can calmly but firmly suggest alternatives to the crisis behaviors. For instance, in talking to Seth during his crisis, the teacher could say "You may go to the magazine area or you may use this time to write in your journal." The teacher must structure the student's activity following the explosive event and communicate support for the student.

In assessing the situation, the teacher must attempt to determine the cause of the crisis. This step is critical in crisis intervention, as it will assist in future efforts and may provide implications for altering the classroom climate in an effort to inhibit crisis development. The disposition is important because the teacher's task during a crisis is to encourage students gradually to believe in their capacities for managing similar situations. Crisis intervention is not complete unless the crisis is followed up to ensure that assistance in appropriate problem-solving techniques are secured.

Counseling interventions have been devised for teacher use during crises. The tenets of two of these interventions (rational emotive therapy and life space interviewing) were presented earlier in discussions on pre-crisis interventions. They are discussed further here as they relate to crisis management. Rational emotive therapy incorporates a crisis intervention model (Wasserman & Kimmel, 1978). The model is proposed to guide teachers through the intervention process. It includes a series of steps that facilitate student perceptions of the event, and subsequent cognitions regarding the event. Additionally, students are encouraged to identify solutions and make recommendations for handling similar events occurring in the future. Figure 11.4 presents steps for implementation.

As you recall, there are two components of life space interviewing— emotional first aid and clinical exploitation of life events. The latter is a counseling approach frequently implemented after a crisis (or problematic behavior) has occurred. General guidelines for its use have been reported. Heuchert (1983) delineated critical teacher behaviors for effective interviewing. The teacher must

---

Figure 11.4 Steps for Implementation

Step 1. Remove student from the situation and evoke description of the event.

- ☐ What happened?
- ☐ How is the event bothering you?

Step 2. Identify the inappropriate cognitions related to the event

- ☐ How did you anger or upset yourself?

Step 3. Identify solutions.

- ☐ What could you have done to avoid, short-circuit, or change the solution?

Step 4. Recommend new feelings and new solutions.

- ☐ How are you feeling now?
- ☐ How can you solve the problem now?
- ☐ What will you do the next time? (adapted from Wasserman & Kimmel, 1978)

---

be aware of both teacher and student affect, have influence on the student's rational thinking, identify the student's motivation for change, and develop a crisis plan with follow-through. According to Wood and Weller (1981), for LSI to be effective students must have awareness of self, events, and others; adequate attention span; communication skills; adequate memory of information; and a trusting relationship with the interviewer. Chapter 10 presented additional guidelines for conducting life-space interviews.

The interviews developed by Redl (1959) are intended to "exploit" the crisis situation. Here they are described with examples.

1. *Reality rub.* As students frequently misrepresent the actual unfolding of events that led to the crisis, this interview provides students with a "reality check." It is important that the teacher begin to increase the child's perception of what happened as soon after the crisis as possible. Redl maintained that students may be socially nearsighted, having trouble perceiving the way events happen. In order to help students correct their distortions, teachers must facilitate a restructuring of the events. First, teachers are charged with finding out student perceptions about the crisis. Second, teachers can correct them when students misinterpret what happened. If Seth, in reconstructing the events leading to his crisis behaviors, reported that the other student was "bothering" him, the teacher would remind him that it was Seth who put his foot across the aisle.

2. *Symptom estrangement.* This interview technique is most useful for students who don't accept responsibility for their actions. When students conveniently blame everyone but themselves, the teacher should confront the inappropriate behavior by keeping it the focus of the discussion. The task involves discouraging the student from using alibis and excuses for the behavior displayed in the crisis situation.

3. *Massaging numb value areas.* Redl believes that some students hold appropriate values but fail to exercise self-control because they have low self-esteem. Since their values suffer from lack of use, they require activities that will stimulate them to use their values to control their behavior. For these students, teachers must consistently seek out opportunities to affirm their individual attributes.

4. *New tools salesmanship.* The goal of this technique is to teach the student socially pleasing alternatives to the behavior displayed in the crisis situation. For example, Seth's teacher could brainstorm with him other ways of dealing with his frustration. After listing several, the teacher could stage a role-play in which she models the alternative behavior. The teacher could then observe as Seth role-plays the alternative.

5. *Manipulation of the boundaries of the self.* This interview is aimed at the students who put the needs of others over their own; for the sake of maintaining "friendships," they allow themselves to be manipulated by others. When the teacher observes this manipulation, he must be careful to help the student gain this insight without causing the student to be defensive and protective of the manipulators.

Reality therapy is another approach to crisis management with children and youth. Glasser (1965) developed this model to emphasize real-life behaviors instead of psychoanalytic interpretations of student behavior. Even though his training was in psychoanalysis, he believed that the causes of misbehavior are unimportant. His model involves using cognition to modify students' behaviors (Newcomer, 1993). It is believed that individuals who engage in inappropriate behaviors do so deliberately; inappropriate behaviors result from bad choices. Reality therapy in crisis intervention is intended for use when the teacher–student relationship is positive. A close relationship should be established in which the teacher is involved in the child's life. This intervention incorporates the following principles, or the 3 Rs.

1. *Responsible behavior.* Glasser believed that being responsible for one's actions is a result of maintaining self-worth and a sense of involvement. When exploring behaviors, the questions posed are Who? What? Where? and How? Asking questions beginning with "why" encourages students

to make excuses and blame others for their behaviors (Clarizio & McCoy, 1983).

2. *Reality.* Students are urged to perceive events that happen realistically. They are discouraged from blaming others for their problems. In addition, attempts are made to get them to associate a behavior with its consequences.

3. *Right and wrong.* Unlike techniques used in other counseling interventions, Glasser espoused attaching values to behaviors. Students are taught that some behaviors are wrong because they may harm themselves and others. For behaviors that are judged wrong, students must learn more appropriate behaviors (Coleman, 1992).

Post-Crisis Phase

As stated earlier in this chapter, teachers play key roles in preventing and managing crises among their students. Their attitudes regarding crises are critical to student management. Granted, crises played out in classrooms are rarely pleasant events for any of those involved. It becomes the teacher's responsibility to remind students of the benefits of conflicts in problem solving. When the student is no longer in crisis, or the need for immediate interventions is no longer present, the student enters the post-crisis, or recovery, phase (Smith, 1981). Teacher behaviors displayed during this phase set examples for students and communicate the learning potential (or lack thereof) inherent in escalated or crisis situations. Hence this period immediately following a crisis can influence the learning of crisis alternatives.

In Seth's case, following the crisis he should be redirected to another area of the classroom, away from the other students. His teacher needs to take several steps to facilitate a healing process. Seth lost control of his behaviors and appeared embarrassed by the uproar he caused afterward. He also wondered what his teacher thought of him for doing so. Seth felt guilty about his actions and was angry at himself for behaving that way in front of everyone.

Wimberley (1985) advised allowing students and teachers time following the crisis to compose themselves and calm down. Morse (1971), however, suggested allowing some of the intensity of the crisis to abate, but ensuring that the student is still charged enough to understand feelings and behavior. Teachers were advised to reconstruct the crisis so the student can practice problem solving.

Any of the mentioned crisis intervention techniques can be used with students in this phase. Students are able to engage in problem-solving activities only after the precipitating and resulting events have been explored. See Figure 11.5 for general guidelines for crisis follow-up.

Figure 11.5   Guidelines for Crisis Follow-up

☐ Identify the problem

☐ Identify the problem's effect on student and others

☐ Discuss the positive/negative values student attaches to the activity

☐ Review past coping efforts

☐ Develop alternative solutions

☐ Make a new plan

☐ Develop positive consequences for alternative behaviors (adapted from Wimberley, 1985)

Crisis Intervention Teams

In handling situations that escalate into crises, the utilization of crisis teams has been supported in the literature (Purvis, Porter, Authement, & Boren, 1991). The purpose of crisis intervention teams is to use the least intrusive intervention designed to allow students to gain self-control. School-based teams consist of various school personnel who are selected because of personal characteristics that facilitate crisis intervention and/or their expertise in working with students who lack behavioral controls. The team may include teachers, behavior specialists, social workers, counselors, psychologists, and administrators who are able to relate positively to students in crisis. The team should also be diverse, to increase the likelihood that students will identify with at least one member and feel that the team is empathetic to, and representative of, their physical and emotional needs. In establishing crisis intervention teams, the following strategies are used (adapted from Purvis et al., 1991):

☐ Identify the goals of the crisis intervention team based on student population characteristics

☐ Perform a needs assessment to reflect areas in which training or resources are needed

☐ Find model programs that respond to similar needs

☐ Develop a membership pool of persons to serve on the teams

☐ Develop a training program which addresses the identified needs

☐ Prepare and maintain a resource list to obtain services for problems experienced in home, school, or community settings.

Physical Interventions

School personnel lament the increasing occurrences of aggression in school settings. There are two types of aggression demonstrated by children and youth. Students who are directly aggressive defy authority and exhibit blatant acts of anger. Students who are passive aggressive are also angry, but don't express it as openly; they use subtle ways to rebel against those in authority (Beck, 1985). Student anger may manifest itself through aggressive and violent behaviors directed at other students, teachers, or themselves. To this end, angry or frustrated students potentially pose harm to involved persons. A proactive stance on behavior management is maintained throughout this book. When signs are present of impending crisis, the selected intervention should first aim to prevent its escalation into a crisis. If those efforts are unsuccessful, the goal should be to intervene therapeutically in the crisis. Unfortunately, there may be occasions when these interventions will not prevent students from becoming aggressive. To maintain a safe environment for students and teachers, physical interventions may have to be employed (Bullock, Donahue, Young, & Warner, 1985).

Physical restraint is characterized as "the direct restriction of a student's movements by applying force to his or her limbs, head, or body" (Schloss & Smith, 1987). This section is not intended to describe procedures for physically restraining students. Instead, the focus centers on issues surrounding the use of physical interventions.

When the use of physical interventions is discussed in the literature, several caveats are addressed. Anyone contemplating using physical interventions should do so only under certain conditions. Specifically, they are:

1. *As a last resort only.* Interventions that teach alternatives to maladaptive behaviors have been implemented and their effects have been documented. Physical interventions should be used as a last resort only (Paul & Epanchin, 1982; Smith, 1980; Wimberley, 1985).

2. *If the student poses harm to self or others.* The assessment must be made that physical intervention is necessary to protect the aggressive student and others in the environment (Ruhl & Hughes, 1982).

3. *When personnel are trained.* Persons employing physical interventions have received specific training in appropriate use (Morgan & Jenson, 1988).

4. *When physical interventions are nonreinforcing.* Physical intervention procedures do not reinforce the students' aggression (Favell, McGimsey, Jones, & Cannon, 1981).

5. *When paired with teaching alternatives.* Physical intervention is followed with instruction in alternatives to aggressive behavior.

6. *When personnel are knowledgeable of policy.* Teachers are aware of national, state, local, and school policy governing the use of physical intervention (Hughes, 1985).

7. *When students are informed.* Students are told in advance of the purpose of physical intervention (Smith, 1980).

8. *When parents are informed.* Parents should be informed in advance of conditions under which physical intervention will be used (Schloss & Smith, 1987).

Conclusions

In summary, there are three phases of crisis development. The teacher has a role in pre, present, and post crisis phases to structure opportunities for students to learn alternatives to crisis behaviors. To the greatest extent possible, the teacher's role in crisis prevention and management is to facilitate students' awareness of thoughts, feelings, and behaviors and to teach them to use alternatives when confronted with stressful situations. The interventions to be used should involve students in understanding and regulating their behaviors. Physical intervention should be avoided because of the risks involved unless there is a threat to the safety of the student or others. Teachers must be apprised of, and adhere to, the guidelines developed to provide procedural safeguards for students to regain control of their behavior. As soon as the student has gained self-control, teachers should resume the use of the other strategies outlined in this chapter. These techniques are proactive, are nonintrusive, provide instructional opportunities, and involve students in efforts to regulate their own behaviors.

Discussion Questions and Activities

1. Develop a plan for recognizing potential crises and preventing the escalation of behaviors.

2. Develop a handbook with information of various community resources to which students and families in crisis can be referred for assistance.

3. Your teaching colleague confided that he has a student in his class who does not trust him. The teacher further stated that he has tried everything to build a relationship with the student and is at wit's end. What advice would you give your colleague?

References

Banks, J.A. & Banks, C.A. (1993). *Multicultural education: Issues and perspectives* (2nd ed.). Boston: Allyn & Bacon.

Beck, M. (1985). Understanding and managing the acting-out child. *The Pointer, 29*(2), 27–29.

Bullock, L., Donahue, C., Young, J. & Warner, M. (1985). *The Pointer, 29*(2), 38–44.

Caplan, B. (1964). *Principles of preventive psychiatry.* New York: Basic.

Center, D.B. (1989). *Curriculum and teaching strategies for students with behavioral disorders.* Englewood Cliffs, NJ: Prentice-Hall.

Clarizio, H.F. & McCoy, G.F. (1983). *Behavior disorders in children* (3rd ed.). New York: Harper & Row.

Coleman, M.C. (1992). *Behavior disorders, theory and practice.* Boston: Allyn & Bacon.

Ellis, A. (1962). *Reason and emotion in psychotherapy.* New York: Lyle Stuart.

Ellis, A. (1973). *Humanistic Psychotherapy: The rational-emotive approach.* New York: McGraw-Hill.

Fagan, S., Long, N. & Stephens, D. (1975). *Teaching children self-control.* Columbus: Merrill.

Fine, R. (1973). Psychoanalysis. In R. Corsini (ed.), *Current psychotherapies.* Itasca, IL: F.E. Peacock.

Froyen, L.A. (1993). *Classroom management: The reflective teacher–leader.* (2nd ed.). New York: Macmillan.

Glasser, W. (1972). *The identity society.* New York: Harper & Row.

Glasser, W. (1965). *Reality therapy.* New York: Harper & Row.

Greenstone, J.L. & Leviton, S.C. (1987). Crisis management for mediators. *Developing Family Mediation, 17,* 39–54.

Guetzloe, E.C. (1993). The special education initiative: Responding to changing problems, populations, and paradigms. *Behavioral Disorders, 18*(4), 303–307.

Heuchert, C.M. (1983). Can teachers change behavior? Try interviews. *Academic Therapy, 18,* 321–28.

Hughes, C. (1985). Physical intervention: Planning and control techniques. *The Pointer, 29*(2), 34–37.

Johnson, D.W. & Johnson, R.T. (1983). Effects of cooperative, competitive, and individualistic learning experiences on social development. *Exceptional Children, 52*(6), 553–61.

Long, N.J. (1974). In J. Kauffman and C. Lewis (eds.), *Teaching children with behavior disorders: Personal perspectives.* Columbus: Merrill.

Long, N.J. (1976). *Conflict in the classroom: The education of emotionally disturbed children* (3rd ed.). Belmont, CA: Wadsworth.

Morgan, D.P. & Jenson, W.R. (1988). *Teaching behaviorally disordered students.* Columbus, OH: Merrill.

Morse, W.C. (1971). The crisis or helping teacher. In N.J. Long, W.C. Morse & R.G. Newman (eds.), *Conflict in the classroom* (pp. 485–90). Belmont, CA: Wadsworth.

Newcomer, P.L. (1993). *Understanding and teaching emotionally disturbed children and adolescents* (2nd ed.). Austin, TX: PRO-ED.

Paul, J.L. & Epanchin, B.C. (1982). *Emotional disturbance in children.* Columbus: Merrill.

Purvis, J.R., Porter, R.L., Authement, C.C. & Boren, L.C. (1991). Crisis intervention teams in the schools. *Psychology in the Schools, 28,* 331–39.

Redl, F. (1959). *The concept of the life-space interview. American Journal of Orthopsychiatry, 29,* 721–34.

Redl, F. (1971). The concept of the life-space interview. In N. Long, W. Morse & R. Newman (eds.), *Conflict in the classroom* (257–66). Belmont, CA: Wadsworth.

Rezmierski, V. & Kotre, J. (1974). A limited literature review of theory of the psychodynamic model. In W.C. Rhodes, *A study of child variance.* Ann Arbor: University of Michigan Press.

Ruhl, K.L. & Hughes, C.A. (1982). Coping with physical violence in the classroom: Holding on and getting out. In B. Algozzine (ed.), *Educator's resource manual for management of problem behaviors in students.* Rockville, MD: Aspen.

Schloss, P.J. & Smith, M.A. (1987). Guidelines for ethical use of manual restraint in public school settings for behaviorally disordered students. *Behavioral Disorders, (12)* 207–213.

Smith, C.R. (1980). Issues to consider in the use of physical restraint and timeout procedures. *Iowa Perspective.*

Smith, P. (1981). *Management of assaultive/physical aggressive behavior.* Unpublished manuscript, Los Angeles County Schools, Los Angeles.

Swanson, H.L. & Rinert, H.R. (1979). *Teaching strategies for children in conflict: Curriculum, methods, and materials.* St. Louis: Mosby.

Wasserman, T. & Kimmel, J. (1978). A rational-emotive crisis-intervention treatment model. *Rational Living, 13,* 25–29.

Waters, V. (1982). Replies to frequently asked questions. *Retwork, 1,* 3.

Wicks-Nelson, R. & Israel, A.C. (1984). *Behavior disorders of childhood* (2nd ed.). Englewood Cliffs, NJ: Prentice-Hall.

Wimberley, L. (1985). Guidelines for crisis management. *The Pointer, 29*(2), 22–26.

Wood, M.M. & Long, N.J. (1991). *Life-space intervention: Talking with children and youth in crisis.* Austin, TX: PRO-ED.

Wood, M.M. & Weller, D. (1981). How come it's different with some children? A developmental approach to life-space interviewing. *The Pointer, 25,* 61–66.

Chapter 12

The Balancing Act: Teachers Helping Self and Others

Julie Simmons is just beginning her final student-teaching experience in a seventh-grade middle school. She is eagerly anticipating it but not sure what to expect in a middle school setting. She has already completed two other student-teaching experiences, one in an elementary school and one in a high school. She loved her high school student-teaching experience and is strongly considering pursuing a high school placement upon graduation. She was surprisingly disappointed in her elementary-school experience because she had always thought she wanted to teach young students.

It took a great deal of reflection for Julie to pinpoint why she was so dissatisfied in her elementary school setting. Comparing her elementary and secondary placements, she found that she equally enjoyed working with the younger and older students and found the lesson plans in both settings to be challenging and exciting. The primary difference between the two settings had more to do with the teachers than the classrooms or the types of students.

It was obvious to Julie that the two teachers had very different personalities, however it took much more time and thought to understand why Ms. Radcliffe seemed to thrive in her chosen career and Ms. Nichols just seemed tired. Both teachers had been teaching for over 20 years, and at the same grade level for about ten of those years. Julie thought Ms. Nichols was very well-organized because she had the whole year planned out by mid-October. When Julie asked Ms. Nichols how she did it, Ms. Nichols told her that once you've initially planned the lesson you can use the same plan over and over—which requires no time and very little preparation. Julie thought this was a great teaching tip until she was placed in Ms. Radcliffe's room. Ms. Radcliffe used the same basic plan but adapted each lesson to fit the new group. Julie asked her why she keeps changing her lesson if the lesson plan she initially designed was successful. Ms. Radcliffe told Julie that each group of students is a little bit different, and even a slight modification of her original plan prompted her continually to evaluate the whats, whys, and hows of each lesson. Julie realized this was one of the reasons Ms. Radcliffe enjoyed teaching, and decided to follow Ms. Radcliffe's teaching tip always to reevaluate and modify plans so that teaching remains alive.

*J*ulie Simmons' student teaching experiences illustrate how the attitudes and beliefs of teachers contribute to positive career development or eventual teacher burnout. The attrition rate of teachers continues to increase at an alarming rate, especially in the area of exceptional education (Dunham, 1983; Iwanicki, 1983; Morsink, 1982; Zabel & Zabel, 1982). In addition, beginning teachers are constantly cautioned to be wary of burnout. Unfortunately, due to the pace of today's classroom, a beginning teacher has little time to reflect on what is causing stress and how to reorganize to avoid burnout. As society changes, the demands of teaching have shifted (Barner, 1982; Crane & Iwanicki, 1986). Some teachers see the shift from simple educator to lifelong learner and collaborator with the community as a positive change. Other teachers continue to blame the system, slowly withdraw from teaching as a profession, and begin to view their chosen profession as just a job where they put in their time until retirement.

Why do some teachers become reflective practitioners who continue to explore new ground, try new ideas, and strive toward reaching each student when faced with such challenging circumstances? A reflective practitioner constantly questions the how and whys of teaching. Reflective questioning is one of the means that educators use to stay active in their field and to continue to grow as professionals. This chapter addresses why maintaining a balance in the workplace is critical for professional educators and emphasizes methods for maintaining that balance.

Stress

Teachers, as with others in the helping professions, are at a high risk of suffering burnout from stress because of the high level of personal interactions that occur consistently over a long period of time (Maslach, 1978; Miller, 1991). A certain amount of stress results in motivation and productivity. As Selye (1974) states, "Complete freedom from stress is death. Contrary to popular public opinion, we must not—and indeed cannot—avoid stress, but we can meet it efficiently and enjoy it" (p. 32). Selye defines stress as the positive or negative reaction to a significant imbalance between the demands of one's life and the capability of the individual to respond to those demands. The positive stress (or *eustress*) enables an individual to be stimulated by the task and results in worthwhile benefits. When the demands of life become greater than the capability of the individual *distress* develops. The body must adapt both physically and mentally to handle the stress overload. These adaptations (Selye, 1984) include the following progressive stages:

Stages of Stress Adaptation

Stage 1	Alarm and reaction
Stage 2	Resistance
Stage 3	Exhaustion

Physical activities help teachers maintain a perspective about stress.

As the distress level advances into each progressive stage, various changes both psychologically and physiologically can result (Bradfield & Fones, 1985). Physical indicators of stress overload may include elevated blood pressure, development of peptic ulcers and digestive disorders, higher incidence of cardiovascular problems, occurrence of sleep disorders, and chronic depression (Kyriacou & Sutcliffe, 1977). Psychological reactions include a decline in quality of work, loss of interpersonal relationships, increased absenteeism at work, and an overall view of a poor quality of life (Rizzo & Zabel, 1988; Schwab, Jackson, & Schuler, 1986; Weiskopf, 1980). In addition, drug and alcohol abuse (Taylor & Salend, 1983) can exacerbate the above behaviors, or drug abuse alone can be the result of too much stress.

Distress also results in a monetary cost. Stress overload results in financial strain to the health care system and to the school system. Holland (1982) reports that stress overload results in a higher incidence of sick days for teachers—thus the need for substitutes, a higher cost for recruiting and orienting new teachers, and a higher cost in attempting to remediate ineffective teachers. What is too much stress? The key to determining one's stress level cannot easily be predicted. *Stress* is defined as a reaction to the imbalance between personal demands and personal capabilities, thus what is stressful to one person may not be stressful to another. Moracco, Gray, and D'Arienzo (1981) contend that an individual's beliefs, temperament, and view of life are the primary determinants for the amount of eustress or distress. Maslach (1982) adds that specific environmental factors seem to be high predictors of distress. The intricate interaction of these two factors seems to determine the difference between eustress and distress for each individual (Iwanicki, 1983; Schwab, 1981; Schwab et al., 1986). The teacher stress and burnout model by Zabel, Boomer, and King (1984) identified the following five factors as specifically pertinent to the stress level of teachers:

- ☐ Expectations

- ☐ School experiences

- ☐ Feelings

- ☐ Behavior

- ☐ Others' reactions

The interaction of these variables seems to have a profound effect on the ability of an individual to handle various levels of stress.

Risk Factors for Stress Overload

Several personal and setting variables have been examined by professionals to determine if there are any specific predictors of stress overload.

Age

No conclusive findings have been noted concerning a specific age group as high risk for stress overload. Numerous investigators have examined age as a factor, resulting in conflicting findings. Banks and Necco (1990) and others (Weber & Toffler, 1989; Zabel & Zabel, 1983) found a correlation between age and level of accomplishment. Younger teachers reported a higher incidence of stress overload (specifically, teachers with less than 6 years' experience). However, Cardinell (1980) reported a surprising finding of increased age as a factor for a stated commitment to teaching, but with a strong feeling of dissatisfaction with the profession. Feitler and Tokar's (1982) investigation revealed a midlife distress level for teacher of ages 31 to 44. No conclusive evidence can be stated concerning age as a factor for stress overload.

Gender

Numerous investigations concerning gender and stress overload indicate no significant findings (Olson & Matusky, 1982). These results could be skewed by the fact that there are a disproportionate number of females to males in public education. In studies that examined stress level and gender (Crane & Iwanicki, 1986), the incidence of a higher level of depersonalization is consistently reported for males more often than females. According to Crane & Iwanicki (1986), this finding may be due to the cultural socialization of females into a role of "nurturer."

Perception of Success

Many individuals select the career of teaching because they believe they can make a difference in a child's life. Conversely, one of the reasons teachers state for leaving the classroom is the inability to make a difference in a child's life because of the many competing variables teachers are faced with on a daily basis (Zabel et al., 1984). These include the external factors teachers have little or no control over, such as students coming to school hungry, lack of adequate clothing or housing for a student, and no family support system for a child. Another compounding variable resulting in stress overload is the perception by teachers that students are making inadequate progress (Marozas & May, 1988). These perceptions occur across grade level and category of setting. Traditionally, only teachers in exceptional education taught "challenging" students. As the population of students changed, both general and exceptional education teachers deal with students with a wide range of differences and unique challenges. Due to the nature of many of these challenged students, teachers do not receive the type of feedback that provides them with a sense of accomplishment. Teachers working with difficult students may receive negative responses that result in a sense of discouragement, disenchantment, and distress with the teaching field (Maslach, 1978).

Educational Level

No conclusive statements can be made concerning educational level and level of stress. Zabel and Zabel (1983) report that master's-level teachers scored lower on indicators of stress such as depersonalization. Johnson, Gold, and Knepper (1984) report a contradictory finding to Zabel and Zabel's investigation. In the Johnson study, educators with a bachelor's degree reported a higher level of personal accomplishment than those teachers with a master's degree.

Teacher Training/Certification

Although numerous studies indicate teachers perceive their preservice training as having inadequately prepared them for the stress of daily teaching (Gold, 1985; Marozas & May, 1988; Ysseldyke & Algozzine, 1982), a majority of investigations indicate no significant difference in stress level between teachers teaching in their certified areas and those with alternative certification. In addition, Banks and Necco (1990) report lower stress levels for those teachers having alternative certification.

Years of Teaching

A common complaint from the field of education is the concern about burnout among teachers who have been in the system 20 or 30 years, but this has not been substantiated. Although some indicators of stress, such as depersonalization, have been noted (Zabel & Zabel, 1983), there does not seem to be a significant correlation between stress overload or burnout and the number of years of teaching (Presley & Morgan, 1982).

Variables in Teaching Settings

Levels of Stress in Exceptional Education Settings

There is no conclusive evidence to indicate that a particular exceptional education setting will accelerate a teacher's stress level (McIntyre, 1983; Presley & Morgan, 1982). Fimian and Blanton (1986) report a higher stress level for secondary special education teachers than for general education teachers, while Zacherman's (1984) investigation refuted the above findings. A significant level of difference in stress level between exceptional education teachers in self-contained classrooms and those teaching in resource-room settings has not been confirmed (McIntyre, 1983; Presley & Morgan, 1982). Faas's (1984) study of 273 educators revealed a fine delineation of levels of stress among teachers not specifically related to self-contained settings or resource-room settings. Faas purports that a difference in stress level is not based on the teaching setting of general or exceptional education but that stress is determined by the responsibilities of a specific job (amount of discipline problems, role of lunch duty, or fear of federal funding being taken away). Faas's investigation revealed that the causes of stress are specific to a particular setting. However, teachers of emotionally handicapped students have reported higher stress levels than those teaching in other exceptionalities (Johnson, Gold, & Vickers, 1982; Zabel & Zabel, 1982).

Levels of Stress in General Education Settings

Level of perceived stress reportedly increases as teachers advance in grade level in the general education setting (Eskridge & Coker, 1985; Feitler & Tokar, 1982). Anderson's (1980) investigation revealed that teachers in elementary settings reported a higher level of personal accomplishment and lower level of depersonalization than their colleagues in secondary settings. A rationale (Anderson, 1980; Miller, 1991) for the above phenomena has been attributed to the belief that behavior problems are less severe, behavioral academic gains are more easily noted, and there is less diversity in the ability of students in the earlier grades.

Class Size as a Variable of Stress Level

Teachers' self-reports indicate that class size is considered a critical variable in stress level (Coates & Thoreson, 1976). This finding is more frequently reported by exceptional education teachers than general education teachers. As highlighted in Bensky and others' (1980) investigation, class size was reported as the number one stressor for exceptional education teachers. However, a statistically significant correlation between class size and level of stress has not been corroborated in additional studies (McIntyre, 1983; Zabel & Zabel, 1983).

Stress can be viewed as the "spice of life" and most would agree, as Selye (1984) aptly states, life would be rather boring if our only experiences were "no runs, no hits, no errors." Eustress is productive and provides an individual with the energy and motivation to complete tasks. Stress becomes problematic when it results in distress. The reaction to stress overload (distress) may result in physiological destruction of the body and psychological destruction of the spirit and mind.

Teachers are considered at high risk for stress overload due to their intense daily interaction with students, parents, and colleagues. In examining specific characteristics or variables that may predispose an individual to stress overload, very few conclusive results can be stated. It is clear that a teacher's perception of what is considered success often results in distress when a vision of teaching does not match the reality of the job. The next section introduces various means to meet stress effectively and possibly even delight in the challenge.

Walking the Balance

As discussed earlier, stress is defined as the positive or negative reaction to a significant imbalance between the demands of one's life and the capability to respond to those demands. Teachers can minimize the imbalance between demands and capability by recognizing the warning signs of stress and maintaining a balance in life. This balance comes about through an examination of various areas of life including personal attitude, time management, support systems, and professional/personal growth.

Recognizing the Signs of Stress Overload

It is possible that distress is such a part of one's life that warning signs are not heeded until serious physical or psychological damage has resulted. In addition, individuals often feel that since no tragic event has recently happened in their life they have no reason to feel over-stressed. All events in a person's life—both pleasant and painful—result in a certain amount of stress. Table 12.1 identifies many so-called positive events as stressors. It presents the life-events scale for college students (Girdano & Everly, 1979, pp. 56–57) in which "beginning a first year of college or ending a final year of college" (often viewed as a very positive event) rank third highest on the indicators of stress.

One sign of stress overload is apathy towards one's work. It is possible that a teacher is unaware of this detached attitude or lack of commitment to teaching. An over-stressed teacher may deny the allegations of stress overload because attendance at work has not shown a significant decrease and all requirements of the job are completed. What is missing is a *commitment to teaching* that encourages learning in students.

A commitment to teaching, although difficult to characterize, has been explored in Rouche and Baker's (1986) investigation of exemplary secondary teachers. Rouche and Baker contend that better teachers are not identified by their level of knowledge but by their ability to encourage learners. The authors have identified three areas where these teachers excel:

☐ Motivation

☐ Effective interpersonal skills

☐ Enhanced teaching skills

Under the area of motivation, these effective teachers perceive their students functioning in a larger arena than the classroom setting. Towards this end they devote time, both in and out of class, which demonstrates their commitment to the students in the class. In addition, these teachers receive personal satisfaction from the knowledge that students are learning. These teachers know they are making a difference through their teaching.

Effective communication skills were identified by the researchers as an integral part of these exemplary teachers' teaching style. Effective teachers are very aware of what is happening throughout the class and have a sense of the climate of the classroom. In communicating with students, these educators listen and empathize with their students through respect and the setting of high but achievable goals.

Table 12.1   Life-Events Scale for College Students

Below are listed events that may occur in the life of a college student. Place a check in the left-hand column for each of those events that have happened to you during the last 12 months.

Life event	Point values
___ Death of a close family member	100
___ Jail term	80
___ Final year or first year in college	63
___ Pregnancy (to you or caused by you)	60
___ Severe personal illness or injury	53
___ Marriage	50
___ Any interpersonal problems	45
___ Financial difficulties	40
___ Death of a close friend	40
___ Arguments with your roommate (more than every other day)	40
___ Major disagreements with your family	40
___ Major change in personal habits	30
___ Change in living environments	30
___ Beginning or ending a job	30
___ Problems with your boss or professor	25
___ Outstanding personal achievement	25
___ Failure in some course	25
___ Final exams	20
___ Increased or decreased dating	20
___ Change in working conditions	20
___ Change in your major	20
___ Change in your sleeping habits	18
___ Several-day vacation	15
___ Change in eating habits	15
___ Family reunion	15
___ Change in recreational activities	15
___ Minor illness or injury	15
___ Minor violations of the law	11

Interpretation: Add up your score. If your total score for the year was under 150 points, your level of stress, based upon life change, is low. If your total was between 150 and 300, your stress levels are borderline; you should minimize other changes in your life at this time. If your total was more than 300, your life-change levels of stress are high.

(Girdano & Everly, 1979, pp. 56–57)

These teachers individually know their students' learning needs and develop programs to meet those needs. In addition, these teachers continually explore new teaching techniques. As professionals they view themselves as life-long learners and enhance this love of learning in their students.

In analyzing career decisions, a reflective teacher needs to compare personal teaching philosophy to that just stated. A warning of stress overload should be considered if a teacher believes the above values are unimportant or impossible to implement. Various scales of stress level, such as the one developed by Girdano and Everly (1979, pp. 67–68) and depicted in Table 12.2, may also assist teachers in determining if eustress has declined to distress.

Other more general warnings of stress overload for teachers have been identified by Rosenberg, O'Shea, and O'Shea (1991, p. 288) in Table 12.3, and may prove beneficial as an initial screening for teachers in determining if stress has become a more serious concern that needs to be addressed.

The results of stress overload do not limit their presentation to the place

---

Table 12.2 *Susceptibility to Overload*

Choose the most appropriate answer for each of the ten statements below and place the letter of your response in the space to the left.
How often do you . . .

____ 1. Find yourself with insufficient time to complete your work?
    (a) Almost always
    (b) Very often
    (c) Seldom
    (d) Never

____ 2. Find yourself confused and unable to think clearly because too many things are happening at once?
    (a) Almost always
    (b) Very often
    (c) Seldom
    (d) Never

____ 3. Wish you had help to get everything done?
    (a) Almost always
    (b) Very often
    (c) Seldom
    (d) Never

____ 4. Feel that people around you simply expect too much from you?
    (a) Almost always
    (b) Very often
    (c) Seldom
    (d) Never

____ 5. Feel overwhelmed by the demands placed upon you?
    (a) Almost always
    (b) Very often
    (c) Seldom
    (d) Never

that causes the stress. For example, stress overload at work may result in diminished personal relations at home and stress overload at home can cause a teacher to perform inadequately at school. Identifying the source of stress may help a teacher to eliminate the cause and move forward in a productive manner.

In most cases, prevention of stress overload is more beneficial for the individual both psychologically and physiologically than reacting after the stress has consumed the person's time and spirit. If stress is kept in balance, less trauma is placed on the body—thus an individual will be mentally and physically healthy. An individual's personal attitude, effective time management, utilization of support systems, and continual professional/personal growth have been identified as key variables in maintaining this delicate balance.

___ 6. Find your work infringing on your leisure hours?
   (a) Almost always
   (b) Very often
   (c) Seldom
   (d) Never

___ 7. Get depressed when you consider all of the tasks that need your attention?
   (a) Almost always
   (b) Very often
   (c) Seldom
   (d) Never

___ 8. See no end to the excessive demands placed upon you?
   (a) Almost always
   (b) Very often
   (c) Seldom
   (d) Never

___ 9. Have to skip a meal so that you can get work completed?
   (a) Almost always
   (b) Very often
   (c) Seldom
   (d) Never

___ 10. Feel that you have too much responsibility?
   (a) Almost always
   (b) Very often
   (c) Seldom
   (d) Never

Score: _____

Scoring: a = 4   b = 3   c = 2   d = 1

Interpretation: Total your points and see how stressed you are by overload. A total of 26 to 40 indicates a high stress level; such an excessive level could be psychologically and physiologically debilitating if steps are not taken to reduce it.

(Girdano & Everly, 1979, p. 67–68)

Table 12.3 Signs and Signals of Stress

☐ Avoidance of school through many absences, continual tardiness, or an intense desire to leave the building before the school day is over

☐ Apathy to students, parents, and teachers

☐ Lower productivity in teaching, especially in teachers who at one time were highly productive

☐ Continual negative self-statements concerning teacher effectiveness

☐ Physical signs including prolonged headaches, stomach pains, or voice problems

☐ Real or imagined mental fatigue over time

☐ Blatant refusal to comply with school policies and rules

☐ Prolonged crying and depression

☐ Deep feelings of loss of control over career, personal life, or business matters

☐ Continual complaints to loved ones

(Reprinted with the permission of Macmillan College Publishing Company from *Student Teacher to Master Teacher* by Michael S. Rosenberg, Lawrence O'Shea, and Dorothy J. O'Shea. Copyright ©1991 by Macmillan College Publishing Company, Inc.)

Attitude

The stories of Charlotte and Marianne illustrates how attitude can "make or break" a teacher. Student teachers are sometimes placed in teaching settings that may not be ideally suited to their personality or learning style. Charlotte and Marianne were two student teachers who were placed in unfortunate student-teaching settings. The end result for Marianne was a positive experience due to her tenacity and positive attitude. Charlotte bitterly complained the entire semester, blaming everyone for the inadequate placement. Charlotte finished her internship with negative feelings and the mistaken notion that as soon as she got "her own, real classroom" things would be much better.

Charlotte had difficulty securing employment because her negative attitude continued to be displayed subtly during job interviews. After finally finding a job, Charlotte returned to her university professor with such comments as "Why didn't you prepare me?" and "I never realized how difficult students can be!" The difference between Charlotte and Marianne has a great deal to do with their attitudes.

How does one foster a positive attitude? A continual reflection upon one's decision to select teaching as a career and a continual self-evaluation of one's abilities will assist educators in determining if their professional choice is right for them, or if a change needs to be made. Self-reflection needs to be made on a continual basis because teaching is an ever-changing process. As Selye (1984) asserts, much of personal distress is due to a negative attitude or viewpoint about one's life situation. Selye's (1984) suggestions for maintaining a balance through a positive attitude are basic strategies that can make the difference between productivity or incapacitation:

- ☐ No one or thing is perfect, so set high but achievable goals.
- ☐ Diligently work at your internal pace, not the pace others set for you.
- ☐ Looking out for yourself is not selfish, but necessary for a healthy lifestyle.
- ☐ Focus on those situations that ameliorate your life.

One of the most basic positive attitudes for coping with the challenges of everyday teaching lies in a teacher's ability to step back from the many frenetic demands and not take life quite so seriously. Self-reflection (Styles & Kavanaugh, 1977) may also help a teacher put life and its many responsibilities into better perspective. In addition, even a brief time spent on reflection may help in sorting out what is really important and what can be left to another day.

A change in viewpoint is often difficult to implement because attitude is such an integral part of an individual's personality. In addition, a negative attitude can be fostered by the people we choose to associate with at school and home. Beginning teachers need to be very aware of their own personal outlook and the negative or positive effects of others' attitudes.

Time Management

Beginning teachers stress that organization and effective time management is what helped them most in their first year of teaching. If a teacher organizes the time on the job, increased time will be made available to plan effective and efficient instruction for students. Teachers can analyze how time is spent in school by examining how they spend their own personal teaching time and how they plan for their instruction. Several effective time-management strategies are discussed in the following sections.

Personal Teaching Time

Prioritizing tasks.   Effective time management requires a teacher to take the time to prioritize not only the demands of school but also the demands of people and activities outside of school. For those jobs that must be completed in school, a written checklist will assist teachers in prioritizing tasks by order of importance and necessary completion date.

Reducing procrastination.   Once activities are prioritized, the next step is completing one task, or some portion of one task. As Styles and Kavanaugh (1977) highlight, procrastination can lead to higher levels of stress as one continues to worry about the consequences of not completing a task and not having enough time to complete the task.

If a task seems overwhelming, Styles and Kavanaugh (1977) suggest breaking it down into segments that can be completed within a reasonable period of time. As each subtask is completed, the satisfaction of reaching closure on an activity will provide the incentive for continuing through the other activities on the prioritized list.

Self-selection of activities. As schools continue to restructure, additional options and opportunities will be provided for teachers above and beyond their traditional role. This will require teachers to determine their own best interests and to be assertive in selecting those activities in which they wish to participate. By doing so, they can successfully complete a manageable number of tasks rather than feeling unsuccessful with many unfinished assignments.

Learning to say no. Teachers must learn to say no. Many teachers report this to be a difficult endeavor because of their need to do as much as they can for their students. In addition, teachers who effectively complete tasks are often asked to take on additional responsibilities. Each teacher must decide what personal limitations are and effectively communicate these limitations to others (Youngs, 1986).

Feeling in control of time. Teachers need to be in control of how time is spent during the teaching day. Hammond and Sparks (1981) recommend re-evaluating how time is spent both daily and weekly to determine if any changes need to be made. These authors suggest that teachers view their time as money. A teacher's investment of time must yield high returns. A high return on a time investment can be enhanced through implementation of the following personal time-management strategies (Hammond & Sparks, 1981):

1. *Return all phone calls at one time.* Make a list of all necessary phone calls and return the calls in consecutive order.

2. *Peruse reading material* if time is not available to read professional information comprehensively.

3. *Set time lines for working on projects.* Any activity can consume all of a teacher's time. Setting a predetermined time frame will assist a teacher in planning realistic goals for completion of projects.

4. *Decisions on administrative paperwork.* As a teacher receives paperwork, it is most efficient to look at the information, make a decision about what needs to be done, and immediately place it in the correct category (to complete, to read, to throw away).

5. *Systemize work space.* Keep a calendar of all upcoming dates and keep immediate work space free from clutter. Use file folders, file drawers, or boxes for categorizing paperwork.

6. *Begin and end all meetings on time.* Respect the time schedules of other professionals, parents, and yourself. Keep meetings to their prearranged time frame.

7. *Wait time materials.* Always carry one or two activities that can be worked on when waiting is inevitable (waiting for a meeting to begin, a doctor's appointment, a drive-thru line). These activities may include reviewing the monthly calendar for upcoming events, updating the to-do list, writing letters to students and parents, and reading professional journals.

Management of "teacher time" enhances the overall organization of the classroom and frees the teacher to plan effective instruction.

Classroom Instruction

Efficient and creative planning of daily classroom instruction ensures that a quality educational program is being provided and maximal time is spent in instruction (McCutcheon, 1982). As a teacher carefully self-evaluates the activities and dynamics among individuals that occur throughout the day, instances of more effective classroom instruction may emerge. This information will provide the teacher with insight on where instruction needs to be adapted, thus minimizing teacher stress and enhancing a positive learning environment.

Transition time. Inefficient time spent in transition can take away as much as one hour of daily teaching instruction. In addition, the climate of the classroom can become negative or chaotic if ineffective transitional patterns are utilized (Bennett, 1978; Gump, 1974). Effective transitional movements include: clear pathways for student movement, organization of materials for easy access (worksheets, textbooks, overheads, chalk, chart paper), cueing students that a transition will occur and expectations for each transition. Chapter 4 details more methods for effective transitional patterns.

Waiting time. An examination of the time students spend waiting may provide a teacher with valuable insight on the classroom climate and answer such questions as why an increase in disruptive behavior occurs during certain time periods. Students spend time a great deal of time waiting for available materials, others to finish an assignment, the teacher to check an assignment, directions for the entire class, and teaching instruction. To reduce the wait time of students and the stress level of teachers who can't get to every student, teachers need to plan creatively and utilize other resources. A ready resource for teachers is the students within the classroom. Some procedural tasks must be completed daily (attendance, lunch count, collection of assignments, classroom clean-up). Many procedural activities can be completed by students, freeing the teacher to spend time on other tasks. Enlisting student help in the daily running of the classroom is advantageous for building a classroom community and enhancing individual student self-esteem. However, teachers must balance the amount of time a student spends "assisting" to guarantee a student's educational program is not suffering. Chapters 4 and 8 discuss creative methods for involving students within the classroom to enhance learning.

Classroom management/student self-discipline. As noted earlier in this chapter, teachers with a high incidence of discipline problems report high stress levels (Faas, 1984). Reduction of discipline problems and increased student self-discipline can be realized through careful analysis of the many factors that affect the climate of the classroom. The focus of this text is on the theory, research, and practical procedures for assisting teachers to create a positive classroom environment. Teachers must synthesize and critically analyze the information and apply it to their own teaching situations. The above practices must occur along with a continual evaluation of the effectiveness of implementation practices.

Instructional time. Instructional time may take place through many venues such as direct teacher lecture, cooperative learning activities, independent activities, small group work, and technological activities. To assure the effective and efficient use of instructional time, a teacher must carefully select a learning setting for delivering instruction. The selection of a specific learning setting is influenced by the type of students and the information to be learned. The difficult task for the teacher is to select a means that will provide the most powerful learning environment for the students. The selection of a learning setting, evaluation of the setting, and continual adjustment of the setting create a positive learning environment for both students and teacher.

Support Systems

The attitude of an individual is strongly influenced by the people with whom the person interacts every day. This daily interaction may provide support to an individual in work and other life activities. Support systems may include colleagues at work, family members, and friends from social, professional, and religious organizations. The support provided by these groups has a positive or negative effect on an individual's outlook regarding career and other aspects of life. Continual "griping" by one team-teaching partner may eventually influence the other team member to focus on the negative aspects of students and teaching. This daily negative influence from others can result in distress and eventual burnout for a teacher.

Setting priorities and taking time to relax with family helps teachers control stress.

A positive support system allows a teacher periodically to "let off steam" in a safe environment. A productive support system also provides a teacher with colleagues who will take the time to brainstorm solutions to problems, encouragement to tackle the problems, and accolades when the situation improves. A positive school community can assist a new teacher in building confidence or save a distressed teacher from burnout.

A new teacher needs to seek out an individual or small group of teachers at school who might provide this type of encouraging environment. If a teacher cannot find a support system at her or his particular school, it is imperative that the teacher reach out to other teachers in other schools or similar settings. Through teacher networking, the planning and creation of new lessons can be shared, thus reducing the work load for any one teacher. If a teacher is having difficulty finding a positive school support group locally, a teacher networking system can be created. District-level administration can assist the teacher in this endeavor by providing for the names and schools of all new teachers in the county. An invitation to other teachers to attend an afternoon open house at one school may be the origin of a new-teacher network.

The type of support system from family and friends outside the teaching environment also affects a teacher's outlook on the chosen career. Isolation and depression can result if a support system is inadequate or lacking. Teachers must seek out a positive support system through professional education organizations or joining other established social, religious, or civic groups.

Teaching is a tough profession, and it requires individuals to continually give a great deal of themselves. A support system is necessary for a teacher to maintain the high energy level and commitment to teaching that assures students a quality educational program. If an individual is feeling isolated or showing signs of severe depression, it is imperative that professional support be provided. An individual continuing to teach with a destructive self-concept will possibly hurt themselves or their students.

Professional and Personal Growth

Ms. Radcliffe was described at the beginning of this chapter as a teacher who seemed to thrive in her chosen career despite teaching for over 20 years. When Julie Simmons, the student teacher, asked her about her teaching style, her response clearly indicated that this teacher continues to grow professionally despite her longevity in the system. Ms. Radcliffe realizes that each student is unique and teaching remains exciting because she continually asks about the what, why, and how of teaching, and she continues to learn with her students.

Teachers need continual rejuvenation for the strenuous and arduous task they face daily. The first step in dealing with fatigue is to seek change. Don't accept that things can't be different. There are many outlets for change. These include joining a professional or political organization. This forum provides a teacher with a group that supports educational change and supports professional educators. In addition, many educational organizations sponsor state and national conferences where professionals from around the state and nation share their research, ideas, and beliefs. Preparing a paper to present at the conference enables a teacher to focus on a specific aspect of teaching and delve into the effectiveness or utilization of a strategy. Funds are often available through the school system or the educational organization to assist teachers in traveling to professional conferences.

Many successful teachers maintain their enthusiasm for teaching because they do not let work consume their lives. A balance in work and play is necessary to allow one to step back and let the challenging events of each day fall into a proper perspective. Tunnel vision can result when a teacher becomes too immersed in teaching. Each event is a crisis, heightening the stress level. Finding an outside interest other than school encourages an individual to focus on another activity for a short period of time, thus reducing tunnel vision. The crisis event can be put in the proper perspective.

Due to the demands of teaching and home life, many teachers neglect their own personal needs and rationalize that they don't have time for themselves because they are too busy taking care of everyone else. Eventually, this pattern of continual physical and mental exhaustion results in the body's shutting down physically and/or mentally. Teachers cannot be effective at school or at home if they are constantly living on the edge of exhaustion.

Teachers need to strive for their own "personal time" to relax and do something for themselves—even for 5 minutes a day! Adequate sleep, exercise, and nutrition builds stamina, increases energy levels, and positively affect one's ability to cope with the stressful events of the day (Selye, 1984). Progressive relaxation, neck and body massage, meditation, and slow breathing exercises are activities that have been found to be beneficial for reducing levels of stress both physiologically and psychologically.

A reflective teacher continually asks the what, why, and how of teaching. If an individual stops asking these questions and begins to show signs of distress such as detachment from the students, an increased number of sick days, lack of planning in teaching, or general incompetence in teaching, intervention is critical. Teachers must continually reflect on their own feelings and provide feedback and support to their colleagues so the stress of teaching is a positive motivator rather than a destructive intrusion.

Conclusions

Teaching often provides the satisfaction that one person can make a difference. But at times teaching provides the frustration that no one seems to make a difference. An effective teacher must continue to probe, question, explore, struggle, work, rejoice, probe, question, explore, struggle, work, rejoice, probe, question, explore, struggle, work, rejoice, and continue. This challenge requires a true commitment to teaching and to lifelong learning. To sustain a high level of commitment to teaching a teacher must maintain a balance in work through a positive attitude, effective time management, utilization of support systems, and continuing professional and personal growth.

Discussion Questions and Activities

1. Reflect on your school experiences and determine who you would identify as your favorite teacher. What characteristics made that teacher "special"? Which of those characteristics do you believe you will carry into your teaching experience and why? Share this information with other preservice teachers.

2. Interview five teachers and ask them to identify, in order of significance, what aspect of teaching causes them the most stress. Share these lists with other preservice teachers and discuss methods for dealing with the five stressors identified most often by the teachers.

3. Discuss the point values for various life events in Table 12.1 (*Life-Events Scale for College Students,* Girdano & Everly, 1979) and complete the table. Discuss those stressors that are under the personal control of each individual and those stressors that seem to beyond the immediate control of an individual.

4. Complete Table 12.2 (*Susceptibility to Overload,* Girdano & Everly, 1979) and determine your stress level. Discuss with other preservice teachers methods for reducing this stress.

5. Interview three teachers and ask them what are the five most important methods they use to reduce stress. Share these methods with other preservice teachers.

6. Complete a personalized stress-reduction activity throughout the semester. Identify one of the areas of stress reduction listed below and highlighted in the chapter. Set a simple objective and keep a daily log towards meeting that objective. Be sure the objective does not add more stress to your life!

   ☐ Time for self-reflection

   ☐ Positive attitude

   ☐ Prioritizing tasks

   ☐ Reducing procrastination

   ☐ Self-selection of activities

   ☐ Learning to say no

   ☐ Feeling in control of time

   ☐ Development of a support system

   ☐ Actively participating in a professional/political group

   ☐ Preparing a professional paper or presentation

   ☐ Development of an outside interest

   ☐ Finding own "personal time"

References

Anderson, M.B. (1980). A study of differences among perceived need deficiencies, perceived burnout, and selected background variables among classroom teachers. Doctoral dissertation, University of Connecticut. *Dissertation Abstracts International 41,* 4218A.

Banks, S.R. & Necco, E.G. (1990). The effects of special education category and type of training on job burnout in special education teachers. *Teacher Education and Special Education, 13,* 187–91.

Barner, A. (1982). Do teachers like to teach? *Pointer, 27* (1), 5–7.

Bennett, S.N. (1978). Recent research on teaching: A dream, a belief, and a model. *British Journal of Educational Psychology, 48,* 127–47.

Bensky, J.M., Shaw, S.F., Gouse, A.S., Bates, H., Dixon, B. & Beane, W.E. (1980). Public Law 94-142 and stress: A problem for educators. *Exceptional Children, 47,* 24–29.

Bradfield, R.H. & Fones, D.M. (1985). Special teacher stress: Its product and prevention. *Academic Therapy, 21,* 91–97.

Cardinell, C. (1980). Teacher burnout: An analysis. *Action in Teacher Education, 2,* 9–15.

Coates T.J. & Thoreson, C.E. (1976). Teacher anxiety: A review with recommendations. *Review of Educational Research, 46,* 159–84.

Crane, S.J. & Iwanicki, E.F. (1986). Perceived role conflict, role ambiguity, and burnout among special education teachers. *Remedial and Special Education, 7*(2), 24–31.

Dunham, J. (1983). Coping with stress in schools. *Special Education: Forward Trends, 10,* 2–6.

Eskridge, D.H. & Coker, D.R. (1985). Teacher stress: Symptoms, causes, and management techniques. *Clearing House, 58,* 387–90.

Faas, L.A. (1984). *Stress producing factors among regular educators and various types of special educators.* Tempe, AZ: Arizona State University. (ERIC Document Reproduction Service No. ED 242 728.)

Feitler, F. & Tokar, E. (1982). Getting a handle on teacher stress: How bad is the problem? *Educational Leadership, 39,* 456–57.

Fimian, M.J. & Blanton, L.R. (1986). Variables related to stress and burnout in special education teacher trainees and first-year teachers. *Teacher Education and Special Education, 9,* 9–21.

Girdano, D.A. & Everly, G.S. (1979). *Controlling stress and tension.* Englewood Cliffs, NJ: Prentice-Hall.

Gold, Y. (1985). Burnout: Causes and solutions. *Clearing House, 58,* 210–12.

Gump, P.V. (1974). Operating environments in schools of open or traditional design. *School Review, 82,* 575–94.

Hammond, J. & Sparks, D. (1981, August). It's August, it's time for time-management ideas. *Instructor, 91* (1), 58–60, 63.

Holland, R.P. (1982, Winter). Special educator burnout. *Educational Horizons,* 58–64.

Iwanicki, E.F. (1983). Toward understanding and alleviating teacher burnout. *Theory into Practice, 22,* 27–32.

Johnson, A.B., Gold, V. & Knepper, D. (1984). Frequency and intensity of the professional burnout among teachers of the mildly handicapped. *College Student Journal, 18,* 261–66.

Johnson, A.B., Gold, V. & Vickers, L.L. (1982). Stress and teachers of the learning disabled, behavior disordered, and educable mentally retarded. *Psychology in the Schools, 19,* 552–57.

Kyriacou, C. & Sutcliffe, J. (1977). Teacher stress: A review. *Educational Review, 29,* 552–57.

Marozas, D.S. & May, D.C. (1988). *Issues and practices in special education.* New York: Longman.

Maslach, C. (1978). Job burnout: How people cope. *Public Welfare, 36,* 56–58.

Maslach, C. (1982). *Burn-out—the cost of caring.* Englewood Cliffs, NJ: Prentice-Hall.

McCutcheon, G. (1982). How do elementary school teachers plan their courses? *Elementary School Journal, 81,* 4–23.

McIntyre, T.C. (1983). The effects of class size on perceptions of burnout by special education teachers. *Mental Retardation and Learning Disability Bulletin, 11*(3), 142–45.

Miller, D.T. (1991). The effects of personal and classroom setting variables on perceived levels of burnout among teachers of emotionally disturbed students. Unpublished doctoral dissertation, University of South Florida, St. Petersburg, FL.

Moracco, J.C., Gray, P. & D'Arienzo, R.V. (1981). *Stress in teaching: A comparison of perceived stress between special education and regular teachers.* Eastern Educational Research Association, Philadelphia, PA. (ERIC Document Reproduction Service No. ED 202 828.)

Morsink, C.V. (1982). Changes in the role of special educators: Public perceptions and demands. *Exceptional Education Quarterly (The Special Educator as a Professional Person), 2*(4), 15–25.

Olson, J. & Matusky, P.V. (1982). Causes of burnout in SLD teachers. *Journal of Learning Disabilities, 15,* 97–99.

Presley, P. & Morgan, H. (1982, Spring). Teacher burnout in special education—myth or reality? *Illinois Council for Exceptional Children Quarterly,* 19–26.

Rizzo, J.V. & Zabel, R.H. (1988). *Educating children and adolescents with behavior disorders: An integrative approach.* Boston, MA: Allyn & Bacon.

Rosenberg, M.S., O'Shea, L. & O'Shea, D.J. (1991). *Student teacher to master teacher.* New York: Macmillan.

Rouche, J. & Baker, G. (1986). *Profiling Excellence in America's Schools.* Arlington, VA: American Association of School Administrators.

Schwab, R.L. (1981). The relationship of role conflict, role ambiguity, teacher background variables, and perceived burnout among teachers. Doctoral dissertation, University of Connecticut. *Dissertation Abstracts International, 41,* 3823A.

Schwab, R.L., Jackson, S.E. & Schuler, R.S. (1986). Educator burnout: Sources and consequences. *Educational Research Quarterly, 10,* 14–30.

Selye, H. (1974). *Stress without distress.* Philadelphia: Lippincott.

Selye, H. (1984). *The stress of life.* (rev. ed.). New York: McGraw-Hill.

Styles, K. & Kavanaugh, G. (1977). Stress in teaching and how to handle it. *English Journal, 66,* 76–79.

Taylor, L. & Salend, S.J. (1983). Reducing stress-related burnout through a network support system. *The Pointer, 27*(4), 5–9.

Weber, D.B. & Toffler, J.D. (1989). Burnout among teachers of students with moderate, severe, or profound mental retardation. *Teacher Education and Special Education, 12,* 117–24.

Weiskopf, P.E. (1980). Burnout among teachers of exceptional children. *Exceptional Children, 47,* 18–23.

Youngs, B.B. (1986). *Stress in children: How to recognize, avoid and overcome it.* Melbourne, Victoria: Nelson Publishers.

Ysseldyke, J. & Algozzine, B. (1982). Critical issues in special and remedial education. Boston, MA: Houghton Mifflin.

Zabel, R.H., Boomer, L.W. & King, T.R. (1984). A model of stress and burnout among teachers of behaviorally disordered students. *Behavioral Disorders, 9,* 215–21.

Zabel, R.H. & Zabel, M.K. (1982). Factors involved in burnout among teachers of exceptional children. *Exceptional Children, 49,* 261–63.

Zabel, M.K. & Zabel, R.H. (1983). Burnout among special education teachers: The role of experience, training, and age. *Teacher Education and Special Education, 6,* 255–59.

Zacherman, J. (1984). Relationship between stress, job, involvement, and teaching of the handicapped. Doctoral dissertation, University of Connecticut, 1983. *Dissertation Abstracts International 44,* 3244A. (University Microfilms International No. 8404990.)

Index